FIRST EDITION

MANAGING
BUSINESS
PROCESS
FLOWS

FIRST EDITION

MANAGING BUSINESS PROCESS FLOWS

Ravi Anupindi

Sunil Chopra

Sudhakar D. Deshmukh

Jan A. Van Mieghem

Eitan Zemel

Kellogg Graduate School of Management
Northwestern University

Prentice Hall, Upper Saddle River, NJ 07458

Acquisitions Editor: Tom R. Tucker
Developmental Editor: Ron Librach
Editorial Assistant: Kerri Limpert
Editor-in-Chief: Natalie Anderson
Marketing Manager: Debbie Clare
Production Editor: Evyan Jengo
Associate Managing Editor: Judy Leale
Manufacturing Buyer: Diane Peirano
Manufacturing Supervisor: Arnold Vila
Manufacturing Manager: Vincent Scelta
Cover Design: Bruce Kenselaar
Composition: Carlisle Communications

Copyright © 1999 by Prentice-Hall, Inc.
Upper Saddle River, New Jersey 07458

Library of Congress Cataloging-in-Publication Data

Managing business process flows / Ravi Anupindi ... [et al.].
    p. cm.
    Includes bibliographical references and index.
    ISBN 0-13-907775-8
    1. Production management.   2. Process control.   I. Anupindi,
Ravi.
TS155.M33217   1999
658.5—dc21   98-30746
                                                   CIP

Prentice-Hall International (UK) Limited, London
Prentice-Hall of Australia Pty. Limited, Sydney
Prentice-Hall Canada, Inc., Toronto
Prentice-Hall Hispanoamericana, S.A., Mexico
Prentice-Hall of India Private Limited, New Delhi
Prentice-Hall of Japan, Inc., Tokyo
Pearson Education Asia Pte. Ltd., Singapore
Editora Prentice-Hall do Brasil, Ltda., Rio de Janeiro

Printed in the United States of America

10 9 8 7 6

Contents

PART IV: PROCESS INTEGRATION   221

CHAPTER 10   Process Synchronization and Improvement   223

Preface

Managing Business Process Flows (MBPF) is a novel approach to studying some of the core concepts in operations, one of the three major functional fields in business together with finance and marketing. MBPF views operations management as the design and management of business processes and uses this process view as the unifying paradigm to study operations.

MBPF uses a logical and rigorous approach to discuss core concepts in three steps. First model and understand the process and its flows. Then study causal relationships between process structure and certain performance metrics. Finally, formulate implications for managerial actions by filtering out managerial levers ("process drivers") and their impact on process performance.

The objective of the book, which consists of four parts, is to show how managers can plan and control process structure and process drivers to achieve desired business process performance.

Part I, Process Management and Strategy, introduces the basic concepts of business processes and management strategy. Processes are core technologies of all organizations for producing and delivering products (including goods and services) aimed at satisfying customer needs. Processes involve transforming inputs into outputs by means of capital and labor resources that carry out a set of interrelated activities. Process management strategy involves establishing competitive priorities about product attributes to provide, and matching the process capabilities with the targeted product attributes.

Part II, Process Flow Measurement, examines key process measures, their relationships, and managerial levers for controlling them. In particular, flow time, flow rate, and inventory are three operational measures that affect the financial measures of process performance. Flow time can be decreased by shortening critical activity times, flow rates can be increased by increasing the process capacity, and inventory can be decreased by reducing the batch sizes. Throughout this part, our focus will be on the average values, ignoring for now the impact of uncertainty in process performance. The average values of flow time, flow rate, and inventory are related through the *Little's Law*.

Part III, Process Flow Variability, studies the effect of uncertainty in flows on the process performance, and the managerial levers to plan for and control it. Safety inventory is used to maintain material and product availability in spite of variability in inflows and outflows. Safety capacity is used to minimize flow times due to variability in inflows and processing times. Safety time is used to provide a reliable estimate of response time to serve a customer. Finally, feedback control is used to monitor and adjust the process performance dynamically over time.

Finally, Part IV, Process Integration, concludes with principles of synchronization of flows of materials and information through a network of processes most economically. The ideal is to eliminate waste in form of excess costs, defects, delays, and inventories. Instead of responding to the economies of scale and variability in flows, the long term approach is to reduce the need for such responses by making processes lean, flexible and predictable. It requires continual exposure and elimination of sources of inefficiency, rigidity, and variability, and use of information technology to integrate various subprocesses. The goal is to design and control the process for continuous flows without waits, inventories, and defects. We conclude with different philosophies of process improvement.

The Appendices contain

- a summary of the "levers" to manage business processes. It is hoped that MBPF Checklist will be useful to the action-oriented reader.
- some background material in probability and statistics. A reader of this book is assumed to have knowledge of these concepts.

Finally, a student version of the simulation software ProcessModel is enclosed with the book. ProcessModel can be used to design, simulate and communicate processes. The capabilities of the software include flowcharting components, simulation logic and animation. Additional features of the software include hierarchical modeling (to develop levels of detail) and layering capability (to organize complex charts), statistical distribution generator, an extensive library of built-in flowcharting graphics, built-in business diagram templates, statistical process control charting capability, and a state of the art flowcharting package. The software comes complete with a built-in comprehensive training program and an online manual.

Several problem sets from the book chapters have been modeled using ProcessModel. These can be accessed from the book web site located at:

http://www.prenhall.com/anupindi

This book has evolved from a set of notes written by the authors and used in teaching the core Operations Management class at the Kellogg Graduate School of Management. We are grateful to the students in the full-time (MM), the part-time (TMP), and the executive masters program (EMP) at Kellogg for their patience and support with the early versions of this manuscript. In addition, several schools other than Kellogg have used the manuscript in its custom published form. We are particularly indebted to Larry Robinson at Cornell University and George Monahan at the University of Illinois at Champaign Urbana, for several in-depth comments on the manuscript that have resulted in significant improvements. At Kellogg, in addition to us, Krishnan Anand has used the manuscript to teach the TMP students. His suggestions and comments, especially the Loan Application Flow example in chapter 3, are greatly appreciated. We are also grateful to several reviewers of early versions of the manuscript for their constructive suggestions.

In addition, we appreciate the efforts of several people at Prentice Hall. The manuscript has benefited significantly from extensive and meticulous reviews from Ronald Librach, our developmental editor, and Carey Lange, our copy editor. Evyan Jengo was our patient and quality-inspiring production manager; she masterfully incorporated our mass of last-minute changes in the manuscript. We appreciate the efforts of Tom Tucker, our editor, in patiently coordinating the entire project. We acknowledge Scott Baird, CEO of ProModel Corporation, for developing some of the exercises in the problem sets using ProcessModel software.

Finally, all of us have been influenced in various ways by how we were taught operations at our respective alma maters. Parts of the book reflect what each of us imbibed from the various classes we took. So, we thank our mentors and other faculty at Northwestern University, Carnegie Mellon University, Stanford University, State University of New York at Stony Brook, and University of California at Berkeley. Last, but not least, we would like to thank our families for their support during this effort.

Ravi Anupindi
Sunil Chopra
Sudhakar D. Deshmukh
Jan A. Van Mieghem
Eitan Zemel

Kellogg Graduate School of Management
Northwestern University

Process Model

ProcessModel is a revolutionary software tool for designing, testing and communicating business processes. It combines the best process flow-charting tool with the ultimate simulation engine to provide an easy-to-use process improvement tool. With ProcessModel you can model and simulate most processes in a matter of minutes. Imagine being able to quickly test different ways to make your business run more efficiently, increase profits and save money—all risk free. You can use ProcessModel to model any business process such as: order fulfillment, production, warehousing and distribution, accounting and collections, purchasing, and retail and office operations. With ProcessModel you can:

- Perform what-if analysis.
- Reduce cycle time and improve efficiency.
- Track resource, material and activity costs.
- More effectively schedule personnel and allocate resources.
- Animate your processes to identify bottlenecks.

ProcessModel makes it easy to model, analyze and improve your processes. The combined flexibility of Micrografx FlowCharter and PROMODEL's powerful simulation technology lets you take control of your business processes and deliver bottom-line results quickly and easily!

What customers say about ProcessModel:

> I love this product! It seems to have been designed by people who really understand the intricacies of process analysis from start to finish. ProcessModel has the complete set of features; process-flow representation, graphic and statistical analysis output, simulation capability programmatic flexibility and killer visualization for effective communication of the results. . . . It is simply the best, cost-effective, process analysis tool on the market!
>
> CHRIS MILLER, EDS

> We are using ProcessModel for modeling the order management process. The tool enables us to model current processes, looking at the resource utilization and the overall process. By removing the manual process we could project how to free up resources, to allow them to participate in revenue generating sales activities. The model was crucial in our project planning and process redesign efforts.
>
> JOHN CAMBELL, SIX SIGMA BLACK BELT, GE PLASTICS

> We had other products but we chose ProcessModel because of its' ease of use and graphical capability. We were able to build the entire model in three days and get immediate results. This saved us a considerable amount of time. One of the main reasons we were able to improve our process so quickly was because management could visually see the process in action and was confident in our recommendations!
>
> JOHN KIM, JOHN DEERE CREDIT

PROMODEL Corporation
1875 South State
Orem, UT 84097
(801) 223-4600
www.processmodel.com

FlowCharter

Micrografx FlowCharter is the most productive diagramming solution to manage business processes. With unique, patent-pending technology, FlowCharter creates incredibly powerful, interactive diagrams of just about any technology.

FlowCharter contains a wealth of useful and unique capabilities not found in other diagramming products. Living FlowChart technology, for example transforms static diagrams into dynamic, interactive processes. FlowCharter does much more than simply present information—it actually works with it. Attach cost components in a LAN schematic, or associate wages with personnel in an organizational chart, while results tabulate on the fly.

FlowCharter is certified Windows 95, Windows NT, Office 95 and Office 97 compliant. It integrates perfectly with the Microsoft desktop, providing a familiar interface along with complete OLE automation and Visual Basic scripting capabilities. With unmatched ease-of-use, FlowCharter delivers the most powerful diagramming solution for the department and the enterprise.

FORD CORPORATION & THE POWER OF MICROGRAFX FLOWCHARTER
In an effort to fully comply with the IS0-9001 quality standard, Ford Motor Company is currently documenting all of its processes worldwide. In order to make those documents easier to read and to standardize the process description, the Ford Customer Service Division uses Micrografx FlowCharter to design process charts and integrate them within their Word documents. FlowCharter saves Ford employees valuable time in understanding and documenting their processes.

Micrografx Corporation
1303 Arapaho Road
Richardson, TX 75801
1 (888) 216-9281
www.micrografx.com

FIRST EDITION

MANAGING BUSINESS PROCESS FLOWS

Process Management and Strategy

CHAPTER
1
Products, Processes, and Performance

All organizations have business processes that produce and deliver products to satisfy customer needs. These processes transform inputs into outputs by means of capital and labor resources. This transformation involves a flow of work through a network of activities performed by available resources. The resulting outputs are products, which may be physical goods, services performed, or both. Products differ in attributes that customers value such as product cost, quality, variety and delivery-response time. The ability to provide desired product attributes from given inputs depends highly on corresponding process attributes such as processing cost, quality, flexibility and flow time. Processes differ along these four attributes, falling along a continuum—from job shops that produce high-variety/low-volume customized products to flow shops that produce low-variety/high-volume standardized products.

Finally, to assess and improve the performance of a process, we must measure it in concrete, quantifiable terms. The process manager needs both external measures of customer satisfaction, as well as internal measures. Performance may be evaluated frequently in operational terms necessary for day-to-day process management, or infrequently, in the aggregate financial terms that interest mainly the company's stockholders. Managing business processes requires both long-term strategic planning and short-term adaptive control.

1.1 INTRODUCTION

The success of every organization—manufacturing or service, private or public, for-profit or nonprofit—depends on its ability to attract and retain customers. It does so by providing them with products that satisfy their needs, desires, and expectations. Even park districts, postal services, tax-collection agencies, and houses of worship must produce services that satisfy customer needs, whether physical (comfort, safety, convenience), psychological (relaxation, peace of mind), social, or spiritual. Otherwise, unsatisfied customers will seek alternative sources, resulting in a loss to the service provider of both revenue and reputation as an effective organization.

Organizations attract and retain customers by providing products that may be either physical goods (cars, shampoo, computers, food, drugs) or services performed (transporting passengers, performing surgery, giving a sermon, providing consultation, entertaining). In fact, products are often bundles of goods *and* services. An automobile manufacturer, for instance, sells not only cars but also financing and emergency road services. Airlines provide not only transportation but also meals, beverages, and other in-flight services.

Organizations produce and deliver goods and services by means of business processes that transform inputs into outputs. Outputs in the form of finished goods, processed information, and services performed for customers may require a large set of inputs, including raw materials, component parts, energy, data, and customers in need of service. This transformation is achieved by means of organizational resources. *Resources* are tangible assets that are usually divided into two categories: *capital* and *labor.*

In this book, we will see how organizations manage business processes to produce and deliver products that satisfy customer needs, wants, and expectations. In this chapter, we introduce *the process view* of organizations and some fundamental concepts of business processes. The process view, with the strategic role of operations that we discuss in chapter 2, will be our two key approaches to evaluating and improving business process. In section 1.2 we characterize any organization as *a process through which inputs flow and exit as outputs.* Processing involves a flow of work through a network of activities performed by organizational resources. In section 1.3 we identify *product attributes that customers value* such as product cost, quality, variety and delivery-response time. We also examine the similarities and differences between processes that provide goods and processes that provide services.

In section 1.4 we study the corresponding *process attributes* that managers can control: processing cost, quality, flexibility, and flow time. We also outline the differences between *two types of processes:* job shop and flow shop. In section 1.5 we describe *process performance measures* that help managers to assess and improve processes. In particular, we distinguish between external and internal measures and between financial and operational measures of performance. In section 1.6 we conclude by distinguishing between *process planning* and *process control decisions* that are discussed in detail in the rest of the book.

1.2   THE PROCESS VIEW OF ORGANIZATIONS

Any organization, or any of its parts, can be viewed as a process. A **process** is a transformation of inputs into outputs and can be represented, at the highest level of abstraction, as a black box (see Figure 1.1). To evaluate and improve the performance of a process—the two key objectives of this book—we must look inside the black box and examine the input-output transformation in greater detail.

The transformation is clearly defined by the **process architecture,** or **structure,** which incorporates five elements:

1. Inputs and outputs,
2. Flow units,
3. A network of activities and buffers,
4. Resources and
5. Information structure.

Inputs and Outputs   The first step in viewing an organization as a process is to identify its inputs and outputs, as well as their entry and exit points that define process

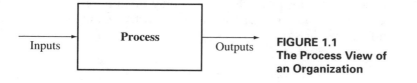

FIGURE 1.1
The Process View of an Organization

boundaries. **Inputs** refer to any tangible or intangible items that flow from the environment into the process. **Outputs**—whether information, material, energy, cash, or satisfied customers—flow from the process back into the environment. Thus, inputs and outputs constitute the organization's interaction with its environment.

As inputs are being transformed, they flow through the process and exit as outputs. Thus, raw materials flow through a manufacturing process and exit as finished goods. Passengers waiting in Location A flow through an air-transportation process and exit as passengers at Location B; along the way, the jet fuel is transformed into energy and pollution. Similarly, data flow through an accounting process and exit as financial statements. Invoiced dollars (accounts receivable) flow through a billing and collection process and exit as collected dollars (cash).

Flow Units   The second step in developing a process view is a clear definition of the **flow units,** the units of flow being analyzed. Depending on the process, the flow unit may be a unit of input (e.g., a customer), a unit of output (e.g., a finished product), a unit of an intermediate product (e.g., a seat in an auto assembly plant), or even a set of inputs or outputs in a multiproduct process (e.g., a set of subassembled components needed for the final assembly). Although the definition of the flow units is quite important for process-performance evaluation or analysis, it is also important when designing the process because (as we shall see later in this book) it directly affects capacity and investment levels. Table 1.1 lists some generic business processes and identifies the flow units that move through the input-output transformation.

A Network of Activities and Buffers   As a third step in adopting the process view, we must identify the various flows *inside* a process that constitute the transformation. In a multiproduct organization, there are typically multiple flows within the process, each associated with one product. To identify these various flows and to understand how they can be managed, we examine the input-output transformation in greater detail. This transformation is achieved by flows through networks of activities that are performed by the various resources at the organization's disposal.

TABLE 1.1   Some Generic Business Processes

Process	Flow Unit	Input-Output Transformation
Order fulfillment	Orders	From the receipt of an order to the delivery of the product
Production	Products	From the receipt of materials to the completion of the finished product
Outbound logistics	Products	From the end of production to the delivery of the product to the customer
Supply cycle	Supplies	From issuing of a purchase order to the receipt of the supplies
Customer service	Customers	From the arrival of a customer to the departure
New product development	Projects	From the recognition of a need to the launching of a product
Cash cycle	Cash	From the expenditure of funds (costs) to the collection of revenues

Activities are building blocks of processes. An **activity** is the simplest form of transformation that we need to consider. It is a mini-process in itself, but for our process-evaluation and -improvement purposes, we are not concerned with further details of any specific activity. In other words, the "art" of process analysis and design is to choose an appropriate level of detail in given activities that define the entire process. Thus, a black box view of activities themselves will suffice. For example, when studying a supply chain (the interorganizational process that includes consumers, suppliers, manufacturers, distributors, and retailers), it suffices to view each organization (plant, warehouse, or store) as one activity or black box. When studying each organization more fully, however, we must study its particular transformation process in more detail by looking closely at its specific activities. At this level, activities include spot welding sheet metal to auto chassis, checking in passengers at airport terminals, entering cost data in accounting information systems, and receiving electronic fund transfers at collection agencies.

Activities are ordered so that the output of one becomes an input into another—hence the term a **network of activities.** This network describes the specific **precedence relationships** among activities—the sequential relationships according to which one activity must be finished before another one can begin. As we will see later, the precedence relationships embodied in network structure heavily influence the time performance of the process. Again, in multiproduct organizations, each product will have a specific set of precedence relationships. Each network of activities can have multiple "routes," each of which indicates precedence relationships for a specific product.

Often the process allows for *storage* of flow units residing in **buffers** between consecutive activities. Storage could be regarded as a special activity that transforms the time dimension of a flow unit by delaying it. In business processes, storage is called *inventory,* and the amount of inventory in the system is an important process-performance measure that we discuss in detail in chapter 3. From Figure 1.2, a network can be represented graphically as a process flow chart consisting of activities (represented by rectangles), storage buffers (represented by triangles), and the routes or precedence relationships among them (represented by solid arrows).

FIGURE 1.2 A Process as a Network of Activities

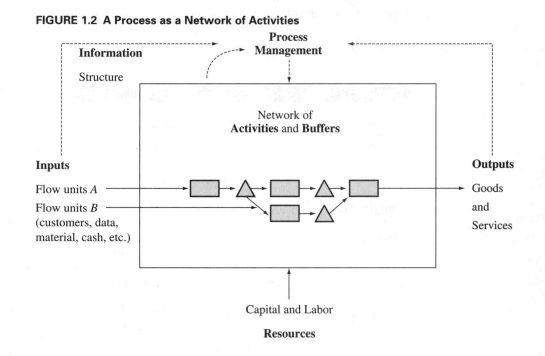

Resources

Resources   The fourth element of the process view consists of organizational resources. **Resources** are tangible assets that are usually divided into two categories:

- **Capital,** fixed assets such as land, buildings, equipment, machines, and information systems, and
- **Labor,** such as operators, customer-service representatives, workers, and clerks.

Resources are the necessary means to perform activities. While inputs are *consumed* during the transformation process, resources are *utilized* but not consumed (except perhaps for depreciation, wear and tear). Some activities require multiple resources (a welding activity, for instance, requires a worker and welding equipment), and some resources can perform multiple activities (some workers can not only weld but also drill). How resources are allocated to activities is an integral part of every process.

Information Structure   The fifth and final element of the process view of an organization is its information structure. The **information structure** shows which information is needed and/or available to manage activities or make managerial decisions. Information flow is usually represented in process flow charts by means of dotted lines.

Thus, we can define a **business process** as *a network of activities performed by resources that transform inputs into outputs.* **Process flow management,** therefore, is *a set of managerial policies specifying how a process should be operated over time*—how and when it should be operated and which resources should be allocated to the activities that constitute it. This process view of organizations will be our tool in evaluating and improving organizational performance. We will see how process structure and process flow management significantly affect the performance of the process and, ultimately, that of the organization.

Among the advantages of the process view is its portability to a variety of organizations—it can be used to represent not only a manufacturing process, but any process in which activities are performed. These processes include such services as those offered by accounts receivable departments, product design teams, computer-rental companies, and hairdressing salons. The process view is the ultimate tool for representing *cross-functional processes,* including production, finance, marketing-related functions, and supplier relationships. By incorporating buffers, we also account for handoffs or interfaces between different people or activities—typically the areas where most improvements can be made. In addition, the process view can be used at a very high level such as that of the supply chain, or at a very detailed level such as that of a manufacturing work cell. The process view is "customer-aware"—it always includes the customer as the person who receives the outputs. Finally, the process view is our tool for performing two functions:

1. Evaluating processes and
2. Studying the ways in which processes can be designed, restructured, and managed to improve performance.

1.3 PRODUCTS

Products are the desired set of process outputs. (The process may also produce other by-products, such as heat, pollution, or scrap, that are not desired by or delivered to customers.) For a specific product type, different customers may have different needs and desires, and if the process is to produce and deliver products that satisfy them, the **process manager**—the person who controls and is responsible for the process—must be aware of these key *product attributes*. As mentioned, products may be physical goods, services performed, or a combination of both. Important differences exist between goods and services that the manager must consider when designing or managing the processes that deliver them. Section 1.3.2 addresses these differences.

1.3.1 Product Attributes

Customers value products because they help satisfy their wants and needs. **Product attributes** refer to those properties customers consider important. For simplicity, we categorize product attributes along the following four dimensions.

1. **Product cost** is *the total cost that a customer incurs to own and experience the product.* It includes the purchase price plus any costs incurred during the lifetime of the product, such as costs for servicing, maintenance, insurance, and even final disposal. Cost is important because customers usually make purchase decisions within budget constraints.

2. **Product delivery-response time** is *the total time that a customer must wait before receiving a product for which he or she has expressed a need to the provider.* Response time is closely related to product availability and accessibility. If a manufactured good is on store shelves, the response time is effectively zero. If it is stocked in a warehouse or a distribution center, response time consists of the transportation time needed to get it to the customer. If a firm does not stock the product and produces only to-order, response time will also include the processing time required to produce the product.

   With services, response time is determined by the availability of resources required to serve the customer—if resources are not immediately available, the customer must wait. Even when resources become available, the customer must often wait while the service is being performed. Thus, even if the product is on the retail-store shelf, the customer may have to wait for a checkout clerk to become available. Generally, customers prefer short response times, as immediate gratification of needs is typically preferred over delayed gratification.

3. **Product variety** indicates *the range of choice offered to the customer to let the product meet his or her needs.* Choice results from the variety of volumes, colors, and sizes from which customers can choose in such outlets as department stores, or from any other product features or aspects that customers can request at custom tailor shops and other made-to-order businesses. Whereas standard, commodity products may offer little variety, custom products may be one-of-a-kind items tailored specifically to customers' unique needs or wishes. For example, when purchasing consumer items such as money-management software in a computer store or clothing in a department store, customers must choose from limited sets of personal finance programs or clothes sizes, colors, and styles. In contrast, when ordering an accounting-information program from a software-consulting company or a suit at a custom tailor, customers can specify products that meet personal needs and desires, providing an almost endless range of product variety.

4. **Product quality** refers to *the degree of excellence—it depends on what and how well the product performs.* Product quality is a function of effective design, as well as production that conforms to the design. It may refer to tangible, intangible, and even transcendental characteristics. Product quality is often the most difficult product attribute to define and measure because subjective judgment and perception play important roles in the estimation of quality. Table 1.2 lists some definitions of quality. Each definition tries to capture something that is elusive, philosophical, statistical, and all-inclusive, largely because quality is a dimension that must be seen from both the customer's and the producer's perspectives.

   From the customer's perspective, quality depends on product features (what it can do), performance (how well it does what it does), and reliability (how consistently it performs over time). Whereas product features and performance are influenced by quality of design, reliability is more heavily influenced by the conformance of the production process to the design. Thus, the styling, size, options, and engine rating of an automobile are its *features.* Acceleration, emergency handling, ride comfort, safety, and fuel efficiency

TABLE 1.2 Quality Is . . .

Quality is recognized by a nonthinking process, and, therefore, cannot be defined!—R. M. Pirstig in
Zen and the Art of Motorcycle Maintenance
That which makes anything such as it is—from *Funk and Wagnall's Dictionary*
Fitness for use—J. Juran and ASQ
Conformance to requirements—P. Crosby
Closeness to target—deviations mean loss to the society—G. Taguchi
Total Quality Control provides full customer satisfaction at the most economical levels—A.
Feigenbaum
*Eight dimensions of quality are: Performance, Features, Conformance, Reliability, Serviceability,
Durability, Aesthetics, and Perception*—D. Garvin

are aspects of *performance,* while durability and failure-free performance over time represent its *reliability.*

A product may thus be defined as a bundle of these four attributes. When these attributes are measured and quantified, we can represent a product by a point in the associated four-dimensional matrix, or *product space,* of cost, time, variety, and quality. (The "product space" image will be a useful metaphor to define strategy in chapter 2.) The choice between different products often involves trade-offs among these attributes. The value of a product to customers is measured by the *utility* that they derive from buying some combination of these attributes at a price within their budget constraints. In general, high-quality products that are available in wide varieties and are delivered quickly and at low cost provide high customer value. Product value (or "utility" in economic terms) is a complex function of these four product attributes. It may be easy to define qualitatively, but difficult to measure in practice. *A reasonable estimate of product value is the price that a specific customer is willing to pay for a product.* (This willingness-to-pay varies from customer to customer, giving rise to the familiar price-quantity market-demand relationship described by economists.)

Although customers prefer products with all attributes (good, fast, and cheap), obvious trade-offs are involved. Customer expectations, for instance, may depend on the availability of—and experience with—competing products. In that case, an important strategic business decision involves selecting the right combination of product attributes that will distinguish an organization's product by its appeal to a particular segment of the market (see chapter 2). Moreover, the dynamics of competition entail continuous improvement in product variety and quality and a decrease in cost and delivery-response time.

1.3.2 Product Types: Goods versus Services

Goods are physical, tangible products delivered by producing organizations. In contrast, services include tangible as well as intangible products experienced by the customer, such as getting a haircut or receiving investment advice. The process of producing goods is typically called **manufacturing** or **production operations.** Processes that deliver services are sometimes called **service operations.** We refer to business processes that design, produce, distribute, and deliver goods and/or services simply as **operations.**

Although goods and services share the same four attributes, significant differences exist between the two product types that make their process management considerably different. Services are inherently "experiential" and require close interaction between the service process and the customer. Services are often delivered and experienced simultaneously and cannot be produced in advance and stored for later consumption. Unlike manufacturing managers, service managers cannot separate the production and consumption aspects of the process output by such buffers as inventory and time delay. Also, service operations "transform the customer" and often require the physical presence of the customer who undergoes or participates in at least part of the process. This places high demands on the service process architecture because factors such as the attractiveness of the process environment and friendliness of the labor resources become important. (The term *backroom operations* refers to those aspects of service operations that are hidden from customers.) Finally, most customer experiences are subjective and often include an intangible component. This complicates the measurement of service process performance and makes its evaluation even harder (see section 1.5).

1.4   PROCESSES

As mentioned, processes produce and deliver products by transforming inputs into outputs by means of capital and labor resources. Performance evaluation of a given process includes an assessment of its ability to provide the desired product attributes from the given inputs. In this section, we describe processing abilities according to the corresponding four dimensions of product attributes. We also classify processes based on these attributes.

1.4.1   Process Attributes

As with products, we use four attributes for measuring the ability of processes to produce and deliver corresponding product attributes.

1. **Process cost** is *the total cost incurred in producing and delivering outputs.* It includes the cost of raw materials and both the fixed and variable costs of operating the process. (For our purposes, we need not be more specific about the ways in which accounting practices allocate costs to time periods and products.)

2. **Process flow time** is *the total time needed to transform a flow unit from input into output.*

3. **Process flexibility** measures *the ability of the process to produce and deliver desired product variety.* Process flexibility is closely linked to the flexibility of its resources. Flexible resources (such as flexible technology and cross-trained workers or "generalists") can perform multiple activities and often produce a variety of products. Dedicated or specialized resources, on the other hand, can only perform a restricted set of activities, typically those designed for one product.

4. **Process quality** refers to *the ability of the process to produce and deliver quality products.* It includes process accuracy (dimensional precision and setting), conformance to design specifications, and process reliability and maintainability.

Not surprisingly, product and process attributes are often interrelated. For example, product quality is closely related to both product and process cost and response time. Thus, product availability, accessibility, and prompt delivery are often critical to service quality, as in retail stores and restaurants. In manufacturing, producing defective products means rework that increases both processing cost and flow time. Shorter processing time may mean fewer opportunities to make mistakes, better accountability for errors, and quicker detection and correction—all of which result in better quality. Conversely, high quality and greater variety may mean higher cost and longer response times, as in the case of handmade (as opposed to machine-made) oriental rugs and customized (as opposed to standard) furniture.

1.4.2   Process Architectures or "Types": Job Shop versus Flow Shop

Although processes differ along their four attributes, most fall somewhere on the continuum between two archetypes: the *job shop process* and the *flow shop process*. The two key differences between these two process types are:

1. *Resource types* used to perform their activities, and
2. *Physical layout* in the processing network.

Job Shops   At one extreme, a **job shop** uses *flexible resources to produce low volumes of customized, high-variety products*. Job shops include artisan bakeries, tool and die shops, management consulting firms, law firms, and architectural and design companies. Job shops use general-purpose resources that can perform many different activities and locate resources with similar functional capabilities in close proximity. This design is called a **functional or process layout,** because it groups organizational resources by processing activities or "functions" in "departments." For example, a job shop manufacturing process (e.g., a tool and die or machine shop) will group all its presses in a stamping department and all its mills in a milling department.

A job shop usually has many products simultaneously flowing through the process, each with its own route. Therefore, it is often more practical to represent a job shop process view with a network of resources instead of a network of activities. In a network of resources, the rectangular boxes represent resources (grouped into departments such as an X-ray, accounts payable, or stamping department) instead of activities. The flow chart on the left in Figure 1.3 shows an example of the functional layout of a two-product process with four resource groups, labeled *A, B, C* and *D*. Resource *A, D* and *B* perform product 1's activities, while product 2 calls for resources *C, B* and *A*. The set of activities for each product is now allocated to the resources with the routes representing the precedence relationships as before.

Because the sequence of activities required to process each product (i.e., the routes) varies from one job to the next, job shops typically display jumbled work flows with large amounts of storage and substantial waiting between activities. To direct work flow, job shops typically use highly structured information systems. In its simplest form, shop paper (in manufacturing) or bill paper (in services) is physically tagged to each flow unit. It specifies the appropriate sequence of activities, together with the resources needed for each specific activity. For costing and control purposes, each operator (or department) reports the time worked on each flow unit.

FIGURE 1.3 Functional or Process Layout (left) versus Product Layout (right)

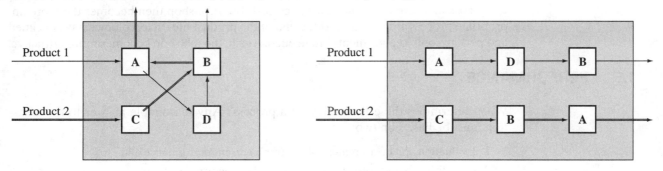

Because of the high variety of products flowing through the job shop, resources often need setups before they can be changed over from the activities required for one product to those required for another. This changeover causes loss of production and a fluctuating workload. Job shop process architectures typically result in high processing costs and long flow times; however, it remains the modern artisan's shop—its hallmark is a high process flexibility that permits product customization.

Flow Shops   At the other extreme, a **flow shop** uses *specialized resources that perform limited tasks but with great precision and speed.* The result is a limited variety of product produced in large volumes. Due to the expertise developed by workers through repetition, quality tends to be more consistent. Although the high processing capacity needed to produce large volumes entails high fixed costs for plant and equipment, these costs are spread over larger volumes, often resulting in the low-variable processing cost that characterizes economies of scale. Resources are located according to the sequence of activities needed to produce a particular product, and limited storage space is used between activities. Because the location of resources is dictated by the processing requirements of the product, the resulting network design is called a **product layout.** The flow chart on the right in Figure 1.3 shows the two-product process now in product layout. Each product is now produced on its own "production line" with product-dedicated resources. Notice that dedicating resources to a product may necessitate the duplication (and investment) of a resource pool, such as resource *A* in Figure 1.3. On the positive side, limiting the product variety of dedicated resources allows specialization. Therefore, a product layout and the high productivity rate of its specialized resources typically results in shorter process flow time than in a job shop.

The most famous example of a flow shop is the automobile assembly line pioneered by Henry Ford in 1913. An *assembly line* is actually an example of the *discrete flow shop,* where products are produced as disjoint items, such as bread, cars, and computers. In contrast, beverage companies, steel plants, oil refineries, and chemical plants are *continuous flow shops.* Sometimes called "processing plants," they produce outputs in a continuous fashion. Resources in flow shops are often rigidly connected by automatic conveyor systems that result in a linear flow and little storage between activities. Although the rigid layout of resources and their highly specialized nature prevent the process from providing significant product variety, the flow shop remains the crown jewel of the industrial revolution—its hallmark is low unit-processing cost and consistent quality despite high volumes.

Real-world processes generally fall somewhere along the continuum between these two archetypes (Schmenner 1994 gives an excellent overview). In the early stages of a product's life cycle, because volumes are low and marketability is uncertain, high capital investment cannot be justified at this stage. Consequently, a job shop is often the appropriate process. As the product matures, however, volume increases and product consistency, cost, and response time become critical. The flow shop then becomes the more appropriate process architecture. At the end of the product life cycle, volumes have declined and perhaps only replacements are needed. Again, the job shop becomes more attractive.

1.5   PERFORMANCE

What determines the effectiveness of a process? Any reasonable answer to this question must be based on two factors:

1. Evaluation and measurement of the firm's current performance and
2. Establishment of future goals as expressed by the firm's strategy.

TABLE 1.3 The Importance of Measurement

*When you can measure what you are speaking about, and express it in numbers, you know
    something about it*—Lord Kelvin (1824–1907)

*Count what is countable, measure what is measurable, and what is not measurable, make
    measurable*—Galileo Galilei (1564–1642)

Data! Data! Data! I can't make bricks without clay—Sherlock Holmes in *The Adventure of
    Copper Beeches,* by Sir Arthur Conan Doyle

In God we trust, everyone else must bring data—W. Edwards Deming

*To assess and improve the performance of a business process, we must measure it in quan-
tifiable terms.* In this section, we identify several quantifiable measures of process performance, both internal and external. We also indicate how performance may be evaluated in both financial and operational terms. The relationship between process
architecture and the firm's strategy will be the topic of chapter 2.

1.5.1 The Importance of Measurement: Management by Fact

Longtime General Motors chairman Alfred Sloan defined a "professional manager" as
someone who manages by fact rather than by intuition or emotion. By capturing facts
in an objective, concrete, and quantifiable manner, measurement provides a scientific
basis for making decisions (see Table 1.3). It allows us to estimate the functional relationship between controllable process attributes and desired product attributes and,
thus, lets us set appropriate performance standards. Finally, performance measurement
is essential in designing and implementing incentive mechanisms for improving both
products and processes and for assessing the extent of our improvements.

1.5.2 Types of Measures: External versus Internal

Process performance should be evaluated in terms of such *external* measures as customer satisfaction; however, we also need *internal* measures, which not only affect customer satisfaction but which the process manager can also control. *Thus, internal measures provide a basis for process-related decisions (e.g., scheduling production) and
external measures indicate the effectiveness of those decisions in satisfying the customer.*

External Measures   External-performance measures estimate a firm's ability to attract and retain customers by providing goods and/or services that satisfy their needs,
wants, and expectations. External performance strongly depends on the **economic environment** of the process, which consists of three elements:

- *Output market,* including market demand and prices for the producer's product and the
  customer's access to alternate product sources (the competition),
- *Input market,* representing the available supply and costs of inputs, and
- *Resource market,* representing the availability and costs of resources.

Managers study the impact of competition through competitive industry analysis and
estimate demand through market research based on customer surveys, relative rankings, and ratings of competing products. These measures can then be used to estimate
the value or utility of goods and services to customers.

  For example, the American Society for Quality (ASQ) and the University of
Michigan have developed the *American Customer Satisfaction Index* (*ACSI*), which
tracks overall customer satisfaction in several manufacturing and service industries and

public sectors. Each score is a weighted average of customer responses to questions relating to perceptions of service, quality, value, and the extent to which products meet expectations and ideals. The overall effect of customer (dis)satisfaction also can be measured indirectly by rates of customer retention, defection, and turnover. It is estimated that organizations typically lose 20% of their dissatisfied customers forever. Thus, customer loyalty and retention rates directly affect the bottom line in terms of expected cash flow over the product's lifetime.

In addition, *the cost of attracting a new customer is estimated to be five times that of serving a current customer.* Because an organization has better information on current customers, it is more economical to serve them than to seek out new ones. Number of warranty repairs, product recalls, and field failures are measurable signs of potential customer dissatisfaction and eventual defection. Although number of customer complaints received is a direct measure of customer dissatisfaction, research shows that *only about 4% of dissatisfied customers bother to complain,* representing only the tip of the iceberg.

Customer-satisfaction measures represent an external market perspective that is objective and bottom-line oriented, because they identify competitive benchmarks at which the process manager can aim. These measures indicate customer satisfaction at an *aggregate,* not at an *individual-customer,* level. They are also more *results oriented* than *action oriented*—they cannot indicate how the manager might improve processes. Finally, they are *lagging,* rather than *leading,* indicators of success—after-the-fact assessments of performance. To be operationally useful, customer-satisfaction measures must be linked to internal measures that the process manager can control.

Internal Measures   As noted, product cost, response time, variety, and quality are four critical product attributes that determine customer satisfaction. Some of these attributes can be easily translated into concrete measures of process performance that the manager can plan, monitor, and control. Processing cost and work flow time, for example, are quantifiable internal measures that relate directly to both product price (and thus ownership cost) and delivery-response time.

External measures can be linked to internal measures using some or all four process attributes. For example, an airline's on-time performance may be translated into the following goal: "Average arrival and departure delays should not exceed 15 minutes." The responsiveness of its reservation system could be measured by "the time taken to answer the telephone," with a specified goal of "30 seconds or less 95% of the time." Similarly, waiting time at a bank teller's window or registration and admission into a hospital can be measured, monitored, and standardized. Product availability also can be measured by such standards as "fraction of demand filled from the stock on hand" or "average number of stockouts per year."

Service (un)availability can be measured by the proportion of customer calls that must wait because all operators are busy. The goal might be to reduce that proportion to "no more than 20%." At an electric utility company, service availability might be measured by "frequency or duration of power outages per year" with a target of "no more than 30 minutes per year." Process flexibility can be measured either by the time or cost needed to switch production from one good or service to another or by the number of different products that can be produced.

When measuring product quality, managers must be specific as to which of the many quality dimensions concern them: product features, performance, reliability, serviceability, aesthetics, and conformance to customer expectations. Reliability, for instance, is measured in terms of durability and frequency of repair. Both product reliability and serviceability, therefore, can be assessed by the following technical measures: *failure rate,* which measures the probability of product failure; *mean time between fail-*

ures (*MTBF*), which indicates how long a product is likely to perform well before needing repair; and *mean time to repair* (*MTTR*), which indicates how long a product is likely to be out of service while under repair.

Although customers can readily identify product features, performance can be appraised only through actual experience. Evaluating reliability usually requires long-term experience. For instance, a high-end stereo system may have few features, but it offers superior performance in terms of sound quality and is highly reliable. In a restaurant, the main service transformation (the product) is "feeding" hungry customers, and ambiance, menu, and a cocktail lounge are among the features. Tasty food prepared by experienced chefs and presented by knowledgeable, friendly, attentive servers provides a quality dining experience—consistency of quality from one visit to the next provides reliability. McDonald's, for example, is a highly consistent fast-food restaurant featuring a limited menu and a dining experience of a very specific kind.

Measuring and standardizing the quality of services is particularly difficult. In addition to the role played by customer perception, services are often intangible and involve a level of human interaction that is inherently variable. Because they are produced and consumed simultaneously, there is little opportunity to detect and correct defects. Nevertheless, certain tangible aspects of services, as well as the responsiveness, accuracy, and reliability of the provider, can be quantified. The quality of an airline's baggage-handling service can be measured and standardized by such goals as "The number of bags lost or damaged per thousand must not exceed five." Flight comfort can translate into legroom and the width, contour, and thickness of seat cushions. Finally, the quality of in-flight service depends on the quality of meals and entertainment, restroom cleanliness, and the number of attendants on board.

Knowing the external product measures applied by customers, the process manager must translate them into internal process measures that affect the external measures. To be effective, internal measures must meet two conditions:

1. They must be linked to external measures that customers deem important, and

2. They must be directly controllable by the process manager.

Measuring and improving a feature that the customer does not value is a waste of time and effort. Moreover, if we do not know how a process variable affects a product measure, we cannot control it. Ignoring one or both of these conditions has sabotaged many process improvement programs (see Kordupleski et al., 1993).

1.5.3   Types of Measures: Financial versus Operational

Ultimately, process performance is summarized and measured by the financial performance of the organization. Each quarter, most organizations report three types of financial measures to shareholders and other stakeholders:

1. *Absolute performance* (revenues, costs, net income, profit),

2. *Performance relative to asset utilization* (accounting ratios such as ROA, ROI, and inventory turnover), and

3. *"Survival" strength* (cash flow).

Though the ultimate judge of process performance, financial measures are inherently lagging, aggregate, and more results oriented than action oriented. They also are reported infrequently.

The operations manager, however, needs *operational measures*—more detailed and more frequent measures that can be controlled and that ultimately have an impact on financial measures. Ideally, companies want operational measures to be leading indicators of financial performance. The three types of financial measures would then mirror operational measures and provide daily support to process management. For example, the percentage of time that a customer-service phone line is busy is an operational measure that can be monitored and controlled daily—reducing this percentage may well increase revenues. A familiar operational measure is **efficiency,** or **input-output measure**—a relative estimate of the amount of input needed to produce a certain amount of output (e.g., labor hours per product). This operational measure links to financial asset utilization ratios.

Like product value, the efficiency of business processes is easier to define than to measure. Often managers can estimate inputs and outputs in common (usually financial) units. The process efficiency measure then becomes quite sensitive to the economic environment and the price of inputs and outputs will reflect not only process performance, but also the economic climate of input and output factors. To be more specific about operational measures—while simultaneously linking them to the three types of financial measures—we examine basic process measures in greater detail in chapter 3.

1.6 PROCESS PLANNING VERSUS PROCESS CONTROL

Process planning involves *choosing or designing a process architecture.* Managers usually begin by defining outputs—the product types and attributes that the firm should focus on providing. Planning also entails *segmenting markets according to products that customers desire and focusing on segments that the firm wants to serve.* Does the company want to be a low-cost or a high-quality provider? Does it want to provide a wide variety of products or to be known for a few that it supplies very well? As we shall see in chapter 2, such choices depend on both the firm's competitive environment and its inherent capabilities.

Once outputs are defined, managers must choose inputs and design the process architecture needed to accomplish the desired transformation. At this stage, planning decisions include plant location and distribution, product and process design, resource choice and investment (capital equipment and labor), and scale of operation. Thus, *process planning involves strategic positioning of both products and processes and entails long-term commitment of resources.*

Finally, when product attributes have been determined and processes designed, managers must develop operational policies and target values for performance measures. Managerial policies—also referred to as **process control**—specify how processes should be operated and controlled over time. The objective is to ensure that actual process performance continually conforms to planned performance. Ensuring process conformance means monitoring its actual performance over time, comparing it with planned performance, and taking corrective action when deviations occur. Control decisions thus include monitoring and correcting product cost, delivery performance, customer waiting time, inventory levels, and quality defects.

THE PLAN OF THE BOOK

The remainder of this book focuses on the management of business processes in general and process flows in particular. Chapter 2 focuses on strategic decisions involving product attributes and the job of matching process capabilities to desired product attributes. In part II, we analyze key process flow measures in detail. Part III is devoted to process planning and control and stresses the means by which managers achieve desired performance in the presence of uncertainty. Part IV concludes with managing flows in processing networks and with the principles of process improvement.

Problem Set

1.1 Following are several examples of organizations. For each, identify underlying business processes in terms of inputs, outputs, and resources employed. Who are the major competitors of each organization? Who are the customers, and what product attributes do they consider important? What process attributes affect these product attributes? How can these process attributes be measured from both internal and external perspectives? What financial and operational measures would you choose to assess the performance of these processes?

- Toothpaste manufacturer
- Personal computer manufacturer
- Fast-food restaurant
- Telephone company
- Inner-city school
- Public park
- Major business school
- Local bank
- Federal penitentiary
- Art museum
- Red Cross
- Law firm

References

R. E. Kordupleski, R. T. Rust, and A. J Zahorik. Spring 1993. "Why Improving Quality Doesn't Improve Quality (or Whatever Happened to Marketing?)" *California Management Review:* 82–95.

R. W. Schmenner. 1994. *Plant and Service Tours in Operations Management.* Prentice Hall, Upper Saddle River, NJ.

CHAPTER

2

Operations Strategy and Management

An effective business process is tailored to business strategy—process structure and management policy work together to support the organization's overall strategic objectives. *Strategy* consists of plans to deliver sustained superior performance. *Strategic positioning* means deliberately focusing on product attributes that are different from those of one's competitors. *Operations strategy* involves developing more effective business processes. *Operational effectiveness* means developing more effective operating policies than one's competitors and doing a better job of managing one's business processes. Both strategic positioning and operational effectiveness are necessary for sustained superior performance.

Focusing operations and matching products with processes are means of facilitating an effective *fit* between strategy and processes. Both evolve over time. Because the best operational practices improve continuously in competitive industries, firms must make continuous improvements in operational effectiveness.

2.1 INTRODUCTION

The word *strategy* derives from the Greek military term *stratégia,* "the general's art." It is

> the art or science of planning a war, and much of the original management thinking on strategy treated business as something of a war and the goal was to win. However, times have changed. CEOs are no longer generals, workers are not soldiers. Today, strategy is a plan to achieve an objective (Hindle, 1994).

The "plan" specifies for managers precisely what they must do to reach corporate objectives. Often the implicitly assumed objective in business strategy is to deliver *sustained superior performance.* To outperform one's rivals, one must be—and remain—different from them. Indeed, because similar firms, especially those in the same industry, perform in much the same way, a sustainable competitive advantage requires some form of differentiation.

Competitive Product Space Figure 2.1 represents the concepts of strategy and differentiation by depicting a firm's product portfolio in the *competitive product space* composed from the measured four product attributes introduced in chapter 1. (For graphical simplicity, we only show variety and cost efficiency, two dimensions of the four-dimensional product space, holding timeliness and quality constant.) An organiza-

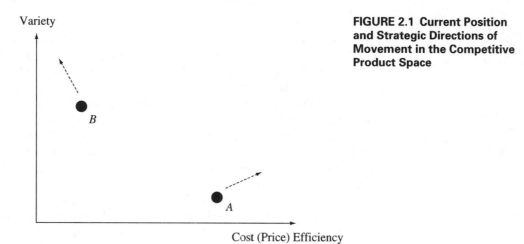

FIGURE 2.1 Current Position and Strategic Directions of Movement in the Competitive Product Space

tion may, for example, differentiate itself by offering customers *value* through a product with a unique combination of those product attributes defined in chapter 1: product cost, quality, variety and delivery-response time.

Measuring and quantifying the current product portfolio value offering along these four dimensions yields a set of *points,* one per product, in the competitive product space. This set of points represents the firm's current strategic *position.* A firm may choose to provide a low-cost standardized product rather than an expensive customized product (the two positions represented in Figure 2.1 by points *A* and *B,* respectively).

Strategic Positioning   Strategic positioning defines those positions that the firm wants to occupy in its competitive product space. Relative to its current position, it defines its future position as a *direction of movement* by assigning relative priorities to each of the four dimensions of strategic positioning. We can represent strategic positioning as an arrow or ray emanating from the firm's current position—its slope represents the relative strategic priorities assigned by the firm to the four dimensions. In Figure 2.1, for example, the provider of product *B* wants to deliver a more customized product, even at the expense of cost efficiency. *A*'s provider, on the other hand, is mainly concerned about cost.

Competitors also occupy positions in the competitive product space. One could conceivably measure the product performance of each competitor, deduce its strategic positioning from the attributes of its products, and represent its current position in the competitive space. Occupying a differentiated position, then, entails producing and delivering different product attributes. This approach means structuring and performing the firm's network of activities—and thus its business processes—in ways that differ from those of competitors.

To deliver superior performance, a firm must strive to select a combination of product attributes and business processes that are distinct from those of the competition. In the automotive industry, for example, whereas Hyundai aims to occupy a low-cost position, Rolls Royce strives for the highest-quality cars. As we will see, each company's business processes will also differ. To deliver better performance some differentiation from competitors is needed. Finally, to *sustain* competitive advantage, a firm must ensure that its competition finds it hard to imitate its chosen position.

Operational Effectiveness In addition to developing a sustainable strategic position, a firm may, of course, distinguish itself through superior operational performance. For example, a company can gain a cost advantage over competitors by performing production and distribution activities more efficiently. **Operational effectiveness** means developing more effective operating policies than one's competitor and managing one's business processes better. "Operational effectiveness includes but is not limited to efficiency. It refers to any number of practices that allow a company to better utilize its inputs by, for example, reducing defects in products or developing products faster" (Porter, 1996). Two automobile companies may have similar assembly-line processes, but one company may perform better because it is better at managing its work flow.

In practice, gaining and sustaining a competitive advantage requires *both* strategic positioning and operational effectiveness. In this chapter, we examine these two concepts and trace their historical development. In section 2.2, we first define *business strategy* in terms of markets, customers, and products, and *operations strategy* as planning the process structure necessary to produce and deliver those products. In section 2.3, we emphasize the importance of a *strategic fit* among three pivotal aspects of a firm's operations:

1. Business strategy,
2. Operations strategy, and
3. Managerial policies.

In section 2.4, we show how focusing on narrow market segments and structuring business processes accordingly facilitates this strategic fit.

Section 2.5 presents an important example of matching products and processes according to variety and volume. In section 2.6, we distinguish between strategic positioning and operational effectiveness by developing the concept of *operations frontier* in the competitive product space of product cost, response time, variety, and quality. Section 2.7 concludes the chapter by tracing the historical evolution of operations strategy and process improvements.

2.2 THE STRATEGY HIERARCHY

Strategic planning spans different levels in an organization. At the highest level of a diversified company, **corporate strategy** defines the businesses in which the corporation will participate and specifies how key corporate resources will be acquired and allocated to each business. Corporate strategy formation is thus like portfolio management—managing a mix of divisions or product lines so as to ensure synergy and competitive advantage.

At the next level, **business strategy** defines the scope of each division or business unit in terms of the products that it will offer, the market segments that it will serve, and the ways in which it will deliver superior performance. At this level, strategy includes what we have described as *strategic positioning*—selecting the key product attributes on the basis of which the business unit will compete. The goal is to differentiate the firm from its competition by establishing competitive priorities in terms of product attributes—cost, quality, variety and response time. Business strategy, therefore, entails a two-pronged analysis:

1. Competitive analysis of the industry in which a business unit will compete and
2. Critical analysis of the unit's competitive skills and resources.

At the next level, we have **functional strategies** for marketing, operations, and finance—the three main functions in most organizations:

- *Marketing* identifies and targets customers that the business unit wants to serve, the products that it must supply to meet customer needs, and the competition that it will face in the marketplace.
- *Operations* involves planning and managing the processes through which the business unit supplies customers with desired products.
- *Finance* deals with the acquisition and allocation of the resources needed to operate all of a unit's business processes.

Each of these functions must translate mid-level business strategy into its own functional requirements by specifying what it must do well to support the higher-level strategy.

In particular, **operations strategy** involves configuring and developing business processes that will enable a firm to produce and deliver the products specified by the business strategy. This task includes selecting and combining activities and resources into a *network architecture* that, as we saw in chapter 1, also defines the other elements of a process, such as inputs and outputs, flow units, and information structure. Operations is also responsible for developing or acquiring the necessary process capabilities and attributes—process cost, flow time, flexibility, and quality—to support the firm's business strategy. Whereas business strategy involves choosing product attributes on which to compete, operations strategy focuses on enabling and executing the business strategy—on *how* to produce and deliver those product attributes.

The difference is that business strategy is concerned with selecting *external output markets* and the *products* with which to supply them, whereas operations strategy involves designing *internal processes* and *interfaces* between input and output markets. It must establish operational objectives that are consistent with overall business goals and develop the process architecture that will accomplish them.

A business strategy based on product cost as a top competitive priority calls for an operations strategy of focusing on efficient and lean business processes. Similarly, if a firm seeks competitive advantage through product variety, its business processes must be flexible enough to produce and deliver customized products. If the goal is to provide short response times, processes must include greater investment in inventories (for manufactured goods) or greater resource availability through excess capacity (for service operations) as we will show in the remainder of the book. Finally, a strategy that calls for producing and delivering high-quality products entails high-quality processes with precision equipment and highly trained workers. In every case, *process capabilities must be aligned with desired product attributes*—operations strategy must be consistent with business strategy. Example 2.1 describes how Wal-Mart achieved such consistency.

2.3   STRATEGIC FIT

The hierarchical framework described in the previous section reflects a *top-down* approach to strategy formulation. Once the firm's business strategy has defined its position in the competitive space (as defined by cost, time, variety, and quality), its business processes are then designed and managed to attain and maintain that position. It is worth pursuing this point because it helps us in answering a fundamental question: *What distinguishes an effective business process?* In manufacturing, the common tendency is to equate an effective process with an *efficient* process. Although *cost efficiency* (achieving a desired level of outputs with a minimal level of inputs) is obviously an

EXAMPLE 2.1

As an example of consistency in hierarchical strategy, consider the case of Wal-Mart, the well-known retailing and distribution company. Figure 2.2 shows how Wal-Mart has positioned itself as a low-cost retailer of medium-quality goods supplied with high accessibility and availability, both in terms of store locations and continuous product availability on store shelves. To support this business strategy, Wal-Mart's operations strategy calls for an efficient distribution process featuring short response times and low inventory levels.

To accomplish both seemingly contradictory objectives, Wal-Mart's logistic process calls for its own transportation fleet and information network, complete with a satellite communications system to connect stores in well-chosen locations. To ensure close communication among retail outlets and suppliers—and thus fast replenishment of depleted stocks—*point-of-sales (POS)*

data are transmitted via *electronic data interchange (EDI)*. Low pipeline-inventory levels are achieved by a system of *cross-docking* distribution centers—incoming trucks dock opposite outgoing trucks so that goods are distributed directly from incoming to outgoing trucks without intermediate storage.

The overall result is impressive: a high inventory turnover rate (four times the industry average), improved targeting of products to markets (resulting in fewer stockouts and markdowns), significantly higher sales per square foot of store space ($379 in 1995—twice that of rival Kmart), dominant market share, and growth (from 20% in 1987 to 47% in 1995). Wal-Mart is thus an outstanding example of a strategically well-positioned firm that has carefully orchestrated operations strategy and process structure in support of business strategy.

FIGURE 2.2 Wal-Mart Strategy and Operations Structure

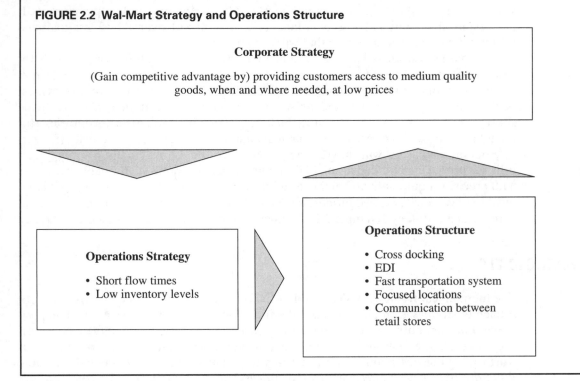

important competitive advantage, firms also may compete on several other strategic positions—such as those based on response time, product variety, or quality. Thus, a business process that is effective for one company may be a poor choice for another company pursuing a different strategy in the same industry.

How, then, does "effective" differ from "efficient"? The key is the need for a *strategic fit* among three main components of a firm's strategy:

- Its strategic position,
- Its process structure, and
- Its managerial policies.

Strategic fit means *consistency between the competitive advantage that a firm seeks and the process capabilities and managerial policies that it uses to achieve that advantage.* Consistency may be absent if top-level managers are insufficiently knowledgeable about basic business processes, or if they delegate important process decisions to technical managers who are unfamiliar with the firm's overall strategy. In either case, the company's strategic position and network of business processes may be incompatible. For example, if top managers are unfamiliar with technology and leave technology-choice decisions to technical managers, then the firm may end up with sophisticated, but inflexible, automated technology (that pleases engineering pride), while it may pursue a strategy of variety and cost-efficiency that could be supported better with old-fashioned, manual technology.

The potential conflict between the top-down view of strategy and the principle of strategic fit was first described in 1969 by Wickham Skinner, who argued that "too often top management overlooks manufacturing's potential to strengthen or weaken a company's competitive ability." As a result, concluded Skinner, "manufacturing becomes the missing link in corporate strategy" (Skinner, 1969). Among other things, Skinner was criticizing the perception of operations as a technical discipline concerned only with low-level day-to-day decisions.

Even though that misperception is still fairly widespread, consultants, educators, and practicing operations managers have made substantial progress in understanding the strategic importance of operations. Indeed, the *business process reengineering* movement of the early 1990s stressed the fundamental rethinking and redesign of business processes as a means of improving performance in such areas as time, cost, quality, and service. This theory advocates radical changes in processes (and, in fact, in the organization as a whole) as an effective means of formulating strategy and designing processes that will result in significant improvements in performance. By *equating organizations with processes,* this view has put business process management on the strategic agenda of top management at numerous firms (Harrison & Loch, 1995).

Market- and Process-Driven Strategies   Although the top-down view is convenient for explaining the concept of strategic fit, some experts urge that the relationship be reversed. Management, contends one team of researchers, should emphasize that "the building blocks of corporate strategy are not products and markets but business processes. Competitive success then depends on transforming a company's key processes into strategic capabilities that consistently provide superior value to the customer" (Stalk, Evans, & Shulman, 1992).

We can summarize by observing that strategic fit may be achieved in two ways:

1. By **market-driven strategy:** One starts with key competitive priorities and then develops processes to support them, or
2. By **process-driven strategy:** One starts with a given set of process capabilities and then identifies a market position that can be supported by those processes.

EXAMPLE 2.2

Shouldice Hospital in Toronto, Canada, offers a good example of a business process custom fit with a focused strategy. Shouldice focuses on a very narrow market segment. It specializes in the repair of external abdominal hernias in healthy male patients. The founder developed and standardized a simple, repeatable surgical procedure that requires only local anesthesia and that encourages patient movement, participation, and socialization through excellent ambulatory care provided in a non-hospital-like environment. The carefully tailored process performed in this highly focused "plant" results in fast recovery, low-cost operations, and high quality in terms of low recurrence rates.

Whereas producers of commodity products tend to be market-driven, technologically innovative companies tend to drive markets. Sony, for example, has a core set of process technologies that allow miniaturization of electronic products. It has leveraged this capability to develop new products and even new consumer markets. Had Sony relied solely on market analysis of current customer needs, the Walkman would never have been introduced.

Generally, strategic fit requires both market- and process-driven strategies. It entails identifying and developing external market opportunities with internal process capabilities until the two are mutually consistent, and it means doing so repeatedly. The resulting view of strategy and fit, argues one review of the field, "inextricably links a company's internal capabilities (what it does well) and its external industry environment (what the market demands and what competitors offer)" (Collis & Montgomery, 1995).

2.4 FOCUSED OPERATIONS

The concepts of strategic fit and sustainable strategic positioning are rooted in the very existence of trade-offs and the need to make choices. As discussed, strategic fit requires business processes that are consistent with a given business strategy; however, because no single process can perform well on every dimension, *there cannot be a process that fits all strategies.* Choosing a strategy, therefore, involves choices: "The essence of strategy," observes Michael Porter, "is what to do and what *not* to do" (Porter, 1996).

Focused Strategy and Focused Processes   Not surprisingly, it is easier to design a process that achieves a limited set of objectives than one that must satisfy many diverse objectives. This fact underlies the concept of **focused strategy:** targeting a limited, congruent set of objectives in terms of demand (products and markets) and supply (inputs, necessary process technologies and volumes). This approach concentrates on serving limited market segments with business processes specifically designed and operated to meet their needs.

In turn, a focused strategy is best supported by a **focused process**—one whose products all fall *within a small region* of the competitive product space. All products emphasize the same competitive priorities. If the area occupied in the product space by the product portfolio is small, then the process is focused. Or, if the product portfolio is more dispersed in the competitive space, then the process is equally less focused. A focused process need not produce only one product. A job shop can be focused on providing variety, as long as all its products have similar quality, cost, and timeliness attributes so that they fall in a small area in the product space. Shouldice Hospital, as described in Example 2.2, offers a good example of a focused service operation.

Even if a strategy calls for serving broader market segments, each requiring different strategic emphasis (or positions in the competitive product space), it can be separated into *substrategies,* each focusing on a limited, consistent, and clear set of objectives. Each

---

EXAMPLE 2.3

Porter cites the case of Continental Airlines's efforts to imitate Southwest Airlines by creating a low-budget carrier called Continental Light—meals and first-class service were eliminated, departure frequency increased, fares reduced, and turnaround time at the gate shortened. Porter indicates that "because Continental remained a full-service airline on other routes [its own position], it continued to use travel agents and its mixed fleet of planes and to provide baggage checking and seat assignments. . . . An airline," Porter concludes, "can copy activities (say, deciding to drop meal service), but it cannot do both (say, having meal service on some flights and not on others) without bearing major inefficiencies" (Porter, 1996).

In short, Continental failed to treat Continental Light as an independent, focused plant-within-a-plant. Granted, financial considerations may have forced Continental to keep its low-budget operations aligned with its full-service operations, but by trying to do both—by refusing to make a choice—Continental engineered a "hybrid" process that could not compete with Southwest's focused operations. Continental aborted Continental Light shortly after takeoff.

---

substrategy can then be supported by its own consistent—or *focused*—business process. Depending on the scale of the business, this approach leads either to a *focused plant* that performs one specific process or to a so-called **plant-within-a-plant (PWP)** that is divided into several "mini-plants," each devoted to a specific mission by performing a process that focuses strictly on that mission.

Most general hospitals, for example, have realized the benefits of focus by separating the emergency room and trauma units from the rest of the facility. Some hospitals (such as Massachusetts General) have gone even further by developing separate units to focus on such routine operations as hip or knee replacement and rehabilitation. Large manufacturers usually operate multiple plants that support the entire *product life cycle*—research and development, prototype labs, production plants, sales and marketing units, financing-service offices, and repair facilities—all housed in physically separate facilities.

This divide-and-conquer strategy also can be implemented on a smaller scale by separating product lines within a plant. Harley-Davidson maintains two separate flow processes—one for its small 883 cc engine and transmission systems and one for its large 1,340 cc power trains. This strategy is logical because each product line requires a different process and has sufficiently high volume to warrant the investment. Similarly, engine maker Briggs & Stratton separates its various production plants and, within each plant, different product assembly lines in PWPs.

Finally, the practice of achieving strategic fit through focused operations provides firms with a powerful deterrent against competitors' efforts to imitate them. Their competitive advantage, therefore, is more sustainable. Although any single activity may be vulnerable to imitation, the greater the number of activities involved, the harder wholesale imitation becomes. Supporting a firm's strategic position with multiple, mutually reinforcing activities creates sustainable competitive advantage, because it is, according to Porter, "harder for a rival to match an array of interlocked activities than it is merely to imitate a particular [activity]" (Porter, 1996). Indeed, copying a focused business process—a complete *network* of activities—amounts to cloning the entire organization. If a firm's process and strategy are both focused, its position is already the result of carefully considered trade-offs made when managers chose their position and its supporting process. (We will say more about trade-offs in section 2.6.) A competitor, therefore, can copy that position only by making similar trade-offs. In so doing, it will inevitably be giving up its own position. Example 2.3 describes Continental Airlines' unsuccessful attempt to imitate focused competitor Southwest Airlines.

2.5 MATCHING PRODUCTS AND PROCESSES

Focused operations make it easier to match the products a firm produces with the process it uses to produce them. A useful tool for matching processes to products is the **product-process matrix** proposed by R.H. Hayes and S.C. Wheelwright (1979). A model of this matrix is shown in Figure 2.3.

The horizontal axis charts product variety, a product attribute, ranging from "low variety" (representing standardized products produced at high volume), to "high variety" (representing one-of-a-kind products produced at low volume). At the right end, we would find such unique products as skyscrapers, tailor-made suits, consulting reports, and plastic-surgery. Such highly customized products are demanded and produced to order in very low volume. The left end exhibits the other extreme—highly standardized commodity products demanded and produced in large volume. Breweries

FIGURE 2.3 The Product-Process Matrix

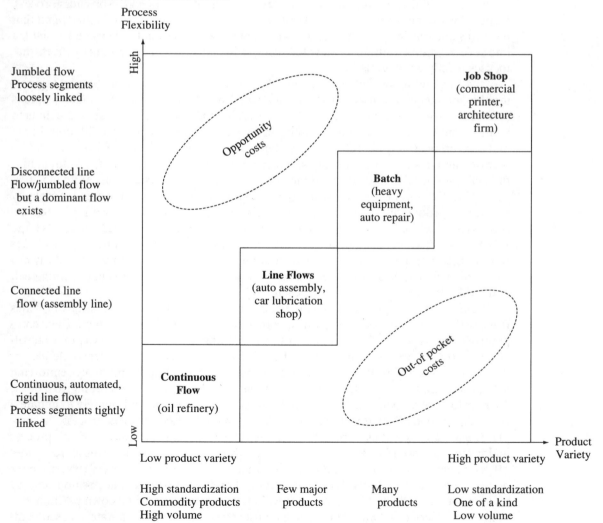

and commercial paper mills produce products at this end of the continuum. Between these extremes fall products with intermediate degrees of customization and volume. Thus, houses built by a real estate developer may be largely similar to a limited variety of model homes while permitting some degree of customization and upgrades.

The vertical axis measures process flexibility, the process attribute on the supply side that corresponds to product variety. At the bottom of the figure, low process flexibility results from a process architecture with rigid, fixed routes and specialized resources that can perform only a narrow set of tasks repeatedly, as in a continuous flow shop. At the top of the figure, high flexibility results from processes that employ general-purpose resources loosely linked so that products can flow along many different routes, yielding "a jumbled work flow," as in a job shop (see chapter 1). Intermediate processes differ in degree of specialization, volume capability, and interlinkage of resources.

Ideally, each process type fits a specific product demand. Job shops, for instance, are ideally suited to produce custom products in low volume, whereas flow shops work best for more standardized products demanded in high volume. *Effective product-process matches occur* on the diagonal *of the product-process matrix*. An off-diagonal position represents a mismatch that can result in unnecessarily high costs—a job shop that produces only one product (resulting in opportunity costs) or a flow shop that undergoes numerous equipment changeovers to produce several products demanded only in very low volume (resulting in cash costs). A diagonal position, though, corresponds to a proper match between product variety and process flexibility.

Note that the product-process matrix connects only one product attribute with one process attribute. A correlation exists between process flexibility and product cost—standardization typically results in economies of scale and thus lower variable product cost. Likewise, a correlation exists between process flexibility and product response time—flow shops typically have shorter flow times than job shops. Product quality, however, bears no direct correlation to layout of resources and connecting routes. Both job shops and flow shops can produce high quality.

2.6 STRATEGIC POSITIONING AND OPERATIONAL EFFECTIVENESS

Once the firm has chosen its operations strategy and process structure, it must manage the process to execute the strategy. As discussed, a strategic position supported by consistent business processes that are managed effectively is essential for superior performance. Sustained competitive advantage requires *both* strategic positioning and operational effectiveness.

Strategic positioning is about choosing a different set of activities or choosing to perform activities in a different way—which entails choosing a different business process architecture. Firms change strategic positioning quite infrequently (typically, once a decade). When managers are considering such a change, they ask: "*What* should we do and not do?" Operational effectiveness, on the other hand, is about performing certain activities better than rivals perform similar activities. When managers are considering changes to the operating policies of a process structure already in place, they ask: "*How* could we better manage the process on a daily basis?"

The Operations Frontier   Earlier, we represented strategic positioning by an arrow or ray emanating from the current point or position of the firm's products in the competitive product space and pointing in the direction of strategic movement. An empirical study of a particular industry might measure and position each firm's product

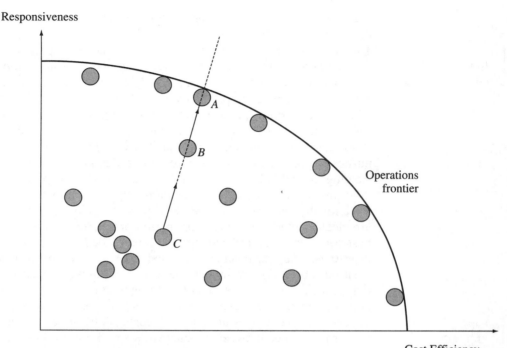

FIGURE 2.4 The Operations Frontier as Minimal Curve Containing All Current Positions in an Industry

offerings in that space. As in Figure 2.4, the measurement could apply to two competitive dimensions (with product quality and variety regarded as constant). One could then define the **operations frontier** as *the smallest curve that contains all current industry positions.* Clearly, the operations frontier then represents the current best practices of world-class firms. Firms located on the same ray share identical current priorities in terms of product attributes. Only those firms on the operations frontier, however, boast superior performance—they have the highest **operational effectiveness** in managing their processes. Operational effectiveness is thus related to the distance between the current position and the (current) operations frontier. The closer a firm is to the frontier, the higher its operational effectiveness will be. In Figure 2.4, the companies delivering products *A, B,* and *C* share identical strategic priorities of movement, yet the company delivering product *A* has the highest level of operational effectiveness. It defines the current set of best practices to manage its business processes (it is on the frontier), while the product *C* company has the lowest level (it is farthest from the frontier, as measured along its direction of movement).

Trade-offs A **trade-off** is *a decision whereby someone must decrease one aspect to increase another.* Because the operations frontier is typically concave, any point *on* the frontier represents a trade-off. To increase performance along one product dimension, a firm must give up some performance along the others. It thus follows that firms not on the frontier do not face strict trade-offs. They can improve along multiple dimensions simultaneously. Trade-offs, therefore, are typically reflected most clearly in the strategies of world-class companies, such as Toyota as described in Example 2.4.

Improved operational effectiveness is not the same as improved strategic positioning. Whereas strategic positioning defines the *direction* of improvement from the current position, operational effectiveness measures the *distance* of the current position

---

EXAMPLE 2.4

In the late 1960s and early 1970s, a small Japanese automobile maker was facing a depressed economy in a country where space was at a premium and, because no firm can survive producing only a single product for small depressed markets, product variety was a necessity. During the 1970s, therefore, Taiichi Ohno and his coworkers developed the *Toyota Production System (TPS)*. The key idea behind TPS was to produce exactly what you need (regardless of variety) exactly when you need it. The potential problem was equally simple: There was no room for error. Suppliers and equipment had to be reliable, production had to be flexible, quality had to be high, and consistency was necessary in every respect. Critical to the success of the system were precisely coordinated relations with suppliers, who had to meet both precise schedules and precise performance specifications while remaining as flexible as the automaker itself.

TPS was in fact the rediscovery of Henry Ford's assembly line or process-flow concept (see section 2.7) with an important modification: Instead of focusing on low cost and zero flexibility, TPS allowed *product variety through process flexibility.* TPS simultaneously permitted wide variety, high quality, low cost, and short response time. In effect, it so completely redefined the operational-effectiveness frontier that competitors worldwide had to scramble to catch up to. Having established TPS as the world-class flow process for discrete manufacturing, Toyota remains the best example of a company that used manufacturing as a competitive weapon in rising from obscurity to the top ranks of its industry.

Initially, when competitors began copying elements of TPS, they saw dramatic improvements in *both* cost and quality. They thought that if such operational effectiveness was possible, perhaps the traditional trade-offs between cost and quality or cost and variety were no longer valid. Most of these rivals, however, were far from the best in their class. In their quest for operational effectiveness, they originally did not have to make genuine trade-offs. Their operations were so generally ineffective that they could simultaneously improve on several dimensions of their processes.

---

to the current operations frontier in the direction of improvement. When a firm's position on the operations frontier is developed according to "the state of best practices," it represents the best attainable *compromise* between the two dimensions at a given time. Any change in such a position necessarily entails trade-offs between the two dimensions. Example 2.5 describes the trade-offs that differentiate an emergency room from other hospital processes.

Note that companies not on the frontier can make simultaneous improvements on both dimensions by moving toward the frontier. In other words, the purpose of operational effectiveness is *to bring a company closer to the frontier.* The purpose of strategic positioning, on the other hand, is *to specify a direction of improvement and thus the position on the frontier the company wants to occupy.*

Improving operational effectiveness is necessary, but often not sufficient, for superior performance. Generally, new management techniques ("best practices") are rapidly diffused and imitated. As a result, they form no basis for *sustained* competitive advantage. In the 1980s many Japanese companies started pursuing *time* as a source of competitive advantage by introducing new products at a faster rate. No single company, however, "won" the race because every competitor was following the same strategy. Customers obviously were reaping the benefits of wider product variety at lower prices, but as sellers and products started to become more similar, each lost any claim to competitive advantage or superior performance (Stalk & Webber, 1993). Well-aligned operational techniques and processes such as the famous Toyota Production System (Example 2.4), however, *do* form a basis for sustained advantage. Indeed, although well documented and diffused, few competitors have managed to implement

EXAMPLE 2.5

If a general hospital tries to handle both emergency and nonemergency cases with a *single* process, the products of that process will have very different strategic emphases. Such process will undoubtedly cover too large an area in the competitive product space and make it difficult for the hospital to be competitive on both dimensions. Suppose that the hospital divides its operations into two distinct plants-within-a-plant (PWPs)—an emergency room and nonemergency facilities. Suppose, too, that each PWP has both its own competitive priority (time or cost) and a consistent process to support the priority. Clearly, an emergency room will employ doctors and staff who are "on call" and will have the flexibility to treat a wide variety of cases rapidly. A general hospital, meanwhile, can afford more specialized labor resources, each geared to the treatment of a small set of cases. In Figure 2.5, the products of each PWP now share similar competitive priorities and thus occupy a smaller area. Each PWP process is more focused, and it is easier for each to perform effectively in its specific strategic direction.

FIGURE 2.5 The Operations Frontier in the Health Care Sector

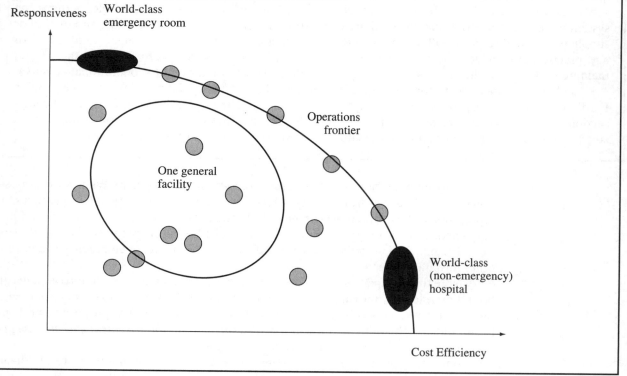

TPS as well as Toyota has. (And Toyota keeps raising the bar by improving its production system.)

Likewise, as both technology and management practices advance, the operations frontier shifts outward, or away from the point of origin in the competitive space. World-class companies achieve either the same response time (or quality or variety) at a lower cost or better response time (or quality or variety) at the same cost. As the dynamics of competition keep pushing the operations frontier outward, world-class firms must continuously improve operational effectiveness merely to maintain their positions.

2.7   THE EVOLUTION OF STRATEGY AND PROCESS MANAGEMENT

Over time, strategies and processes will change in response to changes in the environment or industry in which a company operates or in response to the technology that it uses. In particular, the historical evolution of operations and process management is linked intimately to technological changes and their role in the development of industrialization. Until 1765, the worlds of commerce and technology had changed very little from those known to the Greeks and the Romans. Although advances had been made in the textile, printing, and construction industries, the commercial world of 1765 still faced the same physical limitations as ancient cultures. Transportation speed—whether of people, of goods, or of information—was limited on land by the speed of the fastest horse and on water by the most favorable winds. At the end of the sixteenth century the trip from New York to Boston—a distance of 288 kilometers or 175 miles—took three days (Ambrose, 1996).

The Factory System and Specialization   This situation was destined to change dramatically in 1765, when the **factory system** heralded the start of the industrial revolution and the end of the "artisan" system consisting of craft guilds and decentralized cottage industries. The factory system was the result of three innovations:

1. Scottish economist Adam Smith proposed that the **division of labor** and **functional specialization** would lead to vast improvements in cost and quality (albeit at the expense of flexibility).
2. Scottish engineer James Watt's invention of the steam engine made it possible for powered machinery to replace human labor. Powered by steam, the transportation speeds of goods carriers soon increased by a factor of 20. (Meanwhile, the telegraph removed virtually all limits on the transportation speed of information.)
3. The practice of centralizing work in one facility began.

From Standardization to Mass Production   In 1810, based on the practices of Eli Whitney and Samuel Colt at the national armory at Springfield, Massachusetts, the **American system of manufacturing** introduced the use of interchangeable parts, thereby eliminating the need to custom-fit parts during assembly. Standardization had begun. The end of the nineteenth century brought technological advances that were prominent in such commercial phenomena as the "bicycle boom" of the 1890s—sheet-metal stamping and electrical-resistance welding allowed for new designs and assembly methods. Another fundamental change occurred on April 1, 1913, when Henry Ford introduced the moving assembly line—the first machine-paced flow shop—at his plant in Highland Park, Michigan, and thus dawned the era of **mass production.** "Armory practice and sheet steel work equipped Ford with the ability to turn out virtually unlimited numbers of components. It remained for the assembly line to eliminate the remaining bottleneck—how to put these parts together" (Hounshell, 1991).

Ford's primary mode of competition soon became low cost. Scale economies and the virtual elimination of all product flexibility made cars available in high volume for a mass market. Prior to the development of the assembly line, a Ford Model T required 12.5 hours of assembly-worker time—a limitation that the assembly line reduced to only 1.5 hours. Soon Ford's plant in Rouge, Michigan was a totally integrated facility with the best furnaces, operational equipment, and electrical systems efficiently converting raw materials into cash in 36 hours. It was also a highly focused plant—serving a competitive strategy of low cost and zero flexibility. It produced one product, the

Model T, and Henry Ford's attitude toward the higher costs entailed by product flexibility was uncompromising. Of the Model T he said, "You can have any color as long as it's black."

Flexibility and the Productivity Dilemma   The changeover from Model T to Model A in 1927 was the end of Ford's competitive advantage. Alfred Sloan of General Motors had introduced the concept of "annual models" and the slogan "A car for every purpose and every price." The practice of **flexible mass production** had introduced product variety as a second mode of competition in the automobile industry. It also was accompanied by one of the most significant trade-offs in the history of strategic positioning. Faced with the **productivity dilemma,** manufacturers were obliged to choose between the lower productivity entailed by frequent product changes and the higher productivity that was possible only if they declined to introduce variety into their product lines (Hounshell, 1991).

From Scientific Management to Employee Involvement   The first few decades of the 1900s also witnessed the rise of **scientific management,** based on the time and motion studies conducted by Frederick W. Taylor at the turn of the twentieth century. Taylor's philosophy was to replace subjective management by "objective" management based on science. It centered on three ideas (Hounshell, 1991):

1. Scientific laws govern how much a worker can produce per day;
2. It is management's function to discover and apply these laws to productive operations systems; and
3. It is the worker's function to carry out management decisions without question.

Taylor's "ceaseless quest for the 'one best way' and efficiency changed the very texture of modern life. Taylor influenced Ford's assembly line" (Kanigel, 1996) and led universities to start new 'industrial engineering' departments. His ideas of industrial organization and scientific observation inspired the **statistical quality control** studies of Shewhart at Bell Laboratories in the 1930s and Elton Mayo's celebrated Hawthorne studies of worker motivation at Western Electric, which highlighted the importance of employee involvement and incentive systems in increasing productivity.

Competitive Dimensions After World War II   The period after World War II found the United States with a virtual monopoly on worldwide productivity. With most of Europe and Japan practically destroyed, there was no competition for meeting pent-up consumer demand. Thus, volume and scale economies rose to the top of the American strategic agenda. The 1960s witnessed the rise of enormous integrated economic structures and the emergence of huge capital investments as the main barrier to entry in many industries.

During the 1970s, Japanese manufacturers began to incorporate *quality* into their cost focused strategy. Toyota began developing what, in Example 2.4, we described as the *Toyota Production System (TPS)*. Among other things, TPS gave rise to a fourth competitive dimension: the use of *time* in product development, production, and distribution. The emergence of Japanese manufacturing as a global force in the 1980s led to a renewed interest in manufacturing as a competitive weapon in the rest of the industrialized world. It gave rise to a variety of new management philosophies and practices, including total quality management (TQM), just-in-time (JIT) manufacturing, time-based competition, and business process reengineering. In addition, technologies such as computer-aided design and manufacturing (CAD/CAM), flexible manufacturing systems, robotics, and Internet-based processes now play important roles in modernizing business activities.

WHAT'S NEXT?

In chapter 1, we introduced the concept of processes, and in this chapter, we saw that choosing a process structure, or architecture, is a significant component of strategic positioning. We saw, too, that well-managed processes are a necessary condition for operational effectiveness. Because both activities are necessary for sustained superior performance, we must better understand how changes in process structure and process management can affect a firm's strategic position and operational performance.

In the rest of this book, we study (as our title suggests) *process flows*. The study of process flows is critical when a firm is seeking sustained superior performance based on performing effectively along any of the four dimensions of cost, time, flexibility, and quality.

In the following chapters, we discuss ways in which managers can change both process structure and process management, and we describe in some detail the effect that such changes can have on process performance. Throughout, we focus on levers that managers can use to control structure and to manage the process so as to improve operational effectiveness.

Problem Set

2.1 How do the strategies of your neighborhood supermarket differ from those of Wal-Mart? How do their business processes support those strategies?

2.2 Compare and contrast the strategies and supporting business processes of Southwest Airlines and Singapore Airlines. Compare their business strategies in terms of the four product dimensions, the targeted market segments, and the process architectures.

References

Ambrose, S. E. 1996. *Undaunted Courage.* Simon & Schuster, New York, NY.

Collis, D. J., and C. A. Montgomery. 1995. Competing on Resources: Strategy in the 1990s. *Harvard Business Review:* 93–101.

Harrison, J. M., and C. Loch. 1995. Five Principles of Business Process Reengineering. Manuscript, Stanford University: 1–20.

Hayes, R. H., and S. C. Wheelwright. 1979. Link Manufacturing Process and Product Life Cycles. *Harvard Business Review:* 133–140.

Heskett, J. L. 1989. Shouldice Hospital Limited. *Harvard Business School Case Study:* 1–16.

Hindle, T. 1994. *Field Guide to Strategy.* Harvard Business School Press, Cambridge, MA.

Hounshell, D. A. 1991. *From the American System to Mass Production 1800–1932: The Development of Manufacturing Technology in the United States.* The Johns Hopkins University Press, Baltimore, MD.

Kanigel, R. 1997. The One Best Way: *Frederick Winslow Taylor and the Enigma of Efficiency.* The Penguin Group, New York, NY.

Porter, M. E. 1996. What is Strategy? *Harvard Business Review:* 61–78.

Skinner, W. 1969. Manufacturing—Missing Link in Corporate Strategy. *Harvard Business Review:* 136–145.

Skinner, W. 1974. The Focused Factory. *Harvard Business Review:* 113–121.

Stalk, G., P. Evans, and L. E. Shulman. 1992. Competing on Capabilities: The New Rules of Corporate Strategy. *Harvard Business Review:* 57–69.

Stalk, G., and A. M. Webber. 1993. Japan's Dark Side of Time. *Harvard Business Review:* 93–101.

CHAPTER

3

--- --------------------------------

Process Flow Measures

In this chapter, we introduce the concept of *flows* in business processes. We define three key operational measures—*flow time, flow rate,* and *inventory*—and present a fundamental relationship among them, called *Little's law.* Flow time measures the total time that a flow unit spends in the process. The reciprocal of average flow time is called *inventory turns.* Whereas flow rate measures the number of flow units that flow through the process per unit of time, inventory measures the number of flow units in the process at any point in time. Little's law states that average inventory equals average flow rate times average flow time. When managers understand these three operational measures of process performance, they can determine when a change in a process is an improvement.

3.1 INTRODUCTION

As discussed in chapter 1, the objective of any process is to transform inputs into outputs to satisfy customer needs. As important indicators of buyers' preferences, *external* measures of customer satisfaction are important indicators of product demand; however, managers can control only *internal* measures of process performance, whether financial or operational. If operational measures are chosen appropriately, they can serve as indicators not only of customer satisfaction, but also of financial performance. Operational measures however, can perform this twofold function only if they are carefully correlated with both (external) customer-satisfaction measures and (internal) financial measures. In this chapter, we identify several key operational measures of process performance and show their relationships to some commonly used financial measures.

Throughout this book, we examine processes from the perspective of *flow.* Specifically, we study the dynamics of a process as inputs enter the process, proceed through various activities performed (including such passive activities as waiting in buffer for activities to be performed), and finally exit the process as outputs. Recall that we refer to a unit of flow by the generic term **flow unit,** and as indicated in chapter 1, a flow unit may refer to a patient, a dollar, a pound of steel, an R&D project, or a bank transaction to be processed. To study process flows, we first answer three important questions:

1. On average, how many flow units pass through the process per unit of time?
2. On average, how much time does a typical flow unit spend within process boundaries?
3. On average, how many flow units are within process boundaries at any point in time?

In sections 3.2 through 3.4 we discuss operational measures of process performance that address each of these three questions. In section 3.5 we explain the basic relationship among these three measures, and in section 3.6 we illustrate each measure with examples

■ 37 ■

EXAMPLE 3.1

MBPF Finance Inc. makes loans to qualified buyers of prefabricated garages from its parent company, MBPF Inc. Having just reengineered its application-processing operations, MBPF Finance is now evaluating the effect of its changes on service performance. The subsidiary receives about 1,000 loan applications per 30-day working month and makes accept/reject decisions based on an extensive review of each application.

Prior to January 1998 (under "Process I"), MBPF Finance processed each application individually. On average, 20% of all applications received approval. An internal audit showed that, on average, MBPF Finance had about 500 applications in process at various stages of the approval procedure, but on which no decisions had yet been made.

In response to customer complaints about the time taken to process each application, MBPF Finance called in Kellogg Consultants (KC) to help streamline its decision-making process. KC quickly identified a key problem with the current process. Although most applications could be processed rather quickly, some took a disproportionate amount of time because of insufficient and/or unclear documentation. KC suggested the following changes to the process (thereby creating "Process II"):

1. Because the percentage of approved applications is fairly low, an Initial Review Team should be set up to preprocess all applications according to strict but fairly mechanical guidelines.

2. Each application would fall into one of three categories: type A (looks excellent), type B (needs more detailed evaluation), and type C (reject summarily). Type A and B applications would be forwarded to different specialist subgroups.

3. Each subgroup would then evaluate the applications in its domain and make accept/reject decisions.

Process II was implemented on an experimental basis. The company found that, on average, 25% of all applications were of type A, 25% were of B, and 50% were of C. Typically, about 70% of type A and 10% of B were approved on review. (Recall that all of type C were rejected.) Internal-audit checks further revealed that, on average, 200 applications were with the Initial Review Team undergoing preprocessing. Only 25 were with the Subgroup A Team undergoing the next stage of processing and approximately 150 were with the Subgroup B Team.

MBPF Finance would like to determine if the implemented changes have improved service performance.

---

drawn from various manufacturing and service settings. In section 3.7 we discuss the concept of inventory turns. Finally, in section 3.8 we relate these operational measures to financial measures of process performance as a means of determining when a process change has been an improvement from the operational and financial perspectives.

We can use this basic relationship between operational measures to analyze whether process changes—reengineered process flows or allocation of additional resources—have actually improved process performance. We start this chapter with the story of MBPF Finance Inc. (Example 3.1), a business situation in which such analysis would be particularly useful.

In the rest of this chapter, we introduce concepts that can be used to analyze the situation in Example 3.1.

3.2 FLOW RATE (THROUGHPUT RATE)

One important measure of process-flow dynamics is **flow rate**—*the number of flow units that flow through a specific point of the process per unit of time.* If we denote any given time as *t,* we can focus on the entry and exit points of the process and then denote total inflow and outflow rates through all entry and exit points as $R_i(t)$ and $R_o(t)$, respectively.

EXAMPLE 3.2

MBPF Inc. manufactures prefabricated garages. The manufacturing facility purchases sheet metal, which is formed and assembled into finished products (garages). Each garage needs a roof and a base, and both components are punched out of separate metal sheets prior to assembly. Production and demand data for the past eight weeks are shown in Table 3.1. Observe that both production and demand vary from week to week and are not necessarily identical.

By regarding the MBPF Inc. factory as a *process* and each garage as a *flow unit,* we see that flow rate has fluctuated from week to week. Taking the average production over the eight weeks charted in Table 3.1, we see that the factory has an average flow rate or throughput of $R = 1,000$ garages per week. Suppose that in terms of direct material and labor, each garage costs \$3,300 to produce. If we consider each dollar spent as our flow unit, then the factory has throughput of $R = $ \$3,300,000 per week. Thus, we have evaluated the throughput of the factory using two different flow units—garages and dollars.

As a measure of process performance, throughput tells us *the average rate at which the process produces and delivers output.* Ideally, we want process throughput to match customer demand. Average demand experienced by MBPF Inc. over the eight weeks considered in Table 3.1 is 1,000 garages. Over the eight weeks considered, therefore, average production at MBPF has matched average demand. Finally, production rate is the inflow rate for MBPF and sales is the outflow rate. Because these rates are equal, we conclude that MBPF Inc. is a stable process.

TABLE 3.1 Production and Demand Data for MBPF Inc.								
Week	*1*	*2*	*3*	*4*	*5*	*6*	*7*	*8*
Production	800	1,100	1,000	900	1,200	1,100	950	950
Demand	1,200	800	900	1,100	1,300	1,300	550	850

A specific process is shown graphically in Figure 3.1. This process features two entry points and one exit point. Total inflow rate $R_i(t)$, therefore, is the sum of the two inflow rates, $R_{i,1}(t)$ and $R_{i,2}(t)$, one each from the two entry points. Remember that inputs may enter a process from multiple points and outputs leave a process from multiple points.

Flow Rate and Stability   Inflow and outflow rates generally fluctuate over time. When inflow rate exceeds outflow rate in the short term, the number of flow units within process boundaries increases. The converse is true if outflow rate exceeds inflow rate in the short term. A **stable process** is one in which, in the long run, *average inflow rate is the same as average outflow rate.* When we have a stable process, we can refer to average inflow or outflow rate simply as **average flow rate,** or **throughput rate**—*the*

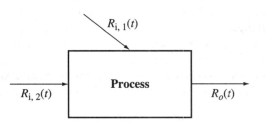

FIGURE 3.1 A Process with Two Entry Points

average number of flow units that flow through (into or out of) the process per unit of time. Average flow rate or throughput is denoted as *R*. These concepts are illustrated in Example 3.2 for MBPF Inc.

3.3 FLOW TIME

As a flow unit moves through the process, one of two things happens to it:

1. It undergoes an activity, or
2. It waits to undergo an activity.

We now follow a specific flow unit from the time it enters the process until it exits. The total time spent within process boundaries is called **flow time.** Some flow units move through the process with no wait (perhaps they require only resources that are available in abundance or they are deliberately expedited). Others may spend a long time in the process, typically waiting for resources to become available. Thus, *flow time varies—sometimes considerably—from one flow unit to another.* Although this variance also occurs in a stable process, we can define an **average flow time** by taking *the average across all flow units that exit the process during a specific span of time.* We denote average flow time as *T.*

Returning to our MBPF factory in Example 3.2, we can track the time spent by each garage in the factory from the point at which raw material enters as sheet metal to the point at which a garage leaves as a finished product. Although flow time for each garage varies, we can ask: *How long does it take, on average, to produce a garage?* We take each garage as the flow unit and look for the average flow time spent by each garage in the factory. Suppose that MBPF has gathered extensive data showing average flow time for a garage to be *T* = 2 weeks.

As a measure of process performance, average flow time indicates the average time needed to convert material inputs (sheet metal) into outputs (garages). This measure includes any time spent by a flow unit waiting for activities to be performed. It is thus useful information for a manager who must promise a delivery date to a customer. It also indicates how long working capital is tied up in the process.

3.4 INVENTORY

The number of flow units present within process boundaries at time t is the **inventory** in the process at time *t,* and is denoted by *I(t).* To obtain process inventory at time *t,* we count all flow units within process boundaries at time *t.* Inventory represents *those flow units that have currently entered the process but have not yet reached an exit point.*

Inventory has traditionally been defined in a manufacturing context as material waiting to be processed or sold. Our definition of flow units allows a broader view. We define *inventory* for *any* process, whether it is a manufacturing, service, financial, or even an information process. It encompasses orders, products, customers, and cash. Our definition of inventory includes all flow units within process boundaries—whether being processed or waiting to be processed. Thus, raw materials, work-in-process (partially completed products), and finished goods inventories are included. When we need to develop a framework for analyzing business process flows, this broader definition of inventory allows us to exploit the fundamental equivalence of flows through all business processes. This advantage allows us to provide a single framework for analyzing flows in all business processes. A clear definition of *flow unit* is thus extremely important.

At time *t,* the **instantaneous inventory accumulation rate,** $\Delta R(t)$, is the difference between inflow (supply) rate $R_i(t)$ and outflow (demand) rate $R_o(t)$. Thus,

$$\Delta R(t) = R_i(t) - R_o(t)$$

EXAMPLE 3.3

MBPF Inc. tracks inventory at the end of each week. Inventory is measured in number of garages, with any inventory of sheet metal, roofs, or bases adjusted so that each flow unit is a finished garage. In other words, a roof and a base on the factory floor are together counted as one garage of inventory. Let $I(t)$ be the inventory at the end of week t. Now suppose that inventory at the end of week 0 is 2,200 units. Thus $I(0) = 2,200$. Assume the production and demand quantities shown in Table 3.1. Production represents inflow rate $(R_i(t))$ of garages and demand represents outflow rate $(R_o(t))$. Weekly inventory thus fluctuates by the inventory accumulation rate $\Delta R(t)$. From Table 3.1, we have $R_i(1) = 800$ and $R_o(1) = 1,200$. Thus $\Delta R(1) = -400$. Since $I(0) = 2,200$, we have $I(1) = I(0) + \Delta R(1) = 2,200 - 400 = 1,800$. We can similarly evaluate in-

ventory for each week. Ending inventory for each of the eight weeks is shown in Table 3.2.

With these data, we can construct an **inventory build-up diagram** that depicts inventory as *a function of time*. Figure 3.2 shows the inventory build-up diagram for MBPF over the eight weeks considered. The horizontal axis shows time (t) by week. The vertical axis shows the starting inventory for that week (which is equal to the ending inventory for the previous week). We have assumed that inventory remains constant during the week and changes only at the end of the week when sales take place. Inventory also may be present in various stages of completion.

Observe that the inventory of flow units (garages) varies over time. From Table 3.2 we can calculate the average inventory over the last eight weeks to be $I = 2,000$ garages.

TABLE 3.2   Ending Inventory Data for MBPF Inc.

Week	0	1	2	3	4	5	6	7	8
Ending Inventory	2,200	1,800	2,100	2,200	2,000	1,900	1,700	2,100	2,200

FIGURE 3.2 Inventory Build-Up Diagram for MBPF Inc.

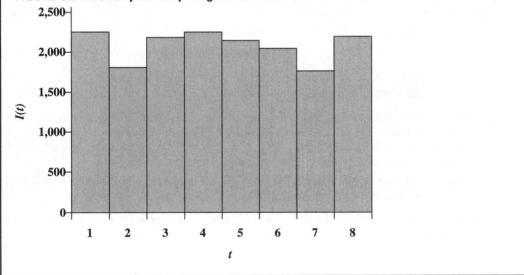

In most applications, process inventory $I(t)$ fluctuates over time in accordance with the instantaneous inventory accumulation rate $\Delta R(t)$:

- If $R_i(t)$ is larger than $R_o(t)$, inventory accumulates at a rate of $\Delta R(t) = R_i(t) - R_o(t)$.
- If $R_o(t)$ is larger than $R_i(t)$, inventory is depleted at a rate of $-\Delta R(t) = R_o(t) - R_i(t)$.

We thus have $I(t) = I(t-1) + \Delta R(t)$.

Even though inventory fluctuates over time in a stable process, we can define average inventory, where the average is taken over time, and denote it as I. Also in a stable process, average inventory accumulation rate ΔR, though not average inventory, must be zero.

As a measure of process performance, average inventory tells us the average number of flow units within the process boundaries. It is useful in identifying the amount of working capital that is tied up in the factory. It also is useful in estimating the amount of storage space required. Example 3.3 illustrates inventories at MBPF Inc.

3.5   RELATING FLOW RATE, FLOW TIME, AND INVENTORY

The three performance measures discussed in sections 3.2, 3.3, and 3.4 answer the three questions about process flows that we raised earlier:

1. On average, how many flow units pass through the process per unit of time?
2. On average, how much time does a typical flow unit spend within process boundaries?
3. On average, how many flow units are within process boundaries at any point in time?

The answers to these three questions are as follows:

1. *Average flow rate or throughput* of the process is the average number of flow units that pass through the process per unit of time.
2. *Average flow time* for a flow unit through the process is the average time that a typical flow unit spends within process boundaries.
3. *Average inventory* is the average number of flow units within the process boundaries.

Little's Law   We can now show that these three performance measures are linked by a fundamental relation of process flows. This relation is known as **Little's law**. It relates average flow rate (i.e., throughput) R, average flow time T, and average inventory I as

$$I = R \times T$$

In Example 3.4 we illustrate Little's law. Two immediate but far-reaching implications of Little's law are as follows:

1. Of the three related operational-performance measures—flow rate, flow time, and inventory—a manager can select any two on which to focus, with the result that the third, according to Little's law, is determined by the levels of the two choices. The manager has the responsibility of deciding which two measures to manage.
2. For a given level of throughput in any process, the only way to reduce flow time is to reduce inventory, and vice versa.

In Example 3.5 we show that Little's law holds for a stable process even when there are short term fluctuations in throughput and inventory.

3.6   EXAMPLES

The following examples illustrate the wide range of applications, both in manufacturing and service operations, in which an analysis based on Little's law can be useful. In section 3.6.6 we use the concepts discussed thus far to analyze changes at MBPF Finance and so complete the problem raised in Example 3.1.

EXAMPLE 3.4

Recall from Example 3.3 that average inventory is $I = 2,000$ garages and from Example 3.2 that average throughput rate is $R = 1,000$ garages per week. Recall also that even though inventory and flow rate vary over time, the MBPF Inc. process is stable. With these facts in mind, we will track a typical flow unit entering MBPF. First, our flow unit encounters an average of $I = 2,000$ flow units, all of

which must be processed at rate $R = 1,000$ per week before our flow unit can leave the process. On average, complete processing takes

$$I/R \text{ time units} = 2 \text{ weeks}$$

—the length of time T that our flow unit spends, on average, in this stable process.

EXAMPLE 3.5

Using numbers from our MBPF illustration, we can give a derivation of Little's law based on the inventory build-up diagram discussed in Figure 3.2. Recall that MBPF tracks inventory over $k(= 8)$ periods of time (weeks). From Figure 3.2, in the first week 2,200 garages spend a week within the MBPF process. Thus, total flow time (across all garages in the process) incurred in the first week is 2,200 garage weeks. In the second week, 1,800 garages spend a week within the MBPF process. Thus total flow time incurred in the second week is 1,800 garage weeks. Covering the entire eight-week period, the area under the bars in Figure 3.2 represents *the total number of garage weeks spent within the process by all garages.* We denote this area as $A(k)$—which, in the case of MBPF, is $A(8)$ and $A(8) = 16,000$ garage weeks.

We also can construct a rectangle with base k and height I that has the same area $A(k)$. In the case of MBPF, this procedure implies a rectangle with a height $I = 2,000$. Carrying the fluctuating amount of inventory over the k periods (eight weeks), as shown in Figure 3.2, is equivalent to carrying I units (2,000 garages) of inventory over the k periods (eight weeks). This equation implies the following relationship:

$$I = A(k)/k = 16,000/8 = 2,000$$

Note that $A(k)$ is also the sum of flow times of all garages that flow through the process during the k periods. By allowing T to be the average flow time here, we arrive at the following equation:

$$A(k) = \text{Total number of flow units through process in } k \text{ periods} \times T$$

This equation implies that:

$$I = (\text{Total number of flow units through process in } k \text{ periods }/k) \times T,$$
$$= \text{Average number of flow units through process per period} \times T, \text{ and}$$
$$= R \times T, \text{ which is Little's law.}$$

At MBPF, the total number of flow units moving through the process over the eight weeks is 8,000—a figure that yields a process throughput of $R = 1,000$ garages per week. From Little's law, therefore, we can derive the following equation:

$$T = I/R = 2,000 \text{ garages}/(1,000 \text{ garages/week}) = 2 \text{ weeks}$$

3.6.1   Material Flow

A fast-food outlet processes an average of 5,000 kilograms (kg) of hamburgers per week. Typical inventory of raw meat is 2,500 kg. The process in this case is the fast-food outlet and the flow unit is a kilogram of meat. We know, therefore, that

$$\textit{Throughput R} = 5,000 \text{ kg/week}$$

and

$$\textit{Average inventory I} = 2,500 \text{ kg}$$

Thus, we can deduce the following:

$$\textit{Average flow time T} = I/R = 0.5 \text{ week}$$

So an average kilogram of meat spends only half a week as raw material inventory. The fast-food outlet may use this information to verify that it is using fresh meat in its hamburgers.

3.6.2 Customer Flow

A restaurant processes, on average, 1,500 customers per 15-hour workday. At any point in time, there are, on average, 75 customers in the restaurant. These people are either waiting to place an order, waiting for an order to arrive, eating, or returning to the counter to order another serving. Because it will tell us how long a customer spends inside the restaurant, we are interested in the average flow time for each customer. The process is the restaurant and the flow unit is a customer. We know, therefore, that

$$\textit{Throughput R} = 1,500 \text{ customers/day or 100 customers/hour}$$

and

$$\textit{Average inventory I} = 75 \text{ customers}$$

Thus, we can deduce the following:

$$\textit{Average flow time T} = I/R = 75/1,500 \text{ day} = 1/20 \text{ day} = 3/4 \text{ hour}$$

So the average customer spends 3/4 hour, or 45 minutes, at the restaurant.

3.6.3 Job Flow

A branch office of an insurance company processes 10,000 claims per year. Average processing time is 3 weeks. Assume that the office works 50 weeks per year. The process is a branch of the insurance company and the flow unit is a claim. We know, therefore, that

$$\textit{Throughput R} = 10,000 \text{ claims/year}$$

and

$$\textit{Average flow time T} = 3/50 \text{ year}$$

Thus, we can deduce the following:

$$\textit{Average inventory I} = R \times T = 10,000 \times 3/50 \text{ claims} = 600 \text{ claims}$$

On average, then, scattered in the branch are 600 applications in various phases of processing—waiting to be assigned, actually being processed, waiting to be sent out, waiting for additional data, and so forth.

3.6.4 Cash Flow

A steel company processes $400 million of raw materials per year. The cost of processing is $200 million per year. Average inventory is $100 million. The value of inventory includes both raw material and processing cost. The process in this case is the steel company and the flow unit is a cost dollar. Throughput corresponds to the $600 million flowing through the process each year. We know, therefore, that

$$Throughput\ R = \$600\ million/year$$

and

$$Average\ inventory\ I = \$100\ million$$

Thus, we can deduce the following:

$$Average\ flow\ time\ T = I/R = 100/600\ years = 1/6\ year = 2\ months$$

On average, therefore, a dollar spends two months in the process—an average lag of two months occurs between the time a dollar enters the process (either in the form of raw materials or of processing cost) and the time it leaves (in the form of finished goods). Thus, each dollar is tied up in working capital at the factory for an average of two months.

3.6.5 Cash Flow (Accounts Receivable)

A major manufacturer sells $300 million worth of cellular equipment per year. Average amount in accounts receivable is $45 million. In this case, the process is the manufacturer's accounts receivable department and the flow unit is a dollar in accounts receivable. We know, therefore, that

$$Throughput\ R = \$300\ million/year$$

and

$$Average\ inventory\ I = \$45\ million$$

Thus, this equation implies the following:

$$Average\ flow\ time\ T = I/R = 45/300\ years = 0.15\ year = 1.8\ months$$

On average, 1.8 months elapse from the time a customer is billed to the time payment is received. Any reduction in this time will result in revenues reaching the manufacturer more quickly.

3.6.6 MBPF Finance

We now analyze the MBPF Finance scenario presented in Example 3.1. Having made changes in the application approval process, the firm wants to analyze the impact of these changes on its service performance.

In this case, the flow unit is a loan application. Recall that, on average, MBPF Finance receives and processes 1,000 loan applications per month. If we start by considering Process I, we know the following:

$$Throughput\ R = 1,000\ applications/month$$

and

$$Average\ inventory\ I = 500\ applications$$

Thus, we can conclude that

$$Average\ flow\ time\ T = I/R = 500/1,000\ months = 0.5\ month = 15\ days$$

In Process I, each application spent, on average, 15 days with MBPF Finance before receiving an accept/reject decision.

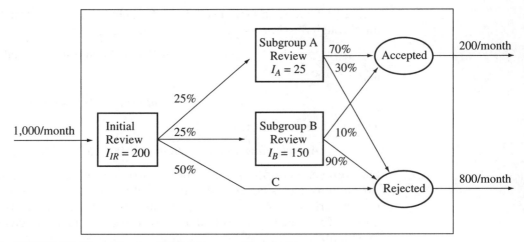

FIGURE 3.3 Flow Chart on MBPF Finance Process II

Now consider Process II. Because this process involves multiple steps, it is worth starting with the process flow chart in Figure 3.3. (We discuss process flow charts more fully in chapter 4.) Note that, on average, 1,000 applications arrive per month for the Initial Review Team. After review, 25% are categorized as type A (looks excellent), 25% are categorized as type B (needs more detailed evaluation), and 50% are categorized as type C (and thus rejected). On detailed evaluation by Subgroup A Team, 70% of type A applications are accepted and 30% are rejected. On evaluation by Subgroup B Team, 10% of type B applications are accepted and 90% are rejected. Thus, an average of 200 applications are accepted each month and 800 are rejected.

As mentioned in Example 3.1, Figure 3.3 shows that, on average, 200 applications are with the Initial Review Team, 25 are with the Subgroup A Team, and 150 are with the Subgroup B Team. Thus, we can conclude (for Process II) that

$$Throughput\ R = 1,000\ applications/month$$

and

$$Average\ inventory\ I = 200 + 150 + 25 = 375\ applications$$

Thus, we can deduce the following:

$$Average\ flow\ time\ T = I/R = 375\ /\ 1,000\ month = 0.375\ months = 11.25\ days$$

Under Process II, each application spends, on average, 11.25 days with MBPF Finance before an accept/reject decision is made. Compared with the 15 days taken, on average, under Process I, this reduction is significant.

Another way to reach the same conclusion is to break down Process II into its three subprocesses: Initial Review, Subgroup A Review, and Subgroup B Review. In Figure 3.3, each application begins in Initial Review. On average, the Initial Review Team has 200 applications. For Initial Review, the performance measures are denoted with subscript *IR* and are as follows:

$$Throughput\ R_{IR} = 1,000\ applications/month$$

and

$$Average\ inventory\ I_{IR} = 200\ applications$$

From this information we can deduce that for Initial Review

Average flow time $T_{IR} = I_{IR}/R_{IR} = 200/1{,}000$ months $= 0.2$ month $= 6$ days

Thus, each application spends, on average, six days in Initial Review.

Now consider the applications classified as type A by Initial Review. Recall that, on average, Subgroup A Review Team has 25 applications. Because 25% of all incoming applications are categorized as type A, on average, 250 applications per month are categorized as type A. We thus have

Throughput $R_A = 250$ applications/month

and

Average inventory $I_A = 25$ applications

Thus, we can deduce the following:

Average flow time $T_A = I_A/R_A = 25/250$ month $= 0.1$ month $= 3$ days

Type A applications spend, on average, another three days in the process with the Subgroup A Review Team.

Similarly, Subgroup B Review Team, on average, has 150 applications and processes 250 applications per month. Thus,

Throughput $R_B = 250$ applications/month

and

Average inventory $I_B = 150$ applications

Thus, we can deduce the following:

Average flow time $T_B = I_B/R_B = 150/250$ months $= 0.6$ month $= 18$ days

Type B applications spend, on average, another 18 days in the process with the Subgroup B Review Team.

Recall that each application received by MBPF Finance is categorized as type A, B, or C by the Initial Review Team. Each application spends, on average, 6 days with the Initial Review Team. Type A applications are then reviewed by the Subgroup A Review Team, where they spend an additional 3 days. Type B applications are reviewed by the Subgroup B Review Team, where they spend, on average, another 18 days. Type C applications are rejected by the Initial Review Team itself. Under Process II, therefore, we know the following:

- All type A applications spend, on average, 9 days in the process;
- All type B applications spend, on average, 24 days in the process; and
- All type C applications spend, on average, 6 days in the process.

In this analysis, we defined flow units according to categories of applications. When evaluating service performance, however, MBPF Finance may want to define flow units differently—as applications, approved applications, or rejected applications. We now evaluate flow times for each of these instances.

We can find the *average flow time* across all applications under Process II by taking the *weighted average* across the three application types. Recall that Type C applications have a throughput of $R_c = 500$/month. Average flow time across all application types is given as follows:

$$T = \frac{R_c T_{IR} + R_A(T_{IR} + T_A) + R_B(T_{IR} + T_B)}{R_A + R_B + R_C}$$

$$= \frac{(500 \times 6) + (250 \times 9) + (250 \times 24)}{1{,}000} = 11.25 \text{ days}$$

Because approved applications represent customers who provide revenue, MBPF Finance would probably benefit more from reducing the flow time for them to less than 11.25 days. Compare the average time that an approved application spends with MBPF Finance under each of the two processes. Under Process I, average time spent by an application in the process is 15 days—regardless of whether it is finally approved. Under Process II, 70% of type A applications (175 of 250 per month, on average) are approved, as are 10% of type B applications (25 of 250 per month, on average). Thus, average time spent in Process II by an application that is eventually *approved* is given as follows:

$$Average\ flow\ time\ for\ approved\ applications = \frac{(175 \times 9) + (25 \times 24)}{175 + 25} = 10.875\ days$$

Meanwhile, average time spent in Process II by an application that is eventually *rejected* is given as follows:

$$Average\ flow\ time\ for\ rejected\ applications = \frac{(500 \times 6) + (75 \times 9) + (225 \times 24)}{500 + 75 + 225} = 11.343\ days$$

Process II, therefore, has not only reduced average overall application flow time, but also has reduced it more for approved customers than for rejected customers. However, 12.5% of all approved applications (25 that are categorized as type B of 200 approved each month) remain longer in Process II than in Process I (an average of 24 days instead of 15 days). This delay can pose a potential problem for MBPF Finance in terms of service performance. These applications represent customers who can potentially provide revenue for the firm. A delay in the approval process may result in a loss of revenue if these customers go elsewhere for financing.

3.6.7 Analyzing Income Statements and Inventory Details

We now return to MBPF Inc. and analyze all or part of three financial statements: the firm's *income statement, balance sheet,* and *cost of goods sold (COGS)* for 1998. With an appropriate use of Little's law, this analysis will help us not only to understand the current performance of the process but also to suggest areas for improvement.

A key financial measure for any process such as MBPF Inc. is *investment in working capital.* Working-capital requirements include *the value of inventories in the process and the value of any accounts receivable.* At a minimum, any reduction in working capital reduces the firm's interest expense. If cash constraints limit a firm's ability to invest in other profitable ventures, a reduction in working capital can make extra cash available for this investment. The following analysis shows us how to find areas within MBPF Inc. in which a reduction of flow time will result in a significant reduction in inventories and, therefore, working capital.

In 1998, MBPF operations called for the purchase of both sheet metal (raw materials) and prefabricated bases (purchased parts). Roofs were made in the fabrication area from sheet metal and then assembled with prefabricated bases in the assembly area. Completed garages were stored in the finished goods warehouse until they were shipped to customers.

To conduct our analysis, we need the data contained in the following tables:

- Table 3.3—MBPF's 1998 income statement,
- Table 3.4—MBPF's consolidated balance sheet as of December 31, 1998, and
- Table 3.5—details concerning process inventories as of December 31, 1998, and production costs for the year 1998.

EXAMPLE 3.6

Our objective is to study *cash flows* at MBPF to determine *how long it takes for a cost dollar to yield revenue.* First, we need a picture of process-wide cash flows. The flow unit here is a cost dollar and the process is the entire factory, including the finished-goods warehouse. Incorporating inventory and cash-flow numbers obtained from Table 3.5, a flow diagram for the entire process (factory + finished-goods warehouse) is shown in Figure 3.4. From Table 3.5, we observe that raw materials (for roofs) worth $50.1 million and purchased parts (finished bases) worth $40.2 million are purchased each year. Labor and overhead costs in roof fabrication total $60.2 million per year and in final assembly total $25.3 million per year. Adding all costs, we obtain annual cost of goods sold—$175.8 million (as shown in Table 3.3). From Table 3.4, we find that inventories at MBPF Inc. total $50.6 million.

Upon analyzing the cash flows, we arrive at the following information:

Throughput
R = $175.8 million/year [cost of goods sold, Table 3.3]

and

Average inventory
I = $50.6 million [inventories, Table 3.4]

Thus, we can deduce average flow time as follows:

Average flow time $T = I/R$ = 50.6/175.8 years
$= .288$ year $= 14.97$ weeks

Alternatively, if we replace the *annual* throughput figure of $175.8 million/year with a *weekly* figure of $3.38 million/week, then we can obtain T in weeks directly as follows:

Average flow time T = 50.6/3.38 = 14.97 weeks

The average dollar invested in the factory spends roughly 15 weeks before it leaves the process through the door of the finished-goods inventory warehouse.

FIGURE 3.4 Flow Diagram for MBPF Inc.

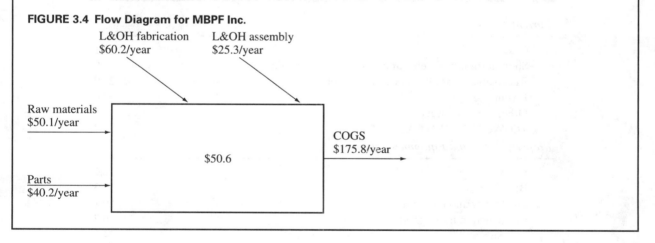

Before proceeding, note that the following stipulations apply to Tables 3.3, 3.4, and 3.5:

- All values are in millions of dollars, except those per common share, which are in dollars.
- All data represent end-of-the-year numbers.
- We will assume, however, that inventory figures represent average inventory in the process.

From Examples 3.6 and 3.7 we see a significant time lag between when a cost dollar is invested and a sales dollar returns. MBPF Inc. would gain significantly if this lag is shortened. A more detailed analysis by stage can help identify specific areas for improvement as shown in Example 3.8.

TABLE 3.3 Consolidated Statements of Income and Retained Earnings for 1998

Net sales	250.0
Costs and expenses	
Cost of goods sold	175.8
Selling, general and administrative expenses	47.2
Interest expense	4.0
Depreciation	5.6
Other (income) expenses	2.1
TOTAL COSTS AND EXPENSES	234.7
INCOME BEFORE INCOME TAXES	15.3
PROVISION FOR INCOME TAXES	7.0
NET INCOME	8.3
RETAINED EARNINGS, BEGINNING OF YEAR	31.0
LESS CASH DIVIDENDS DECLARED	2.1
RETAINED EARNINGS AT END OF YEAR	37.2
NET INCOME PER COMMON SHARE	0.83
DIVIDEND PER COMMON SHARE	0.21

TABLE 3.4 Consolidated Balance Sheet as of December 31, 1998

Current Assets

Cash	2.1
Short-term investments at cost (approximate mkt.)	3.0
Receivables, less allowances of $0.7 mil	27.9
Inventories	50.6
Other current assets	4.1
TOTAL CURRENT ASSETS	87.7

Property, Plant, and Equipment (at cost)

Land	2.1
Buildings	15.3
Machinery and equipment	50.1
Construction in progress	6.7
Subtotal	74.2
Less accumulated depreciation	25.0
NET PROPERTY, PLANT, AND EQUIPMENT	49.2
Investments	4.1
Prepaid expenses and other deferred charges	1.9
Other assets	4.0
TOTAL ASSETS	146.9

TABLE 3.5   Inventories and Cost of Goods Details

Cost of Goods Sold

Raw materials	50.1
Fabrication (L&OH)	60.2
Purchased parts	40.2
Assembly (L&OH)	25.3
TOTAL	175.8

Inventory

Raw materials (roof)	6.5
Fabrication WIP (roof)	15.1
Purchased parts (base)	8.6
Assembly WIP	10.6
Finished goods	9.8
TOTAL	50.6

EXAMPLE 3.7

A similar analysis can be performed for the accounts receivable (AR) department. Our objective here is to determine *how long it takes, on average, between the time at which a dollar enters the AR department and the time at which it is received as payment from the customer.* In this case, process boundaries are defined by the AR department, and the flow unit is a dollar of accounts receivable. Observe in Table 3.3 that MBPF has annual sales (and thus an annual flow rate through AR) of $250 million. Observe in Table 3.4 that accounts receivables total $27.9 million. Incorporating these numbers, Figure 3.5 presents the flow in MBPF's AR department.

When we analyze flows through AR, we arrive at the following information:

Throughput R_{AR} = $250 million/year [net sales, Table 3.3]

and

Average inventory
   I_{AR} = $27.9 million [receivables, Table 3.4]

Accordingly, we can deduce average flow time through AR as follows:

Average flow time
$T_{AR} = I_{AR}/R_{AR} = 27.9/250$ years = 0.112 year = 5.82 weeks

After a sale is made, MBPF must wait nearly 6 weeks before sales dollars arrive from the customer. Overall, an average lag of about 21 weeks (15 weeks in production and 5.8 weeks in AR) occurs between the point at which cost dollars are invested and the point at which sales dollars are received by MBPF. Note, however, that cost and sales dollars are not equivalent. From Table 3.3, we see that 175.8 million cost dollars result in 250 million sales dollars. When considering inventories, MBPF must use cost dollars. Conversely, when considering receivables or revenue, MBPF must consider sales dollars.

FIGURE 3.5 Accounts Receivable Process at MBPF

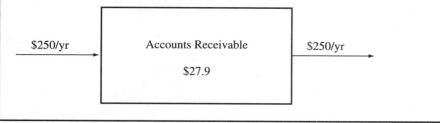

EXAMPLE 3.8

We now consider detailed operations by analyzing dollar flows separately through each of the following stages of the process: raw materials, purchased parts, fabrication, assembly, and finished goods. The flow unit in each case is a cost dollar. A detailed flow diagram is shown in Figure 3.6, with all cost dollar flows in millions of dollars.

For each stage, we obtain throughput as *the cost of input plus any labor and overhead (L&OH) incurred in the department.* The throughput rate through fabrication is $50.1 million per year in raw materials and $60.2 million in labor and overhead for a total of $110.3 million per year. The throughput through the assembly area is $110.3 million per year in roofs, $40.2 million per year in bases, and $25.3 million per year in labor and overhead for a total of $175.8 million per year.

By analyzing the various flows through these four stages, we find the flow times for a cost dollar through each department shown in Table 3.6. (All data originate from Table 3.5.)

Working capital includes the amount of inventory in each department. Flow time in each department represents the amount of time a cost dollar spends, on average, in that department.

Reducing flow time therefore reduces interest expenses incurred by MBPF on its working capital. Knowing this principle, we should be prompted to ask this question: *In which department does a reduction of flow time have the* greatest *impact on working capital?* Because inventory equals the product of flow time and throughput, the value of reducing flow time in any department is proportional to its throughput rate. For example, because throughput through the finished-goods warehouse is $3.38 million per week, reducing flow time here by one week saves $3.38 million in working capital (inventory). Or, because the throughput rate through purchased parts is only $0.77 million per week, a one-week reduction in flow time saves only $0.77 million in working capital. *Current flow time, then, represents the maximum potential reduction in flow time.*

Both current flow times and the value of reducing them are represented graphically in Figure 3.7. For each department, we plot throughput on the vertical axis and flow time on the horizontal axis. Corresponding to each department we have a rectangle whose area represents the inventory in the department.

FIGURE 3.6 Flow Times Through MBPF

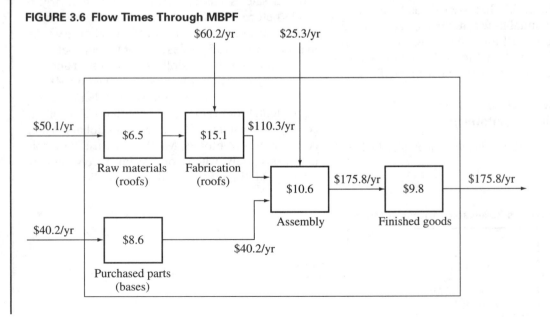

Observe in Figure 3.7 that a one-week reduction in flow time has the largest impact in the AR department, where the rectangle for AR represents the highest flow rate of $5 million per week. The smallest possible impact of a one-week reduc- tion would be in the purchased parts department, which has a flow rate of only $0.77 million. With a flow time of 11.12 weeks, however, the purchased parts department offers the greatest potential to decrease flow time itself.

TABLE 3.6 MBPF Business Flows Process					
	Raw Materials	*Fabrication*	*Purchased Parts*	*Assembly*	*Finished Goods*
Throughput R					
million $/Year	50.1	110.3	40.2	175.8	175.8
million $/Week	0.96	2.12	0.77	3.38	3.38
Inventory I (million $)	6.5	15.1	8.6	10.6	9.8
Flow time $T = I/R$ (weeks)	6.77	7.12	11.17	3.14	2.90

FIGURE 3.7 Inventory Value Representation

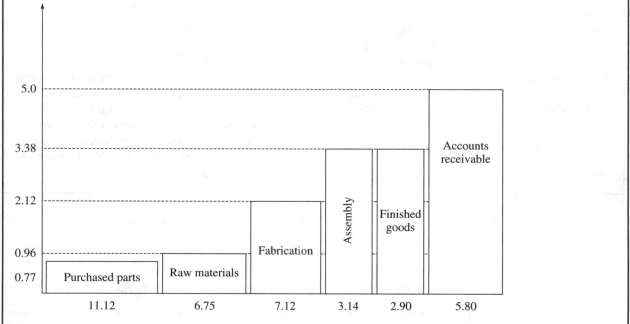

3.7   INVENTORY TURNS (TURNOVER RATIO)

We now introduce the concept of inventory turns, a popular measure in business. We relate inventory turns to measures discussed earlier.

Inventory turns, or **turnover ratio** (henceforth referred to as turns) is defined as *the ratio of throughput to average inventory* and expressed as

$$Turns = R/I$$

EXAMPLE 3.9

We now return to the MBPF financial statements discussed earlier. If we use cost dollar as the flow unit and if we designate the factory and the finished-goods warehouse as the process, then we observe that the process has a turnover ratio expressed as follows:

$$Turns = (\$175.8/year)/\$50.6 = 3.47/year$$

You cannot use a throughput of $250 million per year because that figure is measured in sales dollars whereas inventory is measured in cost dollars. The problem with using sales dollars instead of cost dollars is illustrated in the following example. Assume that in 1999, MBPF Inc. experiences an increase in sales to $300 million (from $250 million in 1998). Cost of goods sold in 1999 is $204 million, and inventories total $60 million in cost dollars. Although the *contribution margin*—the excess of sales revenue over variable costs—has clearly increased from $75 million in 1998 (30% of sales) to $96 million in 1999 (32% of sales), a key question remains: *Has the firm's operational management of its inventories improved?*

If we use sales dollars to measure throughput and inventory turns, MBPF obtains the following figures for turns:

$$250/50.6 = 4.94 \text{ turns in } 1998$$

and

$$300/60 = 5 \text{ turns in } 1999$$

Based on this measure, MBPF would conclude that because turns have increased, inventory was managed better in 1999 than in 1998.

On the other hand, if throughput and turns are measured by cost of goods sold, MBPF obtains the following figures:

$$175.8/50.6 = 3.47 \text{ turns in } 1998$$

and

$$204/60 = 3.40 \text{ turns in } 1999$$

Using this measure, we must conclude that 1998 inventory management was better than 1999 inventory management. This contradicts the conclusion drawn using sales dollars. Observe that flow time in 1998 is

$$50.6/175.8 = 0.28 \text{ years}$$

while flow time in 1999 is

$$60/204 = 0.29 \text{ years}$$

This difference indicates that each cost dollar spent more time within the MBPF process in 1999 than it did in 1998. In this case, the use of sales dollars to measure throughput distorts this important fact and leads to erroneous conclusions. In evaluating turns, therefore, it is advisable to measure throughput in cost dollars.

Using Little's law, the *turnover ratio equals the inverse of average flow time:*

$$Turns = \frac{1}{T}$$

To derive a meaningful turnover ratio, *we must specify flow unit and inventory in the same units.* Some organizations measure turns as the ratio of sales to inventory. This measure has a drawback in that sales (a measure of throughput) are expressed in sales dollars, but inventory is measured in cost dollars. Because both are measured in cost dollars, a better definition of turns is the ratio of cost of goods sold (COGS)—labor, materials, and overhead expenses allocated to the products in question—to inventory. Measuring turns as the ratio of sales to inventory can lead to erroneous conclusions when measuring process performance, as illustrated in Example 3.9.

3.8   WHAT IS AN IMPROVEMENT?

Thus far, we have defined three operational process-performance measures: *flow rate, flow time,* and *inventory.* We also have seen how each measurement can be evaluated for a variety of business-process flows. Because Little's law relates these measures through one equation, we can manage only two of them independently, and the third measure is then automatically determined. We now relate these operational measures to financial measures of process performance. Our goal is *to determine when a process change generates an improvement from both operational and financial perspectives.*

Net Present Value   An absolute measure of financial performance of any business process may be measured by the **net present value (NPV)** of its current and future cash flows. NPV is a model for *computing expected monetary gain or loss by discounting all expected future cash inflows and outflows to their present value.* Given a sequence of cash flows over a period of future time, a firm's NPV is equivalent to a single present sum. In this regard, any risk-neutral investor who is in a position to choose between accepting a future sequence of cash flows and accepting the single sum today will value both the same. NPV is calculated by adjusting future cash flows by a discount factor to reflect the **time value of money**—the principle stating that a dollar you hold today will be worth more than a dollar you expect to receive in the future. The discount factor is based on the **rate of return (*r*).** An investor demands a reward ($ *r*) for accepting payment of $1 delayed by one period of time. Equivalently, our investor is indifferent to whether $1/(1+r)$ is received this period or $1 is received next period.

Let C_t represent the cash flow in period *t,* starting from period $t = 0$ and ending at period $t = k$. The NPV of this set of cash flows is given as

$$\text{NPV} = C_o + \sum_{t=1}^{k} \frac{C_t}{(1+r)^t}$$

where we applied a discount factor of $1/(1+r)^t$ to all cash flows in period *t.*

Sales Volume and Cash Flows   The true throughput for any business process is measured by *sales volume*—number of units sold. If MBPF Inc. produces 2,200 garages per week while market demand is for 1,000 garages per week, an additional 1,200 garages per week will simply build up as inventory. Throughput will be 1,000 garages per week. If, however, production is only 800 garages per week and demand is 1,000 per week, then actual sales—and thus throughput—will be 800 garages per week. *Process throughput, therefore, is the minimum of its output and market demand.* Note that *positive cash flows* result from the revenue received from product sales (there may be other revenue sources, but product sales will be a major contributor). We can assume that positive cash flows are correlated with throughput. An increase in throughput (sales) thus increases positive cash flows.

Negative cash flows typically result from investment in resources, interest expense, and operating expense (labor + overhead). Interest expense is correlated with the amount of process inventory. Reducing inventory in the process reduces the company's working capital requirement. This reduction lowers its interest expense, thereby reducing negative cash flows. **Process cost** is the total cost incurred in producing and delivering outputs. Negative cash flows can also be reduced by reducing process cost, because negative cash flows decrease when the process entails lower cost to produce the outputs.

We are now in a position to know when a change in the process can be called an improvement. From the financial perspective, a change is an improvement *only if it increases NPV.* A change may increase both positive and negative cash flows, which is an improvement only if the NPV of the increase in positive cash flows exceeds the NPV of the increase in negative cash flows. A change can certainly be called an improvement if it either increases positive cash flows without increasing negative cash flows or decreases negative cash flows without decreasing positive cash flows. This situation is equivalent to addressing the following three questions:

1. Has process throughput (amount of sales) risen without any increase in inventories or process cost?
2. Has process inventory declined without any reduction in throughput or increase in process cost?
3. Has process cost declined without any reduction in throughput or increase in inventory?

The first two questions are tantamount to asking if flow time has been reduced without any increase in process cost. All three questions are quite similar to those raised by Israeli physicist E.M. Goldratt in his efforts to identify and characterize process improvement (Goldratt, 1992). All three questions address only simple instances in which we know that NPV will rise because of the change. In more complicated scenarios in which both positive and negative cash flows change, we *must evaluate* NPV before characterizing a change as an improvement.

A relative measure of financial performance is **return on total assets,** which shows how well a firm uses its assets to earn income for the stockholders who are financing it. We can express this measure as follows:

$$Return\ on\ total\ assets = \frac{EBIT - Taxes}{Average\ Total\ Assets}$$

where *EBIT* is **earnings before interest and taxes.** EBIT is also known as *operating income* and compares gross profit with operating expenses. It increases with an increase of annual unit sales and income per unit (assuming a positive income per unit). Average total assets include *fixed assets* (typically those invested in resources) and *working capital* (typically those invested in inventory). An affirmative answer to any of the three questions posed in this section results in an increase in return on total assets.

In this chapter we have established a relationship between the three operational measures and some common financial measures. Our discussion indicates that improvements along the three operational measures also translate into improvements along financial measures.

Problem Set

3.1. The Internal Revenue Service Department of Tax Regulations writes regulations in accord with laws passed by Congress. On average, the department completes 300 projects per year. The *Wall Street Journal* reports that, as of October 11, 1997, the number of projects currently "on the Department's plate" is 588. Nevertheless, the department head claims that average time to complete a project is under six months. Do you have any reason to disagree? Why or why not?

3.2. A bank finds that the average number of people waiting in line during lunch hour is 10. On average, during this period 2 people per minute leave the bank after receiving service. On average, how long do bank customers wait in line?

3.3. At the drive-through counter of a fast-food outlet, an average of 10 cars waits in line. The manager wants to determine if the length of the line impacts on potential sales. Her study reveals that, on average, 2 cars per minute try to enter the drive-through area, but 25% of these cars are dismayed by the long line and simply move on without entering the line and placing orders. Assume that no car entering the line leaves without service. On average, how long does a car spend in the drive-through line?

3.4. Checking accounts at a local bank carry an average balance of $3,000. The bank turns over its balance six times a year. On average, how many dollars flow through the bank each month?

3.5. A hospital emergency room (ER) is currently organized so that all patients register through an initial check-in process. At his or her turn, each patient is seen by a doctor and then exits the process, either with a prescription or with admission to the hospital. Currently, 50 people per hour arrive at the ER, 10% of whom are admitted to the hospital. On average, 30 people are waiting to be registered and 40 are registered and waiting to see a doctor. The registration process takes, on average, 2 minutes per patient. Among patients who receive prescriptions, average time spent with a doctor is 5 minutes. Among those admitted to the hospital, average time is 30 minutes. On average, how long does a patient stay in the ER? On average, how many patients are being examined by doctors? On average, how many patients are in the ER?

3.6. A triage system has been proposed for the ER described in Problem 3.5. As mentioned, 50 patients per hour arrive at the ER. Under the proposed triage plan, patients who are entering will be registered as before. They will then be quickly examined by a nurse practitioner who will classify them as Simple Prescriptions or Potential Admits. While Simple Prescriptions will move on to an area staffed for regular care, Potential Admits will be taken to the emergency area. Planners anticipate that initial examination by the triage nurse will take 3 minutes. They expect that, on average, 20 patients will be waiting to register and 5 will be waiting to be seen by the triage nurse. Recall that registration takes an average of 2 minutes per patient. Planners expect the Simple Prescriptions area to have, on average, 15 patients waiting to be seen. As before, once a patient's turn comes, each will take 5 minutes of a doctor's time. The hospital anticipates that, on average, the emergency area will have only 1 patient waiting to be seen. As before, once that patient's turn comes, he or she will take 30 minutes of a doctor's time. Assume that, as before, 90% of all patients are Simple Prescriptions. Assume, too, that the triage nurse is 100% accurate in her classifications. Under the proposed plan, how long, on average, will a patient stay in the ER? On average, how long will a Potential Admit stay in the ER? On average, how many patients will be in the ER?

3.7. Refer again to Problem 3.6. Once the triage system is put in place, it performs quite close to expectations. All data conform to planners' expectations except for one set—the classifications made by the nurse practitioner. Assume that the triage nurse has been sending 91% of all patients to the Simple Prescription area when in fact only 90% should have been so classified. The remaining 1% are discovered when transferred to the emergency area by a doctor. Assume all other information from Problem 3.6 is valid. On average, how long does a patient stay in the ER? On average, how long does a Potential Admit stay in the ER? On average, how many patients are in the ER?

3.8. Last year, the *Wall Street Journal* reported that " . . . although GM and Toyota are operating with the same number of inventory turns, Toyota's throughput is twice that of GM." The discrepancy, concluded the writer, "could be due to much faster flow times and lower inventories by virtue of Toyota's production system." With which of the following deductions do you agree:

a. The two statements are consistent.

b. The two statements are inconsistent. If both have the same inventory turns, then they have the same flow time but Toyota has higher average inventory than GM.

www.prenhall.com/anupindi

For exercises using Process Model, go to http://www.prenhall.com/anupindi/

c. The two statements are inconsistent. If both have the same inventory turns, then they have the same flow time but Toyota has lower average inventory than GM.

d. The two statements are inconsistent. If both have the same inventory turns, then they have the same average inventory but Toyota has higher flow time than GM.

e. The two statements are inconsistent. If both have the same inventory turns, then they have the same average inventory but Toyota has lower flow time than GM.

CHAPTER

Flow-Time Analysis

This chapter analyzes *flow time* as a measure of process performance. Flow time is *the total amount of time that a flow unit spends in a process,* and it includes the following:

1. *Theoretical flow time*—the minimal time required to process a flow unit if it does not have to wait at any point in the process, and

2. *Waiting time*—the total amount of time that a flow unit spends in the process waiting to be processed.

Flow-time efficiency is *the ratio of the theoretical flow time to the average total flow time.* To determine the theoretical flow time of a process, we model it graphically as a *process flow chart,* which shows both the various activities involved in processing a flow unit and their precedence relations. A sequence of activities that takes the longest total time for completion is called a *critical path.* The total duration of a critical path impacts the flow time.

4.1   INTRODUCTION

In the preceding chapters, we introduced three important measures of process performance:

- Average flow time,
- Average flow rate, and
- Average inventory.

We also showed how Little's law establishes a fundamental relationship among these three measures. In chapter 3, we stressed the importance of these measures and applied Little's law to a macrolevel performance evaluation of a business process. In chapters 4 and 5, we lay the foundation for more detailed process analysis. Our goal is to understand what factors affect the three key performance measures and the levers that can be manipulated to improve process performance along the continuums that they measure.

In this chapter, we begin with the concept of flow time. Recall from chapter 3 that the flow time of a given flow unit is the total amount of time required by that unit to flow through the process from entry to exit. For any given process, various flow units display a great degree of variation in flow time. Thus the average flow time of a process is determined by taking the average across all flow units that exit the process during a specific span of time.

Process flow time is a valuable measure of process performance for several reasons. Consider the following advantages of shorter flow time:

1. Flow time affects delivery response time, a key product attribute that customers value, as discussed in chapter 1. As long as a given flow unit remains within the process, it is

unavailable to its intended customer and earns no revenue for its producer. Shorter process flow times lead to shorter product response times, and thus allow firms to create better value for their customers, and collect revenue earlier.

2. Short flow times in production and delivery processes also reduce the inventory (by Little's law) and associated costs.

3. A shorter flow time in the new product development process of a firm leads to faster product introduction into the market, which is a major source of competitive advantage. Likewise, it can bring more generations of a product to market within a given amount of time.

4. In markets featuring short product life cycles, shorter manufacturing-process flow times allow firms to delay production closer to the time of sale and thus gain valuable market information, avoid product obsolescence, and minimize the inventory required.

5. Finally, the indirect importance of flow time derives from its role as an integrative measure of overall process performance—short flow time frequently requires a high level of overall operational excellence. For instance, a process rife with quality problems would typically display the longer flow times required for inspections, rework, and so forth. Short flow times result in fast feedback and correction of quality problems, as we will see in chapters 9 and 10.

In this chapter, we study the factors that determine process flow time and specify some managerial levers that are available for reducing it. Our first step will be to develop the process flow chart presented in section 4.2. A process flow chart is a graphical representation of a process that breaks down the total processing task into a set of activities and identifies their interrelationships. Such a representation is the starting point of analyzing any process. In section 4.3 we discuss flow-time measurement. We introduce the concept of *theoretical flow time* and show how it relates to the concept of a *critical path* in the process flow chart. We then examine the roles of activity time and waiting time as they relate to total flow time and introduce the concept of *flow-time efficiency*. We will continue to illustrate these principles by returning to our ongoing example of operations at MBPF Inc. Section 4.3 also features an extended illustration from the service sector—the X-ray-service process at Valley of Hope Hospital. In section 4.4 we present a formal version of the critical path method for determining both theoretical flow time and critical paths in complex processes. Finally, section 4.5 identifies some key managerial levers for reducing theoretical flow time. (The levers for reducing wait time will be discussed later in chapters 6, 7, and 8.)

4.2   THE PROCESS FLOW CHART

Recall that in chapter 1 we described a process by five elements; namely inputs and outputs, flow units, network of activities and buffers, resources allocated to activities, and information structure.

Value-Adding and Non-Value-Adding Activities   The activities associated with a given process take time and consume resources. We generally divide activities into two major categories:

1. **Value-adding activities** increase the economic value of a flow unit because they are valued by the customer. Performing surgery, piloting an airplane, serving meals in a hospital, machining a part, and evaluating a loan application are examples of value-adding activities.

2. **Non-value-adding activities,** while not directly increasing the value of a flow unit, are required by the firm's current process structure. The following are common non-value-adding activities:

   - *Transport,* such as moving work (or workers) among various locations;
   - *Support,* such as setting up a machine, filling out a form, maintaining equipment, or scheduling work; and
   - *Testing*, such as auditing and inspection.

The distinction between value-adding activities and non-value-adding activities is not absolute but rather depends on the specific situation being analyzed. For instance, consider the activity of transporting a component part between two locations. In the context of a standard manufacturing process, this activity is non-value-adding—the customer typically does not care about the internal movements of a unit during manufacturing. If, however, we are analyzing the performance of an airline or a railroad, transporting cargo must obviously be treated as value-adding. Similarly, the activity of auditing adds no value to a customer of a manufacturing firm, but is paramount for an auditing firm. In fact, it is difficult to conceive of an activity that cannot be considered as value-adding in some context.

Process Flow Charts A **process flow chart** is *a graphical representation of all the elements that make up a process.* For the purpose of representation, it is useful to separate activities that require a decision (henceforth called **decisions**) from other types of activities. Decisions route a flow unit to one of several (at least two) continuing routes, resulting in a "splitting" of flows. In a process flow chart decisions are represented by diamonds, (remaining) activities by rectangles, precedence relationships between any two activities by solid arrows, buffers by triangles, and information flows by dashed arrows. In addition, it is useful to identify events (e.g., start and end of a process, milestones at which reports are to be issued, and so on) in a business process. Events are represented using ovals in a process flow chart. Finally, process flow charts often depict resources required to carry out activities. Adding resource allocation to a process flow chart is useful when studying the sort of throughput and capacity issues that we consider in chapter 5. One way to incorporate resource allocation is to partition the process flow chart into several horizontally distinct colors or bands, one for each resource. The decision as to which elements of the process should be represented on a given flow chart depends on the application and the level of representational detail desired.

Process flow charts were originally developed to coordinate large projects involving complex sets of activities and considerable resources. They are also useful, however, for understanding, documenting, and analyzing almost any business process. Breaking down a process into its component activities, identifying their interrelationships, and viewing them graphically help to enhance our understanding of the total process. Studying the process also highlights non-value-adding activities and areas for possible improvement. More information about process flow charts can be found in any textbook on project management, on operations management, or on operations research; we provide some references at the end of this chapter.

EXAMPLE 4.1

To illustrate the function of a process flow chart, we consider once again the manufacturing process at MBPF Inc. Recall that MBPF manufactures garages, each of which consists of a roof fabricated in-house and a prefabricated base purchased from an outside supplier. Recently, MBPF made a strategic decision to fabricate the bases in-house as well. The manufacturing process, then, will follow upon procurement of sheets of steel that will be used to form both roofs and bases.

The first step involves separating the material needed for the roof from that needed for the base. Subsequently, the roof and the base can be fabricated "in parallel," or simultaneously. Roof fabrication involves punching and forming the roof to shape. Base fabrication entails punching and forming plus a subassembly operation. Fabricated roofs and bases are then assembled into finished garages

that are subsequently inspected for quality assurance. A list of activities needed to fabricate a roof, fabricate a base, and assemble a garage is given in Table 4.1. The entire garage-making process is shown in Figure 4.1.

TABLE 4.1 Activity List for MBPF Inc.

	Activity
1	Separate the roof and base modules
2	Punch the base
3	Punch the roof
4	Form the base
5	Form the roof
6	Subassemble the base
7	Assemble
8	Inspect

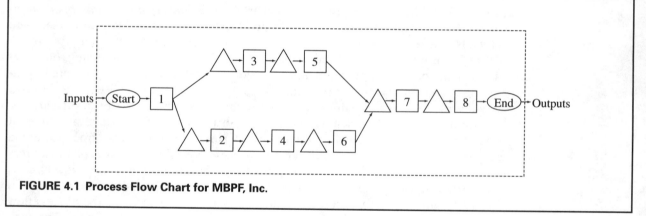

FIGURE 4.1 Process Flow Chart for MBPF, Inc.

Subprocesses and Cascading   In any given representation of a process, such as the flow chart in Figure 4.1, activities are typically treated as indivisible parts of the process. However, any activity may itself be broken down further (exploded) into a set of subactivities. Then the activity can be considered as a process in its own right, with its own set of inputs, outputs, activities, suppliers, customers, and so forth. We then refer to it as a **subprocess** of the original process. How do we decide which parts to treat as indivisible activities and which may be further subdivided into more elementary subprocesses? The answer depends on two factors: the parts of the process on which we wish to focus and the level of detail that we desire. If we wish to represent a given process at several levels of detail simultaneously, we may turn to a technique called **cascading** the process. In Figure 4.2, from a flow chart depicting a simple generic process, activity d has been exploded into a complete subprocess.

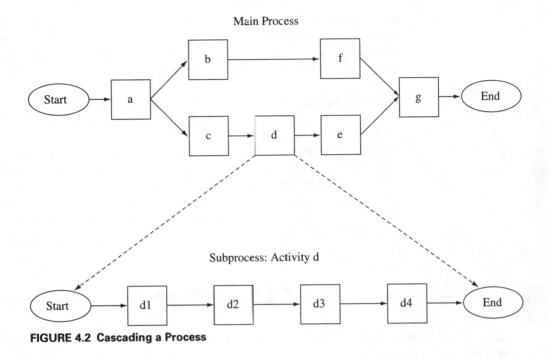

FIGURE 4.2 **Cascading a Process**

4.3   FLOW-TIME MEASUREMENT

The average flow time of a given process can be determined in two independent ways: as a direct measurement or indirectly by application of Little's law. A direct measurement can be made as follows:

1. Observe the process over a specified extended period of time.

2. Take a random sample of flow units over the specified period.

3. For each flow unit in the sample, measure its flow time from entry to exit.

4. Compute the average of flow times measured.

Using the indirect approach, we measure average throughput or flow rate (R) and average inventory (I) and then compute average flow time (T) by using Little's law, which, as you recall, can be stated as

$$T = I / R$$

Both approaches require that flow units, and entry and exit points are carefully specified. If the indirect method is utilized, it is also necessary to ensure that flow time, inventory, and throughput are defined consistently. Although flow-time theory allows us extremely wide latitude in selecting the appropriate specifications for each of these concepts, and in most cases the rough specifications follow quite naturally from the context of the application, we must, nevertheless, be precise and consistent.

To illustrate some of the subtleties involved, consider the production process of a standard manufacturer. Such a process typically handles a given combination or "mix" of distinct models that vary in size, cost, quality level, routing, and so forth. In addition, quality problems may cause a certain fraction of all products to be reworked or scrapped at various points along the process. Finally, each product may consist of several parts or modules that arrive at different times and travel separately through the factory.

Defining the Flow Unit   What is the appropriate definition of a *flow unit* in these cases? Our choices are considerable. We can, for instance, concentrate on units of a particular model or broaden our definition to encompass the entire product mix. In the latter case, we need to consider how to compare the units of the various products that comprise the product mix. We may weight these units equally or account for their differences by weighting them according to the emphasis we wish to place on certain values such as size, cost, price, profitability, or labor content. Moreover, we may choose to include or exclude scrapped units from our definition of a flow unit. We illustrate this concept in Example 4.2.

EXAMPLE 4.2

Consider for instance, MBPF, Inc. If the output of garages in a certain period consists of 100 units of Model A, 200 units of Model B, and 300 units of Model C, how many flow units have been processed? Obviously, the simplest way is to consider each garage (irrespective of model) as a flow unit, ignoring the variations among them. In that case, the number of flow units produced is 600. On the other hand, if the models vary significantly with respect to say, cost, it may sometimes be more useful to assign weights to the various models to signify their relative importance. For instance, suppose the relative costs of the three models are respectively $125, $100, and $67. We may then decide to treat Model B as our standard of flow unit, counting a unit of Model A as the equivalent of 1.25 standard units, and a unit of Model C as the equivalent of 0.67 standard units. In that case the number of flow units produced is $100 \times 1.25 + 200 + 300 \times 0.67 = 526$ units of standard Model B.

Defining the Process Boundaries   We also have choices to make about the process boundaries. When is a flow unit completed? Is it at the moment its construction is completed, when it is shipped to the customer, or when it enters finished goods inventory? What is the exit point for a scrapped unit (in case we decide to include it in our study)? Similar latitude exists in defining the starting point of the process. In some scenarios, the starting point can be defined as the moment at which all required parts or modules are available for production; or in other cases the proper choice is the time at which work starts on any part of the flow unit.

The important point is that each valid set of specifications results in a different interpretation of—and a different numeric value for—flow time. When we adopt Little's law, we must also remember that each different selection requires us to define the concepts of inventory and throughput in a consistent fashion.

4.3.1 Theoretical Flow Time

As a flow unit travels through the process from entry to exit, it typically undergoes a sequence of activities interspersed with periods of waiting in buffers. The unit's total flow time consists of both time during which activities are performed and time spent waiting in buffers. Because waiting time is usually a large part of total flow time in most business processes, it is an important aspect of flow-time management. Eventually we will illustrate the importance of waiting time in flow-time management and define an efficiency measure to capture it. At this point, however, we focus on the *activity* component of flow time. We examine the causes and effects of waiting in section 4.3.2 and in chapters 6, 7, and 8.

The **theoretical flow time** of a process is the minimal amount of time required for processing a typical flow unit—without any waiting. Thus it includes only the activity-time component of the process, ignoring completely the impact of waiting (which is typically significant). For this reason, theoretical flow time represents an idealized target for an actual flow time of the current process that can only rarely be achieved in practice. In this section, we show how theoretical flow time can be computed by combining a process flow chart with information about the time taken by the various activities represented on it.

Activity Time and Work Content   **Activity time** is *the time required by a typical flow unit to complete the activity once.* Rework (fixing defective products so that they conform to specifications) may require that activities be repeated several times. We refer to these repetitions as **visits** to an activity. Since only a certain fraction of the flow units may require rework, the number of visits of an average flow unit to a typical activity may be fractional. The **work content** of a flow unit at an activity is *the activity time multiplied by the average number of visits to that activity.* It measures the average total amount of time required to perform the activity during transformation of a typical flow unit.

In the sequel we will often use the phrase "work content of an activity" to mean the work content of a flow unit at an activity whenever there is no ambiguity about the identification of a flow unit.

Critical Paths and Critical Activities   The work content of a flow unit at various activities, coupled with their precedence structure, now allows us to compute the theoretical flow time. To appreciate the necessary computations involved, first consider a simple process in which all activities are carried out sequentially, one following the other. In this case, the process flow chart consists of a single **path** (or *route*) of activities connecting the entry and exit points of the process. Because all activities along this path must be completed sequentially, the total time required to complete all of them equals the sum of their individual work contents.

A process usually consists of a combination of sequential and parallel activities, resulting in a process chart that graphs several paths running from start to finish. For each path, theoretical flow time of that path is *the sum of the work contents of the activities that constitute the route.* Now, a flow unit can exit the process only after all of the activities along all the paths are completed. Theoretical flow time of the process, therefore, must be the same as the theoretical flow time of the *longest* path(s) in the process flow chart. Any such path is called a **critical path,** and activities on a critical path are called **critical activities.** The work content of these critical activities determines the total flow time of the process. Thus, a delay in completing any critical activity results directly in a corresponding delay in processing the flow unit. As a result, management of critical path is of paramount significance. We illustrate these concepts in Example 4.3.

EXAMPLE 4.3

To demonstrate the computation of the theoretical flow time, we continue the MBPF illustration given in Example 4.1. Table 4.2 complements the information in Table 4.1 by adding *activity times* and *number of visits* for each activity. A fractional number of revisits indicates that only those flow units found to be defective at the end of the specific activity are reworked. For the purpose of measuring theoretical flow time, we define a flow unit to include both inputs that do and do not require rework. Work content is then computed as the product of activity time and number of visits.

Note that our flow chart in Figure 4.1 shows two paths connecting the beginning and end of the process:

Path 1 (roof): Start→1→3→5→7→8→End

Path 2 (base): Start→1→2→4→6→7→8→End

The theoretical flow times of path 1 and path 2 are 90 and 105 minutes, respectively. Therefore, the theoretical flow time of the process is 105 minutes, and the critical path is path 2. Alternately, suppose we define a flow unit to include only those units that *do not* require rework. For such flow units, the number of visits to an activity is 1.0 and the work content of flow unit at an activity is equal to the activity time of that activity. It can then be seen that the theoretical flow times of paths 1 and 2 are, respectively, 80 and 90 minutes, path 2 remains the critical path, and the theoretical flow time of the process is 90 minutes. Thus, due to rework, the theoretical flow time is extended from 90 to 105 minutes.

TABLE 4.2 Activity Times and Work Content for MBPF Inc.

	Activity	Activity Time (Minutes)	Number of Visits	Work Content
1	Separate	10	1	10
2	Punch the base	25	1.2	30
3	Punch the roof	20	1.1	22
4	Form the base	5	1.2	6
5	Form the roof	10	1.2	12
6	Subassemble	10	1.3	13
7	Assemble	10	1	10
8	Inspect	30	1.2	36

For simpler processes the critical path can often be determined by computing the theoretical flow time of each path. For complex processes there may be too many paths and we need a more computationally efficient approach, like the one outlined in section 4.4, to identify the critical path.

4.3.2 Average Flow Time and Flow-Time Efficiency

At this point we can combine the process flow chart with information about waiting in its various buffers to study flow time of a given process.

The following simple three-step procedure can be used:

1. We treat waiting in each buffer as an additional (passive) activity with activity time equal to the amount of time spent in that buffer,

2. We add waiting times in buffers to the theoretical flow time of the appropriate path, and

3. We obtain the average flow time of the process by finding the path whose overall length (activity plus waiting) is maximal.

The amount of waiting along different paths may vary. Thus, when waiting times are added to the analysis, the relative lengths of the various paths—and so the identity of the critical path—may vary.

In some instances, it may not be convenient to separate activity and waiting times. In such cases, we may prefer to aggregate the two into a single measurement. Also recall that rather than measuring them directly, we can use Little's law to compute average time spent in a given buffer (or the total of waiting-plus-activity time associated with a given activity).

EXAMPLE 4.4

To demonstrate these concepts, we revisit MBPF Inc. To calculate the average flow time using Little's law, we need information regarding the average flow rate and the average inventory in various buffers over the time period of interest. Assume that the average flow rate has been measured at 16.5 garages per hour. Assume, too, that average inventories of roofs and bases at relevant buffers were measured and reported as in Table 4.3. For notational purposes, we have numbered each buffer according to the activity that follows it. Because we have two types of flow units—roofs and bases, either of which could be in a buffer—we identify buffer contents with the quantity of each type of flow unit in each buffer.

Upon analyzing the flow time for roofs, we note that the average number of roofs waiting in various buffers is 80 roofs. Because the average flow rate for roofs is 16.5 per hour (the same as the flow rate for garages), we conclude that average amount of waiting for a typical roof is

$$80/16.5 = 4.85 \text{ hours} = 291 \text{ minutes}$$

Now we add to this figure the theoretical flow time of a roof, which is 90 minutes. We therefore get an average flow time for a roof of 381 minutes. (We could also calculate the waiting time spent separately in each buffer and then add those figures, and the result would be the same.) Similarly, average waiting time for a base is

$$90/16.5 = 5.45 \text{ hours} = 327 \text{ minutes}$$

Adding this figure to the theoretical flow time of 105 minutes for a base, we obtain an average flow time of 432 minutes for the bases. The path traversed by a base remains the critical path.

TABLE 4.3 Average Buffers, MBPF Inc.

Buffer	Average Number of Bases	Average Number of roofs
2	30	–
3	–	25
4	10	–
5	–	20
6	20	–
7	10	15
8	20	20
Total	90	80

In Example 4.4, we computed average flow time for two types of flow units— roofs and bases. Because both products are required for assembling a garage, average flow time for a garage is given by the average flow time of the longest path traversed by the bases, which is equal to 432 minutes. Such a flow-time measurement is useful for

TABLE 4.4 Flow-Time Efficiency of Business Processes

Industry	Process	Flow Time	Theoretical Flow Time	Flow-Time Efficiency
Life Insurance	New Policy Application	72 hr.	7 min.	0.16%
Consumer Packaging	New Graphic Design	18 days	2 hr.	0.14%
Commercial Bank	Consumer Loan	24 hr.	34 min.	2.36%
Hospital	Patient Billing	10 days	3 hr.	3.75%
Auto Manufacture	Financial Closing	11 days	5 hr.	5.60%

quoting due dates to customers. We note that under different scenarios (i.e., with different buffer sizes), the relative lengths of these two paths could be identical or even reversed, illustrating the difficulty of quoting realistic due dates (delivery times) on a real-time basis.

Recall that we can classify activities as value-adding and non-value-adding. If, as discussed, flow time consists of work contents plus waiting times, then we may also define the following:

Flow time = Value-adding flow time + Non-value-adding flow time

All waiting time is clearly non-value-adding. Other activities in a given process may be only partially value-adding.

The process itself, however, may have other non-value-adding activities—other than waiting times—that could further be eliminated in an improved process. For example, if the current process involves rework of some flow units at certain activities, the number of visits to these activities will be greater than one, which in turn will affect the theoretical flow time; in Example 4.2 rework increased theoretical flow time from 90 to 105 minutes. A process improvement that reduces the amount of rework clearly decreases the theoretical flow time. If careful analysis reveals that all activities, except waiting, add value, then theoretical flow time is in fact the same as the value-adding flow time.

Flow-Time Efficiency It is instructive to compare the average flow time with the theoretical value. The relation between these two measures of flow time provides an indication of the amount of waiting time associated with the process. This relation is captured by the concept of **flow-time efficiency,** which is defined as follows:

Flow-time efficiency = Theoretical flow time / Average flow time

The values of the flow-time efficiency for a variety of processes were studied by Blackburn (1992) and are excerpted in Table 4.4. Their surprisingly low values underscore the significance of reducing waiting time as a major lever for improving flow-time performance. We discuss this and other levers in chapters 6-8.

We now demonstrate the main concepts of this chapter by taking an extended example from the service sector, as illustrated in Example 4.5.

EXAMPLE 4.5

Valley of Hope (VOH) Hospital has been under recent pressure from stakeholders to improve cost efficiency and customer service. In response, the hospital has undertaken a series of process-improvement initiatives. One of the first processes targeted for improvement is the X-ray service. A major concern identified by both doctors and patients has been the amount of time required to get an X ray. In addition, management would like to make sure that available resources are utilized efficiently.

A process-improvement team was set up to study the X-ray-service process and recommend improvements. The team identified the point of entry into the process as the instant that a patient leaves the physician's office to walk to the X-ray lab. The point of exit was defined as the instant that both the patient and the completed X-ray film are ready to enter the physician's office for diagnosis.

To determine the flow time of the existing process, a random sample of 50 patients was observed over a two-week period. For each patient, the team recorded times of entry and exit from the

X-ray-service process. The difference between these two times was then used as a measure of flow time for each patient. The average of the 50 data points was 154 minutes. This figure, then, serves as an estimate of the average flow time for the X-ray-service process.

To further study process flow time, the team examined the entire process in detail and broke it down into the constituent activities identified in Table 4.5.

The corresponding process flow chart is shown in Figure 4.3. It depicts all activities and the precedence relationships among them. For example, activity 2 must be completed before activity 3 can begin. Meanwhile, activity 1 can be carried out simultaneously with activities 2 and 3.

Next, another sample of 50 patients was studied over a two-week period. For each patient, the times required to perform each activity, as well as the number of visits to that activity, were recorded. Because activities 6, 7, and 8 are repeated once for 25% of the patients, the average number of visits

TABLE 4.5 The X-Ray-Service Process at Valley of Hope Hospital

Activity/Event	Description	Type
Start	Patient leaves the physician's office	Event: Start of process
1	Patient walks to the X-ray lab	Activity: Transport
2	The X-ray request travels to the X-ray lab by a messenger	Activity: Transport
3	An X-ray technician fills out a standard form based on the information supplied by the physician	Activity: Support
4	The receptionist receives from the patient information concerning insurance, prepares and signs a claim form, and sends to the insurer	Activity: Support
5	Patient undresses in preparation for X-ray	Activity: Support
6	A lab technician takes X-rays	Activity: Value added
7	A darkroom technician develops X-rays	Activity: Value added
8	The lab technician checks X-rays for clarity	Activity: Inspection and Decision
	If an X-ray is not satisfactory, activities 7, 8, and 9 are repeated (On Average, 75% of X-rays are found satisfactory the first time around, while 25% require one retake; virtually no units require more than two takes.)	
9	Patient puts on clothes and gets ready to leave lab	Activity: Support
10	Patient walks back to the physician's office	Activity: Transport
11	The X-rays are transferred to the physician by a messenger	Activity: Transport
End	Patient and the X-rays arrive at the physician's office	Event: End of process

to these activities is 1.25. The average work content for each of these activities is thus obtained by multiplying their activity times by 1.25. The data and computations are summarized in Table 4.6.

The team analyzing the process flow chart identified four activity paths:

Path 1: Start→1→4→5→6→7→8→9→10→End

Path 2: Start→2→3→4→5→6→7→8→9→10→End

Path 3: Start→1→4→5→6→7→8→11→End

Path 4: Start→2→3→4→5→6→7→8→11→End

The total work-content of these four paths are 50, 69, 60, and 79 minutes, respectively. *Path 4, therefore, is the critical path, yielding a theoretical flow time of the process as 79 minutes.* What, then, is the flow-time efficiency of the process? Because actual flow time was measured at 154 minutes and theoretical flow time at 79 minutes, flow-time efficiency is expressed as follows:

$$79/154 = 51\%$$

This means that waiting corresponds to roughly half of the time in this process. Obviously the challenge this poses to the management of VOH is whether some of this waiting can be eliminated.

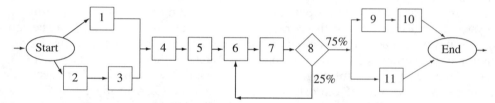

FIGURE 4.3 Flow Chart for the X-Ray-Service Process, VOH Hospital

TABLE 4.6   Work Content in X-Ray-Service Process Activities

Activity	Activity Time	Number of Visits per Flow Unit	Work Content per Flow Unit
Start	—	1	—
1	7	1	7
2	20	1	20
3	6	1	6
4	5	1	5
5	3	1	3
6	6	1.25	7.5
7	12	1.25	15
8	2	1.25	2.5
9	3	1	3
10	7	1	7
11	20	1	20
End	—	1	—

4.4   THE CRITICAL PATH METHOD

In section 4.3 we illustrated a method for finding the critical path of a process. It involved computing the flow time of each path in the process network and identifying the path with the longest flow time. If the process network involves several paths, this procedure can be quite tedious. More efficient procedures for finding the critical paths and computing their total flow time have been developed in the context of project management. As mentioned, all activities that lie along the critical path are labeled critical activities because any delay in executing a critical activity will delay completion of the whole process. Noncritical activities, on the other hand, may be delayed (within limits) without affecting the total process flow time. **Slack time** of an activity is *the extent to which that activity can be delayed without affecting the process flow time.* Obviously, the slack time that can be allowed on a critical activity is zero. We can define a **critical path,** therefore, as a *path consisting of activities all of which have a slack time of zero.* Our task of finding a critical path is thus reduced to finding the slack times of each activity.

To compute the slack times, we must calculate four time values for each activity in the processing network. Recall as you study the following definitions that work content of an activity is defined as activity time multiplied by average number of visits. For each activity,

- **Early start time (*EST*)** is the earliest possible time that we *can* begin that activity.
- **Early finish time (*EFT*)** is the earliest possible time we *can* finish that activity. It is given by the sum of its EST and its work content.
- **Late finish time (*LFT*)** is the latest time at which the activity *must* be finished in order not to delay the rest of the process.
- **Late start time (*LST*)** is the latest we *must* start that activity in order not to delay its finish beyond its *LFT.* It is given by the difference between its *LFT* and its work content.

The slack time of the activity therefore is the allowance between the latest permissible start (or finish) time and the earliest possible start (or finish) time; that is,

$$\text{Slack time} = LST–EST = LFT–EFT$$

We now describe a systematic procedure for computing the various times.

4.4.1   Computing EST and EFT

We begin by visiting all activities in sequence from the events "Start" to "End." The *EST* of an activity can be computed as follows. Set the *EST* of the first activity (activities) after "Start" as zero. Then, proceeding forward, for any activity:

1. Find all activities that are immediate predecessors of the current activity. Immediate predecessors of an activity are the activities that immediately precede it.
2. To the *EST* of each immediate-predecessor activity add its work content to get its *EFT.*
3. Compute the *EST* of the current activity by taking the maximum of the *EFT*s of all of its immediate predecessors.

The rationale for step 3 is that the current activity can start only after *all* of its predecessors have been completed. We then compute the *EFT* of the current activity by adding its work content to its *EST.*

4.4.2   Computing *LFT* and *LST*

To compute the *LFT*s, we work backwards from the last activity (the activity immediately preceding the "End" event). We assume that the *LFT* of the last activity is also its *EFT;* that is, the latest we *must* finish the last activity is the earliest we *can* finish it. Then the *LFT* of any other activity is computed recursively as follows:

1. Find all activities that are successors of the current activity. Immediate successors of an activity are the activities that immediately follow it.
2. From the *LFT* of each immediate-successor activity subtract its work content to get its *LST.*
3. Compute the *LFT* of the current activity by taking the minimum of all the *LST*s of its immediate successors.

The *LST* of the current activity is then simply the difference between its *LFT* and its work content. We illustrate this procedure using Example 4.6.

EXAMPLE 4.6

Reconsider our computations of theoretical flow time and critical path at MBPF, Inc. The first two columns of Table 4.7 list the activities that must be performed to manufacture a garage. Table 4.7 also includes the work content corresponding to each activity, as derived in Table 4.2. To compute *EST, LST, EFT,* and *LFT* for each activity, we assume that the process starts at time 0.

To compute the *EST* of an activity, we need to identify all immediate predecessors of that activity. For example, MBPF's activity 7 is immediately preceded by activities 5 and 6. The early start times of activities 5 and 6 are, respectively, 32 and 46. The *EST* of activity 7, therefore, is equal to the maximum of

$$44 (= 32 + 12)$$

and

$$59 (= 46 + 13)$$

which is 59. In order to compute *LST* and *LFT,* we now work backwards from the last activity,

which in this case is activity 8. We set the *LFT* of activity 8 to equal its *EFT.* To compute the *LFT* of any other activity, we need to identify all its immediate successor activities. At MBPF, for example, the immediate successors of activity 1 are activities 2 and 3 with *LFT*s of 40 and 47, respectively. The *LFT* of activity 1, therefore, is the minimum of

$$10 (= 40 - 30)$$

and

$$25 (= 47 - 22)$$

or 10.

Finally, slack times are computed as *LST–EST* or *LFT–EFT.* The various times at MBPF are listed in Table 4.7. We see, for instance, that activities 1, 2, 4, 6, 7, and 8 have slack times of zero and that the path connecting these activities is the critical path.

TABLE 4.7 Slack Times for Activities at MBPF, Inc.

	Operation	Work Content	EST	EFT	LFT	LST	Slack Time
1	Separate	10	0	10	10	0	0
2	Punch the base	30	10	40	40	10	0
3	Punch the roof	22	10	32	47	25	15
4	Form the base	6	40	46	46	40	0
5	Form the roof	12	32	44	59	47	15
6	Subassemble	13	46	59	59	46	0
7	Assemble	10	59	69	69	59	0
8	Inspect	36	69	105	105	69	0

4.5 MANAGING THEORETICAL FLOW TIME

The average flow time of a process is the sum of its theoretical flow time and waiting time. In this section, we examine some of the levers available for managing theoretical flow time. Levers for managing waiting will be discussed in chapters 6, 7, and 8.

Because theoretical flow time of a process is determined by the total work content of its critical path(s), *the only way to reduce it is by shortening the length of* every *critical path*. There are two basic approaches to reducing the work content of a critical path:

1. Decrease the work content of an activity on the critical path.
2. Move some of the work content off the critical path.

We examine these two approaches more fully in the following subsections.

4.5.1 Reducing the Work Content of Critical Activities

The work content of any activity can be reduced by any combination of the following actions:

1. Eliminate non-value-adding aspects of the activity ("work smarter").
2. Increase the speed at which the activity is performed ("work faster").
3. Reduce the number of repeat activities ("do it right the first time").
4. Change the product mix.

The Application of Scientific Management   The first three actions involve a rational approach to work analysis and methods of improvement. In this respect, the core ideas of the scientific management approach (see section 2.7) are still applicable. Consider, for instance, the four principles of scientific management originated with Frederick Taylor (1911) and his followers such as Frank Gilbreth (1911), *work analysis, work methods, work assignment,* and *work environment.*

Work Smarter   Work analysis involves breaking down a process into component activities to trace the flow of the product through the process. This approach allows us to identify and eliminate such unnecessary, non-value-adding activities as waiting, movement, inspection, and various administrative steps. To eliminate unnecessary steps, however, we must ask the question: *What work* adds *value?* The answer depends on what the customers of the process consider important. Consider, for example, the accounts payable process at Ford Motor Company as reported by Hammer and Champy (1993). The original process involved comparing three documents; the purchase order, the invoice, and the receiving document. If the three documents agreed, payment was authorized. Otherwise, a complicated, long, and resource-intensive process of reconciliation was initiated. Many of the steps involved were not value-adding to the process customers, which included the accounting group at Ford and Ford's suppliers. (Ford needs to ensure that payments are for goods actually ordered and received and must keep track of payments for accounting purposes. Suppliers prefer to be paid in full as fast as possible.) Ford reengineered its account payable process by eliminating many of the non-value-adding steps. In the new process, a purchase order is sent to the supplier and a copy is submitted simultaneously to the Receiving Department. When a shipment of goods arrives, its contents are compared to the purchase order. If they match, the receiving clerk authorizes payment on the spot. Otherwise, the shipment is returned. Note that the invoice was completely eliminated in the new process, since its processing did not add any value to Ford or to its suppliers.

Work Faster   The speed at which an activity is performed can be improved in a variety of ways. Again, among the first steps is to find out why a resource needs the amount of time it does to perform an activity. When human resources are involved, Taylor's (1911) principles of work methods analysis can be used to study the actions and performance of workers—minimizing wasteful motions, for example, reduces time and fatigue in performing physical work. Documenting and following standard operating procedures facilitates training and eliminates confusion about how to perform them. The work environment can be improved by organizing efficient layouts, and ergonomically efficient workplace design reduces fatigue and errors, and improves worker productivity and morale.

Activity time can be further improved by: acquiring faster equipment, increasing resource allocation, or offering incentives to increase output. Increasing performance speed typically requires either financial investment in faster equipment or modified incentives for labor resources. Consider, for instance, a manual checkout counter at a local grocery store. The speed of this operation can be increased by: using bar codes with a scanner, adding a second worker to bag products, or instituting proper incentives for checkout personnel to work faster (without increasing error rates or degrading service quality). In an R&D laboratory, dedicated teams that concentrate fully on one activity rather than working on several projects simultaneously can increase the speed at which a particular research activity is carried out.

Do It Right the First Time   Decreasing the amount of repeat work reduces the average number of visits to an activity and thus decreases its work content. Reductions are often achieved by such process-improvement techniques as statistical process control for early detection of problem sources, product design for facilitating manufacturability, process foolproofing, and workforce training.

Change the Product Mix   If a process produces a mix of products, we can affect theoretical flow time by changing the product mix—in particular, by processing more of the products that require less processing time. Product mix is often dictated by the market, but when they also lead to greater profitability, judicious marketing decisions can still alter mixes for better flow times.

Finally, although reducing the work content of noncritical activities does not reduce theoretical flow time, such reduction may be useful for other reasons—decreasing total processing costs, increasing the process capacity (see chapter 5), and reducing the potential for errors and defects.

4.5.2 Moving Work Off the Critical Path

Theoretical flow time can also be reduced by moving work off the critical path and onto paths that have sufficient slack to pick up more work. This can be accomplished in one of two ways:

1. Move work from a critical to a noncritical activity, or
2. Move work off the critical path to the "outer loop" (to some stage of pre- or post-processing).

Move Work to a NonCritical Path   Moving work from a critical to a noncritical path means examining critical activities that are currently performed sequentially and re-designing the process so that they can be performed in parallel. Scientific-management pioneer Frank Gilbreth, who sought to upgrade performance by finding the most eco-nomical motions for each task, is reported to have trained himself to shave both sides of his face simultaneously, using both hands! (Gilbreth & Carey, 1949).

A prime—and somewhat more practical—example of this approach, especially in the elimination of repeat work, is the contemporary practice of *concurrent engineering*. Traditionally, product design, process planning, and manufacturing are performed se-quentially. By permitting interfunctional coordination of these activities, concurrent en-gineering reduces the total time, cost, and rework necessary to design, produce, and de-liver new products to market quickly.

As another example, consider a typical software-development process. The conventional approach to software development requires five steps in sequence: specification, design, development, production of the user manual, and testing. The last two activities are often performed in parallel. Because the user manual tells the user how to interface with the *finished* product, it does not generally influence the technical details of software development. This allows writing of the user manual to begin before software development and testing are complete. To shorten flow time, many firms develop demo versions of software according to specifications that allow software design, development, and testing to proceed in parallel with production of the user manual.

Move Work to Outer Loop   Moving activities to the outer loop means performing them either before the countdown for the process starts or after it ends, as defined by the process boundary. This approach is also called *pre-* or *postprocessing*. For example, in the VOH Hospital X-ray-service process of Example 4.4, activity 5—receiving the pa-tient's insurance information, preparing and signing a claim form, and sending the form to the insurer—is a critical activity. Some of the work content of this activity can be moved to the outer loop if the following changes are feasible:

- Collect insurance information before the X-ray process starts (e.g., when the patient calls to make an appointment), and
- Complete the insurer's form later in the day, when the receptionist has more time.

Such changes correspond to performing some work before the processing of the flow unit starts and performing some after it has ended—thus, moving it to the outer loop. Although the work must still be done, the critical path is shortened. Con-sider the process of changing a make-to-order production system into a make-to-stock system. For example, instead of assembling a complete hamburger *after* re-ceiving a customer order, fast-food restaurants often precook beef patties and keep them ready *prior to* the lunchtime rush. As far as customer flow is concerned, theo-retical flow time will be reduced because the production of the beef patty has been moved to the outer loop of the order-fulfillment process. However, because make-to-stock produces units prior to demand, this strategy affects the material flow time in the opposite fashion. In case of hamburgers, it may also affect their taste and quality.

4.6   LEVERS FOR MANAGING FLOW TIME

The theoretical flow time and waiting time affect the total flow time of a process. Hence, the key managerial levers for reducing the total flow time are:

1. Decrease waiting time (to be covered in chapters 6 through 8)

2. Decrease theoretical flow time

   a. Reduce the work content of critical activities

   - Eliminate non-value-adding aspects of the activity ("work smarter").
   - Increase the speed at which the activity is performed ("work faster").
   - Reduce the number of repeat activities ("do it right the first time").
   - Change the product mix.

   b. Move some work content off the critical path

   - Move work to a noncritical path.
   - Move work to outer loop.

Problem Set

4.1. This exercise revisits the VOH Hospital X-ray-service process described in Example 4.4. Following are two lists. The first contains a series of hypothetical modifications that can be made to the VOH Hospital X-ray-service process. The second consists of three exercises for evaluating each of these modifications. *Consider each change separately, not cumulatively, and perform each evaluation to each modification.*

Modifications
   a. Install new equipment that enables lab technicians to develop X rays in 10 minutes instead of 12 minutes.
   b. Redesign the messenger route so that the trip from the physician's office to the X-ray lab is reduced from 20 minutes to 15 minutes each way.
   c. Encourage the patient to walk faster to and from the physician's office (using 5 minutes each way instead of 7 minutes).
   d. Encourage patients to dress and undress faster (using 2 minutes instead of 3 minutes).
   e. Fax X-ray requests (taking 1 minute) instead of sending them with a messenger.
   f. Ask patients to carry X-ray requests and completed X rays instead of sending them by messenger.
   g. Improve the method of taking X rays to reduce rework on shots from 25% to 5%.
   h. The hospital serves both inpatients and outpatients with the same X-ray-service process. The current mix is 50% each, but the hospital wants to change it to 75% and 25%, respectively. Shown in Table 4.8, the activity times for these two types of patients differ.

Evaluations
1. Classify the modification in terms of the type of levers described in section 4.6.
2. Indicate the effect of the modification on the work content of the activity in question.
3. Indicate the effect of the modification on the theoretical cycle time of the entire process.

TABLE 4.8 Activity Times for Inpatients and Outpatients

Activity	No. Visits per Flow Unit	Activity Time Inpatients	Activity Time Outpatients
Start	1	—	—
1	1	8	6
2	1	24	16
3	1	6	6
4	1	5	5
5	1	5	1
6	1.25	6	6
7	1.25	12	12
8	1.25	2	2
9	1	5	1
10	1	8	6
11	1	24	16
End	1	—	—

4.2. Kristen[1] and her roommate are in the business of baking custom cookies. As soon as she receives an order by phone, Kristen washes the bowl and mixes dough according to the customer's order—activities that take a total of 6 minutes. She then spoons the dough onto a tray that holds 1 dozen cookies (2 minutes). Her roommate then takes 1 minute to set the oven and place the tray in it. Cookies are baked in the oven for 9 minutes and allowed to cool outside for 5 minutes. The roommate then boxes the cookies (2 minutes) and collects payment from the customer (1 minute).

a. Draw a flow chart for the process described here and determine theoretical flow time from the time of order receipt until the time of payment collection. Assume no waiting over the course of the process.

b. Suppose that each order consists of 2 dozen cookies. Assume that although the mixing bowl can accommodate dough for 2 dozen cookies at a time, the oven can accommodate only 1 tray of 1 dozen cookies at a time. As before, spooning each tray takes 2 minutes, and both trays must be cooled prior to boxing the cookies for customer pickup. Draw a modified flow chart and determine theoretical flow time. Consider the effect on flow time of the following possible alternatives to the system:

1. Buying a second oven that can bake 1 tray of 1 dozen cookies,
2. Buying a second oven that can hold 2 trays of 1 dozen cookies each,
3. Buying a faster convection oven that can bake 1 dozen cookies in 6 minutes instead of 9 minutes,

4.3. MBPF Inc. wants to introduce a new model of its standard garage, which it will call the Deluxe. The basic process of building the Deluxe would be the same as that for the standard model. Activity times and number of visits are detailed in Table 4.9.

a. Compute theoretical flow time for production of the Deluxe garage.

b. Compute theoretical flow time for a product mix of 75% standard, 25% Deluxe garages.

[1]This exercise is based on "Kristen's Cookie Company," Case 9-686-093, published by Harvard Business School.

TABLE 4.9 Activity Times for the Deluxe Model of MBPF Inc.

	Activity	Activity Time (Minutes)	Number of Visits
1	Separate	10	1
2	Punch the base	30	1.5
3	Punch the roof	24	1.25
4	Form the base	5	1.2
5	Form the roof	10	1.2
6	Subassemble	15	1.2
7	Assemble	12	1
8	Inspect	30	1.2

4.4. Honda's 1100cc motorcycle, the "American Classic Edition" or ACE, is assembled in the US from four major subassemblies. The first subassembly produces the engine from three activities: a left and right part of the engine block come out of the automatic mold every two minutes. These two parts are welded together, requiring one minute of the continuous welding machine. Finally, it takes the engine assembler three minutes to insert the two pistons and four valves. The second subassembly produces the frame in two steps: first heavy metal bars are bent in the 10,000 lbs press in 1 minute. Then it takes three minutes to weld the multiple bars together with the continuous welding machine to produce the frame. The third subassembly consists of the front and rear fenders, both of which are formed using the same (as used for the metal bars) 10,000 lbs press for 1 minute each. The fourth subassembly makes the seat. It takes an assembler 7 minutes to cut the padding, put it on a preformed piece of sheet metal and wrap the two with synthetic leather. In final assembly, first the four subassemblies are put together. Adding front and tail lights, wheels, driving shaft, brakes and cables produces a new bike that is ready for test drive. It takes 30 minutes to finish assembly of one motorcycle. Currently Honda ACE staffing is as follows: there is one molding machine operator, one welder, one press operator, one engine assembler, 2 seat assemblers and 10 final assemblers.

- Draw a process flow chart identifying resources, activity times and any potential storage buffers.
- What is the theoretical flow time of the ACE production process?
- Knowing the benefits of flow time reduction, Honda would like to decrease the theoretical flow time of the ACE process. Which specific action(s) do you recommend?

www.prenhall.com/anupindi

For exercises based on Process Model go to http://www.prenhall.com/anupindi

References

Blackburn, J.D. 1992. Time-Based Competition: White-Collar Activities. *Business Horizons,* 35(4), pp. 96–101.

Chase, R.B., N.J. Aquilano, and F.R. Jacobs. 1999. *Production and Operations Management.* 8th ed. Irwin McGraw-Hill, Chicago, IL.

Eppen, G.D. et al. 1998. *Introductory Management Science.* 5th ed. Prentice Hall, Upper Saddle River, NJ.

Evans, J.R. 1994. *Applied Production and Operations Management.* 4th ed. West Publishing Company, Minneapolis, MN.

Gilbreth, F.B. 1911. *Motion Study.* Van Nostrand, New York.

Gilbreth, F.B. Jr., and E.G. Gilbreth Carey. 1949. *Cheaper by the Dozen.* T.Y. Crowell, New York, NY.

Hammer, M., and Champy, J. 1993. *Reengineering the Corporation.* Harper Business, New York, NY.

Kaniegel, R. 1997. *The One Best Way: Frederick Winslow Taylor and the Enigma of Efficiency.* The Penguin Group, New York, NY.

Kerzner, L.J. 1989. *Project Management.* Van Nostrand Reinhold, Princeton, NJ.

Krajewski, L.J., and L.P. Ritzman. 1996. *Operations Management.* 4th ed. Addison Wesley, Reading, MA.

Kristen's cookie company (A1). 1986. Harvard Business School case 9-686-093. Harvard Business School Publishing Company, Cambridge, MA.

McClain, J.O., L.J. Thomas, and J.B. Mazzola. 1992. *Operations Management.* 3rd ed. Prentice Hall, Upper Saddle River, NJ.

Schroeder, R.J. 1993. *Operations Management.* 4th ed. McGraw-Hill, New York, NY.

Shtub, J., F. Bard, and S. Globerson. 1994. *Project Management.* Prentice Hall, Upper Saddle River, NJ.

Taylor, F.W. 1911. *The Principles of Scientific Management.* Harper & Row, New York, NY.

CHAPTER

5

Flow Rate
and Capacity Analysis

This chapter studies the *average flow rate* (or *throughput*) of a given process—the average number of units that flow through the process per unit of time. Processing activities require resources that may form *resource pools*. The *theoretical capacity of a resource pool* is the maximal number of flow units that can be processed by the pool per unit of time if it could be fully utilized during its available time. Resource pools with minimum theoretical capacity are called *bottleneck* resources. Bottlenecks provide an upper bound on the flow rate that we call the *theoretical capacity of the process*. *Capacity utilization* of a resource pool is the ratio of its flow rate to the theoretical capacity of the process.

5.1   INTRODUCTION

Throughput, or **average flow rate** of a process, is *the average number of flow units that flow through the process per unit of time*. **Process capacity** is *the maximum sustainable flow rate of a process*. Throughput and process capacity are important measures of process performance. If the process earns an economic return for each processed flow unit, then it follows that the higher the throughput, the greater the return generated per unit of time. Capacity is also important from the perspective of managing process flow times, since insufficient process capacity may lead to excessive waiting time. In this chapter we study process flow rate and capacity, and some key levers for increasing them.

Like flow time, throughput and capacity depend on all elements of the process:

- The nature and mix of the *flow units,*
- The required *activities*, buffers, and their network structure,
- The *resources* allocated to performing them, and
- The *operating procedures* used to manage required activities.

In section 5.2 we identify the kinds of *resources* and *resource pools* available for performing processing activities. In section 5.3 we define the *theoretical capacity of a resource pool,* show how the *theoretical capacity of the process* depends upon that of its *bottleneck resources,* and introduce the concept of *capacity utilization*. In section 5.4, we examine how product mix decisions impact the theoretical capacity of a process and its profitability. In section 5.5, we discuss factors that affect the process capacity. In section 5.6 we study some key ideas to improve the theoretical capacity of a process. We conclude in section 5.7 with a list of levers for managing the flow rate of a process.

5.2 RESOURCES AND RESOURCE POOLS

As discussed in chapter 1, activities are performed by capital and labor resources. Each activity may require one or more resources, and each resource may be allocated to one or more activities. For example, in the process of making bread, input raw materials—flour, salt, butter, water, and so forth—are transformed into outputs of loaves of bread. The entire process requires performing such activities as mixing the ingredients, kneading and forming dough, loading it in oven(s), and baking the loaves. In turn, these activities utilize such resources as bakers and ovens. A given resource—say, a baker—may be utilized by several activities such as mixing, kneading, and forming dough, while certain activities such as loading ovens may require multiple resources such as both a baker and an oven.

A **resource pool** is *a collection of interchangeable resources that can perform an identical set of activities.* Each unit in a resource pool is called a **resource unit.** Thus, in our bread-making example, three flexible bakers, each of whom can perform any baking activity, would be viewed collectively as *a single resource pool* containing three resource units. Conversely, three individual bakers, each specialized in a separate activity (mixing, kneading, and forming dough, respectively), would be regarded as *three separate resource pools,* each consisting of a single resource unit. Through process investments, however, it is sometimes possible to make the separate resource pools flexible to handle tasks performed by each other. Such investments allow combining separate resource pools into a single resource pool called **resource pooling,** to perform several activities. It is a powerful operational concept that can significantly affect not only process flow rate and process capacity, but also flow time (as we will see in chapter 8).

5.2.1 Unit Loads

In chapter 4 we defined the work content of each activity as the product of activity time and the average number of visits that a flow unit makes to that activity. Since activities are performed by resources, we can extend this concept to compute total work performed by each resource. Specifically, the **unit load** of a resource unit is *the sum of the work contents of all activities that utilize that resource unit.* Unit load is measured in units of time per flow unit (e.g., minutes required to service one customer) and so represents the amount of resource time required to process each flow unit. Example 5.1 demonstrates this computation for MBPF, Inc.

5.2.2 Load Batching

Thus far, we have implicitly assumed that a resource processes flow units, one unit at a time. Often, however, resources can process several flow units simultaneously—a phenomenon referred to as **load batching.** These resources are referred to as *batch resources,* such as the bread-baking oven mentioned earlier that can bake several loaves simultaneously. If the oven can bake up to 10 loaves at a time, then we say that its *load batch* is 10. As we will see shortly, load batching affects the rate at which a resource processes flow units.

5.2.3 Scheduled Availability

Typically each resource unit is scheduled for operation only during a certain portion of the total time (e.g., eight hours per day, five days per week). This period is called the **scheduled availability** of the resource unit. Similarly, the *scheduled availability of a resource pool* is the sum of the scheduled availabilities of all resource units in the pool.

EXAMPLE 5.1

We now revisit MBPF Inc. Table 5.1 lists the following:

- The *activities* required to complete a standard garage,
- The *work content* for each activity, and
- The *resources* (machines, tools, and workers) required to perform these activities.

Table 5.1 lists several types of workers each trained to perform a specific activity. Worker S is trained to perform the "separate" activity. Worker PR operates punch press R and worker

PB operates punch press B. Worker FB operates forming machine B and worker FR operates forming machine R. Worker SA is trained to do the subassembly using the welding gun and worker FA is trained to complete the final assembly. The inspector conducts the final inspection of the garage. By adding the work contents of all the different activities assigned to each member of the resource pool, we can use the data in Table 5.1 to compute the unit load imposed by a standard garage on that resource pool as shown in Table 5.2.

TABLE 5.1 Activities, Work Content, and Resource Pools for a Standard Garage, MBPF Inc.

	Activity	Work Content (Standard Garage) (min. per unit)	Resource Allocated
1	Separate	10	Worker-S
2	Punch the base	30	Punch Press-B, Worker-PB
3	Punch the roof	22	Punch Press-R, Worker-PR
4	Form the base	6	Forming Machine-B, Worker-FB
5	Form the roof	12	Forming Machine-R, Worker-FR
6	Subassemble	13	Welding Gun, Worker-SA
7	Assemble	10	Worker-FA
8	Inspect	36	Inspector

TABLE 5.2 Unit Loads for a Standard Garage, MBPF Inc.

Resource Pool	Unit Load (Standard Garage) (min. per unit)
Worker-S	10
Punch Press-R	22
Punch Press-B	30
Worker-PR	22
Worker-PB	30
Forming Machine-R	12
Forming Machine-B	6
Worker-FR	12
Worker-FB	6
Welding Gun	13
Worker-SA	13
Worker-FA	10
Inspector	36

For example, assume that the oven resource pool at our bakery contains five ovens, each of which is scheduled to bake for eight hours per day. In that case, the scheduled availability of the oven pool is

$$5 \times 8 = 40 \text{ hours per day}$$

Scheduled availability of various resource pools may differ. It is not uncommon, for example, that some departments within a plant operate only one shift per day while others operate two shifts. The scheduled availabilities of the resources in these two departments will differ, and capacity analysis of the plant should take this difference into consideration. Moreover, our choice of *one day* as the time period of measurement for scheduled availability is arbitrary. We have simply assumed that availability patterns repeat on a daily basis, but more complicated patterns are possible. Some resource pools, for example, may be available only on Mondays and Thursdays, with the pattern repeating every week. In that case, we should measure scheduled availability in *number of hours per 1 week.* To simplify matters, however, we will continue to assume that availability patterns repeat on daily bases.

5.3   FLOW RATE MEASUREMENT

Flow rate and process capacity are both expressed in terms of *number of flow units per unit of time,* such as customers per day, tons of steel per shift, cars per hour, dollars per month, and patents per year. The average flow rate (throughput) of a stable process can be determined by the following four-step procedure:

1. Identify a particular entry and exit point in the process.
2. Observe the process over a given, extended period of time.
3. Measure the number of flow units that pass through the selected point over the selected period of time.
4. Compute the average number of flow units per unit of time.

In the sections that follow, we explore ways to estimate the capacity of a process using the concepts developed earlier.

5.3.1   Theoretical Capacity

If we observe a given resource unit during the period of time in which it is available, we will see that it alternates between periods in which it is utilized, or busy processing flow units, and periods during which it is idle. Resource units, for example, may be out of service (due to maintenance or breakdown), occupied for setups (changeovers), or interrupted by other activities. Any one of these events will reduce the time period during which a resource pool is available. The impact of these factors on the flow rate is discussed in section 5.5.

The **theoretical capacity of a resource unit** is *its maximum sustainable flow rate if it were fully utilized* during its scheduled availability (without idle periods.) Likewise, the **theoretical capacity of a resource pool** is *the sum of the theoretical capacities of all the resource units in that pool.* Theoretical capacities of different resource pools may vary. Since all resource pools are required to process a flow unit, no process can produce output any faster than its "slowest" resource pool. Therefore, we define the **theoretical capacity of a process** as *the theoretical capacity of its slowest resource pool.* Like theoretical flow time (in chapter 4), theoretical capacity represents an idealized target that can rarely be achieved in practice. Resource pools with minimum theoretical capacity are called **theoretical bottlenecks.**

Computing Theoretical Capacity The theoretical capacities of various resource pools, and of the entire process, can be computed from the following data:

- Unit loads,
- Load batch of each resource pool,
- Scheduled availability of each resource pool, and
- Number of units in the resource pool.

To better understand the computational procedure, consider a simple process requiring a single resource. Assume that the resource unit load is 10 minutes per flow unit, with a load batch size of one unit and scheduled availability of eight hours per day. The theoretical capacity of the resource unit is then 6 flow units per hour, or 48 flow units per day. (As mentioned earlier, the choice of the time unit for measuring rate is arbitrary.) Because there is only one resource unit in the resource pool, theoretical capacity of the resource pool is also 6 flow units per hour, or 48 flow units per day.

Reconsider our baking-process example in which an oven is our resource. We noted earlier that the oven is a batch resource since it can process multiple flow units simultaneously. Now suppose that the oven can bake 10 loaves of bread simultaneously, which is a load batch of 10 loaves. If baking time is 15 minutes, the theoretical capacity of the oven is

$$\frac{1 \text{ batch}}{15 \text{ minutes}} \times \frac{10 \text{ loaves}}{\text{batch}} \times \frac{60 \text{ minutes}}{\text{hour}} = 40 \text{ loaves per hour}$$

Thus we can compute the *theoretical capacity of a resource unit* as

$$(1 / \text{unit load}) \times \text{load batch} \times \text{scheduled availability}$$

Theoretical capacity of different resource pools should be expressed over their respective scheduled availabilities. Sometimes we may prefer to compute the capacity in units per hour and then account for scheduled availability by simply multiplying the theoretical capacity (of resource pools or process) by their respective scheduled availabilities.

EXAMPLE 5.2

We now compute the theoretical capacity for Standard garages at MBPF Inc. Table 5.3 recapitulates the data on unit load for each resource in the factory process. If the factory operates one shift of eight hours per day, we have a scheduled availability of eight hours per day for all resource pools. Furthermore, the load batch of each resource is one. The number of units of each resource and the theoretical capacity of the resource pool are also listed in Table 5.3.

As shown, the slowest resource pools or bottlenecks are punch press B and worker PB, each with a theoretical capacity of 2.0 garages per hour. Thus, the theoretical capacity of the process—which equals the minimal theoretical capacity of all its resource units—is also 2.0 (standard) garages per hour.

TABLE 5.3   Theoretical Capacity for a Standard Garage, MBPF Inc.

Resource Pool	Unit Load (minutes/ flow unit)	Load Batch (flow units/batch)	Theoretical Capacity of a Resource Unit (flow units per hour)	Number of Units in the Resource Pool	Theoretical Capacity of the Resource Pool (flow units per hour)
Worker-S	10	1	6.00	1	6.00
Punch Press-R	22	1	2.73	1	2.73
Punch Press-B	30	1	2.00	1	2.00
Worker-PR	22	1	2.73	1	2.73
Worker-PB	30	1	2.00	1	2.00
Forming Machine-R	12	1	5.00	1	5.00
Forming Machine-B	6	1	10.00	1	10.00
Worker-FR	12	1	5.00	1	5.00
Worker-FB	6	1	10.00	1	10.00
Welding Gun	13	1	4.62	1	4.62
Worker-SA	13	1	4.62	1	4.62
Worker-FA	10	1	6.00	1	6.00
Inspector	36	1	1.67	2	3.33

5.3.2   Throughput and Capacity Utilization

The throughput of a process is measured as the average number of flow units processed over a given period of time. Throughput of a process is rarely equal to its theoretical capacity due to internal inefficiencies that lead to resource unavailability and idleness as well as external constraints such as low outflow rate (due to low demand rate) or low inflow rate (due to low supply rate).

Working from the notion of theoretical capacity, which is an idealized but easily computable measure of capacity, we can measure the degree to which resources are effectively utilized by a process. To do so, we introduce an important performance measure called **capacity utilization,** defined as:

$$\text{Capacity utilization} = \text{Throughput} / \text{Theoretical capacity}$$

Capacity utilization indicates the extent to which resources (which represent invested capital) are utilized to generate outputs (flow units and ultimately profits).

EXAMPLE 5.3

Assume that over a period of several weeks, the average output at MBPF Inc. has been 1.5 Standard garages per hour. Using the information on theoretical capacity derived in Table 5.3, we can compute the capacity utilization for the various resource pools listed in Table 5.4. Overall capacity utilization—determined by the theoretical bottlenecks at punch press B and worker PB is 75%.

TABLE 5.4 Capacity Utilization for MBPF Inc. Producing 1.5 Garages Per Hour

Resource	Unit Load (minutes / flow unit)	Theoretical Capacity of Resource Pool (flow units/hour)	Capacity Utilization (%)
Worker-S	10	6.00	25
Punch Press-R	22	2.73	55
Punch Press-B	30	2.00	75
Worker-PR	22	2.73	55
Worker-PB	30	2.00	75
Forming Machine-R	12	5.00	30
Forming Machine-B	6	10.00	15
Worker-FR	12	5.00	30
Worker-FB	6	10.00	15
Welding Gun	13	4.62	32.5
Worker-SA	13	4.62	32.5
Worker-FA	10	6.00	25
Inspector	36	3.33	45

We now demonstrate the main concepts developed thus far by applying them to an example from the service sector.

EXAMPLE 5.4

Reconsider the situation at Valley of Hope (VOH) Hospital, first introduced in chapter 4. For the sake of convenience, the activities required for each X ray, with corresponding work content and allocated resources, are repeated in Table 5.5. By observing the number of patients processed over a three-week period, VOH Hospital found that its X-ray unit processes, on average, 44 patients per eight-hour day, or 5.5 patients per hour. All resources are scheduled for operation from 9:00 A.M. to 5:00 P.M. each day, six days per week.

Using the information in Table 5.5, we can compute the unit loads and theoretical capacity of various resource units as given in Table 5.6. Further, with information on the number of resource units in each resource pool, we compute the theoretical capacity of the resource pools as shown in Table 5.6. Note that the theoretical bottleneck resource is the darkroom, with a capacity for processing only 8 patients per hour. The theoretical capacity of the process itself, therefore, is 8 patients per hour.

Finally, based on throughput of 5.5 patients per hour, we summarize the utilization of various resources in Table 5.7.

TABLE 5.5 Work Content and Resources, VOH Hospital

Activity/ Event	Description	Work Content (minutes per patient)	Resources Allocated
Start	Patient leaves the physician's office	—	—
1	Patient walks to the X-ray lab	7	—
2	The X-ray request travels to the X-ray lab by a messenger	20	Messenger
3	An X-ray technician fills out a standard form based on the information supplied by the physician	6	X-ray technician
4	The receptionist receives from the patient information concerning insurance, prepares and signs a claim form, and sends to the insurer	5	Receptionist
5	Patient undresses in preparation for an X ray	3	Changing room
6	A lab technician takes X rays	7.5	X-ray technician, X-ray lab
7	A darkroom technician develops the X rays	15	Darkroom technician, darkroom
8	The lab technician checks X rays for clarity	2.5	X-ray technician
9	Patient puts on clothes and gets ready to leave the lab	3	Changing room
10	Patient walks back to the physician's office	7	—
11	The X rays are transferred to the physician by a messenger	20	Messenger
End	Patient and the X rays arrive at the physician's office	—	—

TABLE 5.6 Theoretical Capacity, VOH Hospital

Resource Pool	Resource Unit Load (minutes/patient)	Load Batch (patients/batch)	Theoretical Capacity of Resource Unit (patients/hour)	No. Units in Resource Pool	Theoretical Capacity of Resource Pool (patients/hour)
Messenger	40	1	1.5	6	9
Receptionist	5	1	12	1	12
X-ray technician	16	1	3.75	4	15
X-ray lab	7.5	1	8	2	16
Darkroom technician	15	1	4	3	12
Darkroom	15	1	4	2	8
Changing room	6	1	10	2	20

TABLE 5.7 Capacity Utilization, VOH Hospital

Resource Pool	Theoretical Capacity of Resource Pool (patients/hour)	Capacity Utilization (%)
Messenger	9	61.11
Receptionist	12	45.83
X-ray technician	15	36.67
X-ray lab	16	34.38
Darkroom technician	12	45.83
Darkroom	8	68.75
Changing room	20	27.50

5.4 EFFECT OF PRODUCT MIX ON THEORETICAL CAPACITY AND PROFITABILITY OF A PROCESS

Firms often produce several products simultaneously. In this section we first show that the theoretical capacity of a process is a function of the product mix that it produces. This observation has an important business implication. In most organizations, sales/marketing departments make product-mix decisions. Since such decisions affect the process capacity—a major driver of profitability—an input from the operations group (responsible for production) is obviously required. We also explore how the interaction between product mix and capacity impacts the profitability of a firm.

5.4.1 Unit Load for Product Mix

For a process that produces several types of products, a flow unit may correspond to a given mix of the various products. We can calculate the unit load for a given product mix by averaging the unit loads of individual products, using weights determined by the mix, as illustrated in Example 5.5.

EXAMPLE 5.5

Assume that, in addition to its Standard garage, MBPF Inc. manufactures another model called Fancy. Unit loads on resources used to produce the Fancy model are given in Table 5.8. Suppose the product mix choice of MBPF Inc. is 75% Standard and 25% Fancy; in other words, MBPF produces 3 Standard garages for each unit of Fancy. Then, for example,

Unit load of punch press B for the 75–25 mix = (75% × *Unit load of punch press B for Standard garage*) + (25% × *Unit load of punch press B for Fancy garage*)

= (75% × 30) + (25% × 50) = 35 minutes

Likewise, the last column in Table 5.8 indicates the unit loads on each resource pool for the same 75%–25% hypothetical product mix.

TABLE 5.8 Unit Loads for a 75%–25% Product Mix at MBPF Inc.

Resource Pool	Unit Load (minutes per unit)		
	Standard	Fancy	75–25% Mix
Worker-S	10	10	10
Punch Press-R	22	30	24
Punch Press-B	30	50	35
Worker-PR	22	30	24
Worker-PB	30	50	35
Forming Machine-R	12	15	12.75
Forming Machine-B	6	10	7
Worker-FR	12	15	12.75
Worker-FB	6	10	7
Welding Gun	13	20	14.75
Worker-SA	13	20	14.75
Worker-FA	10	15	11.25
Inspector	36	40	37

5.4.2 Theoretical Capacity for Product Mix

Since different products may utilize various resources differently, the theoretical capacity of a resource pool—and thus the theoretical bottlenecks and capacity of the process—may depend on the products being produced and on the company's product mix. Computation of theoretical capacity of a resource pool for a product mix follows directly from the unit loads of the product mix only when the load batch at the resource pool is identical across all products in the mix. For simplicity of exposition, we will assume this to be true. A more extensive procedure is necessary when the identical load batch assumption does not hold.

EXAMPLE 5.6

First we compute the theoretical capacity for the Fancy garage by repeating the process utilized in Example 5.2. As you can see from Table 5.9, the theoretical process capacity is 1.2 Fancy garages per hour with punch press B and worker PB as theoretical bottlenecks.

TABLE 5.9 Theoretical Capacity for Fancy Garages, MBPF Inc.

Resource	Unit Load (minutes/ flow unit)	Load Batch (flow units/ batch)	Theoretical Capacity of a Resource Unit (flow units per hour)	Number of Units in the Resource Pool	Theoretical Capacity of the Resource Pool (flow units per hour)
Worker-S	10	1	6.00	1	6.00
Punch Press-R	30	1	2.00	1	2.00
Punch Press-B	50	1	1.20	1	1.20
Worker-PR	30	1	2.00	1	2.00
Worker-PB	50	1	1.20	1	1.20
Forming Machine-R	15	1	4.00	1	4.00
Forming Machine-B	10	1	6.00	1	6.00
Worker-FR	15	1	4.00	1	4.00
Worker-FB	10	1	6.00	1	6.00
Welding Gun	20	1	3.00	1	3.00
Worker-SA	20	1	3.00	1	3.00
Worker-FA	15	1	4.00	1	4.00
Inspector	40	1	1.50	2	3.00

Next, we compute the theoretical capacities of the resources and the process for a product mix of 75% Standard garages and 25% Fancy garages as shown in Table 5.10, which is based on the unit load of the 75%–25% mix derived in Table 5.8.

The theoretical process capacity for a 75%–25% product mix has increased to 1.71 garages per hour while punch press B and worker PB remain theoretical bottlenecks. We see that the theoretical bottlenecks remain unchanged as we go from producing only standard garages to only Fancy garages to a 75%–25% mix of the two. In general, however, product mix decisions may change the theoretical bottlenecks.

TABLE 5.10	Theoretical Capacity for a 75%–25% Product Mix, MBPF Inc.			
Resource	Unit Load (minutes/ flow unit)	Theoretical Capacity of a Resource Unit (flow units per hour)	Number of Units in the Resource Pool	Theoretical Capacity of the Resource Pool (flow units per hour)
Worker-S	10	6.00	1	6.00
Punch Press-R	24	2.50	1	2.50
Punch Press-B	35	1.71	1	1.71
Worker-PB	24	2.50	1	2.50
Worker-PR	35	1.71	1	1.71
Forming Machine-R	12.75	4.71	1	4.71
Forming Machine-B	7	8.57	1	8.57
Worker-FR	12.5	4.71	1	4.71
Worker-FB	7	8.57	1	8.57
Welding Gun	14.75	4.07	1	4.07
Worker-SA	14.75	4.07	1	4.07
Worker-FA	11.25	5.33	1	5.33
Inspector	37	1.62	2	3.24

5.4.3 Optimizing Profitability

Which of the two models made by MBPF—Standard or Fancy—is the more profitable? To answer this question, it is useful to measure capacity and throughput *in terms of financial flows rather than in terms of physical unit flows.*

EXAMPLE 5.7

First, define the **contribution margin** of each flow unit as *its revenue less all of its variable costs.* Assume, for example, that the contribution margins of the Standard and Fancy garages have been determined to be $200 and $260, respectively. Furthermore, market research suggests that the market potential (the maximum number that the firm could sell at its advertised prices) for Standard and Fancy garages is 350 and 150 per month, respectively. Suppose MBPF operates 1 shift (of 8 hours) per day, and a working month of 25 days. The problem is to determine the optimal product mix: the number of garages of each model to make and sell.

At first glance, the Fancy garage, which has a higher contribution margin, seems more profitable. MBPF may decide, therefore, to produce and sell as many Fancy garages as possible and then—only if spare capacity is available—produce as many Standard models as possible. From Table 5.9 we notice that theoretical capacity of Fancy garages is 1.2 units per hour. Multiplying by the duration of the shift and the number of days in a working month, we can express the theoretical ca-

pacity as 240 Fancy garages per month. Since the market potential for Fancy garages is 150 units per month, MBPF has enough capacity to meet the demand. In fact, producing at the rate of 1.2 Fancy garages per hour, the total bottleneck resource (punch press B and worker PB) time required to produce 150 Fancy garages is 125 hours.

Again, operating 8 hours per shift for 25 days each month, MBPF has a total availability of 200 hours per month. Thus after producing 150 Fancy garages—which require 125 hours—MBPF still has 75 hours of time leftover during the month at the bottlenecks which it could use to produce Standard garages. Recall from Table 5.3 that the theoretical capacity of MBPF to produce the Standard garage is 2 units per hour. In 75 hours, therefore, MBPF can produce approximately 150 Standard garages per month. Thus based on unit contribution margins alone, we determine that MBPF should produce 150 Fancy and 150 Standard garages per month, realizing a total monthly contribution of

$$\$(260 \times 150 + 200 \times 150) = \$69,000$$

EXAMPLE 5.8

Can MBPF Inc. do better?

Note that while the contribution margin of a Standard garage is $200, MBPF's theoretical capacity to produce it is 2 units per hour. Its contribution per unit of time is therefore

$$2 \times 200 = \$400 \text{ per hour}$$

Similarly, the contribution margin per unit of time of the Fancy garage is

$$1.2 \times \$260 = \$312 \text{ per hour}$$

Thus based on contribution margin per unit of time, the Standard garage is the more profitable product. Therefore MBPF should first produce as many Standard garages as the market will bear and only then, if excess capacity is available, produce Fancy garages. Since 2 Standard garages are produced in an hour, production of 350 Standard garages (to meet the product's full market potential) would require a total of 175 hours. In the remaining 25 hours of monthly availability, MBPF can produce 30 Fancy garages. Based on contribution margin per unit time, therefore, MBPF should produce 350 Standard garages and 30 Fancy garages to realize a net profit of

$$\$(200 \times 350 + 260 \times 30) = \$77,800$$

which is a 12.71% increase in profits over the decision reached in Example 5.7.

As this example demonstrated, the objective in determining the product mix should be to maximize the flow of **contribution per unit of time** on the bottleneck resource(s) rather than contribution margin (per product). In a simple two-product setting with common bottleneck resources, it is fairly straightforward to derive the optimal product-mix decision. Obviously, more complex settings involving multiple products with multiple and different bottleneck resources involve more difficult tradeoffs. We briefly illustrate a generic approach to solve optimal product mix problems.

5.4.4   A Generic Approach for Optimal Product Mix

Determining the optimal product mix can be stated as a problem of allocating resources to products in order to maximize profits. Suppose a firm can produce two products, labeled 1 and 2, using three resources labeled E, F, and G. We need information regarding the contribution margin and market demand of each product, the scheduled availability of each resource pool, and the unit load imposed by each product on each resource pool. We could also determine the optimal product mix using net availability instead of the scheduled availability; we illustrate the approach using scheduled availability. Let m_1 and m_2 represent the contribution margins of products 1 and 2 and D_1 and D_2 their respective market demand. Let the scheduled availability of resource pools E, F, and G be denoted by b_E, b_F, and b_G respectively. Let the unit load of product 1 on resource pools E, F, and G be denoted by a_{E1}, a_{F1}, and a_{G1} respectively. Similarly, let a_{E2}, a_{F2}, and a_{G2} denote the unit load of product 2 on resource pools E, F, and G. Given this data, we need to compute the quantity of products 1 and 2, denoted by x_1 and x_2, to be produced that will maximize profits while ensuring that we use the resources only during their scheduled availability (known as **resource constraints**) and that we do not produce more than is demanded (known as **demand constraints**). The total contribution generated by producing x_1 units of product 1 and x_2 units of product 2 is given by

$$m_1 x_1 + m_2 x_2$$

Resource constraints entail that the total time required to produce the products on each resource pool is less than the scheduled availability of that resource pool. The total unit load of resource pool E for producing x_1 and x_2 units of products 1 and 2 is given by

$$a_{E1}x_1 + a_{E2}x_2$$

which cannot exceed its scheduled availability, b_E. Similar constraints need to be enforced for resources F and G.

Demand constraints entail that the total production of a product is less than its market demand. That is, for each product 1

$$x_1 \leq D_1$$

An analogous demand constraint applies for product 2. Therefore, the problem of determining the optimal product mix can be stated as the problem of finding appropriate values of x_1 and x_2 that maximize

$$m_1x_1 + m_2x_2$$

subject to

$$a_{E1}x_1 + a_{E2}x_2 \leq b_E$$
$$a_{F1}x_1 + a_{F2}x_2 \leq b_F$$
$$a_{G1}x_1 + a_{G2}x_2 \leq b_G$$
$$x_1 \leq D_1$$
$$x_2 \leq D_2$$

The first set of three constraints represents the resource constraints and the next set of two constraints represents the demand constraints. The theoretical capacity of the process for a *given* mix of products is represented by a point on the boundary of the region defined by the three resource constraints. At the optimal product mix, the theoretical bottleneck resource pools are identified by the resource constraints of those resource pools that are satisfied with equality. If, however, one or more of the demand constraints are satisfied with equality, we say that the corresponding market demand is a bottleneck. The formal optimization technique of *linear programming* can be used for solving these generic optimal product mix problems. Such techniques are detailed in many operations management and research textbooks such as those listed at the end of this chapter.

5.5   OTHER FACTORS AFFECTING PROCESS CAPACITY

The flow rate or throughput of a process is measured as the average number of flow units processed over a given period of time. **Process capacity** has been defined as the maximum sustainable flow rate of a process. Throughput may be less than process capacity solely due to external constraints such as low outflow rate (due to low demand rate) or low inflow rate (due to low supply rate). The process capacity can be computed experimentally (using a modification of the experimental procedure to measure throughput outlined in section 5.3) by assuming that sufficient inputs are always available at the entry point and all flow units exit at the end of processing.

Process capacity is less than the theoretical capacity of a process since the latter assumes, in addition, that all resources are fully utilized during their scheduled availability period. Recall that resource units alternate between periods during which they are utilized and periods during which they are idle. Idle periods may occur for several reasons, either planned or unforeseen:

- *Resource breakdown* Due to unforeseen circumstances, a resource may be unavailable for processing due to equipment breakdown or worker absenteeism.
- *Preventive maintenance* When resources are undergoing scheduled maintenance activities, they are unavailable for processing.
- *Setup/changeover* When assigned to process different products intermittently, a resource may have to be cleaned, reset, and retooled, during which periods—called setup or changeover times—it is unavailable.
- *Starvation* Sometimes resources are forced to be idle because necessary inputs are unavailable.
- *Blockage* Resources may be prevented from producing more flow units because there is no place to store the already processed flow units, or additional processing has not been authorized.

In the case of the first three items on this list, the resource itself is not available for processing, whereas in the case of the last two items, the problem lies elsewhere. We categorize the first three items as **resource unavailability** and the last two as **resource idleness.**

5.5.1   Net Availability

Scheduled availability defines the time period during which a resource unit is scheduled for processing. The **net availability** of a resource unit is *the actual time during which it is available for processing flow units*. **Availability loss** is *the difference between scheduled and net availabilities of a resource unit*. Availability loss represents a loss of resource-unit capacity and thus of theoretical process capacity. **Availability loss factor** is often expressed as a fraction of scheduled availability as shown in the following equation:

$$\text{Availability loss factor} = 1 - (\text{Net availability/Scheduled availability})$$

Availability loss factor for a resource can be determined from data available on historical resource breakdowns, preventive maintenance schedules, time taken for setups or changeovers, worker absenteeism, etc.

A resource will not necessarily be busy processing units during the entire period of net availability. An available resource may be idle because of starvation (lack of input on which to work), blockage (lack of buffer space in which to keep its output), or both.

5.5.2   Effective Capacity of a Process

Recall that we defined the theoretical capacity of a resource unit as its maximum flow rate if it is fully utilized during its scheduled availability (that is, if there are no periods of unavailability or idleness). We now define the **effective capacity of a resource unit** as its *maximum flow rate, if it were fully utilized during its net availability (if there were no periods of resource idleness)*. Clearly, the effective capacity of a resource unit is less than or equal to its theoretical capacity since the net availability of a resource unit cannot be larger than its scheduled availability. The effective capacity of a resource unit can be calculated using the following relation:

$$\text{Effective capacity of a resource unit} = (1/\text{unit load}) \times \text{load batch} \times \text{net availability}$$

The effective capacity of a resource pool is thus the sum of the effective capacities of all the resource units in the pool. Finally the **effective capacity of a process** is *the effective capacity of its slowest resource pools,* called the **effective bottlenecks.** By definition, effective capacity of each resource pool—and of the process itself—is no more than its respective theoretical capacity.

EXAMPLE 5.9

Suppose, for instance, that the MBPF plant is scheduled to run 1 shift of 8 hours per day. Thus, scheduled availability of each resource pool is 8 hours per day. The available resources, with their scheduled availabilities and loss factors, are summarized in Table 5.11. The availability loss factors were estimated by observing each resource pool over a 3-week period. The net-availability column is computed by subtracting availability loss from scheduled availability. If, for example, the loss factor for worker S is 6.25%, then that worker is available 93.75% of the scheduled time of 8 hours. Thus the net availability of worker S is equal to 7.5 hours per day.

To compute the effective capacities, consider, for example, worker S who has a unit load of 10 minutes per flow unit Table 5.2. With a load batch of 1 unit, we compute its effective capacity as

1/10 (batch/minute) × 1 (flow unit/batch) × 7.5 (hours/day) × 60 (minutes/hour)
= 45 flow units per day

Likewise the effective capacity of each resource pool at MBPF can now be computed as displayed in Table 5.11. We see (1) that punch press B and worker PB remain the bottlenecks and (2) that effective capacity of the process is 15.2 garages per day; the theoretical capacity of the process was 2.0 garages per hour or 16.0 garages per day. We see that incorporating loss factors into our availability computations left the bottleneck resource unchanged. In general, however, effective bottlenecks may differ from their theoretical counterparts.

TABLE 5.11 Resource Pools, Availabilities, and Effective Capacity for Standard Garages, MBPF Inc.

| | | Availability | | Effective Capacity of Resource Pool (flow units/day) |
	Scheduled (hours/day)	Loss Factor (%)	Net (hours/day)	
Resource Pool				
Worker-S	8.00	6.25	7.50	45.00
Punch Press-R	8.00	5.00	7.60	20.73
Punch Press-B	8.00	5.00	7.60	15.20
Worker-PR	8.00	5.00	7.60	20.73
Worker-PB	8.00	5.00	7.60	15.20
Forming Machine-R	8.00	10.00	7.20	36.00
Forming Machine-B	8.00	10.00	7.20	72.00
Worker-FR	8.00	6.25	7.50	36.00
Worker-FB	8.00	6.25	7.50	75.00
Welding Gun	8.00	10.00	7.20	33.23
Worker-SA	8.00	6.25	7.50	34.62
Worker-FA	8.00	6.25	7.50	45.00
Inspector	8.00	6.25	7.50	25.00

5.5.3 Effect of Product Mix on Net Availability

As discussed, availability loss factor depends on such factors as changeover times between products. Consequently, the availability loss factor will often be a function of product mix. Suppose, for example, that during an 8-hour shift, a firm is considering production of either 2 products, A and B, or 3 products, A, B, and C. Assume further, that all products require a single resource with one hour of changeover time needed to switch between the production of various products. Suppose that in each case, the changeover between products is only once during a shift. Furthermore, ignore momentarily such factors as resource breakdown and maintenance. Then the availability loss factor of that resource will be one-eighth, or 12.5%, for production of A and B and one-fourth, or 25.0%, for production of A, B, and C. Now consider production of A and B only. If our schedule requires 3 changeovers between products A and B per shift, we will lose 3 hours of productive time per shift, and our availability loss factor will be three-eighths, or 37.5%. That is, the frequency of changeovers for a given mix affects the net availability. In chapter 10 we explore in detail the advantages and disadvantages of the frequency of changeovers for a given product mix.

5.5.4 Comparisons

By definition, effective capacity of a process is less than its theoretical capacity. Due to various operational procedures, it is conceivable that resources would idle even during periods of their net availability. Thus, resource idleness reduces the flow rate of the process even further than its effective capacity. Process capacity measures the reduced flow rate due to resource idleness. Finally, recall that throughput cannot exceed process capacity. We then have the following formula:

$$\text{Throughput} \leq \text{Process capacity} \leq \text{Effective capacity} \leq \text{Theoretical capacity}$$

The inequalities between Process, Effective, and Theoretical capacities are a result of internal inefficiencies and constraints. Conversely, throughput may be lower than the process capacity because of external (to the process) constraints. In such cases, we say that the bottleneck is external to the process.

The separation between the effective capacity (affected by resource unavailability) and the process capacity (affected by both resource unavailability and idleness) also allows us to see which of the two effects—resource unavailability or resource idleness—dominates. That is, suppose we wish to increase the process capacity that is observed to be less than the theoretical capacity. Where should we focus attention? If the effective capacity of a process happens to be close to its theoretical capacity, attention needs to be focused on reducing idleness. Otherwise, we need to work to increase the net availability of the bottleneck resource pools. Finally, data on resource unavailability is more readily available (time lost due to machine breakdowns, preventive maintenance, time spent on changeovers, worker absenteeism, etc.). The effective capacity of a process, therefore, is still relatively easy to compute and it gives a tighter bound than the theoretical capacity on the throughput of a process.

5.5.5 Improving Process Capacity

Increasing the net availability of the bottleneck resource pools and reducing resource idleness can increase process capacity.

- *Increasing net availability* The total loss due to breakdowns and maintenance can be reduced by improved maintenance policies, by scheduling preventive maintenance outside periods of availability, and by effective problem-solving measures that reduce the frequency and duration of breakdowns. The unproductive time incurred in setups and changeovers can be reduced by decreasing the frequency of changeovers, working proactively to reduce the time required for setups (see the more detailed discussion in chapter 10), and by managing the product mix (see section 5.4). To decrease the frequency of changeovers, we need to produce a larger number of units of a product (batch size) before changing over to produce a different product. This increased batch size, however, may lead to higher inventories and longer flow times (see discussion in chapter 6).

- *Decreasing resource idleness* Resource idleness results from starvation or blockage or both. Blockages occur due to limited buffer sizes and rules for managing them. For example, by allowing for a larger buffer size immediately following a resource, we can minimize the blockage of that resource. Proper buffer size selection is discussed in chapter 7 and the impact of buffer size on flow rate is discussed in chapter 8. Starvation results from lack of synchronization between various flows within the process. For example, if components A and B are to be assembled into a product, unavailability of either component can result in idleness of the resource performing the assembly. Process flow synchronization issues are discussed in detail in chapter 10.

5.6 IMPROVING THEORETICAL CAPACITY

To improve theoretical capacity, we must increase the theoretical capacity of each (theoretical) bottleneck. Recall the following formula:

$$\text{Theoretical capacity of a resource} = (1 / \text{unit load}) \times \text{load batch} \times \text{scheduled availability}$$

Since the theoretical capacity of the resource pool is the sum of the theoretical capacities of each resource in the pool, increasing the theoretical capacity of a resource pool requires taking at least one of the following actions:

1. Decrease unit load on the bottleneck resource pool (work faster, work smarter).
2. Increase the load batch of resources in the bottleneck resource pool (increase scale of resource).
3. Increase the number of units in the bottleneck resource pool (increase scale of process).
4. Increase scheduled availability of the bottleneck resource pool (work longer).

5.6.1 Decreasing Unit Load on the Bottleneck Resource Pool

In chapter 4 we showed that the theoretical flow time is decreased by decreasing the work content of *each critical path*. Similarly, the theoretical capacity can be increased by decreasing the unit load of each *theoretical bottleneck resource pool*. We know that the unit load on a resource pool is the total work content of all activities that the resource is assigned to perform. Therefore, the principles that apply to reducing the work content of critical activities also apply to the work content of activities performed by the bottleneck resource pool, thereby increasing its theoretical capacity.

We can emphasize this symmetry with concepts in chapter 4 even further by recalling the levers for managing the theoretical flow time described in sections 4.5.1 and 4.5.2—reducing the work content of critical paths by either (1) decreasing the work content of an activity on the critical path, or (2) moving some of the work content off the critical path. Likewise, because the unit load on a resource pool consists of the total work content of all activities that the resource pool is assigned to perform, we can decrease the unit load on a bottleneck resource pool by taking one of the following actions:

1. Decreasing the work content of an activity performed by the bottleneck resource pool, or
2. Moving some of the work content to nonbottleneck resources.

Essentially, then, these levers are similar to those we developed in chapter 4 to decrease the theoretical flow time. The only difference is in our choice of focus on what to improve: for flow rate we focus on activities performed by bottleneck resources whereas (in chapter 4) we focused on activities along the critical path to reduce the flow time. In either case, we need to decrease the work content of an activity by working smarter, working faster, doing it right the first time, and/or changing the product mix.

Reducing the unit load of a nonbottleneck resource does not affect theoretical capacity. Such reduction may still be useful because it may decrease costs, flow time, and the potential for errors and defects.

Moving part of the work content of bottleneck resources to nonbottleneck resources can also increase the theoretical capacity of a bottleneck resource pool. This, of course, is possible only if the nonbottleneck resources are flexible to perform some of the activities currently performed by the bottleneck resources. If two resources are completely flexible to perform each others' tasks, then we can combine them into a single resource pool—a technique called resource pooling. Note, however, that flexibility of resources increases the theoretical process capacity only when this flexibility helps perform activities currently performed by bottleneck resources. The following example illustrates how flexibility of resources improves theoretical process capacity.

EXAMPLE 5.10

In Table 5.3 we found that the theoretical capacity of MBPF Inc. was limited to 2.0 Standard garages per hour by bottlenecks at punch press B and worker PB. Now suppose we make specific investments such that the punch presses B and R are able to perform both the activities of punching a base and a roof. In addition, we cross-train workers PB and PR to be able to punch both bases and roofs. We rename these flexible resources punch press RB and worker PRB. Observe that we now have two units each of punch press RB and worker PRB. In Table 5.12 we summarize the computation of theoretical capacity when these flexible resources are used.

The theoretical capacity of the process increases to 2.3 Standard garages per hour. Observe that making the resources currently performing the roof and base-forming activities (forming machines R and B, and workers FR and FB) flexible will not impact the theoretical capacity of the process because these resources are not the bottlenecks.

TABLE 5.12   Theoretical Capacity, Standard Garage, MBPF Inc. with Flexible Punch Resources

Resource	Unit Load (minutes/ flow unit)	Load Batch (flow units per batch)	Theoretical Capacity of a Resource Unit (flow units per hour)	Number of Units	Theoretical Capacity of the Resource Pool (flow units per hour)
Worker-S	10	1	6.00	1	6.00
Punch Press-RB	52	1	1.15	2	2.30
Worker-PRB	52	1	1.15	2	2.30
Forming Machine-R	12	1	5.00	1	5.00
Forming Machine-B	6	1	10.00	1	10.00
Worker-FR	12	1	5.00	1	5.00
Worker-FB	6	1	10.00	1	10.00
Welding Gun	13	1	4.62	1	4.62
Worker-SA	13	1	4.62	1	4.62
Worker-FA	10	1	6.00	1	6.00
Inspector	36	1	1.67	2	3.33

The actions outlined to improve the theoretical capacity of the process have different prerequisites and consequences. Working smarter and doing it right the first time require process improvement. Working faster typically involves investments in faster resources or incentives to workers. Changing the product mix and reassigning or shifting work from bottleneck to nonbottleneck resources requires greater flexibility on part of nonbottleneck resources to be able to handle variation in flow rates or to perform the work performed by bottlenecks. To make a resource flexible to perform activities of other resources may require financial investments in tooling, cross-training, and so forth. Moving some (subcontracting) or all (outsourcing) work to a third party may involve swapping operating costs of lower labor and capital for higher costs of inputs (supplies).

5.6.2 Increasing the Load Batch of Bottleneck Resources

Because resources can often process multiple units simultaneously—a phenomenon referred to as *load batching*—one simple way to increase resource capacity is to increase the load batch of the resource. For example, if we have an oven that constitutes a bottleneck because it can bake only 10 loaves at a time, we could increase its capacity by replacing it with an oven that can accommodate 15 loaves at a time.

5.6.3 Increasing the Number of Units of Bottleneck Resources

Adding more units of the resource to the bottleneck resource pool will also increase its theoretical capacity. Because the "slowest" resource pool determines the theoretical capacity of the process, addition of new units to the current bottleneck resource pool could create new bottleneck resource pools. If this happens, we say that *the bottleneck has shifted.* This phenomena is illustrated in Example 5.11.

EXAMPLE 5.11

In Table 5.3, for instance, we found that, limited by bottlenecks at punch press B and worker PB, the theoretical capacity of MBPF Inc. for producing Standard garages was 2.0 units per hour. If we purchased another (identical) punch press and hired another worker to operate it, it would increase the capacities of the resources and hence the theoretical process capacity as well. At first glance, we might expect the theoretical capacity of the process to *double* due to this duplication. From the new resource capacities computer in Table 5.13, however, we see that this need not be the case.

The reason is that the theoretical bottleneck has shifted and our new theoretical process capacity is now constrained by the bottleneck resources of punch press R and worker PR to 2.73 units per hour.

TABLE 5.13 Theoretical Capacity, Standard Garage, MBPF Inc. with Additional Punch Resources

Resource	Unit Load (minutes/ flow unit)	Theoretical Capacity of a Resource Unit (flow units per hour)	Number of Units	Theoretical Capacity of the Resource Pool (flow units per hour)
Worker-S	10	6.00	1	6.00
Punch Press-R	22	2.73	1	2.73
Punch Press-B	30	2.00	2	4.00
Worker-PR	22	2.73	1	2.73
Worker-PB	30	2.00	2	4.00
Forming Machine-R	12	5.00	1	5.00
Forming Machine-B	6	10.00	1	10.00
Worker-FR	12	5.00	1	5.00
Worker-FB	6	10.00	1	10.00
Welding Gun	13	4.62	1	4.62
Worker-SA	13	4.62	1	4.62
Worker-FA	10	6.00	1	6.00
Inspector	36	1.67	2	3.33

Therefore, in selecting the level of financial investment in resources, we should look closely at the process capacity that we are trying to improve. As we relax bottlenecks by adding more resource units, new bottlenecks may appear and the total process capacity may increase, but only at a decreasing rate.

5.6.4 Increasing Scheduled Availability of Bottleneck Resources

Extending the time period during which the bottleneck resource operates (working longer) can increase its scheduled availability. If the oven is the bottleneck in our bread-making process, we could increase its daily capacity by operating it more than 8 hours a day. In both manufacturing and service operations, increasing the hours of operation and employing overtime are common methods to increase process output.

5.7 LEVERS FOR MANAGING FLOW RATE

The flow rate (throughput) of a given process depends on its theoretical capacity, resource unavailability and idleness, and external bottlenecks. Below we summarize the managerial levers to manage flow rate. Financially, these levers are extremely powerful—by increasing the capacity of (typically few) bottlenecks, we better utilize all other resources and increase the flow rate of the entire process.

1. Manage supply and demand to increase the throughput.
   - Have reliable suppliers, produce better forecasts of demand.
2. Decrease resource idleness to increase process capacity.
   - Synchronize flows within the process to reduce starvation.
   - Set appropriate size of buffers to reduce blockage.
3. Increase the net availability of resources to increase effective capacity.
   - Improve maintenance policies, perform preventive maintenance outside periods of scheduled availability, institute effective problem-solving measures that reduce frequency and duration of breakdowns.
   - Institute motivational programs and incentives to reduce absenteeism, increase employee morale.
   - Reduce the frequency of or time required for setups or changeovers for a given product mix or change the product mix.
4. Increase the theoretical capacity.
   - Decrease unit load on the bottleneck resource pool.
     - work faster, work smarter, do it right the first time, change product mix.
     - subcontract or outsource.
     - invest in flexible resources.
   - Increase the load batch of resources in the bottleneck resource pool (increase scale of resource).
   - Increase the number of units in the bottleneck resource pool (increase scale of process).
   - Increase scheduled availability of the bottleneck resource pool (work longer).

Problem Set

5.1 This exercise revisits the VOH Hospital X-ray-service process of Example 5.4 but assumes a 15% availability loss factor across all resources. Following are two lists. The first contains a series of hypothetical modifications that can be made to the VOH Hospital X-ray-service process. The second consists of three exercises for evaluating each of these modifications. Consider each change separately, not cumulatively, and perform each evaluation to each modification.

Modifications

a. Install new equipment that enables lab technicians to develop X rays in 10 minutes instead of 12 minutes.

b. Encourage patients to dress and undress faster (in 2 minutes instead of 3 minutes).

c. Ask patients to carry X-ray requests and completed X rays instead of sending them by messenger.

d. Find an improved method of taking X-ray shots that reduces from 25% to 5% the fraction of shots that must be redone.

e. Reduce the downtime experienced by the darkroom technician to 10%.

f. Reduce the downtime of the darkroom to 0%.

g. Complete the last phase of X-ray development, which takes up 3 of the 12 minutes in the process, so that it takes place outside the darkroom rather than inside. The darkroom technician should still be occupied for the entire 12 minutes.

h. Hire a second receptionist.

i. Install another darkroom.

j. Install another darkroom and merge the tasks of X-ray technicians, darkroom technicians, and receptionist. Basically, train each of your eight employees to perform all eight jobs entailed by the process.

k. Operate the darkroom for 9 hours per shift instead of 8 hours, staggering the schedules of the three darkroom technicians so that each works for 8 hours, but collectively they cover the 9 hours.

l. Change the patient mix to 25% inpatient and 75% outpatient (refer to the data in Example 4.5).

Evaluations

1. Classify the modification according to the type of levers discussed in section 5.7.

2. Compute the impact on unit load, net availability, theoretical capacity, and effective capacity of the resource pool in question.

3. Compute the effect on the theoretical and effective capacity of the entire process.

5.2 Reconsider Kristen's cookie-baking enterprise from Exercise 4.2. Determine the unit load on the three resources in the process—Kristen, her roommate, and the oven. Assuming that all three resources are available 8 hours a day 100% of the time, determine the following:

a. The capacity of the cookie-making process,

b. The capacity utilization of the three resources, and

c. The cumulative effect of each of the following actions on the process capacity and flow rate:

    1. Purchasing another oven, and

    2. Training the roommate to perform the spooning operation.

5.3. MBPF Inc. is considering a new product line, the Super garage, which is projected to yield a per-unit profit contribution of $300. Unit loads for the various resources needed to produce the Super are estimated in Table 5.14.

a. Find the theoretical capacity of the Super garage, in terms of both units and profit contribution per hour.

b. Find the theoretical capacity of a product mix composed of 50% Standard, 25% Fancy, and 25% Super garages.

5.4 Reconsider the ACE production process introduced in chapter 4, Exercise 4.4.

a. What is the theoretical capacity of the ACE production process?

b. Unable to meet demand for this bike, Honda wants to increase throughput. A team member suggests cross-training the engine and seat assemblers. Should this suggestion be implemented? If so, why? If not, why not and what do you suggest?

TABLE 5.14 Unit Loads, Super Garage, MBPF Inc.

Resource Pool	Unit Load (Super Garage) (min. per unit)
Worker-S	10
Punch Press-R	30
Punch Press-B	50
Worker-PR	30
Worker-PB	50
Forming Machine-R	15
Forming Machine-B	15
Worker-FR	15
Worker-FB	15
Welding Gun	20
Worker-SA	20
Worker-FA	26
Inspector	50

www.prenhall.com/anupindi

For exercises based on Process Model go to http://www.prenhall.com/anupindi

---

References

Eppen, G.D., Gould, F.J., Schmidt, C.P., Moore, J.H., and Weatherford, L.R. 1998. *Introductory Management Science.* 5th Edition. Prentice Hall, Inc., Upper Saddle River, NJ.

Goldratt, E.M. and Cox, J. 1992. *The Goal.* Second Revised Edition. North River Press, Inc., Barrington, MA.

Goldratt, E.M. 1990. *Theory of Constraints,* North River Press, Inc., Croton-on-Hudson, New York.

Winston, W.L., 1991. *Operations Research: Applications and Algorithms.* Second Edition. PWS-Kent Publishing Company, Boston, MA.

6

Inventory Analysis

On the one hand, inventories that result from mismatches between process inflows and outflows are costly in both operational and financial terms. Operationally, they increase flow times, delay detection and correction of quality problems, and diminish incentives to improve the process. Financially, they entail costs in both physical storage and tied-up capital. On the other hand, inventory buffers decouple successive stages of processing, thereby permitting their relatively independent operation. Different types of inventory offer different benefits:

- **Theoretical inventory** is essential for maintaining throughput,
- **Cycle inventory** exploits economies of scale,
- **Seasonal inventory** smoothes capacity requirements,
- **Safety inventory** provides stockout protection, and
- **Speculative inventory** profits from price fluctuations.

Inventory management involves the optimal balancing of costs and benefits. The levers for reducing inventory levels include reducing the fixed cost of ordering, adjusting capacity and reducing fluctuations in supply, demand, and prices.

6.1 INTRODUCTION

In addition to flow time and flow rate (throughput), which we studied in chapters 4 and 5, *inventory* is the third basic measure of process performance. As with the other two measures, we first identify the *boundaries* of the process under study. Then we define inventory as the number of *flow units* present within those boundaries. Because average inventory is related by Little's law to both average flow time and average flow rate, controlling inventory indirectly controls flow rate, flow time, or both. Inventory also directly affects cost—another important measure of process performance. Because it affects several dimensions of process performance, inventory is thus a key lever in managing business process flows. In this chapter we analyze different types of inventories. We also show how they fluctuate over time and how they can be structurally controlled to balance costs and benefits.

Process flow management generally involves matching supply (inflows) and demand (outflows). When supply exceeds demand, the excess accumulates as inventory. Conversely, inventory is depleted when demand exceeds supply. Mismatches between supply and demand may be intentional or may result from unforeseen changes in supply, in processing, or in demand. Intentional mismatches usually arise under three conditions:

1. As seen in previous chapters, inventory is intrinsic to all processes, and a minimum level of inventory, referred to as *theoretical inventory,* is necessary to sustain a given throughput

and best achievable flow time. Because each activity takes time, there is always a certain amount of flow units undergoing each activity. Like theoretical flow time, theoretical inventory gives us an optimal target at which to aim.

2. When procurement, processing or transportation activities exhibit economies of scale, a process manager may find it cost efficient to purchase, process or transport multiple items simultaneously. For example, if suppliers offer quantity discounts or if transportation is more cost effective when handled in full truckloads, it may be more profitable to procure or transport many items at once, resulting in an instantaneous increase of inventory that must be depleted over time. Similarly, when baking bread in a large oven, it may be cost efficient to bake many loaves simultaneously.

3. Inventories decouple processing from temporal or seasonal changes in supply and demand and allow constant or level processing—which decreases average capacity requirements. Building seasonal output inventories during the year to sell during the Christmas season allows a uniform processing rate throughout the year. Similarly, keeping input inventories ensures constant availability of inputs even though suppliers may supply only on a weekly basis.

In chapter 7 we will show how inventories can be used as a protection against unforeseen changes in demand or supply. First, however, we begin in section 6.2 with the dynamics of inventory accumulation and depletion over time at various stages of processing. Section 6.3 discusses inventory dynamics under batch purchasing or processing. In sections 6.4 and 6.5 we identify various costs and benefits of carrying different types of inventories. Section 6.6 examines the optimal inventory level that balances these costs and benefits. Section 6.7 studies the effect of lead times on ordering decisions. Finally, section 6.8 concludes by summarizing some key levers for managing various types of inventory.

6.2   INVENTORY STOCKS AND FLUCTUATION

In this section we consider different types of inventories and how they fluctuate over time.

Classes of Inventory   Inventory includes all flow units within the process boundaries. Depending on the inventory's location or stage in the process, we can classify units of inventory as belonging to one of three categories:

1. Flow units that are waiting to begin processing constitute **inputs inventory.**

2. Flow units that are being processed constitute **in-process,** or **work-in-process, inventory.**

3. Processed flow units that have been processed but not yet exited process boundaries accumulate in **outputs inventory.**

Figure 6.1 shows the process flow and the three stages of inventory accumulation.
    If the process under study includes transportation between stages, then **pipeline,** or **in-transit, inventory** is also included with in-process inventory. We begin by establishing the following notations:

$$\text{Average input inventory} = I_i$$
$$\text{Average in-process inventory} = I_p$$
$$\text{Average output inventory} = I_o$$

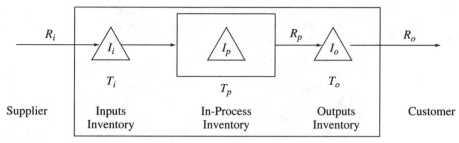

FIGURE 6.1 Process Flows and Inventories

Thus, average total inventory within process boundaries can be expressed as

$$I = I_i + I_p + I_o$$

Similarly, we denote the average times spent by a flow unit in each of the three stages of inventory as follows:

Average time spent in input inventory = T_i
Average time spent in in-process inventory = T_p
Average time spent in output inventory = T_o

Total average flow time, therefore, can be expressed as

$$T = T_i + T_p + T_o$$

If we denote average process flow rate in equilibrium as R, then flow units enter and leave each stage at this rate R. Applying Little's law to the entire process yields

$$I = R \times T$$

while applying it to each individual stage yields the following equations:

$$I_i = R \times T_i$$
$$I_p = R \times T_p$$
$$I_o = R \times T_o$$

To verify consistency we may add these three expressions to yield:

$$(I_i + I_p + I_o) = R \times (T_i + T_p + T_o)$$

or

$$I = R \times T$$

as the relationship among aggregate average inventory, flow time, and flow rate as before.

In a manufacturing operation, inputs inventory consists of raw materials, in-process inventory includes all work being processed, and outputs inventory contains finished goods. In a *service operation,* the flow unit is typically a customer. Inputs inventory, therefore, refers to customers waiting for service and in-process inventory refers to customers being served. If served customers leave the process immediately, there is no outputs inventory. We will analyze the special problems of managing inventories of customers in service operations in chapter 8.

Process Capacity   Although Little's law determines average inventory, an imbalance between inflows and outflows that develops over time will cause actual inventory to fluctuate around this average. Recall from chapter 3, however, that in any stable process—one in which average inflow and outflow rates are the same—long-run flow rates are in equilibrium. Hence, on average

$$\text{Flow rate } R = \text{Inflow rate } R_i = \text{Processing rate } R_p = \text{Outflow rate } R_o$$

where the processing rate is limited by the process capacity. As in chapter 5, every process has a maximal sustainable processing flow rate, which is called **process capacity.** No stable business process can, on a sustainable basis, either produce a higher outflow rate than its process capacity or process at a higher rate than the inflow rate. (When inventory storage space is limited, storage capacity may also constrain flow rate. We will discuss the impact of limited storage capacity in chapter 8. For now, we assume ample storage capacity.)

When inflow (supply) rate exceeds processing rate, inputs inventory accumulates. When processing rate exceeds outflow (demand) rate, outputs inventory accumulates. Even in an ideal situation with perfectly balanced flows—one in which inflow, processing, and outflow rates all equal—we still encounter work-in-process inventory. Indeed, it follows from Little's law and our definition of theoretical flow time T_{th} in chapter 4 that

$$I_p = R \times T_p \geq R \times T_{th} = I_{th}$$

Theoretical Inventory   To remain consistent with the concepts of theoretical flow time and theoretical capacity discussed earlier, we refer to I_{th} as **theoretical inventory.** Much like the concept of theoretical flow time, which represents the minimal flow time, the concept of theoretical inventory refers to *the minimum amount of inventory necessary to maintain a process throughput of R* and can be expressed as

$$R \times T_{th} = I_{th}$$

where T_{th} is the theoretical flow time and R is the throughput rate.

Theoretical inventory is the inventory for a given throughput if no flow unit ever had to wait in any buffer. It represents the minimal amount of flow units undergoing processing activities (no waiting) to sustain a given flow rate. Like theoretical flow time, theoretical inventory gives us an optimal target at which to aim.

Decoupling Processes   Together, input and output inventories form buffers that decouple the process from its environment, thereby permitting relatively independent operation. Input inventory permits the process manager to control processing rates independently of material inflow rates. Output inventory permits controlling the processing rate independently of product outflow (demand) rate.

Stockouts, Lost Sales, and Backlogs   Input and output inventories may be viewed and analyzed in the same way—each has its supplier and customer and each serves as a buffer between the two. If inflow (supply) into the buffer exceeds outflow (demand) from the buffer, the excess is added to the buffer. If outflow exceeds inflow, inventory in the buffer shrinks. If the buffer is emptied, the next stage in the process is "starved" and throughput suffers. Indeed, we maintain buffer inventories, both between different activities and between the process and its environment (consisting of suppliers and customers), precisely to prevent such starvation.

The result of starvation is a **stockout,** which is an event that occurs when current demand exceeds available inventory. A stockout can have different implications, depending on how customers react. Some customers may leave to satisfy their needs elsewhere, resulting in **lost sales.** Other customers may be willing to wait and have their needs satisfied later, in which case their demand is said to be **backlogged.** It is convenient to regard backlog as a **negative inventory level**—one that measures outstanding demand to be filled in the future. When the inventory level becomes nonnegative, the backlog disappears.

Inventory Dynamics   Recall from chapter 3 our definition of instantaneous inventory accumulation rate, the difference between inflow (supply) and outflow (demand) rates $R_i(t)$ and $R_o(t)$, which is expressed as

$$\Delta R(t) = R_i(t) - R_o(t)$$

Thus, it follows that

- If $R_i(t) > R_o(t)$, then inventory is accumulated at a rate $\Delta R(t) > 0$,
- If $R_i(t) = R_o(t)$, then inventory remains unchanged (supply equals demand), and
- If $R_i(t) < R_o(t)$, then inventory is depleted at a rate $-\Delta R(t) > 0$.

The change in inventory over a small time interval from t to $t + \Delta t$ can then be expressed as

$$\Delta I(t) = \Delta R(t) \times \Delta t$$

so that

$$I(t + \Delta t) = I(t) + \Delta R(t) \times \Delta t$$

Given the initial inventory position at time $t_0 < t_1$, adding these increments over time yields the inventory position at any time t_1. Assume, for example, that the inventory buildup rate is constant ΔR during the time interval $[t_0, t_1]$ (or that we use the time-averaged buildup rate ΔR). In this case, the following is true:

$$I(t_1) = I(t_0) + \Delta R \times (t_1 - t_0)$$

By looking at average inventory accumulation rates over certain periods of time, we can easily determine the inventory level, which changes linearly over a given period of time at the corresponding average rate ΔR. Suppose, for example, that while inflow units (supplies) arrive at a continuous rate during the morning only, our process is busy processing the entire day. To have sufficient supplies, the inflow rate during the morning will exceed the processing (or outflow) rate. This situation generates a linear buildup of input inventory during the morning up to time t_1 and is diagrammed in Figure 6.2. During the afternoon, however, even as processing continues, the inflow rate is zero from time t_1 until time t_2. Inventory, therefore, will be depleted at a constant rate (giving rise to a triangular *inventory buildup diagram*).

FIGURE 6.2 Inventory Fluctuation

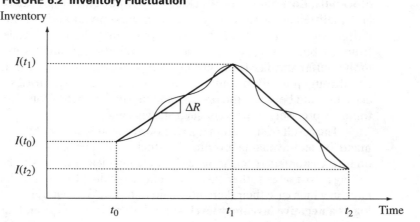

6.3   BATCH PURCHASING (PROCESSING)

We illustrate these concepts as a means of answering two important managerial questions that arise at MBPF Inc. during the processes of purchasing sheet metal (inputs) and producing garages (outputs). Because of transportation economies, MBPF buys sheet metal one full truckload at a time. Production of garages, on the other hand, takes place continuously at a constant rate. MBPF managers must know (1) *when* to purchase a new truckload of sheet metal and (2) *how much* to purchase at a time. Both decisions will affect the firm's balance sheet as they impact costs.

To answer these questions, we will analyze the inventory dynamics of the process view of MBPF (represented graphically in Figure 6.3). We must consider the following procedures that are valid in this purchasing scenario (but equally apply to a production scenario).

1. Inputs are procured (or outputs produced) in multiple units at a time—a system called batch purchasing (or processing), while

2. Processing (or consumption of output units) takes place continuously at a constant rate.

As we shall see, batch purchasing (or batch processing) is done to take advantage of economies of scale in purchasing, transportation, or processing.

Assume that one truck can hold Q rolls of sheet metal. Thus, the purchasing manager buys sheet metal in batches of Q rolls at a time. Because sheet metal is typically purchased in rolls, we treat *each roll* as our flow unit of analysis. The *entry point* is the point at which a batch of Q sheet-metal rolls is delivered to MBPF materials storage and added to the company's input inventory. Assume that MBPF's garage-building process is operating at a constant production rate R with (approximately) constant in-process inventory I_p. Suppose the *exit point* is the point at which completed garages leave the process immediately (instead of being stored for future shipment), MBPF has no outputs inventory, and I_o always equals zero. Total average inventory, therefore, is

$$I = I_i + I_p$$

Finally, assume that initial input inventory, just before the first sheet-metal delivery arrives at time $t = 0$, is zero.

Just after the first batch is received at time 0, we have $I_i(0) = Q$. Total process inventory level is the sum of input inventory and in-process inventory:

$$Q + I_p$$

After the first delivery, inflow rate remains at zero until the next shipment is received. Outflow rate, meanwhile, remains constant at R. After the first delivery, therefore, the process inventory buffer is depleted at a rate R, so that $\Delta R = -R$. To sustain its throughput R, production keeps in-process inventory level I_p constant. Consequently, only input inventory is depleted at rate R, whereby it will reach zero after time t_c, so that $I_i(t_c) = 0$. Thus we have

FIGURE 6.3 Process Flow at MBPF

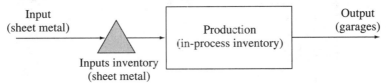

$$I_i(t_c) = Q - R \times t_c = 0$$

so that

$$t_c = Q / R$$

Simply stated, it takes Q/R time units to deplete the purchased input stock of size Q at rate R. If the process manager always orders in batches of size Q, the same cycle is repeated every t_c time units. Over time, the resulting *inventory buildup diagram* displays the sawtooth pattern shown in Figure 6.4. It answers our first question: MBPF should order another batch of sheet metal to arrive just at a time when the total inventory drops to I_p (and thus the input buffer is empty). As a result, MBPF should place its orders so that a batch arrives every t_c time units.

Under batch purchasing and a constant processing rate, the input inventory profile is triangular with height Q. In a typical order cycle, average input inventory, called **cycle inventory,** is then

$$I_i = Q / 2$$

Average total inventory is then

$$I = I_p + Q / 2$$

In terms of flow time, the first flow unit purchased in each batch goes into production immediately. The last unit, meanwhile, spends all of the $t_c = Q / R$ time units in input inventory buffer before its processing can begin. Thus, an average flow unit spends $t_c / 2 = (Q / 2) / R$ time units in input inventory storage. Alternately, we can apply Little's law to determine the average flow time spent in the input buffer as

$$T_i = I_i / R = (Q / 2) / R$$

Similarly, average total flow time is given by Little's law as

$$T = I / R = T_i + T_p = (Q / 2) / R + I_p / R$$

Each flow unit, therefore, spends an average time of $(Q / 2) / R$ in the input buffer and additional time of I_p / R units in process. Example 6.1 illustrates the situation at MBPF, Inc.

FIGURE 6.4 Inventory Buildup Diagram with Batch Size _Q_

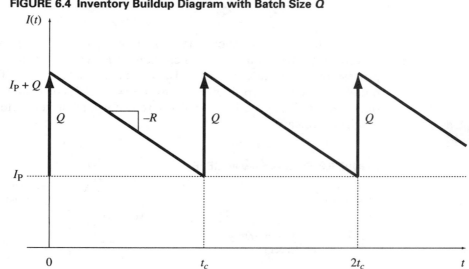

> **EXAMPLE 6.1**
>
> Suppose that MBPF produces 1,000 garages each week and that each garage needs one roll of sheet metal. Assume that MBPF currently purchases 4,000 rolls at a time. The company will thus be ordering once every four weeks, or $t_c = 4$ weeks. Accordingly, average sheet-metal inventory will be $I_i = 4,000 / 2 = 2,000$ rolls, and a typical roll spends an average of two weeks in storage. Thus MBPF carries an average cycle inventory of 2,000 rolls.

6.4   INVENTORY COSTS

Carrying inventory is expensive, both in operational and financial terms. Assume that a firm is carrying a large inventory of work-in-process and outputs. If market demand shifts to new products, the firm is left with two choices. One is to empty the process by scrapping all current work-in-process and liquidating the obsolete outputs inventory at marked-down prices, and then quickly introducing the new product. This results in a significant loss incurred on the old inventory. The other choice is to finish processing all in-process inventory and sell all old inventory before introducing the new product. This delay results in reduced responsiveness to the market.

Large inventories also delay the execution of design changes, because current inventory must be processed and sold first. Moreover, the buildup of inventories between successive processing stages not only obstructs workers' view of the total process, but also discourages teamwork and coordination (because large interstage inventory decouples stages and allows them to operate independently of other process activities). We will discuss these operational inefficiencies from holding inventories further in chapter 10.

Inventory Holding Cost   Carrying inventory also entails a *financial cost* called **inventory holding cost,** which has two components:

1. **Physical holding cost** refers to *the out-of-pocket expense of storing inventory.* It includes all operating costs (insurance, security, warehouse rental, lighting, heating and cooling of the storage) plus all costs that may be entailed before inventory can be sold (spoilage, obsolescence, pilferage, or necessary rework). Physical holding cost per unit of time (typically a year) is usually expressed as a fraction h of the variable cost C of acquiring (or producing) one flow unit of inventory. Thus, the physical holding cost of carrying a unit of inventory for one time unit is hC.

2. **Opportunity cost** of holding inventory refers to the forgone return on the funds invested in inventory rather than in alternate projects. Indeed, inventory shows up as an *asset* on the balance sheet because it is an economic resource that is expected to be of future value. The firm could realize this value by liquidating it and investing the proceeds elsewhere. Specifically, the sooner inventory sells, the sooner it creates accounts receivable and the sooner accounts receivable generates cash. The opportunity cost of holding one flow unit is usually expressed as rC, where r is the firm's rate of return (measured as annual percentage return on capital) and C is the variable cost of acquiring (or producing) one flow unit of inventory (measured as cost / flow unit).

Thus, measured as cost per flow unit held in inventory for one time unit (e.g., a year), unit inventory holding cost is expressed as follows:

$$H = (h + r)C$$

Example 6.2 computes H at our MBPF company.

> **EXAMPLE 6.2**
>
> In our MBPF example, suppose that each roll of sheet metal costs $C = \$1{,}300$. Assume, too, that the company's annual cost of capital is $r = 15\%$. In this case, each dollar's worth of inventory carries an opportunity cost of $\$0.15$ per year in terms of possible alternate uses of the funds. Because $\$1{,}300$ is tied up in each roll of sheet metal, the annual cost of each roll in financial terms is
>
> $$rC = \$(0.15)(1{,}300) = \$195 \,/\, \text{year}$$
>
> MBPF has estimated that the physical holding cost (operating and storage costs) of one roll is about $\$65$ per year: $hC = \$65 \,/\, \text{year}$.
>
> Thus, for every roll stored in inventory for one year, MBPF's holding cost is $H = rC + hC = \$260 \,/\, \text{year}$.

If average inventory level is I, total inventory holding cost per year will be $I \times H$. If we wish to decrease inventory holding cost, we have two levers:

1. Decrease average inventory level I, or
2. Decrease unit inventory holding cost H (typically by getting price concessions on h or C).

6.5   INVENTORY BENEFITS

If inventories are costly, why do firms carry them? One reason follows from Little's law—a minimum level of in-process inventory is necessary to maintain a given process throughput of R:

$$I_p = R \times T_p \geq R \times T_{th} = I_{th}$$

Because theoretical flow time T_{th} is the minimal time needed to transform one flow unit from input to output, theoretical inventory I_{th} represents the absolute minimal inventory needed to maintain a given process throughput of R. Reducing inventories to less than the theoretical inventory will result in a loss of throughput. In transportation and logistics, flow units are transported from one location to another. The units that are being transported (that are en route) at a given point in time constitute *in-transit inventory*. In-transit inventory is necessary to allow the functioning of a business process in which activities are distributed over many locations.

In practice, firms plan and maintain input, in-process, and output inventories, yet we have seen that input inventories arise from supply inflows in excess of processing requirements, and that output inventories arise from processing in excess of demand outflows. The question, therefore, is why do firms intentionally plan for such excesses? In the rest of this section, we will survey four reasons.

6.5.1   Economies of Scale

One reason firms intentionally plan for such excesses is to take advantage of **economies of scale** that may arise from either external or internal causes. If, for example, an external supplier offers quantity discounts, the buyer may find it economical to procure in quantities larger than those needed for immediate processing. Internally, perhaps the buyer finds it more economical to procure or process in large batches because a fixed cost may have to be incurred each time an order is placed or a new batch is processed.

Procuring inputs often involves a **fixed order cost**—the administrative cost of processing the order, transporting the material, and receiving and inspecting the delivery. Each of these costs may add a significant fraction to total cost that is *independent of order size*.

For example, if a truck is dispatched each time an order must be picked up, the cost of the trip does not depend on the quantity ordered (up to the size limit of the truck). In producing outputs, the process of starting a new production run may involve a **fixed setup cost**— the *time and materials required to set up a process* (e.g., clean equipment and change tools). An ice cream maker, for instance, must clean pots before changing from making chocolate to vanilla ice cream. (In the next section we will denote fixed setup or ordering cost per batch as S, which we will measure as cost / batch regardless of batch size.) The effect of batch purchasing (processing) on the cycle inventory was discussed in detail in section 6.3.

With the fixed setup costs, it may be more economical to procure (or produce) infrequently in large batches, thereby spreading the fixed cost over more units. Another reason to procure in larger quantities than immediately required is that external suppliers may offer quantity discounts to help offset their own fixed setup costs. As discussed in section 6.3 this mismatch between inflows and outflows creates **cycle inventory,** which *permits producers to meet constant demand by means of intermittent economic ordering.*

6.5.2   Production and Capacity Smoothing

A related reason for planning supplies in excess of demand is **production and capacity smoothing.** If demand fluctuates seasonally, it may be more economical to smooth (or level) production by *maintaining a constant processing rate,* rather than vary it to chase demand. Leveling the processing rate reduces the fixed costs of making capacity adjustments (hiring or firing workers, using overtime, or keeping resources idle), although a trade-off occurs in the higher variable costs of holding inventory.

Examples of leveling include building inventories of toys throughout the year for the Christmas season or producing lawn mowers year round for spring and summer sale. Demand fluctuations are then absorbed by **seasonal inventories** rather than by intermittent and expensive adjustments in processing capacity. (We will have more to say about leveling in section 6.6.)

6.5.3   Stockout Protection

The third reason for holding inventories is to protect against unexpected supply disruptions on the input side or surges in demand for the output. Any number of events— supplier strikes, fire, transportation delays, foul weather—may reduce input availability. Potential consequences to the buyer include process starvation, downtime, and temporary reduction in throughput. Many producers, therefore, maintain **safety inventories** of inputs to insulate the process from supply uncertainty and continue operation despite supply shortages.

Likewise, because customer-demand forecasts are usually inaccurate, planning process output to meet only forecasted demand may result in stockouts, delayed deliveries, lost sales, and customer dissatisfaction. Thus, many producers maintain safety inventories of outputs to absorb excess demand and to ensure product availability and customer service despite forecast errors. (In chapter 7 we explore in detail the relationship between the degree of stockout protection provided and the level of safety inventory needed.)

6.5.4   Price Speculation

The fourth reason for holding inventories is to profit from probable changes in the market prices of inputs or outputs. In addition to protecting against sudden price increases due to such crises as wars or oil shortages, **speculative inventories** of commodities (such as corn and wheat, gold and platinum) and financial assets (such as stocks, bonds, and currencies) can be held as investments. As prices fluctuate over time, investors can manage their inflows (purchases) and outflows (sales) to optimize the financial value of their inventories. In the semiconductor industry, a rapid price decline of chips over time gives computer manufacturers a strong incentive to delay purchasing chips as inputs and wait to enjoy the latest, and often lowest, purchase price. The process manager then holds little speculative inventory. Although speculative inventories are important in finance and economics, we will not study them in any detail in this book, as our focus is more on processing operations.

6.6 OPTIMAL CYCLE INVENTORY AND ECONOMIES OF SCALE

Process managers want to determine inventory levels that optimally balance costs and benefits of carrying various inventories. As discussed in chapters 4 and 5, theoretical inventory is related to theoretical flow time and flow rates. We will discuss safety inventory in chapter 7. In the remainder of this chapter, we show how to determine the optimal level of cycle inventory—that balances the costs of holding inventory with the benefits of economies of scale. In doing so, we distinguish two causes of scale economies:

1. Economies arising from a *fixed-cost component* in either procurement (order cost) or production (setup cost), and

2. Economies arising from *one-time price discounts* offered by suppliers.

We conclude by indicating how seasonal inventories balance holding costs with the costs of capacity adjustments needed to meet demand fluctuations.

6.6.1 Fixed Cost of Procurement or Production: Economic Order Quantity (EOQ)

As mentioned, our analysis applies equally to input, in-process, and output buffers. Indeed, in the setting of batch procurement or purchasing, we analyze input buffers, while in the setting of batch processing we analyze in-process and output buffers. Suppose outflow from the buffer occurs at a constant rate of R flow units per unit of time (e.g., a year). Assume that the process manager can control inflow into the buffer. Each time the inflow is initiated by the procurement of material (or the production of output), a fixed cost of ordering (or setup) S is incurred, regardless of the quantity procured (produced). It is therefore more economical to procure inputs (produce outputs) infrequently in batches, even though outflow requirements remain steady over time. Let Q be the size of each batch procured at a single time. (From here on we will analyze batch purchasing; our analysis directly applies to batch processing too.) To satisfy an annual outflow rate of R, we must order R/Q times per year. Our annual order cost, therefore, is

$$S \times R/Q$$

This order cost decreases when batch quantity Q increases because the more we order at a given time, the fewer orders we need to place over the course of a year.

Conversely, recall from section 6.3 that average cycle inventory is $I = Q/2$ units. Consequently, annual inventory holding cost is expressed as follows:

$$I \times H = (Q/2)H$$

Note that this cost increases when batch size Q increases.

Finally, we must consider annual cost of materials procured, which is given by

$$C \times R$$

where C is the unit variable cost. This annual purchasing cost is independent of the choice of the batch size Q. (Note that we have assumed the unit variable cost C to be constant and receive no price discounts for purchasing in large quantities.)

Thus, the total annual order, inventory holding, and material purchase cost is given by

$$TC = S\frac{R}{Q} + \frac{Q}{2}H + CR$$

Example 6.3 provides an application.

EXAMPLE 6.3

Suppose that it costs $10,000 each time MBPF places an order for and receives sheet metal regardless of the quantity purchased. Hence, $S =$ $10,000. Recall from Example 6.2 that:

- each roll of sheet metal costs $C = \$1,300$.
- MBPF's inventory holding cost was computed as $H = \$260$ / roll carried per year, and

- MBPF's throughput rate is 1,000 per week, or $R =$ 52,000 / year

If MBPF procures 4,000 rolls in each order, we have $Q = 4,000$. Annual cost can thus be computed as

$$TC = \$68,250,000.$$

Remember that of the total cost TC, the order cost component decreases when batch size increases and the holding-cost component increases when batch size increases. Figure 6.5 shows an optimal batch size Q^* that minimizes total annual cost TC. This optimal order quantity is called the **economic order quantity (EOQ)** and can be found analytically using calculus. Taking the first derivative of the total cost function TC with respect to Q yields

$$\frac{dTC}{dQ} = -S\frac{R}{Q^2} + \frac{H}{2}$$

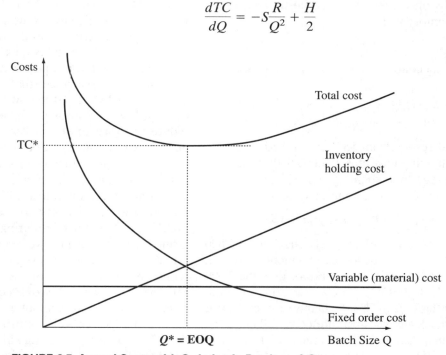

FIGURE 6.5 Annual Costs with Ordering in Batches of Q

If we set the first derivative of the total cost function equal to zero (which is a condition to minimize TC), solving for Q yields

$$Q^* = \sqrt{\frac{2SR}{H}}$$

also known as the **EOQ formula.**

Notice that the optimal order quantity *exactly balances annual order and holding costs.* Thus, we have

$$S\frac{R}{Q^*} = \frac{Q^*}{2}H$$

If we substitute in the total annual cost expression and simplify, we find that minimum annual total cost is

$$TC^* = \sqrt{2SRH} + CR$$

Figure 6.5 shows all costs as functions of the order quantity as well as the economic order quantity and corresponding costs. The optimal order quantity balances order and holding costs. It falls at the intersection of order cost and holding cost. Example 6.4 illustrates inventory management at MBPF, Inc.

EXAMPLE 6.4

In Example 6.3, substituting known information into the EOQ formula yields

$$Q^* = \sqrt{\frac{2SR}{H}} = \sqrt{\frac{2 \times \$10,000 \times 52,000}{\$260}} = 2,000$$

Thus MBPF should order sheet metal in lots of 2,000 rolls, once every 2 weeks. Resulting average cycle inventory will be

$$Q^* / 2 = 1,000 \text{ rolls}$$

We can calculate the minimum annual total cost TC^* as

$$TC^* = (52,000 / 2,000) \times 10,000 + (2,000 / 2) \\ \times 260 + (52,000 \times 1,300) = \$68,120,000$$

This total results from \$520,000 in order and inventory holding cost plus \$67,600,000 in material cost. Average time spent by a sheet-metal roll in the input buffer can be computed as

$$T_i = (Q / 2) / R = 1 / 52 \text{ year} = 1 \text{ week}$$

Suppose that MBPF's full truckload is 2,500 rolls at a time. It may be more convenient, therefore, to order 2,500 rolls at a time rather than the 2,000 specified by the EOQ formula. Deviating from the EOQ (in this case by 25%) will increase total costs, but not much—if we substitute $Q = 2,500$ into the TC formula, we find that total annual cost would be only \$13,000 higher than the minimum. This figure reflects an increase of 0.02% in total cost and 2.5% in order and inventory holding cost.

Thus, the total cost curve is relatively flat around EOQ, as shown in Figure 6.5, and some deviation from EOQ will not significantly increase the total annual costs. EOQ thus provides a ballpark estimate of the range in which we should operate, and we may safely decide to deviate somewhat from the exact value for certain considerations not included in the model. This flexibility makes the model more robust and useful from a practical perspective.

We have already seen that ordering in batches of 2,000 adds 1 week to the flow time of sheet metal through MBPF. Now assume that MBPF wants to reduce batch size to 1,000—a change that would reduce flow time by 0.5 weeks. Changing batch size without changing other factors will increase total cost: Because optimal batch size yields minimum total cost, any deviation from it will increase total cost. Recall, however, that one key lever available to MBPF is reducing fixed ordering (or setup) cost S. Using the EOQ formula, we can infer that in order for 1,000 to be its optimal batch size, MBPF should reduce S to \$2,500 (from the current value of \$10,000). The availability of electronic data interchange (EDI) and computerized ordering has played an important role for firms trying to reduce their fixed ordering costs, making it economical to order smaller quantities more frequently.

Three managerial insights follow from the EOQ formula.

Fixed Order (Setup) Cost Reduction   The optimal batch size Q^* increases if fixed order (setup) cost S increases. The higher the fixed cost, the more we should order at a time to reduce the total number of orders placed per year (or the more we should produce in each batch to reduce total number of setups per year). Conversely, lowering fixed cost would make ordering smaller quantities (producing smaller batches) more economical, which also will reduce average inventory and flow time. As we will see in chapter 10, reducing setup costs will be a major factor in implementing lean operations and Just-in-Time systems.

Inventory vs. Sales Growth   The optimal batch Q^* *is proportional to the square root of outflow rate. Quadrupling* outflow rate, therefore, will only *double* EOQ and the cycle inventory—and thus average flow time in the buffer. Therefore, doubling of a company's annual sales does not require a doubling of cycle inventories. Indeed, optimal inventory management would entail ordering more frequently, so that the 100% growth in throughput can be sustained by a mere 41% (from the square root of 2) increase in cycle inventory.

Centralization and Economies of Scale   The fact that the optimal batch size Q^* is proportional to the square root of the outflow rate R illustrates the scale economies and leads to the idea of inventory centralization. If a firm has two decentralized input warehouses that order independently, it can gain by merging them into one centralized warehouse with centralized purchasing. Indeed, the total average cycle inventory I_i^d for two decentralized, separate warehouses (assuming both face identical cost structure S and H, serve identical processes with same throughput R, and thus both order Q^d according to the EOQ formula) is

$$I_i^d = 2 \times \frac{Q^d}{2} = \sqrt{\frac{2SR}{H}}$$

with total fixed order and holding cost (excluding the variable material cost)

$$TC^d = 2 \times \sqrt{2SRH}$$

If, however, we merge the two warehouses into one central warehouse that will serve a total outflow $2R$ we get an average cycle inventory I_i^c of

$$I_i^c = \frac{Q^c}{2} = \frac{1}{2}\sqrt{\frac{2S(2R)}{H}} = \frac{1}{\sqrt{2}}I_i^d$$

with the total order cost of the centralized warehouse

$$TC^c = \sqrt{2S(2R)H} = \frac{1}{\sqrt{2}}TC^d$$

In conclusion, by consolidating two independent identical warehouses into one central warehouse, we benefit from increased economies of scale—both physical cycle inventory and financial fixed and holding costs decrease by a factor of $1 - \dfrac{1}{\sqrt{2}}$ which is 30%, compared to the decentralized situation. Example 6.5 values the savings to be obtained at MBPF, Inc.

EXAMPLE 6.5

MBPF, Inc. is contemplating expanding into the midwest region of the United States in the year 2000. Preliminary estimates of demand for garages in the midwest region are similar to those in the eastern region currently. That is, the average demand is estimated to be 1,000 garages per week. MBPF, Inc. needs to build a second manufacturing plant in the Midwest region, similar to the current plant. For procurement of raw materials it is considering two options. Option A (decentralized system) is to procure raw material from a regional supplier and store it in a warehouse close to the proposed factory location in the Midwest. Option B (centralized system) is to continue sourcing raw material from the current supplier and store it in the warehouse in the eastern United States. Setup and unit holding costs remain as before (Example 6.2)—both options have identical order setup costs of $S = \$10,000$/order and annual unit holding costs of $H = \$260$. The vice president of operations has to evaluate the implications of these two options.

Under option A, each warehouse will order independently the optimal batch size of 2,000 rolls (see Example 6.4). The total average cycle inventory and cost (excluding material cost) is:

$$I_i^d = 2 \times \frac{2,000}{2} = 2,000 \text{ rolls}$$

$$TC^d = 2 \times \sqrt{2SRH} = \$1,040,000 / \text{yr}$$

Under option B, MBPF would merge the two warehouses into one central warehouse and the new order size would be

$$Q^c = \sqrt{\frac{2S(2R)}{H}} = \sqrt{\frac{2 \times \$10,000 \times 2 \times 52,000}{\$260}} = 2,828$$

Corresponding average cycle inventory and costs are:

$$I_i^c = \frac{2,828}{2} = 1,414 \text{ rolls}$$

$$TC^c = \sqrt{2 \times 10,000 \times 2 \times 52,000 \times 260} = \$735,400/\text{yr}$$

which is about 30% lower than that for the decentralized operation.

6.6.2 Price Discounts: Forward Buying

In addition to fixed ordering costs, suppliers' price discounts for ordering in large quantities can provide scale economies in procurement. Under the practice known as **trade promotion,** the supplier offers incentives in the form of one-time opportunities to procure materials at reduced unit costs, or perhaps notifies the buyer of an upcoming price increase and offers the buyer one last chance to order at the preincrease price. In both cases, *the buyer has an incentive to fill future needs by purchasing a single, large quantity* (Q^f) *at the reduced price.*

Forward Buying   Taking advantage of such an opportunity by purchasing future needs today is called **forward buying.** Once the trade promotion is over, the buyer will resume ordering at the regular (or higher) price in the usual batches of size Q^* (or ordering a smaller batch size at the higher new cost). The resulting inventory buildup diagram is shown in bold in Figure 6.6—forward buying results in a big, one-time increase in inventory. In dotted lines, the figure also shows the usual sawtooth profile without forward buying. We wish to determine the impact of a trade promotion on forward buying by comparing Q^f with Q^*.

Consider process inflow at a normal price of $\$C$ / unit. At this price, the process manager normally orders Q^* units per order, but suppose a supplier offers a one-time discount of $\$d$ / unit, such that for a certain period, the price is

$$(\$C - d) / \text{unit}$$

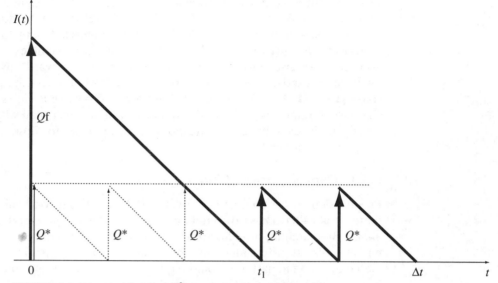

FIGURE 6.6 Forward Buying Q^f versus Regular Buying Q^*

after which regular price $C will resume. The process manager must choose the quantity Q^f to order at the discounted price. To reduce total material purchasing cost, the manager would like to increase order size. This change, however, will increase the amount of inventory held—and thus holding cost. In addition to a lower purchase cost, there will be a savings on fixed ordering cost because the number of orders will be reduced. Our manager's goal is to strike an optimal trade-off that minimizes total cost.

The optimal forward buying quantity is computed in the Appendix at the end of this chapter as:

$$Q^f = \frac{Rd}{(r + h)(C - d)} + \frac{C}{C - d}Q^*$$

If demand up through the next anticipated trade promotion is Q_t, our process manager should order the smaller of Q^f and Q_t. Example 6.6 quantifies the large inventory spikes that can result from forward buying.

EXAMPLE 6.6

Suppose that MBPF's sheet-metal supplier has offered a temporary 5% discount. How much forward buying should the process manager do? Over how many normal order periods will this one-time purchase last?

We will use the numbers from Example 6.4. If we factor in the discount

$$d = (5\%)(\$1,300) = \$65$$

we arrive at the following purchase order (in lots):

$$Q^f = \frac{52,000 \times 65}{0.2 \times (1,300 - 65)} + \frac{1,300 \times 2,000}{1,300 - 65} = 15,789$$

The 5% discount would induce MBPF to increase its order size more than sevenfold! The forward buy, therefore, will cover seven normal order periods. The supplier, of course, will experience an enormous spike in demand followed by very low demand for a long period.

The Effect of Everyday Low Pricing Order increases designed to take advantage of short-term discounts can generate significant increases in inventory—and thus material flow time—in the supply chain. This realization has led many firms to adopt a policy of **everyday low pricing (EDLP).** If retailers charge constant, everyday low prices with no temporary discounts, customers will not exercise forward buying. The same argument can be used upstream in the supply chain. If wholesalers charge **everyday low purchase prices (EDLPP),** retailers will not forward buy. Thus, flows in the entire supply chain will be smoother and total inventories will be lower than when forward buying is practiced. We examine the implications of such policies for flows in supply-chain management in chapter 10.

6.6.3 Capacity Smoothing

Product demand often fluctuates over time. One strategy for dealing with demand fluctuations is called **chase demand strategy**—*producing quantities exactly to match demand.* By matching production with demand, the firm carries no inventory. Unfortunately, it also transfers all demand fluctuations to its processing system. In particular, matching demand patterns would require constantly altering process capacity or its utilization. During one month, for example, the firm may be forced to employ overtime labor, but then be forced to idle full-time workers the next month. The firm may be obliged to hire and lay off workers as needed and to employ outsourcing and subcontracting at times of heavy demand. Even though the firm saves on inventory holding costs, it will find all such capacity adjustments to be costly.

The other extreme is called **level production strategy**—which involves *keeping process capacity and its utilization constant.* Under this strategy, the firm produces at a steady rate, building inventories in periods of low demand and depleting them when demand is high. Because inventories serve as buffers that absorb demand fluctuations, they are called seasonal inventories. Though increasing inventory holding costs, level production strategy minimizes the cost of capacity changes entailed by chase demand strategy.

Which strategy is better—chase demand—or level production? The answer depends on *the relative magnitudes of the fixed costs of altering capacity and the variable costs of holding inventory.* It is wiser to level production if capacity changes are expensive, but wiser to chase demand if inventories are too expensive to carry. Not surprisingly, the true optimum lies somewhere between these two extremes, employing a combination of capacity adjustments and inventory buffers. The problem of finding this optimal combination is called **aggregate production planning,** detailed discussion of which is beyond the scope of this book; we refer the reader to Nahmias (1997).

6.7 EFFECT OF LEAD TIMES ON ORDERING DECISIONS

In many practical settings, process managers will have to make periodic ordering decisions (as opposed to a one-time decision such as the forward buy decision in the previous section). There are two fundamental questions that a process manager then needs to address:

1. How much to order?
2. When to reorder?

The first question depends on the trade-off between some fixed costs of placing orders and the variable holding costs of carrying inventory resulting from ordering in quantities larger than one. An example of this essential tradeoff was discussed in the previous section that led to the Economic Order Quantity (*EOQ*) formula.

The second question depends on how long it takes to replenish inventory. The time lag between the arrival of the replenishment and the time the order was placed is called the replenishment **lead time,** which is denoted by L. Clearly, we should order L units of time before we expect the inventory level to drop to zero. (This was exactly what we did in Example 6.1.)

Instead of keeping track of time, we can keep track of inventory levels and reorder as soon as available inventory drops below a certain **reorder point (*ROP*),** which is the available inventory at the time of placing an order. Clearly, when we process continuously at a constant rate R, we should reorder when we have just enough inventory to cover the requirements during the replenishment lead time L. Thus, the reorder point is found as:

$$ROP = L \times R$$

If the lead time L is less than the time between orders (which we calculated earlier as $t_c = Q/R$ in section 6.3), then the ROP is the inventory that we have on hand at the time of placing an order. The reorder point decisions can be superimposed on the inventory buildup diagram as shown in Figure 6.7. Example 6.7 illustrates the ROP concept.

FIGURE 6.7 Ordering Decisions and the Reorder Point

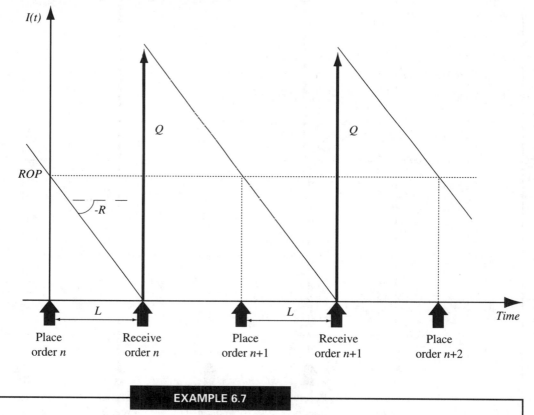

EXAMPLE 6.7

Suppose the replenishment lead time for ordering sheet-metal rolls is $L = 1$ week. With the demand rate $R = 1,000$ rolls/week, the reorder point is:

Thus, whenever the input inventory level drops below 1,000 rolls, the process manager should place a new order with the supplier.

$ROP = L \times R = 1$ week $\times 1,000$ rolls / week $= 1,000$ rolls

EXAMPLE 6.8

Suppose the replenishment lead time for ordering sheet-metal rolls is $L = 3$ weeks (instead of the 1 week assumed in Example 6.7). With the demand rate $R = 1,000$ rolls/week, the reorder point becomes:

$$ROP = L \times R = 3 \text{ weeks} \times 1,000 \text{ rolls / week}$$
$$= 3,000 \text{ rolls}$$

In Example 6.4, we calculated that the optimal order size is $Q^* = 2,000$ so that the time between ordering is $t_c = Q/R = 2$ weeks, which is less than the lead time L. Thus, there will always be one previous order outstanding at the time of ordering. Indeed, in this case the reorder point ROP of 3,000 represents the sum of on-hand inventory (1,000) and one outstanding order ($Q^* = 2,000$) at the time of placing an order. The corresponding ordering decisions over time are shown in Figure 6.8.

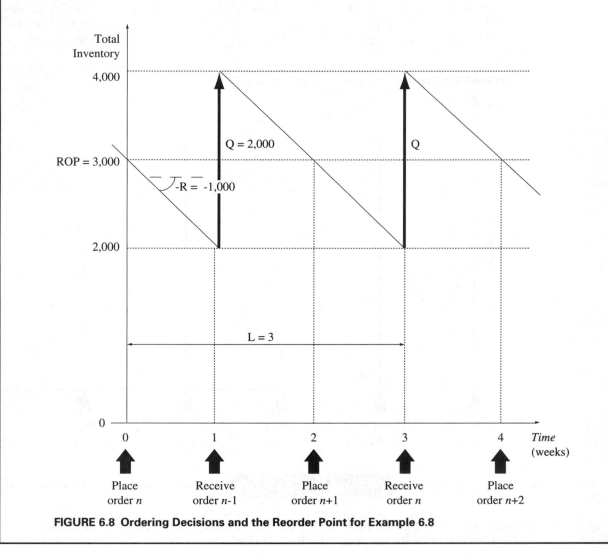

FIGURE 6.8 Ordering Decisions and the Reorder Point for Example 6.8

If, on the other hand, the lead time L is *larger* than the time between orders (i.e., $L > Q/R$), the ROP will be larger than the order quantity Q. This means that at the time we place our current order there will be previous orders outstanding that will be received before the current order is received (at a time L periods from now). In that case, ROP measures the sum of on-hand inventory and all outstanding orders (called **on-order inventory**) at the time of placing an order, as illustrated by Example 6.8.

In reality, there may be uncertainty in both demand rate R and lead time L. We will see in the next chapter how to adjust the reorder point to incorporate a safety cushion, called **safety inventory,** to protect against this uncertainty.

6.8   LEVERS FOR MANAGING INVENTORIES

We conclude this chapter by summarizing the most important ways of controlling the different types of inventories that we have discussed.

Theoretical Inventory   Theoretical in-process inventory, which is expressed as

$$I_{th} = R \times T_{th}$$

is determined by throughput R and theoretical flow time T_{th}. As discussed in chapters 4 and 5, inventory can be controlled by managing these two measures. T_{th} can be reduced by any one of the following measures:

- Reducing critical activity times,
- Eliminating non-value-adding activities,
- Moving work from critical to noncritical activities (as defined in chapter 4), and
- Redesigning the process to replace sequential processing with parallel processing.

Theoretical in-process inventory can also be reduced by reducing process flow rate R. This option will reduce the economic value of output per unit of time. Regardless, theoretical in-process inventory is usually only a small fraction of total inventory, and managers like to reduce it primarily to reduce flow time.

Cycle Inventory   Average cycle inventory is expressed as $Q^*/2$, where Q^* is the optimal batch size given by

$$Q^* = \sqrt{2SR/H}$$

Thus, the only sensible lever for reducing cycle inventory is reducing fixed setup (or order) cost S, which will reduce optimal batch size and average cycle inventory (and flow time). Reducing fixed setup or ordering costs can be achieved by simplifying ordering and by making resources flexible so that setups or changeovers between production runs can be implemented quickly and easily. Excessive cycle inventories resulting from forward buying can be reduced by negotiating everyday low prices with suppliers instead of seeking short-time trade promotions.

Seasonal Inventory   Seasonal inventory results from temporal fluctuations in outflows, coupled with the high costs of adjusting capacity to meet the fluctuations. It can be reduced by using pricing and incentives to promote stable demand patterns. Increasing resource-volume flexibility so that resources can produce at various flow rates to match demand fluctuations will also make it less expensive to adjust seasonal inventory levels. Similarly, using flexible resources to produce counter-cyclical products makes it possible to level the load without building up inventory. A classical example is a company that produces snowblowers in winter and lawn mowers in summer, both with a single flexible production process.

Safety Inventory   Safety inventory cushions the process against unexpected supply disruptions or surges in demand. The basic response to reducing its levels is reducing uncertainty in supply and demand. Ensuring reliable suppliers and stable demand patterns largely eliminates the need for safety inventories. We will discuss the role of safety inventory more fully in the next chapter.

Speculative Inventory   Speculative inventory permits a firm to do one of two things:

1. Reduce the total cost of purchasing materials, or
2. Increase profits by taking advantage of uncertain fluctuations in a product's price.

Negotiating stable prices would eliminate speculative inventories and the associated portfolio risk.

Problem Set

6.1 Suppose you purchase from a supplier at $4 per unit a part with which you assemble red widgets. On average, you use 50,000 units of this part each year. Every time you order this particular part, you incur a sizable ordering cost of $800 regardless of the number of parts you order. Your cost of capital is 20% per year.
   a. How many parts should you purchase each time you place an order?
   b. To satisfy annual demand, how many times per year will you place orders for this part?

6.2 BIM Computers Inc. sells its popular PC-PAL model to distributors at a price of $1,250 per unit. BIM's profit margin is 20%. Factory orders average 400 units a week. Currently, BIM works in a batch mode and produces a 4-week supply in each batch. BIM's production process involves three stages:
   • PC board assembly (the automatic insertion of parts and the manual loading, wave soldering, and laser bonding of electronic components purchased from outside sources),
   • Final assembly, and
   • Testing.

When the firm wants to change production from one model to another, it must shut down its assembly line for half a day. The company estimates that downtime costs one-half hour of supervisory time and an additional $2,000 in lost production and wages paid to workers directly involved in changeover operations. Salaries for supervisory personnel involved amount to $1,500 a day.

Although BIM products are generally regarded as high quality, intense price competition in the industry has forced the firm to embark on a cost-cutting and productivity-improvement campaign. In particular, BIM wants to operate with leaner inventories but without sacrificing customer service. Releasing some of the funds tied up in outputs inventory would allow BIM to invest in a new product development project that is expected to yield a risk-adjusted return of 20%. Assume 50 workweeks in a year and 5 working days in a week.
   a. Determine BIM's total annual cost of production and inventory control.
   b. Compute the economic batch size and the resulting cost savings.

6.3 Victor sells a line of upscale evening dresses in his boutique. He charges $300 per dress, and sales average 30 dresses per week. Currently, Victor orders a 10-week supply at one time from the manufacturer. He pays $150 per dress, and it takes 2 weeks to receive each delivery. Victor estimates his administrative cost of placing each order at $225. Because he estimates his cost of capital at 20%, each dollar's worth of idle inventory costs him $0.20 per year.

    a. Compute Victor's total annual cost of ordering and carrying inventory.

    b. If Victor wishes to minimize his annual cost, when and how much should he order in each batch? What will be his annual cost?

    c. Compare the number of inventory turns under the current and proposed policies.

6.4 A retailer estimates her fixed cost for placing an order at $1,000. Presently she orders in optimal quantities of 400 units. She has, however, heard of the benefits of *just-in-time purchasing*—a principle that advocates purchasing goods in smaller lots as a means of keeping inventory down. If she wishes to order in lots no larger than 50, what should be her fixed ordering costs?

6.5. Major Airlines wants to train new flight attendants in an economically rational way. The airline requires a staff of about 1,000 trained attendants to maintain in-flight service. Due to the nature of the job, attendants have a high propensity to quit, with average job tenure being about 2 years; hence the need to train new attendants. Major's training course takes 6 weeks, after which trainees take 1 week of vacation and travel time before entering the pool from which they are assigned to flight duty as needed to fill vacancies created by attrition. To reduce the dropout rate and ensure the continued availability of trained attendants, Major pays trainees $500 per month while they are training, vacationing, and waiting for assignment.

    The cost of the training itself consists mainly of salaries for instructors ($220 per person per week) and support personnel ($80 per person per week). A training team consists of 10 instructors and 10 supporting personnel. The team is paid only for the time engaged in training, and pay is independent of both class size and the number of classes running simultaneously. Assume 50 workweeks in a year.

    a. Determine the most economical size of a trainee class, the annual total cost of this policy, and the time interval between starting consecutive classes. Draw the inventory buildup diagram, showing when each batch will begin and end training, when each will take vacation time, and when each will be ready for duty.

    b. Now modify the solution in part (a) so that only one class will be in training at one time. Note that this requirement means that a new class must start every 6 weeks. Determine corresponding class size and total annual cost of this operation. Compare your findings for this option with the optimum cost for the option described in part (a) and make a recommendation as to which option Major Airlines should choose.

6.6 Orange Juice Inc.[1] produces and markets fruit juice. During the orange harvest season, trucks bring oranges from the fields to the process plant during a workday that runs from 7 A.M. to 6 P.M. On peak days, approximately 10,000 kg of oranges are trucked in per hour. Trucks dump their contents in a holding bin with a storage capacity of 6,000 kg. When the bin is full, incoming trucks must wait until it has sufficient available space. A conveyor moves oranges from the bin to the processing plant. The plant is configured to deal with an average harvesting day, and maximum throughput (flow rate) is 8,000 kg per hour.

    Assuming that oranges arrive continuously over time, construct an inventory buildup diagram for Orange Juice Inc. In order to process all the oranges delivered during the day, how long must the plant operate on peak days? (Assume, too, that because Orange Juice Inc. makes fresh juice, it cannot store oranges.) Assuming, finally, that each truck holds about 1,000 kg of oranges, at what point during the day must a truck first wait before unloading into the storage bin? What is the maximum amount of time that a truck must wait? How long will trucks wait on average? Among trucks that do wait, how long is the average wait?

www.prenhall.com/anupindi

For exercises based on Process Model go to http://www.prenhall.com/anupindi

---

[1]This problem was inspired by the case "National Cranberry Cooperative," written by J. Jucker, Harvard University, 1983.

References

Hadley, G. and T. M. Whitin. 1963. *Analysis of Inventory Systems.* Prentice Hall, Upper Saddle River, NJ.

Nahmias, S. 1997. *Production and Operations Analysis.* Irwin, Homewood, IL.

Peterson, R., and E. A. Silver. 1979. *Decision Systems for Inventory Management and Production Planning.* John Wiley & Sons, New York, NY.

Sasser, W. 1976. Match supply and demand in service industries. *Harvard Business Review:* November-December.

Chapter 6 Appendix

Calculation of Forward Buying Quantity

The analysis involves comparing inventory pattern and costs with forward buying (indicated in bold lines in Figure 6.6) against the usual sawtooth pattern without forward buying (indicated in dotted lines). Exact analysis is rather complex, because the two cases can only be effectively compared for certain time intervals Δt—those that leave us in the same ending inventory position in both cases. However, we can conduct an approximate analysis as follows (Peterson & Silver, 1979):

1. Assume an interval Δt such that both cases can be effectively compared, and
2. Determine Q^f by maximizing the improvement of total costs over the forward buying interval t_1.

First consider the case of forward buying. At a process throughput of R, a forward-buy order of size Q^f will be consumed by the time interval denoted as

$$t_1 = Q^f / R$$

Total ordering and inventory holding costs during that period can be expressed as follows:

$$TC^f = S + Q^f(C - d) + (r + h)(C - d)\frac{Q^f}{2}t_1$$

Now consider the case without forward buying. We will order EOQ amount

$$Q^* = \sqrt{\frac{2SR}{(r + h)C}}$$

with total costs during the period $[0, t_1]$ (recall that earlier we assumed a time unit of one year). We can thus express total ordering and inventory costs during the period as

$$TC^* = \left(\sqrt{2SR(r + h)C} + CR\right)t_1$$

Noting that $t_1 = Q^f / R$, we would like to select the value of Q^f that maximizes the following cost:

$$TC^* - TC^f = \sqrt{2SR(r + h)c}\left(\frac{Q^f}{R}\right) + CQ^f - S - Q^f(C - d) - (r + h)(C - d)\frac{Q^{f^2}}{2R}$$

Using calculus, we find that at the optimal forwardbuying quantity, the first derivative of this cost differential with respect to Q^f equals zero.

CHAPTER

7

Managing Flow Variability: Safety Inventory

Firms carry *safety inventories* of inputs and outputs as protection against possible stockouts resulting from unexpected supply shortages and demand surges. The goal is to ensure that flow units are available to meet the company's production needs and customer requirements in spite of supply and demand uncertainty. The probability that flow units will be available to satisfy requirements is called the **service level**, which measures the degree of stockout protection provided by a given amount of safety inventory—the higher the level of safety inventory, the higher the level of service provided. The optimal service level balances the cost of carrying the inventory with the cost of incurring stockouts.

Both service level provided and safety inventory required depend on variability in flow rates—reducing variability increases the service level that is provided by a given amount of safety inventory and decreases the amount of safety inventory that is necessary to provide a given level of service. Operational levers for reducing variability—and for improving the service level and lowering inventory costs—include improving forecasts, reducing lead times, coordinating supply with demand requirements, and pooling inventories.

7.1 INTRODUCTION

As discussed previously, matching inflows (supply) and outflows (demand) is a critical aspect of managing any business process. In chapter 6, we focused on economies of scale to explain why firms may plan supply in excess of demand and hold the resulting inventory. Actual supply may still fall short of demand because of unpredictable variability (uncertainty) in either supply or demand. This may result in process starvation, product shortages, lost sales, and customer dissatisfaction. The process manager may respond by holding additional safety inventory as a cushion, or buffer, which absorbs fluctuations and thus maintains stock availability despite variability in supply or demand.

In this chapter we explore this protective function of inventories, its key determinants, and the managerial levers available to control these inventories. As in chapter 6, our discussion applies equally to buffers at any one of three stages in a process: input (raw material), in-process, and output (finished goods). For consistency, however, we refer to inflows into the buffer as *supply* and outflows from the buffer as *demand*.

To plan an adequate level of inventory, the process manager needs to *forecast demand*. The amount of safety inventory required will then depend on the accuracy of that forecast. In section 7.2 we outline some general principles about forecasts and forecast errors that bear on the management of safety inventory. The rest of the chapter then examines these implications in greater detail. In section 7.3 we begin by studying the amount of stockout protection provided by a given level of inventory, and the amount of safety inventory required to provide a given level of protection. In section 7.4 we consider the problem of determining the optimal level of protection that balances the expected costs of overstocking and understocking. Section 7.5 deals with factors affecting variability in supply and demand and thus the extent of safety inventory needed to provide certain levels of service. Sections 7.6 and 7.7 outline operational strategies for reducing variability by means of aggregation of demand and postponement of supply. Finally, section 7.8 summarizes the key levers for managing safety inventory and customer service in the face of demand variability.

7.2   DEMAND FORECASTS AND FORECAST ERRORS

Until now, we have implicitly assumed that product demand is known and constant over time. In reality, of course, demand usually displays variation over time. Although some variation is systematic (e.g., due to trend or seasonality), much of it results from unpredictable, unexplainable, random factors called **noise**. As a process of predicting the future, **forecasting** is, among other things, an effort to deal with noise. Firms forecast a variety of factors, such as future customer demand, sales, resource requirements and availabilities, and interest rates.

Forecasting Methods   A variety of forecasting methods are available, that can be classified broadly as *subjective* or *objective*. The former are based on judgment and experience, and the latter are based on data analysis. Subjective methods include customer surveys and expert judgments. The two primary objective methods are causal models and time-series analysis. **Causal models** assume that in addition to the data, other factors influence demand. For example, future sales could be a function of consumer prices. **Time-series analysis** relies solely on the past data. Objective methods aim to filter out noise and estimate the effect of such systematic components as trends and patterns of seasonality or such causal factors as the effect of price on sales.

Detailed discussion of forecasting methods is beyond the scope of this book. The interested reader should refer to a standard operations management text, such as Chase, Aquilano and Jacobs (1999) or Nahmias (1997). Our focus in this section will be on some general characteristics of forecasts, as identified by Nahmias (1997), that process managers should understand—regardless of the forecasting method that they may use—to make rational decisions about process inventory:

1. *Forecasts are usually wrong!* Even if we could accurately estimate variations in the systematic components of a demand pattern, the presence of random noise that we can neither explain nor control leads to inaccuracy. Therefore, decisions made based on a forecast (specified as a single number) could have unexpected consequences in terms of either higher costs or inadequate service.

2. *Forecasts should, therefore, be accompanied by a measure of forecasting error.* A measure of forecast error quantifies the process manager's degree of confidence in the forecast. Our decisions (e.g., regarding inventory) should change with our confidence in the forecast—the greater the forecast error, the greater the chance of a stockout for a given level of safety inventory. We will study the exact relationship between the safety inventory, the service level, and the forecast error in section 7.3.

3. *Aggregate forecasts are more accurate than individual forecasts.* For example, forecasting demand for sweaters by individual colors is less reliable than forecasting total demand for all sweaters. Intuitively, we know that aggregation reduces variability—or, more precisely, reduces the amount of variability relative to aggregate mean demand. Why? High and low demand patterns among individual products tend to cancel one another, thereby yielding a more stable pattern of total demand. As a result, less safety inventory is needed in the aggregate. This realization underlies the principle of reducing variability and safety inventory by pooling and centralizing stocks discussed in section 7.6.

4. *Long-range forecasts are less accurate than short-range forecasts.* Again, intuitively we know that events further in the future are less predictable than those that are more imminent. Every meteorologist knows that forecasting tomorrow's weather is easier than forecasting next week's weather. Likewise, matching supply and demand in the short run is easier than planning for the long term. The closer to the actual time of demand a manager can make supply decisions, the more information will be available to make those decisions. Demand forecasts, therefore, will be more accurate and less safety inventory will be needed. Section 7.7 focuses on the use of *postponement strategies* to exploit short-range forecasts.

In addition to incorporating hard quantitative data, forecasts should be modified to include qualitative factors such as managerial judgment, intuition, gut feeling, and market savvy. After all, forecasting is as much an art as a science, and no information should be ignored.

7.3 SAFETY INVENTORY AND SERVICE LEVEL

If we grant that forecasts are usually wrong, we must also agree that the planning of supplies merely to match demand forecasts will invariably result in either excess inventories or stockouts, as illustrated in Example 7.1.

Stockouts have critical business implications. In the MBPF situation, sheet metal stockouts imply that garages cannot be produced and customer demands will thus go

---

EXAMPLE 7.1

Consider the procurement decision faced by MBPF in Example 6.4. The throughput rate of sheet metal is 1,000 rolls per week. For a fixed order cost of $10,000 and a holding cost per roll per year of $260, we determined that MBPF should specify 2,000 rolls per order. Because the throughput rate is 1,000 rolls per week, each order of 2,000 rolls is sufficient for 2 weeks of requirement. If we assume that the throughput rate remains steady at 1,000 rolls per week, MBPF would need to order 2,000 rolls every two weeks.

How was the throughput rate of 1,000 rolls per week established? It was perhaps based on some forecast of the number of garages demanded, but the forecast inevitably will involve some error. Recall from Example 6.7 that if the

sheet metal replenishment lead time is 1 week, then the reorder point (*ROP*) set by MBPF's process manager is 1,000 rolls—a reorder is placed when on-hand inventory falls to 1,000 rolls. During that one-week lead time, one of the following events will inevitably occur:

1. Actual requirements will fall below 1,000 rolls, resulting in excess inventory, or
2. Actual requirements will exceed 1,000 rolls, resulting in a sheet metal stockout.

Only by extreme coincidence will actual demand be exactly 1,000 rolls. If demand is equally likely to be above or below 1,000, then the probability that keeping an inventory of 1,000 rolls will result in a stockout is 50%.

unsatisfied. That may mean lost customers and lost revenue, as well as loss of customer goodwill which may lead to lost future sales. To avoid stockouts—and to provide better customer service—businesses often find it wise to keep extra inventory just in case actual demand exceeds the forecast. *Inventory in excess of the average or forecast demand* is **safety inventory** or **safety stock.**

This definition of safety inventory may seem to imply that it is always positive. Depending on costs and benefits of carrying inventory, however, it may be preferable to keep an inventory level that covers less than average demand, which yields a negative safety inventory.

7.3.1 Service Level Measures

To determine the optimal level of safety inventory, the process manager should consider economic trade-offs between the cost of stockouts and the cost of carrying excess inventory. Although inventory carrying costs are quantifiable, the intangible consequences of stockouts unfortunately are difficult to evaluate in monetary terms. Consequently, retailers often decide to provide a certain level of customer service and then determine the amount of safety inventory needed to meet that objective. The two commonly used measures of customer service are as follows:

- **Cycle-service level** refers to either *the probability that there will be no stockout within an order cycle* or equivalently, *the proportion of order cycles without a stockout,* where *order cycle* is the time between two consecutive replenishment orders.
- **Fill rate** is *the fraction of total demand satisfied from inventory on hand.*

These are illustrated in Example 7.2.

Effective inventory policies can be devised to achieve a desired level of either measure of customer service. In most retail settings only information on sales is available, as true demand is rarely observed due to stockouts. This makes it difficult to measure fill-rate which requires knowledge of demand. Furthermore, analyzing inventory policies for the cycle-service level measure is often simpler than for the fill-rate measure. In this book we focus on the cycle-service level and refer to it simply as **service level (*SL*).** Discussions about inventory policies for the fill-rate measure can be found in the standard textbooks on operations management or inventory management listed at the end of this chapter.

In the rest of this section, we wish to determine two items:

1. The service level provided by a given amount of safety inventory, and
2. The amount of safety inventory needed to provide a given level of service.

Before we address these issues, we will describe a modification of the inventory policy (introduced in section 6.7) when demands are uncertain.

EXAMPLE 7.2

Suppose that a process manager observes 100 order cycles with stockouts occurring in 20 cycles. Cycle-service level is then

$$80/100 = 0.8 \text{ or } 80\%$$

Now suppose that in each order cycle in which a stockout occurred, we also measure the extent of the stockout in terms of the number of units by which we were short. Specifically, suppose that total demand during the 100 cycles was 15,000 units, while total number of units short in the 20 stockout cycles was 1,500 units. The fill rate, therefore, is

$$13,500/15,000 = 0.9 \text{ or } 90\%$$

Depending on the business context, an 80% cycle-service level or a 90% fill rate may not be acceptable.

7.3.2   Continuous Review, Reorder Point Policy

In establishing an inventory policy, a process manager must first decide how often the inventory level should be reviewed. The two choices are either reviewing it periodically (weekly, monthly) or continuously. Obviously, this choice will depend on the cost of the review. With the widespread use of information systems, this cost has been declining, and more businesses are opting for a continuous review policy.

Recall the two fundamental questions that a process manager must address once a review policy has been set:

- How much should I order?
- When should I reorder?

The answer to the first question depends on the trade-off between the fixed cost of placing orders and the variable cost of carrying the inventory that results from ordering larger quantities. This trade-off is essentially what led to the development of the economic order quantity (EOQ) formula discussed in chapter 6. Having initially ordered a fixed quantity, the process manager monitors inventory level continuously and then reorders (at a quantity perhaps equal to EOQ) once available inventory level falls to a prespecified reorder point. This order policy, known as a **continuous review, reorder point** policy, is essentially the one described in chapter 6. Here we extend it to include uncertainty in *demand* and replenishment lead time. In this context, R will denote the (uncertain) *demand rate per unit of time* (day, week, month, or year). The average demand rate is R, which now represents the average rate at which inventory is depleted over time. Actual demand rate—and thus inventory level—will vary in an uncertain fashion.

Similarly, the (uncertain) replenishment lead time is denoted by ℓ with an average value denoted by L. This delay can result from a combination of various delays in information, processing, or transportation. The variable is measured in the same time units (days, weeks, months, or years) as R. If R is the average number of flow units demanded per day, week, or month, then L is measured in *the number of days, weeks, or months, respectively, that elapsed between the placing of an order and its receipt.* Thus, when the available inventory level falls to *ROP*, a new order of size Q (a quantity perhaps equal to EOQ) is placed to be received in ℓ time periods. Upon receipt of this new order, available inventory level increases by Q units.

Lead Time Demand   *ROP* inventory is used to meet flow-unit requirements until the new order is received ℓ periods later. The risk of stockout occurs during this period of replenishment lead time. The *total flow-unit requirement during lead time* is called **lead time demand** D_ℓ. In general, if either flow rate R or lead time ℓ is uncertain, total lead time demand D_ℓ will also be uncertain. Uncertainty in flow rate R results from less-than-perfect forecasting (which is inevitable). Uncertainty in lead time ℓ may be due to a supplier's unreliability in delivering on-time orders. When D_ℓ exceeds *ROP*, a stockout occurs as illustrated in the following example.

EXAMPLE 7.1 (REVISITED)

Recall that the average D_ℓ at MBPF was 1,000 units. Suppose, however, that management observes that actual D_ℓ fluctuates between 200 and 1,800 units. *ROP* is set at 1,000 units. Because total D_ℓ is uncertain, actual D_ℓ is less than 1,000 in some replenishment cycles and larger in others. When the latter situation occurs, we have a stockout.

Let the average D_ℓ be denoted by μ. The **standard deviation of D_ℓ** is a statistical measure of variability in lead time demand. It is denoted by σ and indicates *the extent of variation in the actual D_ℓ around its mean μ.*

Suppose that $ROP = \mu$ and that the D_ℓ is normally distributed with mean μ and standard deviation of σ. If we carry just enough inventory to satisfy forecast demand (mean μ), then actual D_ℓ will exceed forecast demand in 50% of our order cycles. We will suffer stockouts and our service level SL will be 50%. To reduce our stockout risk, we may decide to order earlier by setting $ROP > \mu$. The additional amount

$$I_s = ROP - \mu$$

is the safety inventory that we carry in excess of the average requirements μ. Thus, we have a reorder point expressed as follows:

$$ROP = \mu + I_s$$

Figure 7.1 illustrates the continuous review, reorder point system when the lead time demand is uncertain. As shown, inventory level fluctuates over time and is not depleted uniformly. Specifically, the on-hand inventory when an order arrives varies between cycles. When lead time demand is smaller than μ (as in the first cycle in Figure 7.1), the on-hand inventory just before the next order arrives is greater than the safety inventory (I_s). If lead time demand is larger than μ (as in the second cycle in Figure 7.1), the on-hand inventory just before the next order arrives is smaller than the safety inventory. Because the average lead time demand is μ, the average on-hand inventory just before the next order arrives will be equal to the safety inventory (I_s).

Recall from chapter 6 that average inventory with an order of size Q equals $Q/2$ and is called cycle inventory. When lead time demand is uncertain, we carry safety inventory I_s, as well, so that the total average inventory is now

$$I = Q/2 + I_s$$

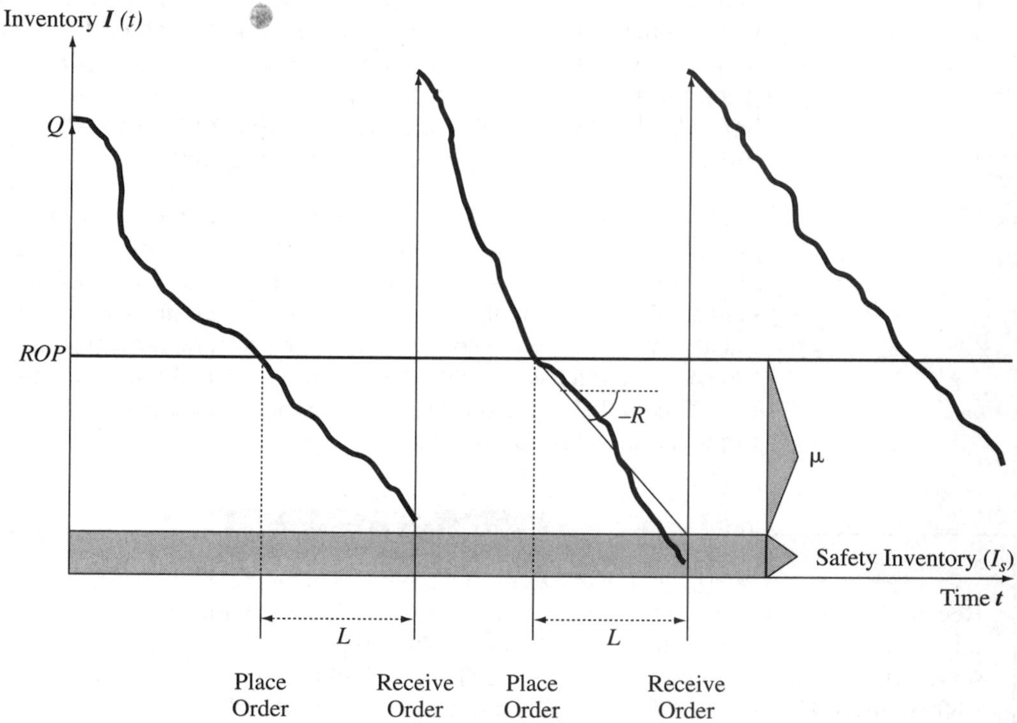

FIGURE 7.1 Continuous Review, Reorder Point Policy

Because the average flow rate is R, the average flow time is expressed by Little's law as follows:

$$T = I / R = (Q / 2 + I_s) / R$$

It represents *the average amount of time a typical flow unit waits in inventory before being used.*

7.3.3   Service Level Given Safety Inventory

Service level SL is measured by the probability (or the proportion of time) that the actual D_ℓ will not exceed ROP—when the inventory of ROP will be sufficient to satisfy D_ℓ. Thus, the formula for finding service level is as follows:

$$SL = \text{Prob}(D_\ell \leq ROP)$$

To compute this probability, we need to know the probability distribution of random variable D_ℓ. It is common to assume that D_ℓ is normally distributed with mean μ and standard deviation σ. (Analysis with other distributions can be performed analogously.) Thus, its probability density function is bell shaped—symmetric around μ with a spread representing the magnitude of σ—where larger values of σ correspond to a more dispersed distribution. Figure 7.2 illustrates the relationship between the distribution of lead time demand D_ℓ, the reorder point ROP, and the corresponding service levels SL. In Figure 7.2, the area under the density curve to the left of ROP is the probability SL that D_ℓ will be less than ROP.

To calculate this area, recall first that if D_ℓ is normally distributed with mean μ and standard deviation σ then

$$Z = (D_\ell - \mu) / \sigma$$

is also normally distributed with mean 0 and standard deviation 1, and is known as the **standard normal random variable.**

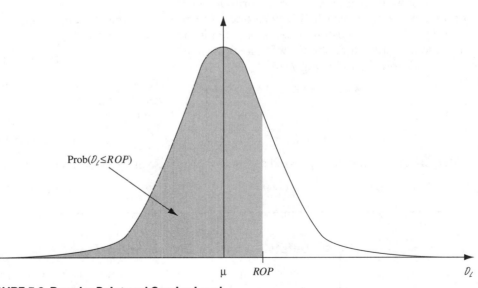

Prob($D_\ell \leq ROP$)

μ ROP D_ℓ

FIGURE 7.2 Reorder Point and Service Level

Furthermore, a given level of safety inventory, I_s, can be measured as a multiple, z, of the standard deviation, σ, of D_ℓ. Thus, we can say the following:

$$I_s = z \times \sigma$$

Using the fact that $ROP = I_s + \mu$, we write

$$z = \frac{ROP - \mu}{\sigma}$$

Therefore, we can say the following:

$$SL = \text{Prob}\,(D_\ell \leq ROP)$$

$$= \text{Prob}\left(\frac{D_\ell - \mu}{\sigma} \leq \frac{ROP - \mu}{\sigma}\right)$$

$$= \text{Prob}\,(Z \leq z)$$

For any given value of z, SL can now be read from the standard normal table given in Appendix 2. SL can also be computed directly in Microsoft Excel as follows:

$$SL = \text{NORMDIST}(ROP, \mu, \sigma, \text{True})$$

Example 7.3 illustrates the computation of service level for a given safety inventory.

EXAMPLE 7.3

The average weekly demand for garages at MBPF, Inc. is determined to be 1,000 units. Actual demand, however, varies weekly. Suppose, then, that the standard deviation of weekly usage is 250 units and that the supplier needs 1 week to deliver. MBPF currently orders a 2-week supply of raw material each time inventory level drops to 1,200 units. Determine service level in terms of the proportion of order cycles over which MBPF will stockout and thereby fail to meet customer demand. What is the average total inventory and the average flow time?

We know the following: D_ℓ has

$$\text{mean } \mu = 1,000$$

and

$$\text{standard deviation } \sigma = 250$$

Safety inventory can be expressed as follows:

$$I_s = ROP - \mu = 1,200 - 1,000 = 200$$

which, when measured as the number of standard deviations, corresponds to

$$z = 200 / 250 = 0.8$$

Using the standard normal tables (Appendix 2), we now find service level to be:

$$SL = \text{Prob}\,(Z \leq 0.8) = 0.7881$$

Note that this equation is identical to Microsoft Excel equation

$$SL = \text{NORMDIST}\,(1200, 1000, 250, \text{True})$$

To summarize, in 78.81% of the order cycles, the retailer will not have a stockout. Average total inventory is

$$I = Q / 2 + I_s = 2,000 / 2 + 200 = 1,200 \text{ units}$$

Average flow time, therefore, is

$$T = I / R = 1.2 \text{ weeks}$$

7.3.4   Safety Inventory Given Service Level

Suppose we want to determine the safety inventory and reorder point required to provide a desired level of service. In that case, we know the area SL and want to compute

ROP. To proceed, we must reverse the computational procedure in section 7.3.3. Knowing *SL*, we first determine the *z* value from the standard normal tables such that

$$SL = \text{Prob}(Z \leq z)$$

We can then compute the safety inventory

$$I_s = z \times \sigma$$

and then the reorder point

$$ROP = \mu + I_s$$

The corresponding formula for *ROP* using Microsoft Excel is:

$$ROP = \text{NORMINV}(SL, \mu, \sigma)$$

Thus, to determine the *ROP* for a desired service level, we need information regarding the average D_ℓ and its standard deviation. These in turn will depend on the flow rate *R* (its average and standard deviation) and the lead time of supply ℓ (its average and standard deviation). To keep our focus on the interaction between service levels and safety inventory, we assume in this section that the average D_ℓ and its standard deviation are known. We discuss methods for estimating information about lead time demands in section 7.5. Example 7.4 illustrates the computation of the safety inventory and *ROP* to achieve a given service level.

EXAMPLE 7.4

Reconsider Example 7.3. We determined that with a safety inventory of 200 units, the provided service level was 78.81%. Recently, the production manager has started complaining about the frequent stockout of raw materials. In response, the purchasing manager is considering increasing service level but does not know how much the increase may cost in extra inventory. He wishes to evaluate the cost of providing service levels of 85%, 90%, 95%, and 99%. How much safety inventory should be carried to provide these levels?

Recall first that the average (μ) and standard deviation (σ) of D_ℓ were 1,000 and 250 units, respectively. Now consider a service level of 85%. To determine the corresponding value of *z* such that

$$\text{Prob}(Z \leq z) = 0.85$$

Using the standard normal tables, one can read the *z* value for 85% service level as 1.04. Safety inventory is therefore

$$I_s = z \times \sigma = 1.04 \times 250 = 260 \text{ units}$$

and the reorder point is

$$ROP = \mu + I_s = 1,000 + 260 = 1,260 \text{ units}$$

We repeat this process for each desired service level—reading the *z* value, computing the safety inventory, and calculating the reorder point. The results are summarized in Table 7.1, where we observe that required safety inventory increases with service level. Whereas an increase of 5% in service, from 85% to 90%, requires an additional safety inventory of 60 units, the next 5% increase in service level, from 90% to 95%, requires an additional safety inventory of 92.5 units. Thus, we observe *a nonlinear relationship between safety inventory and service level.*

TABLE 7.1   Safety Inventory versus Service Level

Service Level (%)	z value	Safety Inventory I_s	Reorder Point ROP
85	1.04	260.00	1260.00
90	1.28	320.00	1320.00
95	1.65	412.50	1412.50
99	2.33	582.50	1582.50

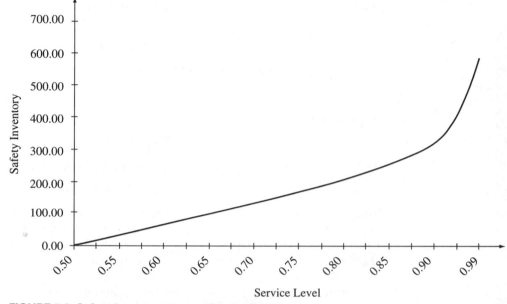

FIGURE 7.3 **Safety Inventory versus Service Level**

Increasing service level increases the required safety inventory *more than proportionately*—as seen in Figure 7.3. Because providing higher levels of service gets increasingly more expensive in terms of inventory holding cost, the process of selecting service and safety inventory levels is an important strategic decision. A firm may choose, for instance, to provide high-quality service in terms of product availability, or it may choose to be a low-cost supplier by holding down inventory costs. In either case, the firm is positioning itself along the service/cost trade-off curve displayed in Figure 7.3. Our aim in providing Example 7.4 and Table 7.1 was to show how that position could be operationalized. For example, if our computer retailer decides to position itself as a company providing high service at a 99% level, then it must carry a safety inventory of 582.50, along with the entailing cost.

7.4 OPTIMAL SERVICE LEVEL: THE NEWSVENDOR PROBLEM

Thus far we have derived safety inventory for a desired level of customer service, but now what level of service should a firm offer? An optimal service level should balance the benefits of improved service in terms of supply continuity and customer satisfaction with the additional costs of holding required safety inventory. In this section, we analyze this problem in a simpler context with a problem involving only one order cycle. The *qualitative* principles that emerge in the upcoming discussion carry over to this discussion of the reorder point model.

A large proportion of retail sales involve "fashion goods" with short product life cycles of a few months. Usually, the retailer has only one or two buying opportunities, and at the end of the product life cycle, remaining items must be marked down for sale or even disposed of at a loss. Newspapers and magazines, for example, have limited lives (a day, a week, a month) at the end of which they lose most of their value. Perishable grocery items—fish, produce, bread, milk—also have limited shelf lives and must be discarded after expiration dates. Seasonal items such as Christmas trees, snowblowers and lawn mowers, and summer and winter apparel are bought and sold at only certain times of the year. In these cases, purchasing too few or too many items in relation to uncertain customer demand entails tangible costs. Because margins are usually high before the end of the season, retailers with insufficient inventory lose potential profits. Conversely, because postseason markdowns can be significant, those with excess inventory lose money through lower margins.

Thus, it is important to perform an economic analysis to determine the optimal order quantity. Such an analysis should balance the *expected costs of ordering too much* (such as markdowns and disposal costs) with the *expected costs of ordering too little* (such as customer dissatisfaction and the opportunity cost of lost revenue). In the operations literature this dilemma is referred to as the **newsvendor problem.** It differs from the *EOQ* inventory model, which focuses on scale economies and, more importantly, assumes no uncertainty. The newsvendor model, which is a basic model for decision making under uncertainty, highlights the role of uncertainty, assumes no scale economies, and boasts a wide variety of applications. Consider the following example.

EXAMPLE 7.5

MBPF is considering introduction of a new product, called Insulated, a specially-designed garage made of a unique material ideal for insulation. It plans to test market this in a small northeast region of the United States. Based on preliminary market research, MBPF estimates that the demand for this new garage will be between 10 and 23 units with probability weights as given in Table 7.2. Each Insulated garage can be sold at $5,500. The cost of materials per garage is estimated to be $3,000. MBPF needs to purchase materials in advance for production of these garages. Any unsold raw material can be salvaged for $2,800. MBPF needs to determine the amount of raw material to be purchased.

Using data from Table 7.2, the forecast of sales of the new garage given by the **expected value** (weighted average) of the demand is as follows:

$$\mu = E(R) = \sum_{r=10}^{23} rf(r) = 16.26 \text{ garages}$$

If there were no uncertainty in demand for the Insulated garage, then raw materials should be purchased to produce exactly 16 garages. With uncertain demand, however, there is a 49% probability that actual demand will exceed 16, resulting in a stockout and lost revenue. There is also a 35% chance that raw material for at least one garage will be leftover to be salvaged at a loss. Let us evaluate the expected profit from ordering raw material for $Q = 16$ garages. First we recall the following facts:

- If actual demand R is 16 or higher, all 16 garages will be built and sold at a profit of $2,500 each.
- If the demand is fewer than 16 garages, some of the raw material for 16 garages will have to be disposed of at a loss of $200 each (the difference between the purchase price and the salvage value).

Thus we can express the expected profit from ordering raw material for 16 garages as follows:

$$(10 \times 2500 - 6 \times 200) \text{ Prob}(R = 10)$$
$$+ (11 \times 2500 - 5 \times 200) \text{ Prob } (R = 11)$$
$$+ (12 \times 2500 - 4 \times 200) \text{ Prob}(R = 12)$$
$$+ \ldots + (16 \times 2500) \text{ Prob}(R \geq 16) = \$37,705$$

A similar approach can be used to determine the expected profit resulting from an order quantity of $Q = 10, 11, \ldots, 23$. The expected profits for each of these order quantities are displayed in Table 7.3. The order quantity that yields the maximum profit equals 20 garages—which is our desired order quantity. The optimal order size is larger than expected demand because with uncertain demand, we do not simply order the expected value of demand. Rather, our decision depends on a broader range of economic considerations, including price, purchasing cost, and salvage value of the unit.

TABLE 7.2 Demand for Insulated Garages at MBPF Inc.

Demand	Probability	Cumulative Probability	Complementary Cumulative
r	$f(r)$	$F(r) = Prob(R \le r)$	$Prob(R > r) = 1 - F(r)$
10	0.01	0.01	0.99
11	0.02	0.03	0.97
12	0.04	0.07	0.93
13	0.08	0.15	0.85
14	0.09	0.24	0.76
15	0.11	0.35	0.65
16	0.16	0.51	0.49
17	0.20	0.71	0.29
18	0.11	0.82	0.18
19	0.10	0.92	0.08
20	0.04	0.96	0.04
21	0.02	0.98	0.02
22	0.01	0.99	0.01
23	0.01	1.00	0.00

TABLE 7.3 Order Quantity versus Expected Profits

Order Quantity (Q)	Expected Profit ($)
10	25000
11	27473
12	29892
13	32203
14	34298
15	36150
16	37705
17	38828
18	39411
19	39697
20	39713
21	39621
22	39475
23	39302

The generic problem can be stated as follows: Consider a retailer who sells a certain seasonal product. Let the demand for this product be denoted by R. Every unit sold during the season fetches retail price of p per unit. Any item not sold during the season can be disposed of at a markdown price of v per unit. The unit-purchase cost (wholesale price paid by the retailer) of an item is w. The retailer must decide how many units to order. Suppose the retailer decides to order Q units. If we let E represent the *expected value operator*, we can compute the expected profit from ordering Q units when the seasonal demand R is a random variable, as follows:

$$E(\text{Profit}) = pE[\min(Q, R)] + vE[\max(Q - R, 0)] - wQ$$

In this equation, the three terms represent the following values:

- The first term $pE[\min(Q, R)]$ is the expected revenue from selling, at the regular price (p) the quantity available or demanded, whichever is smaller.
- The second term $vE[\max(Q-R, 0)]$ is the expected revenue from selling leftover quantity, if any, at the markdown price (v).
- The last term wQ is the cost of purchasing the total quantity at unit wholesale price (w).

Optimizing the profits over the decision variable Q will give us our desired order quantity.

Marginal Analysis   A more insightful approach to understanding the trade-offs involved in deciding optimal order quantity entails **marginal analysis:** *comparing expected costs and benefits of purchasing each incremental unit.* First we must define the following:

- The **net marginal benefit** from each additional unit, denoted by B, is its contribution margin. If the unit retail price is p and the unit purchase cost is w, then

$$B = p - w$$

  In practice, it may also include the opportunity cost of lost goodwill had the unit not been stocked but was demanded.
- The **net marginal cost** of stocking an additional unit, denoted by C, is the effective cost if the unit remains unsold under conditions of low demand. If the unit salvage value is v and the purchase cost is w, then

$$C = w - v$$

We receive the net marginal benefit only when the additional unit sells. At any order quantity, Q, the expected marginal benefit from ordering an additional unit is

$$B \times \text{Prob}(R > Q)$$

At the same time, we suffer the net marginal cost only when the additional unit does not sell. The expected marginal cost of having a unit leftover is

$$C \times \text{Prob}(R \le Q)$$

Note that *while the expected marginal benefit from purchasing an additional unit is decreasing, expected marginal cost is increasing in the order quantity Q.* As long as expected benefit is greater than expected cost, Q should be increased until the reverse is true. Thus the optimal Q is the first value Q^* for which the expected cost of ordering an additional unit exceeds the expected benefit; that is

$$C \times \text{Prob}(R \le Q^*) \ge B \times \text{Prob}(R > Q^*)$$

Since

$$\text{Prob}(R > Q) = 1 - \text{Prob}(R \le Q)$$

this condition can be rewritten as follows:

$$C \times \text{Prob}(R \le Q^*) \ge B \times [1 - \text{Prob}(R \le Q^*)]$$

EXAMPLE 7.6

We now apply these principles to the problem of ordering raw material for Insulated garage at MBPF Inc.

Recall that

$$B = p - w = 5,500 - 3,000 = \$2,500$$

and

$$C = w - v = 3,000 - 2,800 = \$200$$

Thus,

$$\frac{B}{B + C} = (p - w) / (p - v) = 0.926$$

Look again at the cumulative distribution of demand in Table 7.2. Here we find that because

$$F(20) = 0.96$$

and

$$F(19) = 0.92$$

the smallest Q such that $F(Q) \geq 0.926$ is $Q = 20$.

Recalling the following notation for *the cumulative distribution of demand D:*

$$F(Q) = \text{Prob}(R \leq Q)$$

and rearranging terms we arrive at an optimal order quantity as *the smallest value Q^* such that*

$$F(Q^*) \geq \frac{B}{B + C}$$

Thus computing optimal order quantity is a two-step procedure:

1. Compute the ratio $B / (B + C)$,
2. Determine optimal order quantity, Q^*, from the cumulative distribution of R.

We illustrate this procedure in Example 7.6.

We can simplify this procedure even further. It is often more convenient, for instance, to assume that demand is a continuous random variable, whereby all (non-integer) values of R and Q become possible. If we make this assumption, then at optimal Q we can exactly balance out the marginal benefit of increasing Q (by a fractional amount) with the loss of keeping Q at its current level. Thus,

$$C\,\text{Prob}(R \leq Q^*) = B\,[1 - \text{Prob}\,(R \leq Q^*)]$$

which gives us an optimal order quantity Q^* that satisfies the following formula:

$$F(Q^*) = \text{Prob}(R \leq Q^*) = \frac{B}{B + C}$$

Recall from section 7.3 that cycle-service level was defined as the probability of not stocking out in a cycle. If demand is represented by R and order quantity by Q, then cycle-service level is

$$\text{Prob}(R \leq Q) = F(Q)$$

Because Q^* is optimal order quantity determined by the economic trade-off between costs of under- and overstocking, $F(Q^*)$ is the optimal probability of not stocking out. Therefore, optimal service level SL^*, given by $F(Q^*)$, is equal to the ratio

$$\frac{B}{B + C}$$

EXAMPLE 7.7

Recall that in Example 7.5, $\mu = 16$. The variance of R can be computed as *the average squared deviation from its mean,* or

$$\sigma^2 = \sum_{r=10}^{23} (r - \mu)^2 f(r) = 6.15$$

Taking its square root gives the standard deviation $\sigma = 2.48$ garages—a figure that measures the variation in actual demand around its mean. We need Q^* such that

$$F(Q^*) = 0.926$$

Looking up the normal tables or alternately using

$$= \text{NORMINV } (0.917, 16, 2.48)$$

yields 19.59, which is close to our earlier answer. The discrepancy arises because we approximated discrete demand probability density in Example 7.5 with a continuous probability density.

Note that SL^* depends only on the net marginal benefit and cost of stocking a unit, and not on the probability distribution of demand. Furthermore, it increases with the net marginal benefit, B, and decreases with the net marginal cost C. Thus, *the more expensive the stockouts and/or the lower the cost of disposing of the excess inventory, the higher the optimal service level.* For Examples 7.5 and 7.6, optimal service level is computed as equal to

$$\frac{B}{B + C} = 0.926$$

Knowing our SL^*, we can now determine optimal order quantity from the probability distribution of demand. Assume, for example, that demand is normally distributed with mean μ and standard deviation σ. In that case, Q^* can be determined in one of two ways:

1. From the standard normal tables given in Appendix 2, or
2. From the Excel function NORMINV (SL^*, μ, σ)

We illustrate this computation in Example 7.7

In the newsvendor model $Q- \mu$ is the single-order equivalent of safety inventory I_s that we considered in the preceding section. Thus, the qualitative conclusions of this section apply to the preceding discussion. With uncertain demand, therefore, we determine the optimal service level—and corresponding safety inventory—by balancing the expected marginal benefit of an additional unit with those of expected marginal cost. Intuitively, we rationalize that if the net marginal benefit is twice the net marginal cost, we need an order quantity that gives us a probability of overstocking that is twice the probability of understocking. To summarize, the optimal service level increases with the net marginal benefit and decreases with the net marginal cost. The order quantity increases with the optimal service level, and the mean and the standard deviation of demand.

7.5   LEAD TIME DEMAND VARIABILITY

The rest of this chapter considers sources of demand variability and operational strategies for reducing this variability.

Recall that lead time demand D_ℓ refers to the flow unit requirement from the time an order is placed until it is received. We carry safety inventory I_s to satisfy this requirement a proportion of time corresponding to SL. As discussed, both I_s and SL depend critically on the variability in D_ℓ—if D_ℓ were constant and known, we could guarantee that $SL = 100\%$ with $I_s = 0$. In this section, we consider factors that affect SL and I_s by contributing to variability in D_ℓ.

7.5.1   Fixed Replenishment Lead Time

For the sake of simplicity, we first consider the case of known (fixed) replenishment lead time L measured in periods (days, weeks, months). We assume that our supplier is perfectly reliable and postpone the discussion of variability in lead times to subsection 7.5.2.

First, let R_t denote demand in period t. For a supply lead time of L number of periods, total lead time demand will be

$$D_L = R_1 + R_2 + \ldots + R_L.$$

We assume that demand levels between periods R_t are independent and follow the same distribution—that is, they are **independent and identically distributed random variables.** Average D_L therefore, will be given by

$$\mu = L \times R$$

where L is lead time in number of periods and R is average demand per period. Since L is constant, variability in D_L arises from variability in R_t. As noted, the statistical measure of variability is its standard deviation. Let σ_r be the standard deviation of demand (flow rate) per period (day, week, or month). To compute the standard deviation σ of D_L, it is convenient to estimate first the variance of D_L given by σ^2 as

$$\sigma^2 = \sigma_r^2 + \sigma_r^2 + \ldots + \sigma_r^2 = L\sigma_r^2$$

This follows from the fact that the variance of the sum of L independent random variables equals the sum of their variances. Thus, standard deviation of lead time demand is

$$\sigma = \sqrt{L}\,\sigma_r$$

If we know the lead time of supply and the variability in demand per period, then we can compute safety inventory to achieve a desired level of service.

In addition to its dependence on service level (discussed in section 7.3), safety inventory also depends on the standard deviation of lead time demand, which depends in turn on both the length of supply lead time and the variability in demand. Specifically, greater variability in lead time demand results from longer lead time, more variable demand per period, or both. More safety inventory is also needed to provide a desired level of service.

The effect of lead time on safety inventory also has implications for purchasing. Suppose we can choose between two suppliers, one offering a lower price but a longer lead time and the other offering a shorter time but a higher price. As shown in Example 7.8, selecting a supplier on the basis of the price alone could result in the need to carry larger safety inventory—a decision that may increase total cost.

7.5.2   Variability in the Replenishment Lead Time

In addition to its duration, variability in lead time is also an important contributor to the variability in D_ℓ. To develop some intuition for the effect of variability in lead time, suppose that while demand rate R is fixed and known, lead time is a random variable ℓ, with mean L and standard deviation σ_l. In this case, uncertain lead time demand is expressed as

$$D_\ell = R \times \ell$$

EXAMPLE 7.8

MBPF Inc. wants to know if it can reduce material costs. An alternate (overseas) sheet-metal supplier who is willing to supply MBPF at a lower cost than the one it currently pays has recently approached the purchasing department. Lead time of supply, however, is 2 weeks. MBPF needs to know the ramifications of lower material costs coupled with longer supply lead time. If MBPF decides to switch suppliers, the increase in lead time of supply will entail larger safety inventory.

To quantify this increase in safety inventory, we proceed in the following manner. Recall that the standard deviation of demand per week, σ_r, is 250 rolls. For new lead time $L = 2$ weeks, we can compute the standard deviation of D_L as follows:

$$\sigma = \sqrt{L}\,\sigma_r = (\sqrt{2})\,(250) = 353.55$$

For 95% service level, required safety inventory is expressed as

$$I_s = z \times \sigma = 1.65 \times 353.55 = 583.36 \text{ units}$$

Thus, to achieve a desired service level of 95%, MBPF must accept an increase in safety inventory from 412.50 to 583.36 units (or 41.4%) when supply lead time increases from 1 week to 2 weeks. Whereas the alternate supplier can lower its material-procurement costs, MBPF must increase safety inventory and therefore holding costs by 41.4% if it wants to maintain the same service level.

It has mean

$$\mu = R \times L$$

and variance

$$\sigma^2 = R^2 \sigma_l^2$$

The last expression follows from the fact that *the variance of a constant times a random variable is equal to the square of that constant times the variance of the random variable.*

More generally, suppose that both demand rate R and lead time L are random variables. If so, D_L is *the sum of a random number of random variables.* To compute the required safety inventory, therefore, we must compute the mean and the variance of D_L. Since the average lead time is L and the average flow rate is R, it is clear that the average D_L is

$$\mu = L \times R$$

The variance of D_L can be computed by combining two special cases:

1. Variance of D_L when the flow rate is random but the lead time is fixed (a situation discussed in the previous subsection), and

2. Variance of D_L when the flow rate is constant but the lead time is random (a situation discussed at the beginning of this subsection).

Total variability in D_L is then the sum of the two individual effects:

$$\sigma^2 = L\sigma_r^2 + R^2\sigma_l^2$$

The standard deviation of D_L is then computed by taking the square root of the variance of D_L. The exact derivation of the above intuitive explanation can be found in Ross (1972). The impact of variability in lead time on safety inventory is illustrated in Example 7.9.

EXAMPLE 7.9

Return for a moment to Example 7.4 and suppose that the sheet-metal supplier's lead time has recently become more variable. Specifically, suppose that the replenishment lead time has a mean of 1 week and a standard deviation of 0.3 week (with all remaining data as specified in Example 7.4). How much safety inventory does MBPF need to provide a 95% service level?

Again, we start with the following data:

$$L = 1, \sigma_l = 0.3, R = 1000, \sigma_r = 250.$$

Thus, we see that

$$\sigma^2 = 1(250)^2 + (1000)^2(0.3)^2 = 152,500$$

or

$$\sigma = 390.51$$

Therefore, the safety inventory must be

$$I_s = 1.65 \times \sigma = 644.35 \text{ rolls}$$

compared with only 412.50 rolls needed if the lead time were exactly 1 week for sure.

We can arrive at an intuitive understanding of this increase. With variability in lead time, it is likely that actual lead time of supply will be larger than 1 week. The process manager must now account for this increase by carrying more safety inventory.

Thus, variability in lead time of supply increases the safety inventory. Lead time variability, therefore, has a significant impact on safety inventory requirements (and on material cycle time). Reliable suppliers who make on-time deliveries contribute directly to a firm's bottom line and level of customer service.

In summary, we have shown how uncertainty in demand and supply affects raw material and product availability. To provide better service in the face of uncertainty, firms carry safety inventory. Three key factors affect the amount of safety inventory that a company carries under given circumstances:

1. The level of customer service desired,
2. The average and the uncertainty in demand, and
3. The average and the uncertainty in replenishment lead time.

In turn, there are two primary levers for reducing the level of safety inventory:

1. Reducing both the average and standard deviation replenishment lead time, and
2. Reducing demand variability.

Although improved forecasting can reduce variability in demand, too many firms tend to think of it as their only option. Better forecasting can help, but it is not a panacea. As discussed, reducing the lead time and reducing its variability are also important levers. In sections 7.6 and 7.7 we explore two further ways of reducing variability: aggregating demand and using shorter-range forecasts.

7.6 POOLING INVENTORIES THROUGH AGGREGATION

Recall from section 7.2 the third characteristic of forecasts: aggregate forecasts are more accurate than individual forecasts. The basic concept of **aggregation**—*pooling demand for several similar products*—can be applied broadly. Indeed, firms often aggregate sales according to various geographical regions and/or types of products. Improved forecast accuracy due to aggregation is simply a statistical property, and we can devise important operational strategies to exploit this property in effective inventory management.

7.6.1   Physical Centralization

Suppose a firm stocks its product in multiple warehouses to serve geographically dispersed customers. Because all the locations face uncertain demand, each should carry some safety inventory. Assume that the company's warehousing operations are *decentralized*—that each warehouse operates independently of the others. It is possible then that one warehouse will be out of stock while another has the product in stock. Although the total distribution system has sufficient inventory, it may be held at the wrong location. As a result of this maldistribution of inventory some customer demand may not be satisfied.

Suppose, however, that the firm can consolidate all its stock in one location from which it can serve all its customers. We call this alternative system the **physical centralization** of inventory. Because centralization eliminates the possibility of stock maldistribution, all customer demand will be met as long as there is inventory in the system. The centralized system, therefore, will provide better customer service than the decentralized network and will do so with the same total inventory. Equivalently, to provide the same level of service, the centralized system would need less inventory than the decentralized system.

Let us make these claims more precise. Suppose that a firm serves locations 1 and 2, and assume that the lead time demand—$D_{\ell 1}$ and $D_{\ell 2}$—are statistically identically distributed, each with mean of μ and variance of σ^2. To provide desired level of service *SL,* each location must carry safety inventory

$$I_s = z \times \sigma$$

where z is determined by desired *SL* (as discussed in section 7.3). If each facility faces identical demand and provides identical service levels, the total safety inventory in the decentralized system, denoted by I_s^d, is $2z\sigma$.

Independent Demands   Consider centralizing the two inventories in one location when lead time demands at the two locations are independent. This centralized pool will now serve the total lead time demand

$$D_\ell = D_{\ell 1} + D_{\ell 2}$$

Recall that the mean and the variance of a sum of independent random variables are, respectively, equal to the sum of their means and variances. The mean of the total lead time demand D_ℓ is thus

$$\mu + \mu = 2\mu$$

Its variance is

$$\sigma^2 + \sigma^2 = 2\sigma^2$$

The standard deviation of D_ℓ, therefore, is $\sqrt{2}\,\sigma$. Note that although consolidation of demands doubles the mean, the standard deviation increases only by a factor of

$$\sqrt{2} = 1.414$$

Intuitively we understand that high and low demands in the two locations will tend to counterbalance each other, thereby yielding a more stable total demand. Safety inventory carried in the centralized system is then equal to

$$I_s^c = z \times \sqrt{2}\,\sigma$$

Comparing the safety inventories carried by decentralized (I_s^d) and centralized (I_s^c) systems, we observe that when both systems offer the same level of service, the

---

EXAMPLE 7.10

Recall the situation in Example 6.5 in which MBPF, Inc. is contemplating expanding into the midwest region of the United States in the year 2000. Preliminary estimates of demand for garages in the midwest region are similar to those in the eastern region currently. That is, the average demand is estimated to be 1,000 garages per week with a standard deviation of 250. MBPF, Inc. needs to build a second manufacturing plant in the midwest region. For procurement of raw materials it is considering two of the options introduced in Example 6.5. Option A (decentralized system) is to procure raw material from a different supplier and store it in a warehouse close to the proposed factory location in the midwest. The replenishment lead time from the alternate supplier is still one week. Option B (centralized system) is to source raw material from the current supplier and store it in the warehouse in the eastern United States. The vice president of operations has to evaluate the implications of these two options to ensure a 95% service level to the production plants.

Under option A, each warehouse will order independently of the other warehouse. The average weekly demand for each warehouse is 1,000 units with a standard deviation of 250 units per week. The safety inventory required at each warehouse to provide a 95% service level to the corresponding production plant is

$$I_s = 412.50$$

as computed in Example 7.4. Thus the total safety inventory carried in the two warehouses is

$$I_s^d = 2 \times 412.50 = 825$$

Under option B, the single warehouse faces a total lead time demand with mean

$$\mu = 2 \times 1000 = 2000$$

and standard deviation,

$$\sigma = \sqrt{2} \times 250 = 353.55$$

To provide a 95% service level, the warehouse must carry a safety inventory:

$$I_s^c = 1.65 \times \sigma = 1.65 \times 353.55 = 583.36$$

Thus we see that the required safety inventory under option B is less than that required under option A by a factor of $\sqrt{2}$.

---

total safety inventory required by the decentralized operation is $\sqrt{2}$ times the required total safety inventory in the centralized operation. That is, the safety inventory in a centralized operation is less than in a two-location decentralized system by a factor of $1/\sqrt{2}$. We can generalize our analysis of the benefits of centralizing two locations to consider the centralization of N locations. In so doing, we would find that consolidating stocks in N locations with independent and identically distributed demands into one centralized location results in reducing the total safety inventory by a factor of $1 / \sqrt{N}$. The concept of centralization is illustrated in Example 7.10.

Square Root Law   The savings from Example 7.10 results from the **square root law,** which states that *total safety inventory required to provide a specified level of service increases by the square root of the number of locations in which it is held.* This principle is displayed graphically in Figure 7.4.

In addition to the benefits of reducing the safety inventory, centralization also reduces the cycle inventory, as we saw in chapter 6. The reduction in the cycle inventory results from the fact that centralization allows better use of the economies of scale in procurement and production. Physical centralization is a common practice for retailers with catalog and mail-, telephone-, or Internet-order operations.

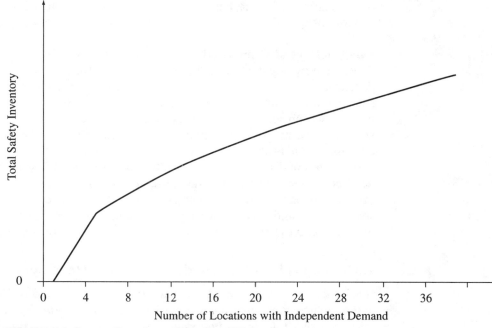

Number of Locations with Independent Demand

FIGURE 7.4 Square Root Law of Pooling Efficiency

Correlated Demands   In the previous discussion we have shown the benefits of centralization when demands in the various locations were independent. Does centralization offer similar benefits when demands in the multiple locations are correlated? Suppose that a firm serves locations 1 and 2 with lead time demand—D_{L1} and D_{L2}, that are statistically identically distributed but correlated with a correlation coefficient of ρ. The mean of the total lead time demand D_L is thus

$$\mu + \mu = 2\mu$$

Its variance is

$$\sigma^2 + \sigma^2 + 2\rho\,\sigma^2 = 2\,(1 + \rho)\sigma^2$$

Therefore, the total safety inventory in the centralized system is

$$I_s^c = z \times \sqrt{2(1 + \rho)}\sigma$$

The total safety inventory required in the decentralized system is

$$I_s^d = 2 \times z \times \sigma$$

Therefore, the safety inventory in the two-location decentralized system is larger than in the centralized system by a factor of

$$\sqrt{\frac{2}{(1 + \rho)}}$$

When demands of the two locations are independent, the correlation coefficient $\rho = 0$ and the safety inventory in the decentralized system is larger by a factor of $\sqrt{2}$ as we discussed earlier. The advantage of a centralized system increases as the demands on the two locations become negatively correlated. On the other hand, the advantage of a centralized system diminishes as the demands on the two locations become positively correlated. In fact, only if demand is perfectly positively correlated (that is, $\rho = 1$)

centralization offers no benefits in the reduction of safety inventory. The benefits of economies of scale discussed in chapter 6, however, remain.

Disadvantages of Centralization   If centralization of stocks reduces inventory, why doesn't everybody do it? In the previous analysis, we assumed that both centralized and decentralized operations have *identical response times* (a value from the customer's perspective) and *identical shipment costs*. In practice, typically a centralized location is farther away from some customer locations than are some decentralized locations; centralization may entail longer response times when units must be shipped to more distant customers. It may also be more expensive to transport products to customers located at vastly different distances from the central location. Finally, the seller's total demand may be affected if some customers decide to not use its central location (because of distance or other inconvenience). In such situations, decentralized locations may improve response times and service levels. With decentralized locations, proximity to customers may also lead to better understanding their needs and developing closer relationships.

7.6.2   Principle of Aggregation and Pooling Inventory

It is important to stress that these benefits result from the statistical **principle of aggregation,** which states that *the standard deviation of the sum of random variables is less than the sum of the individual standard deviations.* In all of the examples discussed in section 7.6.1, total inventory is physically located at a central location to enable the seller to aggregate demand across various regions. Physical consolidation, however, is not essential. As long as the available inventory is shared among various sources of demand—a practice known as **pooling inventory**—we achieve the benefits of aggregation. As the following examples indicate, the concept of pooling inventory can be applied in various ways other than physical centralization.

Virtual Centralization   Consider a distribution system with warehouses in two locations, A and B. Each location carries some safety stock to provide a given level of service. Suppose now that at a given time, demand for a product in location A exceeds the available local stock. The product, however, is available at location B. Customer demand at location A can then be satisfied with stock at location B. Likewise, if at any time location B is out of stock that is available at location A, the product can be shipped to location B to satisfy customer demand. To accommodate this option, however, a system must satisfy two criteria:

1. Information about product demand and availability must be available at both locations, and
2. Shipping the product from one location, B, to a customer at another location, A, must be fast and cost-effective.

If these two requirements are met and correlation of demands is less than 1, pooling is effective—inventory at any location can be shared by demands at all other locations. Because pooling is achieved by keeping the inventories at decentralized locations (instead of physically consolidating them at one location), we may call it **virtual centralization.**

Machine-tool builder Okuma America Corporation, a subsidiary of Japan's Okuma Corporation, is an example of a company that is moving its distribution network toward virtual centralization. Each of its 46 distributors in North and South America has access to Okumalink, a shared information-technology system that provides information about the location and availability of machine tools stored in Okuma warehouses in Charlotte, North Carolina, and in Japan. Okumalink is currently being upgraded to allow channel members to connect with one another directly, thereby facilitating intrachannel exchanges of products and parts (Narus & Anderson, 1996). Similarly, Wal-Mart shares point-of-sales data on product demand and availability by means of a sophisticated satellite-communication system that links its geographically dispersed stores with its Arkansas headquarters. It also operates its own fleet of trucks for fast interstore transfers.

Specialization   A firm may have several warehouses, each of which stocks several products. Safety inventory for each product, however, may be allocated to a particular warehouse that specializes in that product. Even though there are several warehouses, there is for each product only one specialized warehouse that carries the entire safety inventory. Each warehouse effectively pools with all the others the inventory for the product in which it specializes.

This system is particularly useful when the local demand that each warehouse serves is more or less unique to the product. For example, suppose there are two warehouses, one each at locations A and B. Suppose inventory consists of two products, P1 and P2. In addition, suppose a large fraction of demand at location A is for product P1 and a large fraction of that at location B is for product P2. Then location A warehouse may be specialized to carry all the safety stock for product P1, and location B may be specialized for product P2. If location B (or A) requires any units of P1 (or P2), it could be shipped from location A (or B). Under this arrangement, safety inventory for each product is reduced because each inventory is now centralized at one location. Furthermore, because centralization is based on the local demand patterns, transportation time and costs are also less than they would be if all products were physically centralized at one warehouse.

Component Commonality   Our examples thus far have focused on pooling efficiency by means of aggregating demand across multiple geographic locations. The concept of pooling can also be exploited when aggregating demand across various products. Consider a computer manufacturer (such as Dell, Compaq, or IBM) that typically offers a wide range of models. Although models vary considerably, a few common components are used across product lines, such as similar central processing units or CD-ROM drives.

To offer variety, firms have a few options. They can, for instance, produce adequate units of each model in anticipation of product demand—a **make-to-stock** strategy. To provide a desired service level, the firm needs sufficient safety inventory of each product. Conversely, the firm may decide to produce after customers place orders—a **make-to-order** strategy. Under this strategy, a firm keeps all its inventory in components, and builds product as and when customers place orders. To determine the safety inventory of those components common to various product lines, the firm aggregates demand for the products that share specific components. Component commonality thus allows the firm to reduce inventory investment while maintaining the same level of service and offering product variety.

Risk pooling of common-component demand across various products is akin to the practice of physical centralization that we described earlier. Safety inventory of common components will be much lower than the safety inventory of different components stored separately for different finished products. In addition, in a make-to-order situation holding costs will be less because inventory of components has accumulated no added value. There is, however, at least one key drawback. In a make-to-order situation, the customer must wait for the firm to produce the goods, whereas the make-to-stock product is available for immediate consumption. Therefore, if production lead times can be shortened until they are *shorter in duration than the wait that the consumer is willing to endure,* then a make-to-order strategy has significant benefits.

Product Substitution   Often, one product can substitute to fill excess demand for another. The ability to provide substitute products improves effective level of service by pooling safety inventory across multiple products. Substitution, therefore, reduces the level of safety stock needed for a given level of customer service. To exploit this, however, a firm needs to have information on substitution patterns.

7.7   SHORTENING THE FORECAST HORIZON THROUGH SUPPLY POSTPONEMENT

As noted in section 7.2, forecasts further into the future tend to be less accurate than those of more imminent events. Quite simply, as time passes, we get better information and so can make better predictions. Because shorter-range forecasts are more accurate, inventory-planning decisions will be more effective if supply is postponed closer to the point of actual demand.

Postponement (or Delayed Differentiation)   Consider a garment manufacturer who makes blue, green, and red T-shirts. The firm is considering two alternate manufacturing processes:

1. Process A calls first for coloring the fabric, which takes one week, and then assembling the T-shirt, which takes another week.

2. Process B calls first for assembling T-shirts from white fabric, which also takes one week, and then coloring the assembled shirts—a process which, as in process A, takes one week.

Both processes, therefore, take two weeks. Does one have any advantage over the other? With process A, the manufacturer must forecast demand for T-shirts in every color that will sell in two weeks. Although total flow time per T-shirt is the same under both processes A and B, by reversing the assembly and dyeing stages, process B has essentially postponed the color differentiation until one week closer to the time of sale. This practice is well known as **postponement** or **delayed differentiation.** Because it is more accurate to forecast demand for different-colored T-shirts next week than demand that will come forth two weeks into the future, process B will entail less safety inventory of colored T-shirts than process A.

Process B has another advantage. In deciding the number of white T-shirts to assemble in the first phase, the manufacturer can make an aggregate forecast across all colors (as discussed, aggregation reduces variability). Process B, then, boasts reduced variability for two reasons:

1. It aggregates demands by color in the first (assembly) phase, and

2. It requires shorter-range forecasts of individual T-shirts needed by color in the second (dyeing) phase.

Both result in less demand variability and hence require less total safety inventory.

Clothing maker Benetton (Signorelli & Heskett, 1989) was an early pioneer in postponement strategies. Another company that has found this particular process innovation beneficial is Hewlett Packard (HP), which builds Deskjet printers for worldwide sales (Kopczak & Lee, 1994). For example, one major difference between printers destined for North America and those bound for Europe is their power-supply rating. Initially, the HP Deskjet printer was designed to include a specific power supply (110V or 220V) in the assembly process—the plant would make printers specific to each geographical location. In rethinking its distribution system, however, HP redesigned the printer so that the power-supply module could be installed at the very end of the production process (in fact, it is installed by the distributor). Thus, the plant was producing a generic printer and postponing differentiation until the distribution stage. The more recent HP deskjet printers carry the postponement concept even further. These printers can be used as either color or black-and-white printers simply by inserting the appropriate cartridge. Because this customization process is actually performed by the consumer, HP has no need to forecast separate demand for color and black-and-white printers.

7.8   LEVERS FOR REDUCING SAFETY INVENTORY

In this chapter, we first recognized the role of uncertainty and variability in process inflows and outflows, and introduced the notion of *safety inventory* as a buffer against uncertainty in supply and/or demand.

We can identify the following levers for reducing flow variability and the required safety inventory (and thus flow time):

1. Reduce demand variability through improved forecasting.
2. Reduce delivery lead time.
3. Reduce variability in delivery lead time.
4. Pool safety inventory for multiple locations or products, whether through physical/virtual centralization or specialization or some combination thereof.
5. Exploit product substitution.
6. Use common components.
7. Postpone product-differentiation processing until closer to the point of actual demand.

Problem Set

7.1 We now revisit Exercise 6.2 on BIM Computers. Currently, BIM produces a 4-week supply of its PC Pal model when stock on hand drops to 500 units. (It takes 1 week to produce a batch.) Factory orders average 400 units per week, and standard deviation of forecast errors is estimated at 125 units.
   a. What level of customer service is BIM providing to its distributors in terms of stock availability?
   b. Let us say that BIM wants to improve customer service to 80%, 90%, 95%, and 99%. How would such improvements affect the company's reorder policy and its annual costs?

7.2 Weekly demand for diskettes at a retailer is normally distributed with a mean of 1,000 boxes and a standard deviation of 150. Currently, the store places orders via paper that is faxed to the supplier. Assume 50 working weeks in a year and the following data:
   • Lead time for delivery of an order is 4 weeks.
   • Fixed cost (ordering and transportation) per order is $100.
   • Each box of diskettes costs $1.
   • Holding cost is 25% of average inventory value.
   • The retailer currently orders 20,000 diskettes when stock on hand reaches 4,200.
   a. Currently how long, on average, does a diskette spend in the store? What is the annual ordering and holding cost under such a policy?

b. Assuming that the retailer wants the probability of stocking out in a cycle to be no more than 5%, recommend an optimal inventory policy (a policy regarding order quantity and safety stock). Under your recommended policy, how long, on average, would a box of diskettes spend in the store?

c. Claiming that it will lower lead time to 1 week, the supplier is trying to push an EDI system on the retailer. In terms of costs and flow times, what benefits can the retailer expect to realize by adopting the EDI system?

7.3 Johnson Electronics sells electrical and electronic components through catalogs. Catalogs are printed once every two years. Each printing run incurs a fixed cost of $25,000, with a variable production cost of $5 per catalog. Annual demand for catalogs is estimated to be normally distributed with a mean of 16,000 and standard deviation of 4,000. Data indicate that, on average, each customer ordering a catalog generates a profit of $35 from sales. Assuming that Johnson wants only one printing run in each two-year cycle, how many catalogs should be printed in each run?

7.4 As owner of Catch-of-the-Day Fish Shop, you can purchase fresh fish at $18 per crate each morning from the Walton Fish Market. During the day, you sell crates of fish to local restaurants for $120 each. Coupled with the perishable nature of your product, your integrity as a quality supplier requires you to dispose of each unsold crate at the end of the day. Your cost of disposal is $2 per crate. You have a problem, however, because you do not know how many crates your customers will order each day. To address this problem, you have collected the several days' worth of demand data shown in Table 7.4. You now want to determine the optimal number of crates you should purchase each morning.

7.5 A mail-order firm has four regional warehouses. Demand at each warehouse is normally distributed with a mean of 10,000 per week and a standard deviation of 2,000. Holding cost is 25%, and each unit of product costs the company $10. Each order incurs an ordering cost of $1,000 (primarily from fixed transportation costs), and lead time is 1 week. The company wants the probability of stocking out in a flow to be no more than 5%. Assume 50 working weeks in a year.

a. Assuming that each warehouse operates independently, what should be the ordering policy at each warehouse? How much safety stock does each warehouse hold? How much average inventory is held (at all four warehouses combined), and at what annual cost? On average, how long does a unit of product spend in the warehouse before being sold?

b. Assume that the firm has centralized all inventories in a single warehouse and that the probability of stocking out in a cycle can still be no more than 5%. Ideally, how much average inventory can the company now expect to hold, and at what cost? In this case, how long will a unit spend in the warehouse before being sold?

TABLE 7.4 Demand at Catch-of-the-Day Fish Shop

Demand	0	1	2	3	4	5	6	7	8	9	10	11	12	13	14	15
Frequency	0	0	0	1	3	2	5	1	6	7	6	8	5	4	1	3

www.prenhall.com/anupindi

For exercises based on Process Model go to http://www.prenhall.com/anupindi

References

Chase, R., and N. Aquilano and F.R. Jacobs. 1999. *Production and Operations Management.* 8th ed. Irwin-McGraw Hill, Chicago, IL.

Kopczak, L., and H.L. Lee. 1994. Hewlett Packard: Deskjet printer supply chain. *Stanford University Case Study:* 385–395.

Nahmias, S. 1997. *Production and Operations Analysis.* Irwin, Homewood, IL.

Narus, J., and J.S. Anderson. 1996. Rethinking distribution: Adaptive channels. *Harvard Business Review:* 112–120.

Ross, S.M. 1972. *Introduction to Probability Models.* Academic Press, New York, NY.

Signorelli, S., and J.L. Heskett. 1989. Benetton (A). *Harvard Business School Case Study:* 1–20.

8

Managing Flow Variability: Safety Capacity

Service processes display significant variability in both inflow and processing times. Variability degrades process performance in terms of delay and congestion experienced by customers who must wait in line, or *in queue,* before being served. A central message from analysis of queuing processes is that *flow times and inventories increase rapidly with capacity utilization and/or variability in interarrival and processing times.* In the presence of variability, therefore, the service provider must trade off flow-time performance against capacity utilization. To decrease flow times and inventories, process managers can take one or both of two actions:

1. Increase capacity by adding servers or reducing average processing time.
2. Reduce the variability of both processing time (e.g. through process standardization) and inter-arrival time (e.g. through scheduling).

Appropriate capacity investment balances the cost of capacity with the benefit of reduced flow times and inventories. Pooling safety capacity also improves flow-time performance.

8.1   INTRODUCTION

Our analysis of flows and inventories in chapters 6 and 7 focused primarily on manufacturing operations. In these operations, raw materials flow into input buffers and are then processed into finished products that are stored in output buffers until needed to fill customer demand. Excess inflow is accumulated as inventory that entails holding costs but also has two important benefits: permitting economies of scale and providing stockout protection against variability in inflows and outflows. The optimal level of inventory, then, balances these costs and benefits.

Service Operations   Similarly, in service operations, customers in need of service (as inputs) arrive at (flow into) the process, are served (processed), and leave (flow out) as satisfied customers (outputs). Customers arriving at bank teller windows, at drive-through restaurants, and at supermarket checkout counters are service inputs, as are passengers arriving at airline check-in counters, patients coming to hospital emergency rooms, and telephone calls ringing at call centers. Inflows may also take the form of job orders arriving at job shops or ships or trucks arriving at loading docks. In each case, the service process manager, unlike his manufacturing counterpart, has only limited control

EXAMPLE 8.1

We return for a moment to garage maker MBPF Inc. Suppose MBPF makes all sales over the telephone to customers who call a toll-free number (see Figure 8.1). Each incoming caller to the MBPF customer-service department may get a sales representative, be put on hold, or worse, get a busy signal. Customers who are "blocked" by busy signals are denied admission and may not enter the system at all. Those put on hold for excessive lengths may simply decide to hang up (abandon the process). They may try to call back later, or they may call competitors, thereby costing MBPF in lost sales.

When serving a customer, sales representatives take customer orders, establish order numbers and delivery due dates, and provide information to customers. MBPF customers have been complaining that they have difficulty accessing the call center to place orders and that they experience excessive time spent on hold waiting for sales representatives. Because the call center is the firm's only source of order taking, MBPF management is quite concerned about service performance and its effect on the bottom line. The company wants to identify appropriate changes in call-center design and operations that would improve performance.

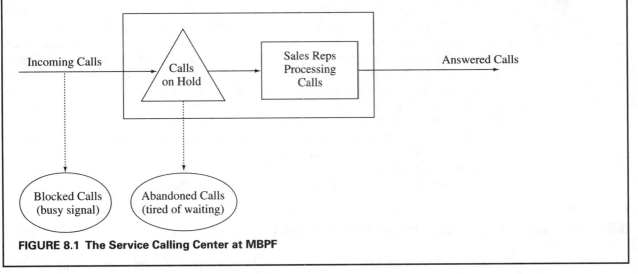

FIGURE 8.1 The Service Calling Center at MBPF

over customer inflow, even when utilizing reservations, appointments, and careful scheduling. Customer inflow now represents *demand for service.* In the context of service operations, customer inflow patterns may display significant variability. As we will discuss, this variability has significant impact on process performance.

Moreover, given the high degree of customization involved in service delivery, individual activity times and total processing times are also significantly more variable than those in manufacturing. For example, in a hair salon, the time taken for each customer is likely to differ, since each customer may have different needs. Finally, because many services cannot be produced and stored in advance for later consumption, arriving customers must wait for service if the resources necessary for processing them are not immediately available.

Service Inventory   In service operations, flow-unit inventory consists of customers waiting for service, which is a significant source of customer dissatisfaction.

Customers have to wait, of course, because servers are not available to provide immediate service. In the case of physical goods, this is equivalent to customers having to wait because of the absence of finished goods inventory. Reducing customer waits and queues requires a twofold approach—increasing processing capacity and/or reducing variability in both inflows and processing times, and each involves costs. In this chapter, we examine the managerial decisions that balance these costs with the benefits of reduced waits, inventories, and flow times. Although we emphasize service operations in this chapter, the concepts discussed here are equally applicable to manufacturing operations.

The situation at MBPF Inc. in Example 8.1 is typical of the situations faced by many businesses, and in this chapter we show how such processes can be modeled and analyzed to provide managerial insights into corrective measures. In section 8.2 we define the terminology used to discuss service processes and define appropriate measures of process performance. The terminology is related to that developed in earlier chapters in the context of general business processes. In section 8.3 we consider the buildup of queues in the absence of variability. In section 8.4 we study the key drivers in queuing processes, namely variability and capacity, that affect various performance measures. In section 8.5 we stress the effect of variability on process performance.

Section 8.6 examines ways in which utilization, capacity decisions and process design affect process performance. Section 8.7 focuses on the effect of limited input buffer capacity on process performance, and section 8.8 focuses on the appropriate allocation of processing and buffer capacity in a queuing process. In section 8.9 we show how synchronization of variability in arrival and variability in processing affect process performance. In section 8.10 we explain why it may be more appropriate to consider the distribution of performance measures (e.g., queue length and waiting time in queue) rather than just their average values. In section 8.11 we discuss how customer perceptions and expectations can be managed to improve performance. Finally, section 8.12 summarizes the key levers for improving process performance.

8.2   SERVICE PROCESS AND PERFORMANCE MEASURES

Recall that any business process is defined by its inputs, outputs, network of activities and buffers, resources, and information flows. In the previous chapters we have emphasized flow rate, flow time, and inventory as the key operational measures of process performance. We have also discussed various levers that drive these measures of process performance.

Although emphasized in a manufacturing setting, any service process can also be studied using this framework. As discussed in chapter 1, a key characteristic of service processes is the fact that most services cannot be produced in advance and held in inventory. In such a situation the use of output inventories to satisfy demand is not feasible. Because a service has to be produced after demand for it occurs, capacity becomes a key lever in managing variability in service processes. Given this special characteristic of service processes, it is useful to specialize the general terminology for business processes introduced in earlier chapters. In this section we introduce the terminology that is more suited to study service processes. We should make clear at the outset that even though the focus of discussion in this chapter is on service processes, most concepts and definitions are also applicable to manufacturing.

Service Processes   In this chapter we will refer to any service process under study as a **queuing process** simply because we envision customers waiting in queues. In Example 8.1, the call center at MBPF Inc. is a queuing process. The basic components of a queuing process are as follows:

- A flow unit arriving for service at a queuing process will be referred to as a **customer** or an **arrival.**
- The input buffer where arrivals wait to be processed is referred to as a **queue.**
- There are three possible customer flows (outputs) in a queuing process.
  1. Customers may be blocked from entering the process and leave without entering.
  2. Customers may abandon the process before being served, after a long wait in queue.
  3. Customers may be served and leave the process subsequently.
- Each resource in the resource pool that processes arrivals will be referred to as a **server.**

A customer may undergo multiple activities performed by different servers in a general queuing process. In a **single-phase queuing process,** each customer is served by only one server and we combine all tasks performed by the server into a single activity. An example is the call center at MBPF where each sales representative serves one customer at a time. In a general **processing network,** multiple servers process each customer, each server performing distinct activities in the order defined by the process flow chart of the service process. For example, customers in a barbershop have their hair washed first and then cut. The washing and the cutting activities form two phases in the network and are performed by different resources.

In this chapter we restrict attention to single-phase queuing processes since they are simpler to analyze and bring out most of the managerial insights on which we wish to focus. Single-phase queuing processes may involve multiple servers in the resource pool. Each server, however, performs the same set of tasks. If the process has multiple servers, it may feature a single queue for all servers, or multiple queues, one for each server. In a single-phase queuing process there is no output buffer since flow units exit the process as soon as they are processed. For example, in the call center at MBPF, customers hang up and exit the process as soon as a sales representative completes service.

Queuing Process Attributes   We now list attributes that help define a queuing process. The queuing process terminology is related to general business process terminology introduced in chapters 3, 4, and 5 where appropriate.

- The average inflow rate of customers (flow units) to a queuing process is referred to as the average **arrival rate** and denoted by R_i.
- The **arrival time** of a customer is the instant at which the customer enters the queuing process. The inverse of the average arrival rate $1/R_i$ is the average time between successive customer arrivals at a queuing process and is referred to as the average **interarrival time.**
- The **departure time** of a customer is the instant at which the customer departs the queuing process.
- The average activity time spent by a customer at a server is referred to as the average **service time** or **processing time** and denoted by T_p.
- The inverse of the average processing time $(1/T_p)$ is referred to as the average **service rate** of a server or **server capacity.** Since we are considering single-phase queuing processes, each server has a load batch of size 1, and the server capacity is equal to the theoretical capacity of a server.
- The servers (resources) in the queuing process form a single resource pool. The number of servers in the queuing process is denoted by c.
- The total capacity across all servers is referred to as the **processing capacity** of the queuing process and denoted by R_p. If we have c servers (if c units of a resource are in the resource

pool), and $c \geq 1$, then the process will be operating at 100% capacity when all servers are processing, that is, if there is a customer being processed at each of the c servers. Then, applying Little's law, we can express the processing (or theoretical) capacity to be the maximal total processing rate:

$$R_p = c / T_p$$

- **Safety capacity,** denoted by R_s, is the difference between the processing capacity of the queuing process and the average arrival rate. We thus have

$$R_s = R_p - R_i$$

- The maximum number of flow units that can wait in the queue is referred to as **buffer capacity** or **queue capacity** and denoted by K.

- **Queue-service discipline** refers to the order in which customers are served. We assume that customers are served in order of their arrival. This queue-service discipline is *first-come/first-served* or *first-in/first-out* (FIFO).

Average Performance Measures for Queuing Processes   Key performance measures of a queuing process are closely related to performance measures discussed earlier for general business processes.

1. *Inventory related measures*

- The average inventory in the queue (input buffer) is referred to as average **queue length** and denoted by I_i.
- The average inventory in process in the queuing process is referred to as average **number in service** and denoted by I_p.
- The average total inventory in the queuing process is referred to as the average **total number in process** and is denoted by I. We have $I = I_i + I_p$.

2. *Flow time related measures*

- The average time spent by a customer (flow unit) in the queue (input buffer) is referred to as average **waiting time in queue** and denoted by T_i.
- The average flow time spent by a customer (flow unit) in a queuing process is referred to as average **total time in process** and denoted by T. We have $T = T_i + T_p$.

3. *Flow rate related measures*

- The average fraction of customers blocked from entering the queuing process because the input buffer is full is referred to as **proportion blocked** and denoted by P_b. The average rate at which incoming customers are blocked is referred to as the **blocking rate** and denoted by R_b. We thus have

$$R_b = R_i P_b$$

The rate at which customers enter the queue is given by

$$R_i - R_b = R_i(1 - P_b)$$

- The average fraction of waiting customers who, because of long waits, abandon the queue and depart before being served is referred to as **proportion abandoning** and is denoted by P_a. The rate at which waiting customers abandon the queue is referred to as the **abandoning rate** and denoted by R_a. We thus have

$$R_a = R_i(1 - P_b)P_a$$

- The rate at which customers (flow units) exit the queuing process after being served is referred to as the **throughput** and denoted by R. We thus have

$$R = R_i - R_b - R_a = R_i(1 - P_a)(1 - P_b)$$

This relationship is an expression of flow conservation with total inflow rate (R_i) equal to total outflow rate ($R + R_b + R_a$).

4. *Process cost related measures*

- **Capacity utilization** of a queuing process is denoted by ρ and is the ratio of throughput to processing capacity (consistent with the definition in chapter 5).

Relationships between Performance Measures for Queuing Processes   From the definitions we can establish relationships between various performance measures. Capacity utilization (ρ) can be expressed as follows:

$$\rho = \text{throughput / processing capacity} = R / R_p = RT_p / c$$

Capacity utilization (ρ) may be interpreted as either:

1. The average fraction of time that each server is busy, or

2. The average fraction of all servers that are busy.

The average number of busy servers is then:

$$\rho c = RT_p$$

Since each server processes one customer at a time, ρc is also the average number of customers being processed simultaneously, or the average number in service I_p. We thus have

$$I_p = \rho c = RT_p$$

With flow rate R, we can apply Little's law to derive relationships between the number of customers and flow times. We can determine relationships between

- average waiting times in queue (T_i) and average queue length (I_i) as $I_i = RT_i$,
- average service time (T_p) and average number in service (I_p) as $I_p = RT_p$, and
- average time in process (T) and average total number in process (I) as $I = RT$.

If no customers are blocked or abandon the queue, throughput (R) equals the arrival rate (R_i). All the above relationships can be modified appropriately. In particular, if no customers are blocked, or abandon service, and the processing rate is larger than the arrival rate, we can link safety capacity and utilization. We have

$$R_s = R_p - R_i = R_p - \rho R_p = (1 - \rho)R_p$$

We derived these general relationships in previous chapters, and in this section we are simply reinterpreting them in the context of queuing processes. (In fact, Little's law was originally derived from an analysis of queuing processes.)

Variability of Performance Measures   Sometimes assessing these performance measures in terms of *average* values alone may not be sufficient. For example, actual waiting times and flow times typically vary among customers; some customers may have to wait for long times, others may be served immediately. Typically, a customer's waiting tolerance decreases in proportion to the duration of the wait. Thus, it is not enough to promise that the average wait across all customers will be less than a prespecified duration. Those who have to wait for longer times will be more dissatisfied than those who have to wait for shorter times. Ideally, we would like to know the entire probability distribution of the flow time, or at least the probability that customers will have to wait longer than a specified period.

Suppose, for example, that average flow time is 10 minutes. Because of variability, however, 5% of customers experience a flow time of over 100 minutes. In this case, 100 minutes corresponds to the 95th percentile of the flow-time distribution. It is cold comfort for customers spending over 100 minutes to be told that the average customer waits only 10 minutes. If we refer to the average alone to quote all customers a response time of, say, 10 to 15 minutes, we could not keep that promise in a large percentage of cases. We would frustrate customers and ultimately lose business. In such instances, a better measure of service performance would be "95% of our customers are served within *t* units of time," not "On average, our customers are served in *t* units of time." Using such a measure, we can limit the percentage of customers who will not be served within the promised length of time.

Process Performance and Financial Measures   The average values or percentiles of these operational measures directly affect the financial measures of process performance. For example, on customers blocked from entering the call-center process, MBPF loses potential revenue if those customers fail to call back. If queues are long and callers have to wait on hold for a long period of time, MBPF must pay telephone charges incurred while customers are kept on hold. In addition, long waits also mean customer dissatisfaction, with some customers abandoning the queue. Once again, MBPF loses potential revenue when an abandoning caller decides not to call back. Such inconvenience also shows up as lost future revenue if disgruntled customers decide to take their business elsewhere. Capacity utilization represents the fraction of time that each sales representative is productively used; idleness represents a waste of resources. Thus each of the operational performance measures for queuing processes has a direct bearing on process revenues or costs or both.

Operational performance measures may depend on queuing process attributes and customer behavior. For instance, abandon rate depends on both the customer's waiting time in queue and his or her tolerance for wait, which in turn may depend on available alternate sources of supply (the competition). In the remainder of this chapter, we study ways in which managers can control process attributes and influence customer behavior to improve key performance measures.

8.3 DELAY AND CONGESTION IN A QUEUING PROCESS WITHOUT VARIABILITY

Congestion in a process occurs when a queue builds up, and any congestion clearly imposes delays on customers in queue. The question is *Why* do queues form?

The Interaction between Inter-Arrival and Processing Times   Example 8.2 illustrates a key observation about single-server queuing processes without variability: *Assuming that interarrival times and processing times are constant, queues will develop if interarrival time is shorter than processing time. Queues will not develop if interarrival time is longer than processing time.*

The same principle can be expressed in terms of arrival rate and processing capacity. Whereas customer arrival rate R_i measures demand for service, processing capacity R_p is the maximum supply of service. If no calls are blocked or abandoned, process flow rate (or throughput) R is given by the minimum of arrival rate and processing capacity:

$$R = \min(R_i, R_p)$$

The fact that the arrival rate R_i does not exceed the processing capacity R_p will be referred to as the **stability condition.** Under this condition, implied throughput, therefore, is R_i. Capacity utilization (ρ) can thus be expressed as follows:

$$\rho = \text{throughput} / \text{processing capacity} = R_i / R_p = T_p / T_i$$

and the stability condition described above requires that processing capacity be sufficient to handle all the demand. Equivalently, the above observation about single-server

---

EXAMPLE 8.2

Returning to the MBPF call center, suppose the following:

- The call center is staffed by a single sales representative,
- There is infinite buffer capacity, so that no arrivals are blocked and $P_b = 0$,
- No one abandons the queue until service completion, so that $P_a = 0$.

Suppose that calls arrive and are served in a uniform or deterministic fashion at evenly spaced points in time; both inter-arrival time and processing time for each customer are constant. Specifically, suppose that call arrivals are exactly 10 minutes apart and that it takes exactly 9 minutes to process each call. In Figure 8.2, we track process flow time and inventory graphically. Each solid block represents the time spent in the process by the caller identified on the vertical axis.

Because calls arrive every 10 minutes and it takes 9 minutes to process each call, there will obviously be no queue. Flow time for each call will be 9 minutes and waiting time will be 0 minutes. The plot in Figure 8.2 can also be viewed as a call-by-call analysis of inventory in the process. Analyzing any queuing process is tantamount to analyzing the inventory (of customer calls) within process boundaries.

Now suppose that calls come in *every minute* and that it still takes 9 minutes to process each call. As shown in Figure 8.3, a queue will develop. The queue will continue to grow if calls come in faster than the rate at which they are being processed and the process will not be stable. Like inventories in manufacturing, *queues in service processes build up whenever inflow rate exceeds processing rate.*

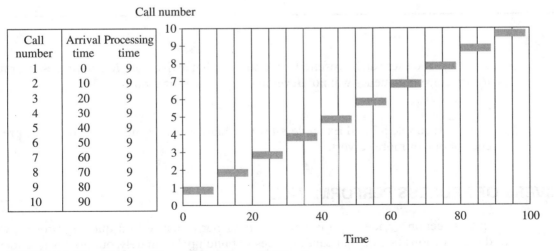

Call number	Arrival time	Processing time
1	0	9
2	10	9
3	20	9
4	30	9
5	40	9
6	50	9
7	60	9
8	70	9
9	80	9
10	90	9

FIGURE 8.2 Flow Times with an Arrival Every 10 Minutes

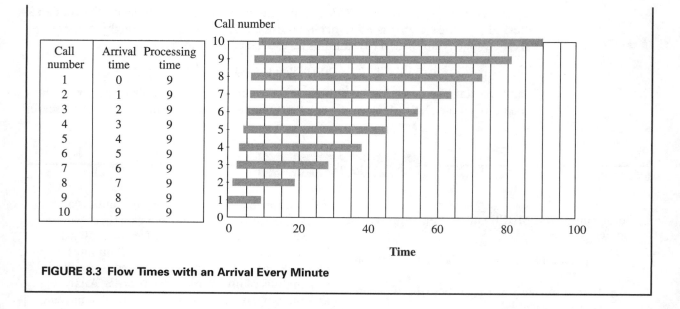

FIGURE 8.3 Flow Times with an Arrival Every Minute

EXAMPLE 8.3

In our MBPF example, we have a single server and constant arrival and processing rates of

$$R_i = 1 / 10 \text{ call per minute}, R_p = 1 / 9 \text{ call per minute}$$

Because no calls are blocked or abandoned, throughput is given by

$$R = \min(R_i, R_p) = 1 / 10 \text{ call per minute}$$

and capacity utilization is given by

$$\rho = R / R_p = 0.9$$

Queues, therefore, will not develop. With calls arriving every 10 minutes and each call being processed in 9 minutes, our server will be busy 90% of the time and idle the remaining 10%. We avoid congestion since ρ, which also represents the average fraction of time that a server is busy, is less than 1.

---

queuing processes can be restated as: Assuming that arrival rate R_i and processing rate R_p are constant, queues will not develop if capacity utilization

$$\rho = R_i / R_p < 1.$$

In Example 8.3 and Example 8.4 we evaluate capacity and utilization in the presence of one or more servers.

8.4 DRIVERS OF PROCESS PERFORMANCE

In this section, to identify the key drivers of performance in a queuing process, we discuss various factors that cause queues to build up. Ultimately, our goal is to understand the effect of these drivers and to identify levers that managers can use to improve performance.

EXAMPLE 8.4

In our MBPF example, let us assume that we have three sales representatives. In this case we have c = 3 servers. The processing capacity of the call center is given by

$$R_p = c / T_p = \tfrac{1}{3} \text{ call per minute.}$$

Because no calls are blocked or abandoned, throughput is given by

$$R = \min(R_i, R_p) = \tfrac{1}{10} \text{ call per minute}$$

Capacity utilization is thus obtained as

$$\rho = R / R_p = 0.3$$

On average, each server is busy 30% of the time. The average number of busy servers is given by

$$\rho c = 3 \times 0.3 = 0.9$$

which is the same as in Example 8.3. On average, 0.9 servers will be busy (serving I_p = 0.9 customers), and 2.1 servers will be idle.

Stochastic Variability   Our analysis in Example 8.2 was based on the assumption that inflow times and processing times are known and constant. We saw that in the absence of variability, we can guarantee that flow units will not have to wait by ensuring that processing capacity exceeds inflow rate by keeping some safety capacity. As mentioned in section 8.1, however, service processes are characterized by a high degree of variability in customer arrivals and processing requirements. At the MBPF call center, for example, customers are not likely to call exactly every 10 minutes, nor is a sales representative likely to spend exactly the same amount of time with each caller. Both interarrival and processing times are likely to vary from one caller to the next. This type of random variability is called **stochastic variability.** Example 8.5 illustrates how stochastic variability may lead to the build up of a queue.

Synchronizing Interarrival and Processing Times   Before we proceed, we should point out that queues build up primarily because variability in processing times is not synchronized with variability in interarrival times. In Example 8.5, customer 3 has a short interarrival time and arrives 1 minute after customer 2. Customer 2, however, has a long processing time of 12 minutes, causing customer 3 to wait for 11 minutes. When interarrival and processing times are synchronized or positively correlated, waiting times can be significantly reduced. Indeed, if short interarrival times are coupled with short processing times and long interarrival times are coupled with long processing times, then queues may not build up.

Thus, in Example 8.5, if processing times of the 10 arrivals were 11, 1, 7, 16, 3, 7, 10, 10, 15, and 10 (recall that arrival times are 0, 12, 13, 20, 41, 44, 51, 62, 75, and 90), then there will be no queue despite variability in interarrival and processing times because variability in the two cases is synchronized or positively correlated. Short interarrival times are coupled with short processing times and long interarrival times are coupled with long processing times. The first customer leaves at time 11 while the second customer arrives at time 12. The second customer leaves at time 13 just as the third customer arrives. As before, the capacity utilization is 0.9. Synchronization between interarrival and processing times is discussed more fully in section 8.9.

To reiterate: Queues build up under two conditions EVEN if capacity utilization $\rho < 1$:

1. If interarrival and processing times are variable, and
2. If variability between the two times is not synchronized.

EXAMPLE 8.5

Let us examine the effect of stochastic variability on process performance at the MBPF call center. Suppose that during certain 10-minute periods multiple customers call in, and during other 10-minute periods there are no incoming customer calls. In the long term across all customers, however, *average* interarrival time is still 10 minutes. Can you expect some customers to wait? What if, as in Example 8.2, interarrival times are constant at 10 minutes, but variability in orders placed produces unevenness in processing times even though average processing time is still 9 minutes?

Figure 8.4 shows how queues build up when both interarrival and processing times display variability. We can see that interarrival times over the 10 customers are 12, 1, 7, 21, 3, 7, 11, 13, and 15, so average interarrival time is 90/9 = 10 minutes. The 10 customers thus arrive at times 0, 12, 13, 20, 41, 44, 51, 62, 75, and 90. Meanwhile, processing times for the 10 customers are 7, 12, 15, 13, 8, 9, 7, 4, 9, and 6, with an average processing time of 90/10 = 9 minutes. As before, capacity utilization, is $\rho = 9/10 = 0.9$. Variability in arrivals and processing, however, causes queues to build up, with all customers other than customers 2 and 10 having to wait.

FIGURE 8.4 Queuing Effects of Variability in Arrivals

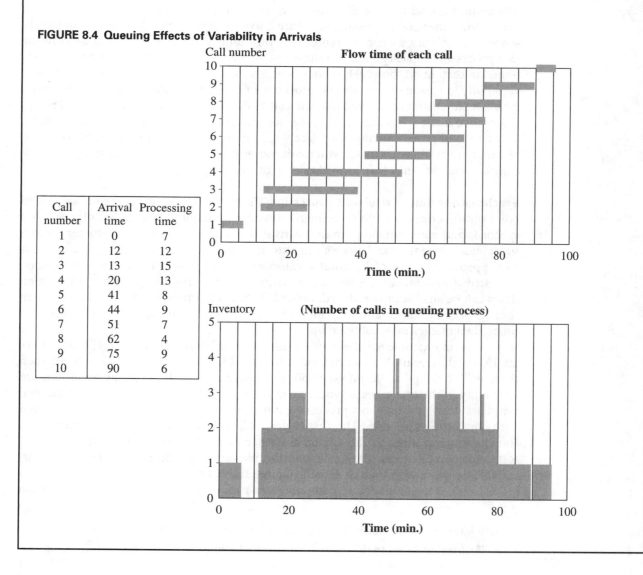

Call number	Arrival time	Processing time
1	0	7
2	12	12
3	13	15
4	20	13
5	41	8
6	44	9
7	51	7
8	62	4
9	75	9
10	90	6

We refer to the two times as not synchronized if there is less than perfect positive correlation between them.

In the presence of variability, some customers may have short interarrival times while others have long interarrival times. Similarly, some customers may have short processing times while others have long processing times. When short interarrival times coincide with long processing times (as may happen if the two times are not synchronized), queues build up. In essence, this situation results simply from an imbalance between inflows and outflows.

A *negative variation* is said to occur when the processing time of an arrival is greater than the interarrival time of the next arrival; a *positive variation* occurs when the interarrival time of an arrival is greater than the processing time of the previous arrival. Waiting effects are counterintuitive because positive and negative variations do not necessarily cancel out.

Negative variations cause queue buildup because they require servers to work longer on each customer while others wait. In contrast, positive variations yield idle time, which cannot be stored for the future and is thus lost forever. The idle time from positive variations cannot, therefore, be used to compensate for negative variations. Thus, we may state the following observation about the corrupting influence of stochastic variability: Queues form when the customer arrival rate is—at least temporarily—greater than the processing rate at which customers are being served. If interarrival and/or processing times display variability that is not synchronized, queues may form EVEN IF average interarrival time is longer than average processing time—that is, even when there is some safety capacity.

In the rest of this chapter, we assume that interarrival and processing times are not synchronized but independent. The previous examples illustrate how queuing process performance is affected by two factors:

1. The mean and variability of interarrival times, and
2. The mean and variability of processing times.

When planning for process capacity, managers generally take into account mean arrival and processing rates. The key lesson to be learned from Example 8.5 is that variability in these rates also has a significant impact on process performance in terms of congestion and delay.

In practice, interarrival times can be measured by tracking either *arrival times* or *total number of arrivals* during a fixed time period. Likewise, processing times can be measured for different customers. We then estimate mean interarrival and processing times by computing the averages. We determine variability in interarrival and processing times by its variance (or standard deviation), which indicates its dispersion around the mean. Variance itself is an insufficient measure of variability—processing times with standard deviation and mean of 1 minute display more relative variability than processing times with standard deviation of 1 minute and mean of 100 minutes.

Coefficient of Variation   We need, therefore, a standardized or relative measure of stochastic variability. One such measure is the **coefficient of variation,** which is defined as *the ratio of the standard deviation to the mean*. We denote the coefficients of variation of interarrival and processing times by C_i and C_p, respectively. Thus, the ratio of the standard deviation of interarrival time to mean interarrival time is C_i and the ratio of the standard deviation of processing time to the mean processing time is C_p.

Queue Length Formula   If arrival rate R_i is less than or equal to processing rate R_p and no arrivals are blocked or abandoned, throughput of the process equals the arrival rate R_i, and utilization is given by

$$\rho = R_i \, / \, R_p$$

We can see from our discussion thus far that utilization, as well as the mean and variability of interarrival and processing times, is a key driver of queuing-process performance, at least in terms of average queue length and average waiting time in queue. This relationship can be expressed mathematically for the case in which we have independent variability and

$$R_i < R_p$$

and no customers are blocked or abandon the queue. The following expression approximates the relationship among average queue length and utilization, number of servers, and coefficient of variation of interarrival and processing times (details may be found in chapter 8 of Hopp & Spearman [1996]):

$$I_i = \frac{\rho^{\sqrt{2(c+1)}}}{1 - \rho} \times \frac{C_i^2 + C_p^2}{2}$$

This formula will be referred to as the **queue length formula** throughout the rest of the chapter.

Utilization and Variability Effects   Observe that average queue length I_i is a product of two factors. The first factor

$$\frac{\rho^{\sqrt{2(c+1)}}}{1 - \rho}$$

captures the **utilization effect,** which shows that *queue length increases rapidly as utilization ρ increases to 1—When capacity utilization nears 100%, average queue length approaches infinity.*

The second factor

$$\frac{C_i^2 + C_p^2}{2}$$

captures the **variability effect.** In this factor, note that the effects of arrival-time and processing-time variability are similar and additive (because we have assumed that they are independent). We must reemphasize that when there is variability in arrivals or processing—as there is in practice—queues will build up and some waiting will occur even with a positive amount of safety capacity, or, equivalently, even if utilization is less than 100%.

Although the queue length formula is an approximation and not an exact relationship, it turns out to be exact if there is a single server ($c = 1$) and interarrival and processing times are both independent and exponentially distributed (see appendix A.2.2). If interarrival and processing times are both exponentially distributed, we have

$$C_i = C_p = 1$$

and with $c = 1$ we obtain

$$I_i = \rho^2/(1- \rho)$$

Exact results for other queuing systems are often impossible or discouragingly difficult to calculate. To learn procedures for obtaining exact relationships in more complex

EXAMPLE 8.6

Suppose that the MBPF call center has only one sales representative (*SR*), who takes calls in the order received. If the *SR* is busy, the caller is put on hold. Suppose, too, that there are enough telephone lines for all callers to get into the system without receiving a busy signal. We also assume that no one abandons the system. Calls arrive at an average rate of 20 per hour, and it takes an average of 2.5 minutes to process a call (to complete the order entry). Finally, suppose that interarrival and processing times are well approximated by exponential distributions. The *SR* is paid $20 an hour. MBPF estimates that each minute a customer spends on hold costs $2 in telephone charges, customer dissatisfaction, and loss of future business. Estimate the average hourly cost of operating the MBPF call center.

Solution.   In this example we have a process with a single server ($c = 1$) and unlimited queue capacity. Mean arrival rate is $R_i = 20$ calls per hour, or $\frac{1}{3}$ call per minute, and mean processing time is $T_p = 2.5$ minutes. Processing capacity, therefore, is $R_p = 1/2.5$ call per minute, or 24 calls per hour. Since arrival rate is less than processing capacity and no callers are blocked or abandon the queue, we have a flow rate (throughput) of $R = R_i = 20$ calls per hour or $\frac{1}{3}$ call per minute. Capacity utilization is thus

$$\rho = R_i / R_p = 20/24$$

Note that because interarrival and processing times are exponentially distributed, $C_i = C_p = 1$. Using the queue length formula with $c = 1$, $C_i = C_p = 1$, we have the following average queue length:

$$I_i = \rho^2 / (1 - \rho) = 4.167$$

On average, there will be 4.167 customers on hold. The average number being processed is

$$I_p = RT_p = (\tfrac{1}{3}) \times 2.5 = 0.833$$

On average, then, there are

$$I = I_i + I_p = 5 \text{ callers in the process}$$

Of the 5 callers in the process on average, 4.167 are on hold and 0.833 are being processed. If we apply Little's law, we see that each customer spends an average of $T = I/R = 15$ minutes in the process, and $T_i = I_i / R = 12.5$ minutes waiting in the queue (on hold).

Each customer kept on hold costs $2 per minute, or $120 an hour, and at any point in time, there are, on average, I_i customers on hold. Average cost of customer wait, therefore, is

$$\$120 I_i = \$500 \text{ per hour}$$

Alternately, each customer waits, on average, for $T_i = 12.5$ minutes before being served by the *SR*, which costs MBPF, on average,

$$12.5 \times \$2 = \$25 \text{ per caller}$$

Since, on average, 20 customers call in each hour, MBPF incurs a total waiting cost of

$$(\$25)(20) = \$500 \text{ per hour}$$

The equivalence of the two computations is a result of Little's law $I_i = RT_i$. Because the *SR* is paid $20 per hour, MBPF incurs a total cost of $520 per hour, which is the cost of customer wait plus the cost of processing capacity.

Finally, note that one *SR* can process, on average, $R_p = 24$ callers per hour. Meanwhile, customers are calling in at the rate of $R_i = 20$ calls per hour. The call center, therefore, has the following safety capacity:

$$R_s = R_p - R_i = 24 - 20 = 4 \text{ callers per hour}$$

Variability, however, causes the queue to build up despite the presence of this safety capacity. If (as in our examples in the preceding section) there were no variability, there would be no queue or wait.

queuing systems, see Kleinrock (1975). In this text, we will continue using the queue length formula because it is a good approximation in many instances and effectively illustrates the impact of various factors on queuing-process performance. Upon computing I_i from the queue length formula, we can use Little's law to obtain $T_i = I_i/R$. The total flow time in the process is then $T = T_i + T_p$. The queue length formula illustrates how these measures of process performance depend on variability and utilization.

Therefore, the key levers for decreasing average waiting and flow times are:

1. Decreasing the variability in interarrival and processing times, or
2. Decreasing the capacity utilization $\rho = R_i / cR_p$ either by:
   a. Decreasing arrival rate or
   b. Increasing the server capacity or number of servers.

The average number of customers in the process given by *the sum of the number in queue and the number being served* is

$$I = I_i + I_p = I_i + \rho c$$

In Example 8.6, we use the queue length formula to evaluate queuing-system performance at MBPF.

8.5   THE EFFECT OF VARIABILITY ON AVERAGE PROCESS PERFORMANCE

As discussed, the variability of interarrival and processing times is measured in terms of the coefficients of variation of interarrival-time and processing-time distributions. Note that average length of the queue (and waiting time in queue) is proportional to *the sum of the squares of the two coefficients of variation.* Our basic observation of cases in which there is no limit on queue capacity can thus be stated as follows: *For any stable queuing process in which mean interarrival and activity times are held fixed, average waiting time in queue (or average length of the queue) increases with an increase in the coefficient of variation of either the interarrival or the processing time.*

Hence one lever to decrease queue lengths and waiting time is to reduce variability in arrival and processing times. Reducing variability in arrival times means planning for more regular arrival patterns. In manufacturing, it means choosing more reliable suppliers with less variable lead times. (Recall from chapter 7 that less leadtime variability also leads to reduced safety-inventory requirements.)

Demand Management Strategies   Even in service operations, in which there is limited control over customer inflows, it is possible to make customer arrivals more predictable through better forecasting, scheduling, differential pricing, and appointments. Because all these actions/tactics affect demand, we call them **demand management strategies.** For example, most customer-service departments at health-insurance organizations inform callers of busy periods and encourage them to call during off-peak periods. Similarly, airlines, hotels, medical offices, and restaurants try to match supply with uncertain demand by means of reservations and appointments.

To reduce variability in processing times, the firm must consider the source of this variability. In some instances, the same resource is responsible for producing a variety of products with very different processing times. In such situations, firms can reduce processing-time variability by limiting product variety. Examples of this tactic include express meal packs at fast-food restaurants, specialized teller windows at banks, and different extensions for different types of telephone calls at a variety of businesses. In some cases, processing-time variability results from a lack of process standardization or a lack of workforce training in standard operating procedures. In such instances, the solution is to set up a standardized process or an appropriate training program. Toyota, for example, defines a standardized sequence of activities for each workstation, which results not only in a reduction of processing-time variability, but also in a reduction of average processing time as well.

Regardless of the strategies that a firm employs, however, it is hard to eliminate all sources of variability. Banks, for example, cannot ensure that customers will come in at regular intervals; after all, each and every customer makes an independent decision about going to the bank. Likewise, banks cannot eliminate processing-time variability because different customers have different transaction needs. Most processes will involve some variability in both inflows and processing, and therefore managers must consider other levers to improve flow-time performance.

8.6   THE EFFECT OF UTILIZATION ON AVERAGE PROCESS PERFORMANCE

As discussed in section 8.2, safety capacity and utilization in a queuing process are closely related:

$$\text{Safety capacity} = (1 - \rho) \times \text{processing capacity}$$

We have also shown in section 8.4 that changing safety capacity—and thus utilization—has an effect on process performance. Increasing safety capacity (decreasing utilization) results in a decrease of average queue length and average waiting time in queue. Safety capacity (or utilization, or both) may change as a result of either changing the arrival rate, server capacity, or the number of servers.

As in chapter 5, total processing capacity R_p can be increased by either:

1. Adding more servers, thus increasing c, or
2. Working faster, thus decreasing T_p

Increasing processing capacity R_p then reduces the capacity utilization

$$\rho = R_i/R_p$$

and increases safety capacity

$$R_s = R_p - R_i$$

For a given processing rate R_p, utilization can be decreased by decreasing the arrival rate R_i. To summarize, the following measures decrease the average queue length and waiting time:

1. Decreasing processing time T_p,
2. Decreasing arrival rate R_i, or
3. Increasing the number of servers c.

Consequently, both total flow time and average total number in process will also decline.

On the other hand, increasing capacity also involves costs in employing more servers or making them work faster. The cost of providing sufficient capacity to avoid all delays under all circumstances generally cannot be justified economically. The role of the operations analyst, therefore, is to design service processes that achieve an acceptable balance between operating costs and the delay suffered by customers. From the information presented here, we must conclude the following: If customers are time-sensitive, it is not optimal, in the presence of stochastic variability, to balance capacity with demand; one should also invest in some safety capacity. In a time-sensitive environment, managers should shy away from operating at a level near full utilization.

8.6.1 Effect of Arrival Rate and Processing Time on Average Process Performance

In this section, we consider the effect of changing arrival rates and processing time (and, as a result, changing utilization) on average queue length and waiting time in queue. A reduction in arrival rate is generally not desirable because it reduces revenues. However, firms use higher prices during peak arrival periods to shift some of the arrivals to off-peak periods.

Table 8.1 shows how process performance (as measured by average length of queue and waiting time in queue) changes with changes in processing time while keeping arrival rate fixed; all evaluations are made using the queue length formula and Little's law. Recall that interarrival-time and processing-time distributions are exponential, implying a coefficient of variation of 1 in each case. Now note that, as resource utilization increases—as safety capacity decreases—average queue length and waiting time in queue increases rapidly. In this case, although we keep average throughput (arrival rate) the same, we measure the effect of changing utilization by changing processing time.

In Table 8.2 we show the effect of varying arrival rate (while keeping processing time fixed) on process performance.

Throughput-Delay Curve Note that average queue length in the two instances is the same because utilization is the same. Average waiting time, however, is different in the two cases because throughput is different. It is clear, however, that as utilization gets

TABLE 8.1 Performance Measures for Varying Processing Time

Throughput $R = R_i$ [number/min]	0.333	0.333	0.333	0.333	0.333
Average processing time T_p [min]	2.5	2.6	2.7	2.8	2.9
Utilization ρ	0.833	0.866	0.899	0.932	0.966
Safety capacity $R_s = R_p - R_i$ [number/min]	0.067	0.052	0.037	0.024	0.012
Average queue length I_i	4.155	5.597	8.002	12.774	27.446
Average waiting time $T_i = I_i / R_i$ [min]	12.5	16.8	24.0	38.4	82.4

TABLE 8.2 Performance Measures for Varying Arrival Rate

Throughput $R = R_i$ [number/min]	0.333	0.346	0.360	0.373	0.386
Average processing time T_p [min]	2.5	2.5	2.5	2.5	2.5
Utilization ρ	0.833	0.866	0.899	0.932	0.966
Safety capacity $R_s = R_p - R_i$ [number/min]	0.067	0.054	0.040	0.027	0.014
Average queue length I_i	4.155	5.597	8.002	12.774	27.446
Average waiting time $T_i = I_i / R_i$ [min]	12.5	16.2	22.2	34.2	71.1

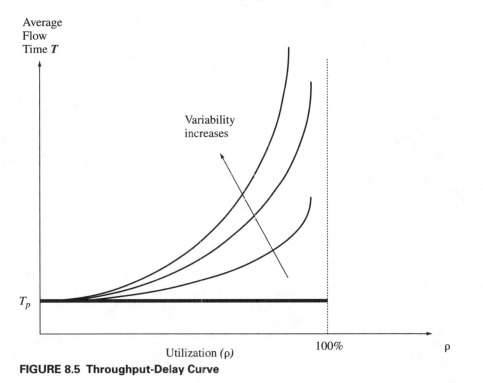

FIGURE 8.5 Throughput-Delay Curve

the two cases because throughput is different. It is clear, however, that as utilization gets closer to 1, average queue length and average waiting time increase rapidly. Recall that in section 8.5, we measured the effect of variability on average waiting time. If we combine the effects of variability with those of utilization, we see that the relationship between average flow time (average waiting time + average processing time) and utilization (for various levels of variability) is as shown in Figure 8.5.

This graph is known as the **throughput-delay curve.** It shows that *average flow time increases rapidly as capacity utilization and/or variability increase.* From this observation, we must conclude that in the presence of variability, high capacity utilization is accompanied by long flow times. In designing service processes, therefore, the manager must trade off the advantages of high capacity utilization against the disadvantages of long flow times.

8.6.2   The Effect of Number of Servers on Average Process Performance

In the previous section, we focused on the effect of changing the processing time or arrival rate on process performance. In this section, we focus on the effect of changing the number of servers on performance. As we shall see, not only the number of servers but the means by which they are organized in the design of the queuing process have a significant impact on process performance.

We return to the MBPF call center described in Example 8.6. Assume that Charles, a process manager, is investigating the potential benefits of increasing the number of *SR*s in the call center. In addition to increasing capacity, he must produce an optimal process layout design by determining the best way to organize available capacity.

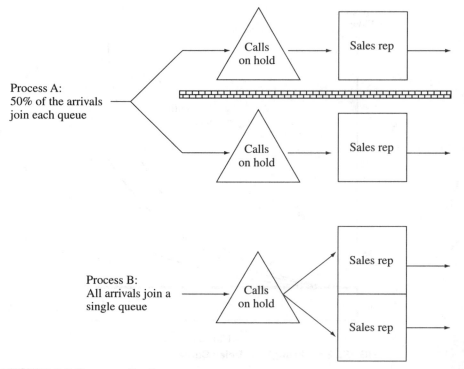

FIGURE 8.6 Resource Pooling

With regard to adding a second *SR,* Charles has two choices of process designs shown in Figure 8.6:

- Process A serves customers with two servers (resources), each with his or her own queue. (This system would be the same as one in which each of the two *SR*s had his or her own phone number, with customers calling one or the other.)
- Process B pools the two servers by placing customers in a single queue that feeds both. (This system would be the same as one in which customers called a common number, waited on hold in a common queue, and were routed in turn to the first available server.)

For purposes of this analysis, suppose that with process A, an arrival randomly chooses one of the queues with equal probability and then remains in that queue. We would like to compare the performance characteristics of the two proposed configurations for the MBPF call center. We first evaluate the performance of process A in Example 8.7.

In Example 8.8 we evaluate the total cost of a process structured like process B, in which a single queue feeds both servers. Remember that in a case with multiple servers, the waiting-time formula is only an approximation. Exact formulas for cases featuring exponential interarrival and processing times may be found in the appendix at the end of this chapter. Recall that we have assumed no limit on buffer capacity. Thus, in this example, when using the formulas in the appendix we set buffer capacity *K* (which we will discuss more fully in section 8.7) to be a very large number. Although the process is a little tedious, these formulas in the appendix can be programmed in an Excel spreadsheet. The reader is invited to download such a spreadsheet (for those cases in which inter-arrival-time and activity-time distributions are exponential), called queuMMcK.xls, from the MBPF Website at

http://www.prenhall.com/anupindi

EXAMPLE 8.7

We begin by reconsidering the data in Example 8.6. Suppose MBPF hires a second *SR*, who is assigned a new telephone number. Customers are equally likely to call either of the two numbers. Once put on hold, customers reckon that the wait at the other number could be worse and tend to stay on line rather than hang up and call the other number. Assuming an unlimited buffer capacity, determine the hourly cost of this process.

Solution   The call-center process described here is similar to process A in Figure 8.6. It features two identical independent servers processing two separate queues. The total process, therefore, can be divided into two identical subprocesses, each with a single server and a single queue. For each of these two subprocesses the following data obtain:

Arrival rate: $R_i = (\frac{1}{3})/2 = \frac{1}{6}$ per minute, or 10 per hour,

Processing rate: $R_p = \frac{1}{2.5}$ per minute, or 24 per hour,

Number of servers: $c = 1$, and

Capacity utilization: $\rho = 0.4167$.

Using the queue length formula and Little's law, we see that average number of arrivals waiting on hold will be

$$I_i = 0.298$$

and average waiting time on hold will be

$$T_i = I_i / R_i = 1.79 \text{ minutes}$$

With the cost of customer waiting being $120 per customer per hour, average waiting cost in each subprocess will be

$$\$120I_i = (120)(0.298) = \$35.76 \text{ per hour}$$

The total waiting cost across the two subprocesses in process A will be $2 \times \$35.76 = \$71.52$ per hour. Because each *SR* is paid $20 per hour (for a total of $40), MBPF now incurs a total cost of

$$71.52 + 40 = \$111.52 \text{ per hour}$$

This figure is a significant improvement over the $520 per hour incurred with a single *SR* under the process described in Example 8.6.

Now we evaluate the amount of safety capacity entailed by process A. Recall that although each *SR* has the capacity to process 24 calls per hour, each handles, on average, only 10 calls per hour and therefore has a safety capacity of 14 calls per hour. Total safety capacity in the process is thus 28 calls per hour.

In Example 8.8, we list the results obtained by using the approximate waiting-time formula and the exact results obtained by using the available spreadsheet.

The Advantage of Pooling Safety Capacity   Why does the situation under process B have a lower waiting time than under process A? Observe that when safety capacity is not pooled, the following situation may arise: While one server has a queue built up, the second server is idle. If safety capacity is pooled, a server will be idle only if there is no queue in the process. Consider, too, the fact that in process A, the waiting time of a customer is dependent on the processing times of those ahead in the queue. When there are independent single queues for each server, this dependence is very strong. If two servers serve a single queue, however, a customer's waiting time is only partially dependent on each preceding customer's processing time. If a preceding customer requires a long processing time, chances are high that the other server will become available to serve the waiting customer before the first customer has been served. This situation not only reduces our customer's waiting time, but also makes it less dependent on the processing times of preceding customers. This process can significantly reduce waiting times. This insight leads us to the following important observation: Pooling all

EXAMPLE 8.8

We analyze the same situation as described in Example 8.7. Now, however, we suppose that both *SR*s are assigned the same toll-free number and that customers on hold form a single queue. The caller at the head of the queue is automatically directed to the first available *SR*. Compute the total hourly cost under this configuration.

Solution This situation involves a queuing process with two servers, and the following data:

> *Arrival rate: $R_i = \frac{1}{3}$* per minute, or 20 per hour,
>
> *Number of servers: c* = 2, and
>
> *Processing time: T_p* = 2.5 minutes.

Using the exact formulas from the appendix at the end of the chapter (we have used the spreadsheet to simplify calculations), we obtain the average number of callers on hold to be

$$I_i = 0.1767$$

The average waiting time on hold will then be

$$T_i = I_i / R_i = 0.53 \text{ minutes}$$

At $120 per customer per hour of waiting, we obtain an hourly average waiting cost of

$$\$120 I_i = \$21.20 \text{ per hour}$$

Each *SR* is paid $20 per hour (for a total of $40), therefore, MBPF now incurs a total cost of

$21.20 + 40 = $61.20 per hour

Note that this is a significant improvement over the $111.52 per hour incurred with process A.

If we use the approximate waiting-time formula to evaluate the various quantities, we obtain the following figures:

- $I_i = 0.4016,$
- $T_i = I_i / R_i = 1.20$ minutes,
- Waiting cost of 120I_i = \$48.19$ per hour, and
- Total cost of 48.19 + 40 = $88.19 per hour.

Note that our approximation overestimates waiting time and costs in this case.

Briefly consider safety capacity under this process. We have two *SR*s, each capable of serving, on average, 24 customers per hour, or a total of $R_p = 48$ customers per hour. The total number of incoming calls remains, on average, $R_i = 20$ per hour. The process, therefore, has a total safety capacity of $R_s = 28$ calls per hour. Note that this safety capacity is exactly the same as that afforded by process A. The only difference in the use of available capacity is that in process B, all safety capacity is pooled and made available to all callers. This results in reduced waiting time in queue.

available safety capacity improves the performance of a queuing process if the processing time distributions of arriving customers are identical.

It is worth noting the similarity of this statement to the one about safety inventory that we made in chapter 7. There we observed that the centralization (pooling) of inventories improves customer-service level for the same total inventory investment. Likewise, we have just seen here that pooling safety capacity improves service in terms of the average queue length and waiting time.

Finally, note that doubling our processing capacity by adding a second server (while maintaining a single queue) reduces average waiting time from 12.5 minutes to 0.53 minute. If we add a third server (and assume that the servers are pooled), waiting time decreases to 0.067 minute. The advantage of adding a third server to the first two is quantitatively less than that of adding a second server to the first. Moreover, the decrease in waiting time that we gain by adding a fourth server is even less. The key observation here is clear: The marginal value of additional servers (and thus of additional safety capacity) displays diminishing returns in terms of customer waiting time.

8.7   THE EFFECT OF BUFFER CAPACITY ON AVERAGE PROCESS PERFORMANCE

Until now, we have assumed that the flow rate in a process is limited only by its input-flow rate and the maximal processing rate of its resources, as no calls are blocked. This assumption implies that the size of the input buffer never constrains flow rate. If, however, storage space is limited, it may also limit process flow rate (throughput) by blocking inflows. In most real-world operations, input buffers (e.g., calls on hold at a call center) have limited capacity to hold arrivals waiting to be processed. As defined in section 8.2, K is the maximum number of waiting arrivals who can be accommodated in the input buffer. As soon as the buffer is full, any new arrivals are blocked from entry into the process. In the MBPF call center, for example, there may be a limited number of telephone lines; in that case, K refers to the maximum number of callers who can be put on hold. When that number is reached, any new caller receives a busy signal. Blocked arrivals represent loss of business if customers do not call back.

In this section, we evaluate the performance characteristics of such processes, including average wait time (T_i), average number in queue (I_i), and probability of being blocked (P_b). First note that with finite buffer capacity, even though the arrival rate is R_i, only fraction $1 - P_b$ gets through. If no customers abandon the queue, throughput rate, therefore, is limited to

$$R = R_i (1 - P_b)$$

Capacity utilization then becomes

$$\rho = R_i (1 - P_b) / R_p$$

Average waiting time T_i now refers to the waiting time only of those customers who gain access to the system.

With finite buffer capacity, we can no longer use the queue length formula. We must now resort to more complicated formulas or simulation. For those cases in which interarrival-time and processing-time distributions are exponential, these formulas are provided in the appendix at the end of this chapter and are also programmed on the spreadsheet queuMMcK.xls that we mentioned earlier.

From these formulas, other performance measures follow by their definitions and by Little's law. In Example 8.9 we evaluate the impact of queue capacity on performance. All calculations use the queuMMcK. xls spreadsheet.

8.8   CAPACITY INVESTMENT DECISIONS

As discussed in the previous section, a manager may use one of two capacity levers to influence queuing-system performance: processing capacity or buffer capacity. In this section, we use simple examples to show how managers may use the analytical tools that we have introduced thus far in making optimal investment decisions.

The Economics of Buffer Capacity   Consider first the economics of increasing input-buffer capacity. Although adding buffer capacity is costly, it will decrease blocking rate and increase throughput. Adding buffer capacity, however, also increases waiting time as in Example 8.9. The goal, then, is to find an optimal tradeoff. This is discussed in Example 8.10.

EXAMPLE 8.9

As in Example 8.6, suppose that the MBPF call center has one *SR* who takes an average of 2.5 minutes to process a call; calls come in at an average rate of 20 per hour. Suppose, too, that there are six telephone lines, so at most, five callers can be put on hold. MBPF would like to identify the proportion of callers who get a busy signal. MBPF is thinking of adding more telephone lines and would like to investigate the effect of doing so on various performance measures.

Solution In this case, we have a queuing process with finite buffer size. We also have the following information:

Arrival rate: R_i = 20 per hour,
Processing rate: R_p = 24 per hour,
Number of servers: c = 1, and
Buffer capacity: K = 5.

Together, these data imply the following (using the queuMMcK.xls spreadsheet):

$$P_b = \text{Probability of blocking} = 0.077$$

$$T_i = \text{Average waiting time in queue} = 4.95 \text{ minutes}$$

This implies that 7.7% of the callers get a busy signal. On average, the rate of calls that are blocked can be expressed as

$$R_b = R_i \times P_b = 20 \times 0.077 = 1.54 \text{ calls per hour}$$

Throughput rate, therefore, is

$$R = R_i - R_b = 20 - 1.54 = 18.46 \text{ calls per hour,}$$
or 0.3077 call per minute

Equivalently,

$$R = R_i (1 - P_b) = 20 \times (1 - 0.077) = 18.46 \text{ calls per hour}$$

According to Little's law, the average number of calls in queue is

$$I_i = RT_i = (0.3077)(4.95) = 1.522$$

Capacity utilization is

$$\rho = R / R_p = 18.46 / 24 = 0.769$$

Thus, the *SR* is busy only 76.9% of the time. Due to variability, however, there are enough periods during which 5 callers are on hold that 7.7% of all callers get a busy signal.

To study the effect of adding more telephone lines, we can change the value of K and see how it affects key performance measures. Table 8.3 summarizes the results. Observe that as the buffer capacity changes from 4 to 10, the blocking probability declines from 10.1% to 2.5%. Due to blocking, some of the calls do not get through to a representative; thus, throughput rate is lower than arrival rate of 20 calls per hour. As we increase the number of telephone lines, we admit more callers into the system. The probability of blocking, therefore, decreases and throughput increases. Interestingly, however, waiting time experienced by callers who are admitted *increases* as buffer capacity increases. This phenomenon agrees with Little's law—as we increase buffer capacity, average inventory may increase, resulting in increased average flow time.

TABLE 8.3 Effect of Buffer Capacity on Process Performance

Number of lines	5	6	7	8	9	10	11
Number of servers c	1	1	1	1	1	1	1
Buffer capacity K	4	5	6	7	8	9	10
Average number of calls in queue I_i	1.23	1.52	1.79	2.04	2.27	2.48	2.67
Average wait in queue T_i [min]	4.10	4.95	5.73	6.44	7.09	7.68	8.22
Blocking probability P_b [%]	10.1	7.7	6.1	4.8	3.9	3.1	2.5
Throughput R (number/hr)	17.98	18.46	18.78	19.04	19.22	19.38	19.50
Capacity utilization ρ	0.749	0.769	0.783	0.792	0.800	0.808	0.813

EXAMPLE 8.10

Let us take Example 8.9 a little further. First assume that any caller who receives a busy signal simply hangs up and orders from a competitor. Also assume that the loss to MBPF in contribution margin per lost call is $100. With a single server and MBPF's current total of six telephone lines, what is the hourly loss due to the inability of some callers to get through? In addition, suppose that after a customer call gets in, each minute spent waiting on hold costs MBPF $2. If each telephone line costs $5 per hour, what is the appropriate number of telephone lines that MBPF should lease for its call center?

Solution   We know that MBPF incurs four types of costs:

1. Cost of servers ($20 per server per hour),
2. Cost of lost contribution margin for callers getting busy signals ($100 per blocked call),
3. Cost of waiting on the part of callers on hold ($2 per minute per customer), and
4. Cost of leasing a telephone line ($5 per line per hour).

With $c = 1$ and $K = 5$, we determined in Example 8.9 the average blocking rate as

$R_b = 1.54$ customers lost per hour due to busy signals

The loss of contribution margin due to blocking is therefore

$$\$100 \, R_b = \$1.54 \times 100 = \$154 \text{ per hour}$$

Similarly, we determined that, on average, $I_i = 1.52$ customers wait on hold. If each one of them costs $2 a minute, or $120 an hour, the hourly waiting cost will be

$$\$120 I_i = \$182 \text{ per hour}$$

Finally, the cost of six telephone lines is ($5)(6) = $30 an hour. Total cost, therefore, is

$$\$(20 + 154 + 182 + 30) = \$386 \text{ per hour}$$

Similarly, changing the number of lines to get different values of buffer capacity K, we can compute the different results for total cost per hour shown in Table 8.4. As shown, total cost minimization means that leasing a total of six lines (the current situation) is indeed appropriate for MBPF. With one SR, the optimal buffer capacity K, in this case is 5.

Observe that the total cost increases if an additional line is leased to raise buffer capacity beyond $K = 5$. In fact, total cost goes up as a result of leasing any additional lines: MBPF must not only pay for additional lines, but also bear the cost of increased waiting time experienced by callers. In this instance the waiting time of the caller is so expensive that the firm is better off blocking some callers from entering the process than admitting them and then subjecting them to long waits. Conversely, leasing fewer lines also turns out to be more expensive, because increased blocking leads to a significant loss of contribution margin.

TABLE 8.4   Effect of Buffer Capacity on Total Cost

Number of lines	5	6	7	8	9	10
Number of servers c	1	1	1	1	1	1
Buffer capacity K	4	5	6	7	8	9
Average number of calls in queue I_i	1.23	1.52	1.79	2.04	2.27	2.48
Hourly cost of waiting [$/hr] = $I_i \times 120$	148	182	215	245	272	298
Contribution margin lost/hr from blocking [$/hr]	202	154	122	96	78	62
Total cost per hour (includes line cost) [$/hr]	375	366	372	381	395	410

In Example 8.11 we consider the problem of determining optimal processing capacity (number of servers) for a given buffer capacity so as to minimize total cost. Again, total cost include losses due to blocking, waiting-time cost, and cost of capacity. In Example 8.11 we return to MBPF, which now wants to know, assuming six leased lines, the number of SRs needed to staff its call center.

The cost of waiting and the cost of lost sales may be difficult to estimate in practice. In such situations, the previous approach may be used to determine costs for which current staffing level may be optimal. Managers can then determine whether the results are reasonable. In Example 8.11 we have assumed the number of lines to be fixed and then optimized over the number of servers. In general, a manager will optimize over both quantities.

EXAMPLE 8.11

Suppose MBPF has a total of six telephone lines and an hourly average of 20 incoming calls. As before, each caller getting a busy signal generates a contribution-margin loss of $100 and each minute spent by a customer on hold costs MBPF $2 per customer. An SR takes 2.5 minutes to process each call, and each SR is paid $20 per hour. How many SRs should MBPF hire to staff its call center?

Solution   Note that because the total number of telephone lines is fixed at six, buffer capacity depends on the number of servers

$$K = 6 - c$$

For example, if there are two servers, no more than four callers can be on hold while two are being served. Total hourly cost, then, consists of the following:

- *Cost of blocking:* $100R_b$,
- *Cost of waiting:* $120I_i$, and
- *Cost of providing service:* $20c$.

For six lines, the line charge is fixed at $30 per hour. Our computations are summarized in Table 8.5, from which it follows that MBPF should staff its call center with three SRs.

TABLE 8.5   Effect of Number of Servers on Cost

c	K	Blocking P_b %	Lost calls R_b [number/hr]	I_i	Total cost [$/hr]
1	5	7.70	1.54	1.522	$30 + 20 + 1.522 \times 120 + 1.54 \times 100 = 387$
2	4	0.43	0.086	0.158	$30 + 40 + 0.158 \times 120 + 0.086 \times 100 = 98$
3	3	0.09	0.018	0.021	$30 + 60 + 0.021 \times 120 + 0.018 \times 100 = 94$
4	2	0.04	0.008	0.003	$30 + 80 + 0.003 \times 120 + 0.008 \times 100 = 111$

8.9   SYNCHRONIZATION OF CAPACITY AND DEMAND

As we have seen, in the presence of variability, a lack of **synchronization** between arrival and processing rates causes queues to build up. Although it may be hard to synchronize the two rates, people often work faster when queues get longer. This phenomenon alone has the effect of introducing a certain degree of synchronization between interarrival times and processing times.

In a manufacturing setting in which output from one station becomes input into the next, managers can synchronize arrival and processing rates by limiting the maximum size of the buffer allowed to build up between the two stations—the station providing input is forced to stop once the input buffer is full. This form of synchronization will decrease waiting time but (as we saw earlier) may also result in some loss of throughput.

Synchronizing Capacity with Demand   The process of synchronizing available capacity with arrival rate (i.e., demand) entails managing either the supply side (capacity) or the demand side (arrival rates). Short-term synchronization is practiced in supermarkets, fast-food restaurants and drugstore outlets that open extra checkout counters when the size of any queue exceeds a specified limit. In this case, servers involved with less time-critical tasks (replenishing shelves or cleaning up aisles) staff the newly opened counters—add to the resource pool—for the short term. Once the queue diminishes, servers return to their original duties. This tactic is also common in call centers where backroom employees or management personnel involved in less time-critical tasks staff phone lines when queues get too large. They, too, return to their duties when the queue declines.

This approach to synchronization is a form of **pooling available capacity across different tasks,** and is possible only if all personnel are trained to perform the jobs required of the resource pool. Another key to the success of this tactic is a threshold policy or mechanism that clearly specifies the server who will join the resource pool once the queue reaches a certain size. For example, several drugstores advertise that a new counter will open if the length of any queue reaches four customers. A queue size of four customers, therefore, serves as the threshold mechanism that directs another worker to open a new counter. If such short-term synchronization succeeds, then customer waiting time will decline.

If we move to a slightly longer time frame, then we find that synchronization is easier to implement. In several operations—call centers, banks, fast-food restaurants—demand for service varies by both time of day and day of the week. The key aspect of this form of variability is that much of it is predictable and can be forecast with a fair degree of accuracy. Managers can therefore schedule available capacity (personnel) so that it is synchronized with expected demand. McDonalds, for instance, is said to manage to synchronize available capacity in 15-minute intervals. Scheduling of breaks, server start times, and part-time employees is an effective mechanism for this type of synchronization.

Managing Demand   In some instances, varying the number of servers to synchronize processing capacity with demand can be too expensive or quite difficult. For example the number of rooms in a hotel or tables in a restaurant must remain fairly constant. In such cases, it may be more efficient to manage demand. Off-season hotel rates, "early bird" restaurant specials, and peak-load pricing by electric utilities are examples of price incentives designed to even out demand and make it more predictable. Once demand has been managed, it is easier to synchronize it with available capacity.

8.10 VARIABILITY OF PROCESS PERFORMANCE

Our entire discussion thus far has focused on *average* queue length and waiting times as measures of queuing-process performance. In Example 8.12 we show why limiting ourselves to average measures of performance may be insufficient.

EXAMPLE 8.12

Figure 8.7 shows the distribution of total time in process (obtained by simulation) of the call center as characterized in Example 8.6. Recall that, we calculated average waiting time as $T_i = 12.5$ minutes and average flow time as $T = 15$ minutes. Figure 8.7, however, shows that 15 minutes of total time in process corresponds roughly to the 65th percentile; 35% of all customers will experience total time in process of more than 15 minutes. Note also from Figure 8.7 that approximately 95% of all customers are served in less than 40 minutes. Of all customers, 5% still wait more than 40 minutes before being served and these customers will be the ones who complain. Thus 95th percentile of total time in process along with average total time in process provides us additional information on process performance.

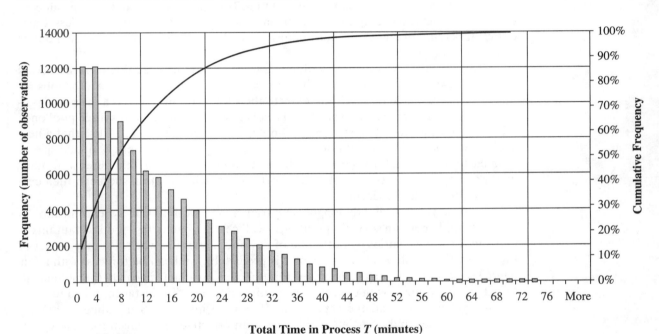

Total Time in Process T (minutes)

FIGURE 8.7 Distribution of Total Time in Process at MBPF

In a queuing process, average waiting time accounts both for customers with very long waits and for those with short or no waits. A customer with a wait of 30 minutes is unlikely to be satisfied by the statement that average waiting time was only three minutes and that nine other customers did not have to wait at all. It is, therefore, appropriate to focus on the range of customers with long waits (i.e., on the upper tail of the probability distribution of the flow time) because this range highlights problematic or unacceptable service. This point is illustrated in Example 8.12.

A firm may wish to give a service guarantee by stating that all callers will be served within t_{DD} units of time. Since guaranteeing a total time in process t_{DD} valid for all customers may yield a conservatively chosen high number, the firm can set a service level (SL) which specifies the probability of achieving the stated guarantee. For example, if $SL = 0.95$, the firm wants to guarantee a total time in process of t_{DD} for 95% of its customers. Usually the service level desired will be such that t_{DD} will be larger than the average total time in process (T). We then define safety time T_s (analogous to safety inventory and safety capacity) as

EXAMPLE 8.13

Suppose that MBPF would like to announce to all callers that they will be served in t_{DD} units of time. Suppose, too, that MBPF wants to meet this service guarantee for 95% of its customers. Thus, SL = 95%. Assuming that the distribution of total time in process is exponential, we get

$$t_{DD} = -(T_i + T_p) \, ln(0.05) = 3(T_i + T_p)$$

In other words, flow time for the 95th percentile is *three* times the average total time process of all customers. Recall from Example 8.6 that we determined the following information:

$$T_i = 12.5 \text{ minutes}$$

and

$$T_p = 2.5 \text{ minutes}$$

Thus,

$$t_{DD} = 3 \times 15 = 45 \text{ minutes}$$

Consequently, the 95th percentile for the distribution of total time in process is 45 minutes (which is close to the figure that we obtained by simulation). This figure means that 5% of all callers spend more than 45 minutes in the MBPF call center—even though it only takes, *on average*, 2.5 minutes to process a call! The average time in process for a customer is $T = T_i + T_p$ = 15 minutes. If we provide a service guarantee of t_{DD} = 45 minutes, we have a safety time of $T_s = t_{DD} - T = 45 - 15 = 30$ minutes.

$$T_s = t_{DD} - T,$$

or,

$$t_{DD} = T + T_s$$

Just as in chapter 7, the amount of safety time required for a desired SL will depend on the probability distribution of the flow time as follows:

$$\text{Prob(Total time in process} \le t_{DD}) = SL$$

Clearly, the larger the safety time, the greater is the probability of achieving the guarantee. In make-to-order manufacturing operations (like one at MBPF) the practice of quoting a time frame within which a product can be expected after an order has been placed is called **due-date quotation.**

For a queuing process with a single server and in which interarrival and processing times are exponentially distributed, we can show that total time in process is exponentially distributed with a mean of $T = T_i + T_p$. Thus,

$$\text{Prob(Total time in process} \le t_{DD}) = 1 - e^{-t_{DD}/(T_i + T_p)}$$

The relationship between t_{DD} and SL is then given by

$$t_{DD} = -(T_i + T_p) \, ln(1 - SL)$$

where *ln* denotes the natural logarithm with

$$e^{ln(x)} = x$$

The exponential distribution is also a good approximation of the distribution of total time in process for many other interarrival and processing time distributions. Alternately, for more complex processes, the distribution of the total time in process can be estimated through simulation.

TABLE 8.6 Due Date and Safety Time Versus Capacity Utilization for $SL = 0.95$				
Utilization ρ	60%	70%	80%	90%
Average Waiting Time T_i	$1.5T_p$	$2.33T_p$	$4T_p$	$9T_p$
Average Total Time in Process				
$T = T_i + T_p$	$2.5T_p$	$3.33T_p$	$5T_p$	$10T_p$
Due date t_{DD}	$7.5T_p$	$10T_p$	$15T_p$	$30T_p$
Safety time $T_s = t_{DD} - T$	$5T_p$	$6.67T_p$	$10T_p$	$20T_p$

Relating Utilization and Safety Time   It should be clear that since both the average total time in process and its distribution depend on the utilization, the safety time needed to guarantee a given service level (SL) will change with the utilization. Table 8.6 shows the effect of capacity utilization on safety time for $SL = 0.95$. In Table 8.6, average waiting time (T_i), quoted due date (t_{DD}), and safety time (T_s) are all reported as functions of the processing time T_p.

Observe that the higher the utilization, the larger the due date and safety time needed to guarantee the due date. Recall that utilization is closely connected to safety capacity; safety capacity decreases as utilization increases. Thus Table 8.6 establishes a dependence between safety capacity and safety time. A larger safety capacity allows a firm to have a smaller safety time and hence quote a shorter due date.

8.11 MANAGING CUSTOMER PERCEPTIONS AND EXPECTATIONS

In this section we focus on managing customer perceptions and expectations to improve queuing process performance. Making the wait in queue as tolerable as possible is an effective mechanism for making the customer less sensitive to longer waits, thereby reducing the cost (to the service process) of waiting experienced by the customer. This cost materializes in the form of customer dissatisfaction and loss of future business.

Various approaches, each dealing with the management of waiting-time perceptions and expectations, are detailed in Maister (1985). One approach calls for occupying the customer with some activity of interest while he or she waits. Hotel guests complain much less about the wait for elevators in hotels that have installed mirrors nearby —the experience of waiting, it seems, is much less disagreeable when you are looking at yourself. As a result, the customer is less sensitive to the duration of the wait. Similarly, restaurants often let guests look at menus and order drinks while waiting for tables (this tactic boasts the added advantage of extra revenues and reduced processing times once guests arrive at tables). Some restaurants provide customers with pagers and inform them when a table becomes available—allowing customers to occupy themselves with other activities while waiting.

Several studies have shown that uncertainty about length of wait seems to make customers more impatient. Customers are willing to wait longer if they are informed of the expected waiting time when they join the queue. Florida Power and Light found that customers were willing to wait up to 94 seconds for a service representative to respond to a call. If, however, the customers are informed of the expected wait at the outset, then they were willing to wait an additional 105 seconds, for a total of 199 seconds, without complaining. Another example comes from various amusement park waiting lines. Parks have found that customer complaints dropped significantly once parks started displaying expected waiting times. Customers are especially patient when pessimistic estimates are posted and they are generally pleased to wait less time than they had expected.

Customers are often willing to wait longer if the service itself is time consuming. At supermarkets customers with full carts are willing to wait longer than those purchasing only a few items. Another key factor is fairness of the wait. Customers often complain more readily if they perceive that later arrivals have been served first (even if their own wait is not long). Conversely, fair processes in which customers are served in order of arrival usually elicit fewer complaints, even if waits are longer. Thus, managing customer perceptions of the wait is as important as the actual waiting time itself.

8.12   LEVERS FOR MANAGING FLOW TIMES IN SERVICE OPERATIONS

In this chapter, we have seen that waiting occurs because of the following factors:

1. High variability (coefficient of variation) in interarrival and processing times C_i and C_p and lack of synchronization.
2. High capacity utilization ($\rho = R_i / R_p$) or low safety capacity ($R_s = R_p - R_i$). This occurs because of high inflow (throughput) rate (R_i) or low processing capacity ($R_p = c / T_p$).

Following are the most appropriate managerial levers for reducing the cost of waiting and flow times for a service system:

1. *Decrease variability*
   - *Inflows* Use reliable suppliers, better forecasts, reservations, appointments.
   - *Processing* Employ standardized operating procedures, better training, specialized servers.
2. *Manage safety capacity:*
   - *Increase safety capacity*
     a. *Scale* (e.g., add servers or part-timers, initiate customer participation)
     b. *Speed* (e.g., simplify, adopt efficient methods and information technology)
   - *Pool available safety capacity*
3. *Synchronize flows:*
   - *Manage capacity to synchronize with demand* (e.g., scheduling of breaks, start times, part-time employees)
   - *Manage demand to synchronize with available capacity* (e.g., off-season rates)
   - *Synchronize flows within the process* (e.g., processing only if there is downstream demand)
4. *Manage customers' psychological perceptions to reduce the cost of waiting* (cf. Maister, 1985):
   - *Make waiting more comfortable* (e.g., providing a cocktail bar and television in a restaurant lounge)
   - *Distract customer's preoccupation with the wait by entertaining them* (e.g., playing music or reading stock quotes for customers on hold)
   - *Manage the perception of wait, either by starting a part of the service early or by explaining the reasons for the wait* (i.e., avoid "blind wait")
   - *Overstate somewhat the wait involved so that customers are pleasantly surprised when it turns out to be less than announced* (e.g., padding schedules by airlines)

Problem Set

8.1 A call center has a total of 12 lines coming into its customer-service department, which are staffed by five customer-service representatives. On average, two potential customers call the call center every minute. Each customer-service representative requires, on average, 2 minutes to serve a caller. After great deliberation, management has decided to add another line, increasing the total to 13 lines. As a result, the call center can expect that:

a. The proportion of potential customers getting a busy signal will:
  - increase,
  - decrease, or
  - remain unchanged.

b. Average flow time experienced by customers will:
  - increase,
  - decrease, or
  - remain unchanged.

c. Average utilization of customer-service representatives will:
  - increase,
  - decrease, or
  - remain unchanged.

8.2 A mail-order company has one department for taking customer orders and another for handling complaints. Currently, each department has a separate telephone number. Each has 7 lines served by two customer-service representatives. Calls come into each department at an average rate of one call per minute. Each representative takes, on average, 1.5 minutes to serve a customer. Management has proposed merging the two departments and cross-training all workers. The projected new department would have 14 lines served by four customer-service representatives. As process manager, you expect that:

a. The proportion of callers getting a busy signal will:
  - increase,
  - decrease, or
  - remain unchanged.

b. Average flow time experienced by customers will:
  - increase,
  - decrease, or
  - remain unchanged.

8.3 As a new business concept, John Doe is thinking of starting Pizza-Ready Inc., which would accept pizza-orders-for-pickup over the phone. Pizza-Ready's strategy is to compete with superior, fresh, made-to-order deep-dish pizza while providing excellent service. As part of his advertising campaign, Doe will publish an ad stating that "If your pizza is not ready in 20 minutes, that pizza plus your next order are on us." Doe has done extensive research on the pizza-cooking process and knows that all fresh deep-dish pizzas require 15 minutes' oven time and 2 minutes' preparation. Moreover, as part of its excellent service, Pizza-Ready will accept orders when customers place them, and a marketing study estimates that Pizza-Ready can count on an average demand of 20 pizzas per hour. Doe, therefore, has ordered five individual-pizza-size ovens and is now looking for a silent partner to help carry the financial burden of his start-up company. Given the structure of this business, a potential partner has asked you whether Pizza-Ready would be a profitable investment. What would you recommend?

8.4 M. M. Sprout, a catalog mail-order retailer, has one customer-service representative (CSR) to take orders at an 800 telephone number. If the CSR is busy, the next caller is put on hold. For simplicity, assume that any number of incoming calls can be put on hold and that nobody hangs up in frustration over a long wait. Suppose that, on average, one call comes in every 4 minutes and that it takes the CSR an average of 3 minutes to take an order. Both interarrival and activity times are exponentially distributed. The CSR is paid $20 an hour, and the telephone company charges $5 an hour for the 800 line. The company estimates that each minute a customer is kept on hold costs $2 in customer dissatisfaction and loss of future business.

a. Estimate the following:
   - Proportion of time that the CSR will be busy,
   - Average time that a customer will be on hold,
   - Average number of customers on line, and
   - Total hourly cost of service and waiting.

b. More realistically, suppose that M. M. Sprout has four telephone lines. At most, therefore, three callers can be kept on hold. Assume, too, that any caller who gets a busy signal because all four lines are occupied simply hangs up and calls a competitor. M. M. Sprout's average loss, in terms of current and potential future business, is $100 per blocked caller. Estimate the total cost of the following:
   - Providing service,
   - Waiting, and
   - Average hourly loss incurred because customers are blocked and cannot get through.

c. Suppose that M. M. Sprout is considering adding another line to reduce the amount of lost business. If the installation cost is negligible, can the addition of one line be justified on economic grounds? How would it affect customer waiting time?

d. In addition to adding another line, suppose M. M. Sprout wants to hire one more CSR to reduce waiting time. Should the firm hire another CSR? (Hint: Use the queuMMcK.xls spreadsheet.)

8.5 Heavenly Mercy Hospital wants to improve the efficiency of its radiology department and its responsiveness to doctors' needs. Administrators have observed that, every hour, doctors submit an average of 18 X-ray films for examination by staff radiologists. Each radiologist is equipped with a conventional piece of viewing equipment that reads one film at a time. Due to complications that vary from case to case, the actual time needed for report preparation is exponentially distributed with a mean of 30 minutes. Together, the cost of leasing one piece of viewing equipment and each radiologist's salary is $100 an hour. Although it is difficult to put a dollar value on a doctor's waiting time, each doctor would like to get a radiologist's report within an average of 40 minutes from the time the film is submitted.

a. Determine the number of radiologists that the hospital should staff to meet doctors' requirements regarding job flow time. Compute the resulting hourly cost of operating the radiology department.

b. The hospital could also change its diagnostic procedure by leasing more sophisticated X-ray viewing devices. Administrators estimate that the new procedure would reduce a radiologist's average film-processing time to 20 minutes. At the same time, however, higher equipment rental and salaries for additional support personnel would boost the hourly cost per radiologist to $150.

   Determine the number of radiologists that the hospital should staff under this new arrangement. Would the new arrangement be economically advantageous? (Hint: Use the queuMMcK.xls spreadsheet.)

8.6 First Local Bank would like to improve customer service at its drive-in facility by reducing waiting and transaction times. On the basis of a pilot study, the bank's process manager estimates the average rate of customer arrivals at 30 per hour. All arriving cars line up in a single file and are served at one of four windows on a first-come/first-served basis. Each teller currently requires an average of 6 minutes to complete a transaction. The bank is considering the possibility of leasing high-speed information-retrieval and communication equipment that would cost $30 an hour. The new equipment would, however, serve the entire facility and reduce each teller's transaction-processing time to an average of 4 minutes per customer. Assume that interarrival and processing times are exponentially distributed.

a. If our manager estimates the cost of a customer's waiting time in queue (in terms of future business lost to the competition) to be $20 per customer per hour, can she justify leasing the new equipment on an economic basis?

b. Although the waiting-cost figure of $20 per customer per hour appears questionable, a casual study of the competition indicates that a customer should be in and out of a drive-in facility within an average of 8 minutes (including waiting). If First Local Bank wants to meet this standard, should it lease the new high-speed equipment? (Hint: Use the queuMMcK.xls spreadsheet.)

8.7   Since deregulation of the airline industry, increased traffic and fierce competition have forced Global Airlines to reexamine the efficiency and economy of its operations. As part of a campaign to improve customer service in a cost-effective manner, Global has focused on passenger check-in operations at its hub terminal. For best utilization of its check-in facilities, Global operates a common check-in system—passengers for all Global flights queue up in a single "snake line," and each can be served at any one of several counters as clerks become available. Arrival rate is estimated at an average of 52 passengers per hour. During the check-in process, an agent confirms the reservation, assigns a seat, issues a boarding pass, and weighs, labels, and dispatches baggage. The entire process takes an average of 3 minutes. Agents are paid $20 an hour, and Global's customer-relations department estimates that for every minute a customer spends waiting in line, Global loses $1 in missed flights, customer dissatisfaction, and future business.

a. How many agents should Global staff at its hub terminal?

b. Global has surveyed both its customers and its competition and discovered that 3 minutes is an acceptable average waiting time. If Global wants to meet this industry norm, how many agents should it hire? (Hint: Use the queuMMcK.xls spreadsheet.)

www.prenhall.com/anupindi

> For exercises based on Process Model go to http://www.prenhall.com/anupindi

References

Bhat, U.N. 1984. *Elements of Applied Stochastic Processes.* John Wiley & Sons, New York, NY.

Chase, R.B., and N.J. Aquilano. 1995. *Production and Operations Management.* 7th ed. Irwin, Chicago, IL.

Hopp, W.J., and M.L. Spearman. 1996. *Factory Physics.* Irwin, Chicago IL.

Kleinrock, L. 1975. *Queueing Systems.* John Wiley & Sons, New York, NY.

Larson, R.C. Perspectives on queues: Social justice and the psychology of queuing. *Operations Research* 35(6): 895–905.

Maister, D. 1985. The psychology of waiting lines. In J.A. Czepial, M.R. Solomon, and C.F. Suprenant, eds., *Service Encounter.* Lexington, KY.

McClain, J.O., L.J. Thomas, and J.B. Mazzola. 1992. *Operations Management.* 3rd ed. Prentice Hall, Upper Saddle River, NJ.

Chapter 8 Appendix

FINITE BUFFER CAPACITY FORMULAS
FOR EXPONENTIAL DISTRIBUTION

For those cases with finite buffer capacity, we present formulas in the special case that meets the following criteria:

- Interarrival and processing times are independent and exponentially distributed random variables with mean arrival rate R_i and mean processing rate R_p (mean interarrival time $1 / R_i$ and mean processing time T_p),
- There are c servers, and
- Input buffer capacity is K (with $K + c$, therefore, as the maximum number in the process).

Explicit formulas are available for computing performance characteristics of such a system (for details, see Kleinrock, 1975). In particular, the probability P_n that there are n customers in the system or, equivalently, that inventory $I = n$ is

$$P_n = \begin{cases} \dfrac{1}{n!}(T_p R_i)^n P_0 & if \;\; 0 \le n < c \\[2em] \dfrac{1}{c!c^{n-c}}(T_p R_i)^n P_0 & if \;\; c \le n \le c + K \end{cases}$$

where P_0 is the probability that total number in process is zero:

$$\frac{1}{P_0} = \begin{cases} \displaystyle\sum_{n=0}^{c-1} \frac{1}{n!}(T_p R_i)^n + \frac{(T_p R_i)^c}{c!} \frac{(1 - (T_p R_i)^{K+1})}{(1 - T_p R_i)} & if \;\; R_i \ne R_p \\[2em] \displaystyle\sum_{n=0}^{c-1} \frac{1}{n!}(T_p R_i)^n + \frac{(T_p R_i)^c}{c!}(K + 1) & if \;\; R_i = R_p \end{cases}$$

Note that blocking probability P_b is the probability that there are $K + c$ customers in the process. Thus, $P_b = P_{K + c}$. Utilization of such a queuing process is given by

$$\rho = \frac{R}{R_p} = \frac{R_i(1 - P_b)}{R_p} = \frac{T_p R_i(1 - P_{K+c})}{c}$$

Define $r = R_i / cR_p$. We then have

$$I_i = \frac{P_0(cr)^c r}{c!(1 - r)^2}[1 - r^{K+1} - (1 - r)(K + 1)r^K]$$

$$I = I_i + c - P_0 \sum_{n=0}^{c-1} \frac{(c - n)(rc)^n}{n!} ; \; T_i = \frac{I_i}{R} ; \; T = \frac{I}{R}$$

These formulas may also be used when there is no limit on buffer capacity by setting buffer capacity K at a very large number. As mentioned, these formulas have been programmed on a spreadsheet called queuMMcK.xls that can be downloaded from the MBPF Website at

http://www.prenhall.com/anupindi

From these, other performance measures follow by their definitions and by Little's law.

CHAPTER

9

Managing Flow Variability: Process Control and Capability

Flow units vary in terms of cost, quality, availability, and flow times, and this variability often leads to customer dissatisfaction. In this chapter, we study some graphical and statistical methods for measuring, tracking, analyzing, controlling, and reducing this variability. In particular, we study short-term *process control*, which involves dynamically monitoring process performance over time to identify excessive variability and to eliminate its causes. The goal of process control is an internal one of ensuring that actual performance does not vary excessively from planned performance. *Process capability*, on the other hand, measures the ability of a process to meet external customer requirements consistently. Improving process capability requires long-term investment in superior product and process design to reduce chances of variability and its effect.

9.1 INTRODUCTION

In chapters 7 and 8 we analyzed the effect of stochastic variability in supply (lead time and processing time) and demand (quantities and customer arrivals) on customer service in terms of product availability and response time. We assumed that the stochastic nature of supply and demand variability was stable and known. Our response to this variability was then a *static plan* of building in safety nets (such as safety inventory, safety capacity, or safety time) to absorb variability in actual supply and demand, so as to provide a desired level of performance, *on average*.

In practice, however, the statistical laws governing variability may themselves be unknown, and moreover, may be changing through time. In this chapter, we study methods for measuring, analyzing, and *dynamically controlling* variability in actual performance over time. We also introduce the concept of *process capability* in terms of its ability to meet customer requirements. Greater capability corresponds to a more robust process with a greater safety margin so that flow units will meet customer needs even with unexpected shifts in process variability. Our discussion is applicable to problems of controlling variability in *any* measure of performance, including cost, quality, availability and response time. For purposes of illustration, however, we will stress *quality* as the key attribute, because we have concentrated on the others in the previous chapters.

In section 9.2 we discuss performance variability in general and emphasize its importance in process management. In section 9.3 we present some graphical and statistical methods for measuring, organizing, and analyzing variability. In section 9.4 we focus on short-term process control based on the principle of feedback control to identify and eliminate abnormal variability. This principle involves monitoring key performance measures over time, comparing them with expected levels of performance, and taking corrective actions when observed variability appears excessive. In particular, we outline the general structure of a *control limit policy* that specifies investigation and correction only when observed performance measure exceeds certain critical thresholds. We describe statistical process control (SPC) as the most prominent example of such a policy for managing process variability, and indicate its connection to methods for controlling inventory, flow time, and cost.

While the objective of process control is an internal one—to maintain a process in a stable state of statistical equilibrium with only normal variability—process capability measures how well process output meets the external customer requirements, which is the subject of section 9.5. In section 9.6 we indicate some methods for improving process capability through process adjustment and variance reduction. Section 9.7 discusses some principles of product and process design to reduce chances of variability and its impact on product performance. Finally, section 9.8 concludes with a summary of the levers for planning and controlling process variability. Several examples discussed throughout the chapter are illustrated using Process Model software, which can be accessed at "http://www.prenhall.com/anupindi".

9.2   PERFORMANCE VARIABILITY

All product and process performance measures—both external and internal—display variability. Results of external measurements (such as customer satisfaction indices, relative product rankings, and number of customer complaints) vary from one market survey to the next. Internally, in business processes, flow units vary with respect to cost, quality, and flow times. For instance, no two cars rolling off an assembly line are exactly identical. Even under identical circumstances, the time and cost required to produce and deliver an identical product may be quite different. Two different customers (in fact, the same customer on two different occasions) may perceive the quality of a restaurant dining experience quite differently. The cost of operating a department within a company generally varies from one quarter to the next. Bank customers conducting apparently identical transactions may need different processing times. Even with carefully planned safety inventory, a department store may run out of stock of an item one month and have excess inventory the next. Sources of all this variability may be either internal to the process (imprecise equipment, untrained workers, lack of standard operating procedures) or external (inconsistent raw material, delivery delays, economic conditions, environmental disturbances, changing customer requirements and perception).

In general, *variability* refers to a *discrepancy between the actual and the expected performance.* It usually leads to higher costs, longer flow times, lower quality, and ultimately to dissatisfied customers. A powerful multimedia computer that crashes unexpectedly may be judged as inferior to a basic no-frills model that is nevertheless reliable. We saw in chapter 7 that producers can reduce safety inventory if materials suppliers have consistent delivery lead times. Finally, as noted in chapter 8, customers often prefer predictable—even if long—waits (e.g., in a restaurant or on the telephone) over "blind" waits. Thus, processes that display performance variability are generally judged less satisfactory than those with consistent, predictable performance. A sharpshooter whose shots are, on average, centered on the bull's-eye but widely dispersed around it cannot be considered a dependable bodyguard. An old adage reminds us that one can drown in the middle of a lake, even though it is, on average, only 5 feet deep! In short, *performance variability—not only its average— matters.*

Customers generally perceive any variation in product or service from its expected performance as a loss in value. Japanese quality engineer Genichi Taguchi suggests measuring this loss by *squared* deviation in the actual performance from its target, the implication being that loss in value rises more rapidly as the actual performance deviates further from the planned target. Thus, Taguchi loss function emphasizes the importance of being on target, as opposed to merely meeting specifications. In fact, customer satisfaction itself may be broadly defined in terms of the variability between their expectation of and experience with the product. It may be due to a gap between the following:

- What the customer wants and what the product is designed to do,
- What the product design calls for and what the process for making it is capable of producing,
- What the process can produce and what it actually produces,
- How the produced product is expected to perform and how it actually performs, and
- How the product actually performs and how the customer perceives it.

Each of these sources of variability from the target may ultimately lead to customer dissatisfaction.

We can broadly classify a product as being "defective" if its cost, quality, availability, or flow time vary significantly from their expected values. In quality management literature, **quality of design** refers to *how well product specifications aim to meet customer requirements.* It specifies product or service attributes that we plan to deliver. **Quality of conformance**, on the other hand, refers to *how well the actual product or service attributes conform to the chosen design specifications.* A well-made Toyota Tercel may have a better quality of conformance than a poorly made Camry, although Camry may have a better quality of design in terms of specifying more power, comfort, and safety features. Quality of design, therefore, refers to *what* we promise to customers (in terms of what the product can do), whereas quality of conformance measures *how well* we keep our promise. **Quality function deployment (QFD)** is a conceptual framework often used for translating customers' functional requirements of product (such as the ease of door operation or durability) into concrete design specifications (such as the door weight should be between 75 kg to 85 kg). The objective of QFD is to provide a common platform for incorporating the "voice of the customer" into the product design process. Details of QFD may be found in Hauser and Clausing (1988).

Given design specifications, quality of conformance is measured by such factors as "number of defects per car" and "fraction of output that does not meet specifications." In a bank, for instance, degree of product conformance can be measured by the error rate in check processing and in monthly statements, or the percentage of customers who have to wait longer than 5 minutes for service. In the information-services department of a company, conformance measurements may include number of errors per 1,000 lines of code, percentage of milestones met on time, frequency and magnitude of project cost overruns, number of software-program rewrites, or frequency of system crashes. In an airline, they may include percentage of flights delayed by more than 15 minutes, number of bags lost per 1,000 flown, or number of reservation errors per 1,000 customers. Degree of conformance to design specifications thus measures performance variability that results in defective products and customer dissatisfaction, leading to loss of reputation, market share, and competitive position. It is therefore critical to measure, track, analyze, and reduce variability in product and process performance.

9.3   ANALYSIS OF VARIABILITY

In this section, we first present some simple graphical methods for collecting, organizing, and displaying information about performance variability. Because statistics is the science of variability, we then outline some statistical methods for analyzing observed variability. Our goal is to provide a few diagnostic tools to monitor actual process performance over time, analyze variability in performance, uncover the root causes of that variability, and eliminate them. Throughout, we illustrate concepts and methods by examining operations at garage maker MBPF Inc., whose business motto is "Guaranteed Total Satisfaction." MBPF managers want to know how their customers perceive the total experience of doing business with the company and how it can be improved. Accordingly, they have tried to identify factors that affect customer satisfaction with MBPF's product and service, and how to measure and improve them.

9.3.1   Check Sheets

A **check sheet** is simply *a tally of problems with flow units documented by type of defect as illustrated in Example 9.1.*

EXAMPLE 9.1

Suppose MBPF's customer service department surveyed 1,000 current and past customers, asking them to rate their experiences with each of the following aspects of MBPF's products and services:

- Cost of purchasing and maintaining a garage,
- Response time from ordering to installation of a garage,
- Customization in accommodating individual preferences,
- Service quality in terms of order placement experience with a sales representative, and

- Garage quality in terms of
  - Fit and finish,
  - Ease of garage-door operation, and
  - Durability.

If customers rated their experience as "unsatisfactory" along any of these dimensions (indicating variability between their expectations and experiences), the pertinent flow unit (order) was considered "defective." MBPF then compiled the check sheet shown in Figure 9.1.

FIGURE 9.1 Check Sheet of MBPF Customer Feedback

Type of Defect	Number of Defective Flow Units
Cost	~~||||~~ ~~||||~~
Response Time	~~||||~~
Customization	|||||
Service Quality	~~||||~~ ~~||||~~ ~~||||~~
Garage Quality	~~||||~~ ~~||||~~ ~~||||~~ ~~||||~~ ~~||||~~

9.3.2 Pareto Charts

After counting defects by type, our next step is to determine which problem should be tackled first. All defects are not created equal, either in terms of their importance or frequency of occurrence, so given the limited time and resources at our disposal, we would like to identify a few critical ones on which we should focus. We may rank-order defects by frequency of occurrence or, more accurately, according to frequency weighted by importance. Problems usually distribute themselves according to the principle of "vital few and trivial many." Thus, the **80-20 Pareto principle** states that *20% of problem types account for 80% of total defects.*[1] A **Pareto chart** is simply a bar chart that *plots frequencies of problem-type occurrence in decreasing order.*

EXAMPLE 9.2

The customer survey record, or check sheet, in Figure 9.1 can be graphed as the bar chart in Figure 9.2. This chart identifies garage quality as the problem that MBPF should address first.

After identifying garage quality as the main concern voiced by MBPF customers, we could try to pin down exactly what aspects of our garage quality dissatisfies them most. We could again use a check sheet, this time classifying each defective garage according to a new list—poor fit and finish, not easy or safe to operate, not durable, and so forth.

Suppose the second Pareto chart reveals that, with quality addressed, the most frequent problem is ease of operation of garage door, followed by its durability. MBPF might assign an en-

gineering team to determine what factors contribute to these two main problems. Suppose all this detective work ultimately leads to identifying the weight of the garage door as the critical quality characteristic that affects both problems: If a door is too heavy, it is difficult and unsafe to balance and lift; if it is too light, it tends to break down frequently or not close properly. Suppose engineers determine that the optimal door design calls for a minimum weight of 75 kg and a maximum weight of 85 kg, thereby specifying the *design quality.* To determine the *conformance quality,* the MBPF team will now collect data on the actual door weights of 100 garages sampled randomly from monthly production of almost 2,000 doors.

FIGURE 9.2 Pareto Chart of Customer Complaints at MBPF

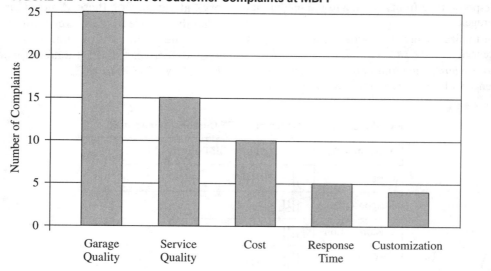

---

[1]The Pareto principle is named after Vilfredo Pareto who concluded in a 1897 study of the distribution of wealth in Italy that about 80 percent of the wealth was in the hands of 20 percent of the population.

The Pareto chart tells us, for example, that we should aim our process-improvement efforts first at reducing the tallest bar by one-half rather than trying to completely eliminate a short one. To solve the dominant problem, more data needs to be collected and analyzed and solution strategies need to be devised. Once the dominant problem is solved, we may collect new data to uncover a new tallest bar on which to focus our efforts next. A Pareto chart, therefore, can be used as a dynamic tool for making constant improvement by continually identifying, prioritizing, and fixing problems.

9.3.3 Histograms

A **histogram** is a bar plot displaying the *frequency distribution of an observed performance characteristic*. A preliminary statistical analysis of the performance characteristic would involve summarizing the distribution in terms of its **mean** which is defined as the *expected value around which the distribution is centered* and the **standard deviation** which *measures the spread of the distribution around the mean*.

EXAMPLE 9.3

Suppose five doors from each of the past 20 days' production runs were weighed and recorded as in Table 9.1. As shown, door weights display variability from door to door within each day's sample as well as between samples from different days. Our goal will be to analyze this variability, determine what action—if any—is necessary to keep it in control, and finally how it can be reduced to improve conformance of actual door weights to design specifications. The garage-door weight data in Table 9.1 are displayed in the histogram in Figure 9.3, which shows that 14% of the doors weighed 83 kg, 8% weighed 81 kg, and so forth.

We can compute key statistics: mean weight $\mu = 82.5$ kg and standard deviation $\sigma = 4.2$ kg (or the variance of $\sigma^2 = 17.64$ kg^2), based on our 100 observations. Thus μ measures the average weight of garage doors produced, and σ measures the variability in weights from door to door. An increase in the value of μ shifts the entire distribution to the right, indicating that all doors are consistently heavier than before. An increase in the value of σ means a wider spread of the distribution around the mean, so that many doors are much heavier or lighter than the mean.

TABLE 9.1 Garage-Door Weight Data

Time\Day	1	2	3	4	5	6	7	8	9	10
9 A.M.	81	82	80	74	75	81	83	86	88	82
11 A.M.	73	87	83	81	86	86	82	83	79	84
1 P.M.	85	88	76	91	82	83	76	82	86	89
3 P.M.	90	78	84	75	84	88	77	79	84	84
5 P.M.	80	84	82	83	75	81	78	85	85	80

Time\Day	11	12	13	14	15	16	17	18	19	20
9 A.M.	86	86	88	72	84	76	74	85	82	89
11 A.M.	84	83	79	86	85	82	86	85	84	80
1 P.M.	81	78	83	80	81	83	83	82	83	90
3 P.M.	81	80	83	79	88	84	89	77	92	83
5 P.M.	87	83	82	87	81	79	83	77	84	77

FIGURE 9.3 Histogram of Garage-Door Weights

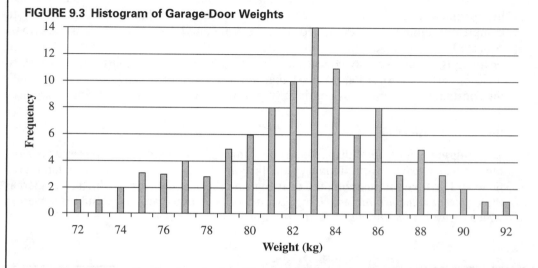

The discrete distribution depicted by isolated bars in Figure 9.3 may be conveniently approximated by a continuous curve which in this instance would appear as a bell-shaped normal distribution that is symmetric around its mean. Recall the properties of normal distribution that we discussed in the context of safety inventory in chapter 7 (also see the Appendix 2). From these properties, we know, for example, that 68.26% of all doors will weigh within ± 1 standard deviation from the average weight—within 82.5

± (1)(4.2), or between 78.3 kg and 86.7 kg. Likewise, we know that 95.44% will fall within ± 2 standard deviations from the mean (between 74.1 kg and 90.9 kg), and 99.73% will fall within ± 3 standard deviations from the mean (between 69.9 kg and 95.1 kg). Standard deviation (or variance) of output, therefore, is a measure of the variability in the door-making process. A precise, consistent process would produce doors of nearly identical weights, resulting in predictable quality in terms of the ease of operation and durability.

Similar statistical analysis can be performed on the mean and variance of response time, cost, and customer experience with the order fulfillment process, as well as any other performance measure that may be of importance to MBPF's customers. The key fact is that process performance typically varies from one flow unit to another, and we would like to measure, estimate, and reduce its variability, with the goal of making it more predictable and consistent with customers' expectations.

Combined with mean and variance, the histogram summarizes overall process performance in the aggregate, but it does not show how performance varies over time.

EXAMPLE 9.3 *(continued)*

Suppose that over the past 20 days there has been an upward trend in our door weights from an average of 80 kg to 85 kg, or 0.25 kg per day. When we aggregate the 20-day data, we may get the same histogram, mean, and variance as we would if we had made all our observations from the output of day 10, which also has an average weight of 82.5 kg. What

can we say, then, if we had to predict door weights on day 21 of production? On the basis of the histogram alone, we would consider it to be a random sample from the normal distribution with a mean of 82.5 kg and a standard deviation of 4.2 kg. With knowledge of the trend over time, however, our estimate of the mean weight on day 21 would be 85.25 kg.

Thus, if we rely solely on the performance summary provided by a histogram, we lose the time value of information. In the next subsection we emphasize how performance varies over time, which is consistent with our flow perspective throughout this book.

9.3.4   Run Charts

A **run chart** is a *plot of some performance measure monitored over time.* It displays variability in process output across time, and helps identify structural variability such as trend and seasonality.

EXAMPLE 9.4

To track variability in door weights over time, we may plot weights of garage doors sampled at two-hour intervals from each day's production. Sup-pose we plot the 100 door weights recorded over time in the past 20 days. The resulting run chart is shown in Figure 9.4.

FIGURE 9.4 Run Chart of Door Weights Over Time

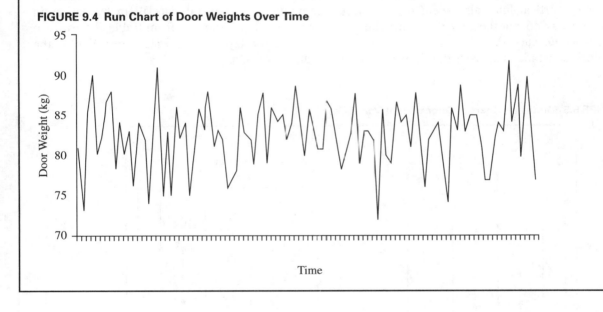

9.3.5   Multi-Vari Charts

To analyze the observed variability in door weights further, we may wish to separate (a) variability among doors produced on the same day, and (b) variability between doors from one day to the next. Isolating the dominant type of variability would then help us search for and eliminate its sources.

Multi-vari chart *is a plot of high-average-low values of measurements sampled over time.* The range between high and low measurements within a sample at a given time indicates variability among flow units produced at one time, while changes in the sample average values show variability over time.

EXAMPLE 9.5

Figure 9.5 plots the data in Table 9.1 as a multi-vari chart. The length of each vertical line represents the range of door weights observed on a given day, which indicates the amount of variability among the doors produced *within* that day's batch. The middle dot on the vertical line represents the average weight of doors produced on that day. Fluctuation in the average weight from one day to the next then indicates variability *between* days, which is tracked by the lines connecting the dots across time.

From this multi-vari chart, we see little fluctuation in averages observed across time. We may therefore conclude that there is no apparent trend or cyclical pattern over time that affects door weights *between* days (ruling out, for example, possibilities of "Friday afternoon" or "Monday morning" effects on worker performance). Similarly, the lengths of vertical lines also seem to vary little from one day to another, so that variability in weights *within* each day also appears stable. We therefore conclude that each day looks more or

less the same as every other, and therefore our estimates of the process mean and variability appear to be stable. Since variability from one day to the next appears to be less pronounced than variability within each day, in our search to reduce variability we should look for causes of process variability that are common to all days.

To quantify these observations, we may summarize the data on weights from each day's production in terms of two statistics:

- Average weight $\overline{X}$ (pronounced *X-bar*), and
- Range *R*—the difference between the highest and the lowest weights.

Average is a measure of expected performance, while range measures variability in performance (analogous to standard deviation but easier to compute). We then tabulate them by day as in Table 9.2. For example, from Table 9.1, we can compute for day 1, the average door weight in the sample of five as

FIGURE 9.5 Multi-Vari Chart of Door Weight Variability

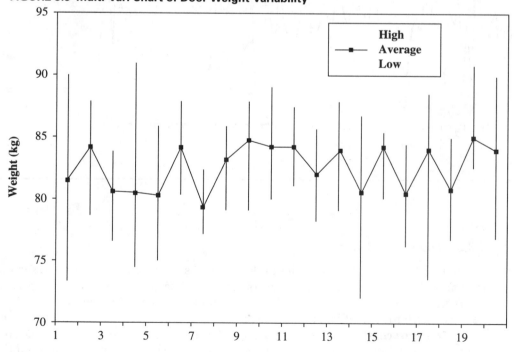

$$\overline{X}_1 = (81 + 73 + 85 + 90 + 80)/5 = 81.8\,\text{kg}$$

and the difference between the heaviest and the lightest door in that sample as

$$R_1 = 90 - 73 = 17\,\text{kg}$$

Similarly, the average weight on day 2 is $\overline{X}_2 = 83.8$ kg with the range of $R_2 = 10$ kg, and so on. Both the average weight and the range of weights vary from one day to the next.

We may now plot averages and ranges across time from Table 9.2 in charts as shown in Figures 9.6 and 9.7, which summarize performance variability between days and within days, respectively. They are essentially run charts of averages and ranges over time.

TABLE 9.2 Average and Range of Door Weights Over Time									
Day	1	2	3	4	5	6	7	8	9	10
$\overline{X}$	81.8	83.8	81.0	80.8	80.4	83.8	79.2	83.0	84.4	83.8
R	17	10	8	17	11	7	7	7	9	9
Day	11	12	13	14	15	16	17	18	19	20
$\overline{X}$	83.8	82.0	83.0	80.8	83.8	80.8	83.0	81.2	85.0	83.8
R	6	8	9	15	7	8	15	8	10	13

FIGURE 9.6 Performance Variability between Days: Variability in Sample Means $\overline{X}$

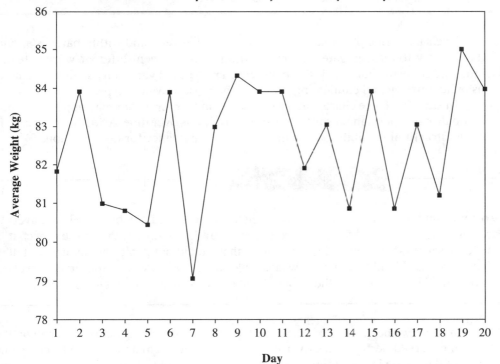

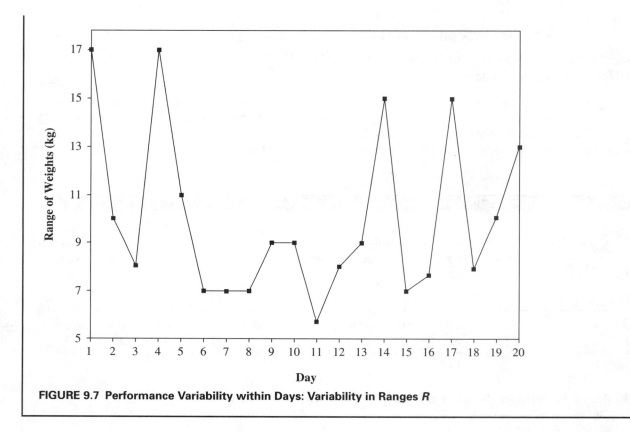

FIGURE 9.7 Performance Variability within Days: Variability in Ranges R

The same principle of separating variability between and within batches applies when we try to disaggregate variability within and between different worker teams, shifts, and so forth. Our goal is to isolate different types of variability so that we can focus on identifying and eliminating causes of the most prevalent type.

In studying these charts, we try to discern any patterns that may appear—trends, seasonality, or a permanent shift in performance levels over time. Aside from such identifiable structural variability, the charts provide no guidance for taking actions.

EXAMPLE 9.5 (continued)

From Figure 9.6, for example, we note that on day 19 average door weight observed was 85 kg—the highest of all averages observed so far and 3.8 kg above the previous day's average. Should we have taken any action back on day 19 to try to reduce the door weight? Well, we did not, but luckily the average dropped to 83.8 kg on day 20. In retrospect, it was good that we did not panic and act hastily, but what should we do if, on day 21, we observe an average weight of 86 kg? Is that too high to be ignored?

In short, we need some operational decision rule for taking actions on-line on the basis of observed performance over time. The same problem arises when tracking any series of data evolving over time—an investor must decide when to buy or sell a stock as its price fluctuates; the central bank must decide when to raise or lower interest rates on the basis of economic data collected over time. We devote the next section to analysis of this important problem of deciding when to act and when not to act.

9.4   PROCESS CONTROL

There are two aspects of process management: Process planning and process control. **Process planning** involves designing process architecture and operating procedures and setting such key process measures as capability, capacity, and efficiency. The long-run goal of process planning, as discussed in chapter 2, is to produce and deliver products to satisfy targeted customer segments. The goal of **process control,** on the other hand, is to continually ensure in the short run that actual process performance conforms to planned performance. Actual performance typically will deviate from planned performance due to various causes. Process control involves tracking variability between the two, and identifying and eliminating its sources.

9.4.1   The Feedback Control Principle

Central to managing process performance over time is the principle of **feedback control** of dynamic systems, which involves two steps:

1. Collecting information about critical performance measures over time, and
2. Taking corrective actions based on observed variability in real time.

It means periodically monitoring actual performance (in terms of cost, quality, availability, and response time), comparing it to planned levels of performance, investigating causes of observed variability between the two, and taking corrective actions to eliminate those causes.

Figure 9.8 shows the feedback control principle, which is similar to the concept of *plan-do-check-act (PDCA) cycle* for problem solving and continuous improvement. A thermostat is a classic example of a feedback control mechanism. We set it at a planned temperature, and a thermometer monitors the actual temperature (which may fluctuate due to air leaks, door openings, and so forth). Depending on the current temperature, the controller automatically turns the furnace on and off. Automobile cruise control is also a feedback control mechanism. It maintains car speed by monitoring actual speed and adjusting fuel supply to ensure that actual speed remains close to planned speed.

In both examples, monitoring and adjustments are performed continuously and automatically. In managing business processes, continuous and automatic feedback

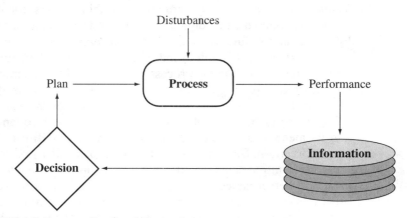

FIGURE 9.8 Process Feedback Control

control may not be economical (or even possible). The manager must therefore make two decisions:

1. How frequently to monitor process performance, and
2. How to react in response to observed performance.

Frequent observation improves both the chance of discovering any degradation in performance and the likelihood of speedy recovery. Unfortunately, it also increases the cost of monitoring. Optimal frequency of monitoring would balance the cost of monitoring with the cost of nonconformance resulting from excessive variability. Thus, for example, the EKG and blood pressure of a heart patient should be monitored more frequently than those of a healthy person because the cost of monitoring is insignificant in comparison with the cost of heart attack.

The next question is how to act on the basis of observed performance. Managers often decide what to do by comparing the current period's performance with that of the previous (or comparable) period only. Thus, cost and productivity-variance reports typically show percentage gains or losses from one period to the next. Managers then base actions (such as granting rewards and reprimands) on whether variances are favorable. Unfortunately, some variances may be due to factors beyond a subordinate's control, so any incentive scheme based on such variance reports may be distorted. According to quality guru W. Edwards Deming, using incentives based on factors that are beyond a worker's control (that he called "system causes") is like rewarding them according to a lottery. To use observed performance data rationally, we must identify which variability is due to factors that are within a subordinate's control and which are beyond his or her control. We must understand different types of performance variability and their causes, because the appropriate managerial actions that are required to attack each will differ.

9.4.2 Types and Causes of Variability

The performance of a process is determined by its architecture (e.g., layout, resources used), operational procedures (e.g., resource allocations, schedules) and the environment (e.g., levels of demand and/or supply). As discussed, a key characteristic of any process performance is variability—a process rarely performs consistently over time. Some of this variability is *normal*—to be expected of any process of a given design operating in a given environment—whereas *abnormal* variability occurs unexpectedly from time to time.

Normal variability is *statistically predictable and includes both structural variability and stochastic variability.* Structural variability refers to systematic changes in the external environment, including seasonality and trend factors. Stochastic variability arises by chance and is due to a stable system of *random* (or *common*) causes that are inherent to every process. Random causes are many in number, but each has only a small and unpredictable effect on the process performance. They cannot be easily isolated and removed without redesigning the entire process. For example, the weight of garage doors varies from door to door as a result of many factors bearing upon the precision of MBPF's production process. A histogram shows the frequency distribution of weights, and its mean and standard deviation summarize MBPF's process target and performance precision. Beyond that we cannot explain why two consecutive doors from the same day's output can have different weights, as *the production process is inherently imprecise.* If performance variability is normal, due to random causes only, we say that the process is in a stable state of *statistical equilibrium*—parameters of its distribution (such as mean and variance) are unchanging—or that the process is performing as expected, given its design. How can we remove these random causes and increase consistency of our process performance? Only by improving process design. It involves purchasing more precise equipment, hiring better-skilled workers and training them more effectively, purchasing better-quality materials, and so forth. All of this process redesign takes both time and investment of resources over the long term and is therefore management's responsibility. It is unfair to expect workers to produce consistent output when the process and the environment they are operating within are inherently imprecise.

In contrast, **abnormal variability** is *unpredictable and disturbs the state of statistical equilibrium of the process by changing parameters of its distribution in an uncertain way.* Abnormal variability results from *assignable* or *special* causes that are externally superimposed from time to time. The existence of abnormal variability means that one or more of the factors affecting process performance—architecture, procedures, or environment—may have changed. Although assignable causes are few in number, each has a significant effect on the process performance. On the upside, however, they can be isolated, investigated, and eliminated, even in the short run. A particular batch of raw material might be defective, the machine may be incorrectly set, or the operator may not be attentive on that day. Because such causes are readily identifiable and correctable in the short run, at the local level, and without large capital expenditures, they are the operator's responsibility. *The goal of process control is to identify whether the observed variability is normal or abnormal, so that an appropriate action can be taken at an appropriate level to eliminate it.*

Ironically, another source of abnormal variability is *tampering*—unnecessary adjustments made in trying to compensate for normal variability. Deming's "marble experiment" illustrates this principle beautifully. A subject is asked to drop a marble through a funnel repeatedly, the goal being to hit a target underneath. If the marble misses the target, the subject usually tries to compensate for the deviation by moving the funnel in the opposite direction. This unnecessary tinkering, however, results in an *increase* in the variability of the marble's final position. The correct strategy, of course, is to aim the funnel right on the target and let the marble land around it, its final position exhibiting stochastic variability due to random causes. The idea is to avoid overreacting to random fluctuations (normal variability) in the short run. In the long run, we may wish to reduce even random fluctuations by redesigning the process—for example, by lowering the funnel, using a less bouncy marble, or leveling the landing surface.

In statistical terms, normal variability is observed among random draws from a given probability distribution of process performance. Abnormal variability occurs when the parameters of the probability distribution (such as its mean or variance) are changed in an uncertain way. Thus, in the short run, our goal is fourfold:

1. To estimate normal variability,
2. To accept it as a factor to be expected of a given process and avoid unnecessary tampering with the process,
3. To detect the presence of abnormal variability in process performance, and
4. To isolate and eliminate any assignable causes of abnormal variability.

Our long-term goal is to reduce normal variability also by improving process precision. Short-term adjustments could and should be delegated to those workers whose activities are closest to the sources of abnormal variability. Long-term process improvements, which may involve considerable investment of resources, time, and effort, are the manager's responsibility.

We deal first with the problem of short-term process control. In the following sections, we assume that structural variability has already been accounted for and that tampering is avoided. As we monitor process performance over time, we want to determine whether observed variability in performance is normal or abnormal. If it is normal—due to random causes only—we say that the process is *in control*. We should then accept observed variability as an expected part of process performance that we cannot eliminate in the short run. It represents the best effort of the process, and we should leave it alone. If, on the other hand, performance variability is abnormal—due to an assignable cause—we conclude that the process is *out of control*. In this case, we should stop the process, investigate, identify, remove assignable causes, and bring the process back into a state of control. The fundamental problem therefore is deciding whether observed variability is normal or abnormal.

9.4.3 Control Limit Policy

The structure of this type of "threshold policy" for making decisions based on the observed performance has an intuitive appeal, and is known to be optimal in a wide variety of situations. At the most basic level, we establish a **control band,** which represents *an acceptable range of performance variability*. Any variability within this range is to be interpreted as normal, due to known structural causes or random causes that cannot be readily identified or eliminated in the short run. Therefore, we should not tamper with the process. Any variability outside this range, on the other hand, should be considered abnormal, due to an assignable cause, warranting detailed investigation and correction.

For example, we might monitor the performance of our car by tracking the gas mileage we get from one fill-up to the next. If we get 30 miles per gallon (1 mpg is about 0.4 km per liter) on average, a combination of random causes (weather and traffic conditions, gasoline quality) and assignable causes (incorrect ignition timing, burnt spark plugs, leaking gas tank) will cause actual mileage to hover around 30 mpg. Our decision rule may be to set a lower limit (e.g., 20 mpg): If actual mileage falls below this limit, we should take the car to a mechanic for a checkup; if it is above this limit, we should drive the car as is. Similarly, in the house thermostat example, the controller may be set at 20°C, and may turn the furnace on if the temperature drops 2°C below the set temperature and shut the furnace off if the temperature rises 2°C above the set value. As a result, the house temperature will be maintained between 18°C and 22°C. A more finely tuned and sensitive controller may be more expensive, but would maintain the temperature closer to the setting by turning the furnace on and off more frequently.

Although the concept of process control is usually applied in managing product quality, the principle is general enough to be applicable to *any* measure of process performance over time. For example, we have already seen an application of control limit policy in managing inventory and capacity. In chapter 7, we saw that inventory control with uncertain demand involves monitoring inventory level over time and ordering Q units as soon as inventory drops below a preestablished reorder point *(ROP)* level. In this context, *ROP* constitutes a control limit, and the action taken, when necessary, consists of ordering Q units. Reorder point determines safety inventory, which controls product availability in terms of the probability of stockout. Similarly, in managing process capacity and unit flow time, as in chapter 8, we may monitor the length of the waiting line (or the duration of customer waiting time). As soon it reaches some *upper* limit *U,* we may increase capacity (for example, by adding a server), and when it reaches a *lower* limit *L,* we may decrease the capacity. Such operating policies are routinely followed in decisions to open and close checkout counters in supermarkets. The goal in establishing control limits *U* and *L* is to control the customers' waiting time most economically. In the area of cost management, accountants use unit cost and productivity variance reports to track the cost performance and to specify managerial actions when observed cost exceeds a certain threshold or when productivity drops below a critical level. In short-term cash management, a firm's (or an investor's) cash position may fluctuate over time. If it falls below a certain level *L,* the firm may liquidate some of its assets to raise cash, whereas if the cash position reaches some higher level *U,* the firm may invest the excess cash in an asset. Finally, in stock trading, investors can place "limit orders" to purchase (or "stop loss" orders to sell) a stock if and when its price drops to a specific level. Computerized "program trading" automatically executes trades when prices reach prespecified trigger levels. Thus, a control limit policy provides guidelines in the form of critical thresholds for taking actions on line, in light of current information in a variety of contexts.

9.4.4 Control Charts

Statistical process control generally involves setting a range of acceptable variability in process performance around its average μ. As long as observed performance varies within this range, we accept it as normal and conclude that we do not have sufficient evidence to suspect the presence of an assignable cause, and therefore refrain from tampering with the process. Any variability outside this range, however, should be regarded as abnormal; we should stop the process, search for an assignable cause, and eliminate it.

In setting an acceptable *control band* around the average performance μ, we should consider the following two factors:

1. The normal variability of the process, as measured by the standard deviation σ of its historical performance, and

2. The degree to which we wish to control the process, as represented by a number *z;* the smaller the number *z,* the tighter the control desired.

We then allow *z* standard deviations around the mean as an acceptable control band of normal variability. We specify an *upper control limit (UCL)* and a *lower control limit (LCL),* and denote the control band as [*LCL,UCL*]. The general formulas for determining the two **control limits** are

$$LCL = \mu - z\sigma$$

and

$$UCL = \mu + z\sigma$$

Figure 9.9 shows a generic **control chart,** which is like a run chart of process performance with control limits overlaid to give it decision-making power. If the observed performance variability is within the control limits, we infer that variability is normal and the process is *in control.* Performance measurements falling outside control limits,

FIGURE 9.9 Process Control Chart

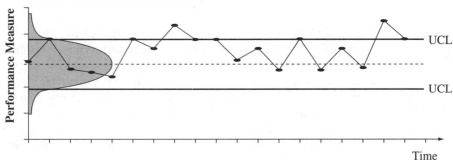

however, indicate that the process is *out of control,* signaling probable existence of an assignable cause. In addition to comparing observed performance against the control limits, we may try to identify any trend or seasonal patterns over time. Various additional rules of thumb may also be used to make inferences about variability and to decide on when to act. For example, one rule recommends that if seven consecutive observations are above (or below) the average performance, we should investigate the process even though it appears to be in control.

Operational Interpretation   Note that a control chart allows performance variability within $z\sigma$ around the expected performance before taking action. Therefore $z\sigma$ may be referred to as *safety quality* to absorb normal variability analogous to safety inventory in chapter 7, and safety capacity and safety time in chapter 8.

Statistical Interpretation   A reader familiar with statistics may recognize the relationship of control limits to *confidence intervals* and *hypothesis testing.* We start with a *null hypothesis* that the process is in control (stable) at mean level μ; the alternate hypothesis is that the process mean has shifted to some other level. Based on observed performance, we must determine if the process mean has shifted. The decision rule is to accept the null hypothesis by default and take no corrective action if the process performance measure falls within control limits. If it falls outside the control limits, we conclude that there is overwhelming evidence to reject the null hypothesis and look for an assignable cause that should be identified and removed.

   This decision rule is not mistake-proof: the presence of stochastic variability may lead to wrong decisions following this rule. Sometimes, even when the process is in control, its performance may fall outside the control band simply due to normal variability. In that case, we conclude—wrongly—that the process is out of control, and look for an assignable cause that does not exist. This chance of a false alarm is called a **type I** (or **α**) **error,** and it results in an expensive wild-goose chase. Conversely, our process performance measure may fall within the control band even if there is an assignable cause of abnormal variability. In this case, we conclude—again, wrongly—that the observed variability is normal and warrants no investigation. This possibility of misinterpreting abnormal variability as normal is called a **type II** (or **β**) **error,** and it results in failure to investigate and eliminate a genuine assignable cause.

   In our gas-mileage example, suppose we normally get an average of 30 mpg and our lower control limit is set at 20 mpg, so that we take the car to a mechanic when the mileage drops below 20 mpg. It is possible that even when nothing is wrong with the car, our mileage may drop below 20 mpg purely by chance, and hence we erroneously conclude that it should be checked out by a mechanic, which results in an unnecessary cost.

Optimal Degree of Control   The magnitude of both types of errors and their costs depends on the narrowness of our control band, as measured by z. Recall that a smaller value of z represents a narrower control band, in which case we end up looking for assignable causes more often than we should, resulting in frequent unnecessary—and expensive—investigation. At the same time, however, tight control band ensures that assignable causes, when present, will be detected faster, thus saving on the cost of operating the process that is out of control. Conversely, a larger z—and a wider control band—means looser control and less frequent investigation, but also a higher cost of failing to adjust an out-of-control process.

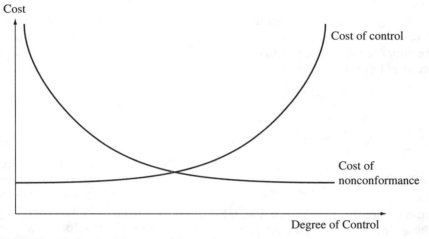

FIGURE 9.10 **Optimal Degree of Control**

The correct choice of z would balance the costs of investigation with failure to eliminate assignable causes of variability. We are thus left with two conclusions graphically displayed in Figure 9.10:

1. Monitoring frequency and tightness of the control band determine the degree of control exercised, and

2. The optimal degree of control is one that balances the costs and benefits of designing and implementing a finely tuned control mechanism.

Both traditionally and in practice, a value of $z = 3$ is used in statistical process control. If the performance measure is normally distributed, then 99.73% of all observations will fall within the following range:

$$\mu \pm 3\sigma$$

In practice, we do not know the true process mean μ and standard deviation σ, representing its expected performance and normal variability, respectively. We therefore estimate these parameters by sampling and use sample mean and sample standard deviation in determining the control limits. We illustrate this with an example.

EXAMPLE 9.6

We return to our garage-door example. Suppose we monitor supplier performance in terms of $\overline{X}$— our sample mean or the average door weight in our sample of five doors inspected each day. From Table 9.2 we can compute the mean of 20 $\overline{X}$'s as

$$\mu_{\bar{x}} = 82.5 \text{ kg}$$

and the standard deviation of $\overline{X}$ as

$$\sigma_{\bar{x}} = 1.6 \text{ kg}$$

(Recall from section 9.3.3 that the standard deviation of door weights X was calculated to be $\sigma = 4.2$ kg—the average $\overline{X}$ of samples of five doors is less variable than individual door weight X. The theoretical relationship between the two is given by

$$\sigma_{\bar{x}} = \sigma/\sqrt{n}$$

where n is the sample size. In our example, with $n = 5$, and $\sigma = 4.2$ kg, our estimate of $\sigma_{\bar{x}}$ would be

$4.2/\sqrt{5} = 1.88$ kg, whereas our sample of 20 produced 1.6 kg.)

If we adopt the standard practice of setting $z = 3$, our control limits on $\overline{X}$ become

$$82.5 \pm (3)(1.6)$$

so that

$$LCL = 77.7 \text{ kg}$$

and

$$UCL = 87.3 \text{ kg}$$

If we compare the 20 values of $\overline{X}$ in Table 9.2 against these limits, we see that all of them fall within our control band. We can therefore conclude that there is no statistical evidence to indicate the presence of an assignable cause of variability that affects the process mean—there is no reason to believe that door weights vary significantly between days. Likewise, we can compute from Table 9.2 average range

$$\mu_R = 10.1 \text{ kg}$$

with standard deviation

$$\sigma_R = 3.5 \text{ kg}$$

We can then compute control limits on values of observed ranges as

$$(10.1) \pm (3)(3.5)$$

yielding

$$LCL = -0.4$$

and

$$UCL = 20.6$$

Note that we should set the LCL of –0.4 to zero because the range of our measurements cannot be negative. When we compare observed ranges with these control limits, we see that they are all less than 20.6 kg. We therefore conclude that no day's output varies significantly, or rather, that there is no assignable cause of variability within each day's performance. Our production process is thus *in control* because it seems to display only normal variability.

We can superimpose these control limits on the charts in Figures 9.6 and 9.7 to yield $\overline{X}$ and R control charts. We can now visually check that all fluctuations in averages and ranges of garage-door weights are within the control limits, so we conclude that $\overline{X}$ and R charts are in control. In conclusion, as far as garage-door weights are concerned, the garage-door-making process appears to be statistically stable.

To highlight the essence of statistical process control, we have described its technical details in simplified form. A complete exposition involves using the average range of observations to estimate the standard deviation of process output and its range. Details may be found in standard books on quality control such as Grant and Leavenworth (1988).

Although we have described process control in terms of quality of its output, the same principles would apply if we considered X as unit flow time or cost. Likewise, our performance measure may be a *continuous variable* (door weight, average of weights in a sample, customer waiting time, unit processing cost) or a discrete variable (product is defective or not, number of defects per flow unit produced, number of customer complaints). In a continuous case, we use normal distribution, as above, while in a discrete case we use appropriate discrete probability distribution, such as *binomial* or *Poisson distribution*. Although the control band formulas differ, the basic principle of establishing control limits remains the same.

Suppose we count the annual number of order taking errors at MBPF. It may be modeled by the Poisson distribution (see Appendix) in which case we have:

Mean = Variance = μ, the average number of errors in the transactions recorded.

Then we may set the following control limits:

$$\mu \pm z\mu^{1/2}$$

If the actual number of errors exceeds the upper control limit, it indicates serious degradation in performance that should be investigated. Conversely, number of errors less than the lower control limit would indicate better-than-expected performance that should be recognized and rewarded—and perhaps institutionalized. In either case, when we get a signal that performance variability is abnormal, we must look for an assignable cause—favorable or unfavorable—and act upon it.

9.4.5   Cause-Effect Diagrams

Upon detecting the presence of abnormal variability, we may use a **cause-effect diagram** (**fishbone** or **Ishikawa diagram**) to identify the *root cause(s)* of the observed variability. It shows a chain of cause-effect relationships ultimately leading to observed abnormal variability. Through discussion and brainstorming, we first try to generate hypotheses about possible causes. According to one guideline, an investigator who diligently pursues a sequence of *Why?* questions five times will ultimately arrive at the root cause of a problem. For example:

- Why are these garage doors so heavy?
  Because the sheet metal used to make them was too thick.
- Why was the sheet metal too thick?
  Because the rollers at the supplier's mill were set incorrectly.
- Why were the supplier's rollers incorrectly set?
  Because the supplier is incapable of producing accurately to our specifications.
- Why did we select a supplier who cannot meet our specifications?
  Because our project supervisor was too busy "getting the product out" to invest time in vendor selection.
- Why did he find himself in these circumstances?
  Because he gets paid to meet production quotas.

Thus the root cause of the door weight problem may be MBPF's incentive structure. A simplified fishbone diagram of this problem may look like the one in Figure 9.11. The tail of each arrow shows a possible cause of the effect indicated at the head of that arrow.

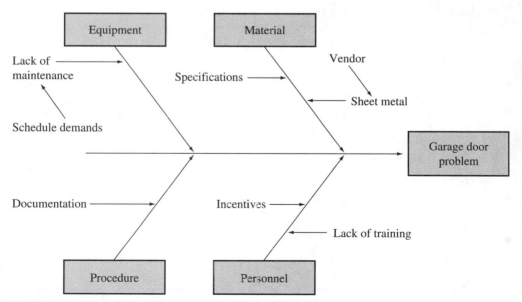

FIGURE 9.11 Cause-Effect Diagram of the Garage-Door Problem

Although a cause-effect diagram enables us to identify a qualitative relationship between a process variable and its effect on the product characteristic that a customer cares about, to take a concrete action, we need to understand the precise quantitative relationship between the two, as indicated in the next subsection.

9.4.6 Scatter Plots

Suppose we have identified the supplier's sheet-metal rolling process as the root cause of the door-weight problem. This problem affects the ease of door operation and its durability that customers value. We would now like to measure the exact relationship between the two, so that we will be able to control the door weight by changing the settings on the supplier's rolling mill.

To estimate this relationship, we may experiment with various settings on the rolling mill, measure the effect on the garage-door weights, and plot the results on a graph called a **scatter plot.** In the scatter plot shown in Figure 9.12, the horizontal axis represents the sheet-metal thickness setting in millimeters and the vertical axis shows the weight of garage doors produced. The two variables seem to be "positively correlated"—increasing the roller setting to a higher thickness of the steel roll would increase the door weight. One could continue with statistical regression analysis to estimate the strength of this relationship, but we will not go into details here.

In summary, process control involves dynamically monitoring performance over time to ensure that variability is due to random causes only; it entails identifying and correcting any variability due to assignable causes. A process being "in control" simply means its performance variability is stable through time, so that its output is statistically predictable. Being in control makes a statement about the *internal* stability of the process. It does not necessarily mean that process performance is satisfactory in terms of its output from the *external* customer's perspective. It behooves managers, therefore, to assess internal process performance against external customer requirements—a topic that we take up in the next section.

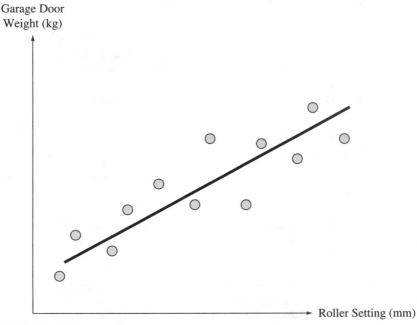

FIGURE 9.12 Scatter Plot

9.5   PROCESS CAPABILITY MEASUREMENT

In our study of process control at MBPF Inc., we have thus far identified the external product measures that customers desire (ease of operation and durability) and linked them to internal measures (door weight) that the manufacturer can control. We have translated performance desired by customers into the necessary upper and lower specification limits (from 75 kg to 85 kg). We have also seen how a process that is in control ensures that its output variability is normal and statistically predictable, i.e., the process is stable and our estimates of the process mean and standard deviation are reliable. Based on these estimates, we would like to determine **process capability,** which may be defined as *its ability to meet customer requirements.* Although we can measure process capability in a variety of ways, here we describe three that are closely interrelated.

9.5.1   Fraction of Output within Specifications

One measure of process capability is *the fraction of output that will fall within the upper and lower specifications,* denoted as *US* and *LS,* respectively. We can compute this fraction either by actual observation or by using a probability distribution as in Example 9.7.

EXAMPLE 9.7

Recall that in the MBPF example, specifications of the garage-door weight are *US* = 85 kg and *LS* = 75 kg. Also recall that in Figure 9.3, each bar height corresponds to the fraction of doors with a specific weight. Adding all the bar heights between 75 kg and 85 kg yields the total fraction of door output that meets design specifications. We see that 74 out of the 100 doors observed fall within the specifications. We may therefore say that the process is currently 74% capable of meeting customer requirements; it is producing approximately 26% defectives.

Alternatively, we may employ normal distribution as continuous approximation and compute the area under the normal probability density curve between 75 kg and 85 kg. If door weight *W* is a normal random variable with mean μ = 82.5 kg and standard deviation of σ = 4.2 kg, then the proportion of doors falling within specification limits is given by

$$\text{Prob}(75 \le W \le 85) = \text{Prob}(W \le 85) - \text{Prob}(W \le 75).$$

If we then let *Z* denote the standard normal variable (with mean 0 and standard deviation of 1), we can use the standard normal tables in Appendix 2 (or in Microsoft Excel, as described in chapter 7) to compute Prob($W \le$ 85) in terms of

$$Z = (W - \mu) / \sigma$$

as

$$\text{Prob}[Z \le (85 - 82.5) / 4.2] = \text{Prob}(Z \le 0.5952) = 0.7240.$$

Similarly, we find from the standard normal tables that

$$\text{Prob}(W \le 75) = \text{Prob}(Z \le (75 - 82.5) / 4.2) = \text{Prob}(Z \le -1.79) = 0.0367.$$

Then:

$$\text{Prob}(75 \le W \le 85) = 0.7240 - 0.0367 = 0.6873.$$

With normal approximation, therefore, the MBPF's process is capable of producing about 69% of doors within the specifications. Thus, MBPF is delivering about 31% defective doors.

Note that, on average, doors weigh 82.5 kg, which is well within specification limits, but that is not a relevant criterion in satisfying customer requirements. Specifications refer to individual doors, not averages: MBPF cannot explain to a customer that, on average, its doors are meeting MBPF specifications; after all, 30% of its customers are getting doors that are either too light or too heavy. It is the variability between doors—not only the average—that matters in determining how capable the process is in meeting customer requirements. This quantitative analysis supports the qualitative discussion of importance of variability from section 9.2.

9.5.2 Process Capability Ratios: C_{pk} and C_p

Another related measure of process capability, which is easier to compute than the fraction of output meeting specifications, is called **process capability ratio,** denoted as C_{pk}. This ratio is based on the observation that in a normal distribution, if the mean is 3 standard deviations above lower specification LS (or below upper specification US), there is very little chance of a product falling below LS (or above US). Consequently, we compute

$$(US - \mu) / 3\sigma$$

and

$$(\mu - LS) / 3\sigma$$

as surrogate measures of how well process output would fall within our specs. The higher these values, the more capable the process in meeting specifications. In fact, (to be on the conservative side) we may take the smaller of these two measures and define a single measure of process capability as

$$C_{pk} = \min [(US - \mu) / 3\sigma, (\mu - LS) / 3\sigma]$$

A process with a higher value of C_{pk} is said to be more capable than one with a lower value. Typically, a process with C_{pk} of 1 or more represents a capable process that will produce at least 99.73% of the output that meets customer specifications.

The C_{pk} measure is also useful when our product specifications are one-sided—when we need to ensure that measurements are not too high (or too low). For example, if we need to measure processing cost, delivery time or number of errors per transactions processed, we may specify only the upper specification limit US. The C_{pk} is then given by the single term in the previous expression that is relevant, the first one in these examples.

As a special case, if the process is centered at the middle of the specification range, we could define C_{pk} by either

$$(US - \mu) / 3\sigma$$

or

$$(\mu - LS) / 3\sigma$$

Equivalently, for a process that is correctly centered at the middle of the specification range, we may simply define the **process capability ratio** C_p as

$$C_p = (US - LS) / 6\sigma$$

This ratio has a nice interpretation. Its numerator specifies the level of product variability that the customer is willing to tolerate (and so represents the "voice of the customer"). The denominator, meanwhile, denotes the level of variability that the process can deliver (thus indicating the "voice of the process"). Recall that with normal distribution, most process output—99.73%—falls within ± 3 standard deviations from the mean. That is, most process variability is within 6 standard deviations around the mean. Consequently, 6σ is sometimes referred to as the *natural tolerance of the process.*

EXAMPLE 9.8

In our garage door weight example, since mean is 82.5 kg and standard deviation is 4.2 kg, we have

$$C_{pk} = \min\left[(US - \mu)/3\sigma, (\mu - LS)/3\sigma\right]$$

$$= \min\left[0.1984, 0.5952\right] = 0.1984$$

If the process is centered at 80 kg, we can define the process capability ratio as

$$C_p = (85 - 75)/[(6)(4.2)] = 0.3968$$

In Example 9.8, note that $C_{pk} = 0.1984$ (or $C_p = 0.3968$) does *not* mean that the process is capable of producing 19.84% (or 39.68%) of the output within the customer specifications; we computed that figure previously to be 70%. There is, however, a close relationship between the process capability ratio and the proportion of output meeting the specifications. Table 9.3 summarizes this relationship, wherein defects are counted in parts per million (ppm) or parts per billion (ppb). Thus, if we would like no more than 100 defects per million (0.01% defectives), we should have the probability distribution of weights produced so closely spread around the mean that the standard deviation is 1.282 kg, which corresponds to $C_p = 1.3$.

TABLE 9.3   Relationship Between Process Capability Ratio and Proportion Defective

Defects (ppm)	10,000	3,000	1,000	100	10	1	2 ppb
C_p	0.86	1	1.1	1.3	1.47	1.63	2

9.5.3   Six-Sigma Capability

A third equivalent measure of process capability that is used by Motorola, General Electric, and other quality-conscious companies is called the **Sigma measure,** which is computed as

$$S = (US - LS)/2\sigma$$

in which case, the process is called an *S-sigma process.*

MBPF's garage door-making process is a

$$(85 - 75)/[(2)(4.2)] = 1.19 \text{ sigma process}$$

Thus with a *three-sigma process,* upper and lower specifications are three standard deviations away from the mean, which corresponds to $C_p = 1$ and 99.73% of output meeting specs. Similarly, a *six-sigma process* is one with a standard deviation σ so small that upper and lower specifications are *six* standard deviations from the mean. This level of performance represents an extraordinarily high degree of precision which corresponds to $C_p = 2$, and only 2 defective units per *billion* produced! For the garage door process to be a six-sigma process, its standard deviation must be

$$\sigma = (85 - 75)/[(2)(6)] = 0.833 \text{ kg}$$

which is about one fifth of its current value of 4.2 kg.

Adjusting for Mean Shifts   Actually, given the sigma measure, Motorola computes the fraction defective after allowing for a shift in the mean of ± 1.5 standard deviations from the center of specifications. Allowing for this shift, a six-sigma process amounts to producing an average of 3.4 defective units per million units. Such a high standard represents, although not quite "zero defects," at least "virtual perfection," and a goal to strive for. If we use this measure and allow for a 1.5-sigma shift, we arrive at the sigma measure, its relationship with C_p, and defective ppm tabulated as in Table 9.4.

TABLE 9.4 Fraction Defective and Sigma Measure				
Sigma	3	4	5	6
C_p	1	1.33	1.667	2
Defects (ppm)	66,810	6,210	233	3.4

Why Six Sigma?   From the table note that improvement from a three-sigma to a four-sigma process calls for a 10-fold reduction in fraction defective; going from a four-sigma process to a five-sigma process requires 30-fold improvement, and going from a five-sigma process to a six-sigma process requires 70-fold improvement. Experts estimate that an average company delivers about 4-sigma quality, whereas best-in-class companies aim for six-sigma quality. Why should we insist on such high—and perhaps unattainable—standards? For one thing, even if individual parts (or processing steps) are of extremely high quality, the quality of the entire product (or process) that requires *all* of them to work satisfactorily will be significantly lower. For example, if a product contains 100 parts and each part is 99% reliable, the chance that the product will work is only

$$(0.99)^{100} = 0.366$$

or 36.6%. Moreover, even if defects are infrequent, the cost associated with each may be very high. Deaths caused by faulty heart valves, automobile brake failures, or defective welds on airplane bodies, however infrequent, are too expensive to the manufacturers (in terms of lawsuits and lost reputation), customers (in terms of lives), and ultimately the society. Moreover, competition and customer expectations keep rising constantly, and ambitious companies and their leaders continue to set such stretch goals.

Safety Capability   In general, we may also express process capability in terms of the *design margin* $[(US - LS) - z\sigma]$, and interpret it as *safety capability*, analogous to safety quality, safety inventory, safety capacity, and safety time encountered in section 9.4.4, chapter 7 and chapter 8. Each of these safety margins represents an allowance $z\sigma$ planned to meet customer requirements of product quality, availability, and delivery response time in face of variability in supply or demand.

Greater process capability, for instance, means less variability and less chance of a product failing to meet customer specifications. Moreover, if the process output is closely clustered around its mean, in relation to the width of customer specifications, most of the output will fall within the specifications even if the mean is not centered at the middle of specifications. Higher capability therefore means less chance of producing defects even if the process goes out of control due to a mean shift off from the center of the specifications. Thus process capability measures the *robustness* of the process in meeting customer specifications. A robust process will produce satisfactory output even when it is out of control.

9.5.4   Capability and Control

In our MBPF example, we see that the production process is not performing well in terms of its output meeting the customer requirements under any of the measures of process capability described above. Yet recall that in the preceding section, we concluded that the MBPF process was "in control"! It is therefore important to emphasize that *being in control and meeting specifications are two very different measures of process per-*

formance. Whereas the former indicates *internal* stability and statistical predictability of the process performance, the latter indicates its ability to meet *external* customer requirements. Being in control is a necessary but not a sufficient condition for satisfactory performance of a process. Observations of a process in control ensure that the resulting estimates of the process mean and standard deviation are reliable, so that our measurement of process capability is accurate. The next step is then to improve process capability so that its output will be satisfactory from the customer's viewpoint as well.

9.6   PROCESS CAPABILITY IMPROVEMENT

Since each measure of process capability defined above depends on the process mean and/or standard deviation, we must try to adjust one, or the other, or both.

9.6.1   Mean Shift

Given the probability distribution of process output, changing the process mean will shift the distribution and increase the proportion of output within the specifications as well as the process capability ratio.

EXAMPLE 9.9

The MBPF door process mean of 82.5 kg is much too high in relation to the company's specifications of 75 kg to 85 kg. The histogram in Figure 9.3 reveals a symmetric shape of door weight distribution around its mean. If we can adjust the process mean to the center of the specifications, it would bring a greater proportion of process output within specs. Thus if our supplier turns down the thickness setting on his sheet rolling mill, he can reduce the mean weight to $\mu = 80$ kg, thereby shifting the entire distribution of door weights to the left. Under these conditions, the proportion of sheets falling within specifications increases to

$$\text{Prob}(75 \leq W \leq 85) = \text{Prob}(-1.19 \leq Z \leq 1.19)$$
$$= (2)(0.383) = 0.766$$

Figure 9.13 shows the improvement in the proportion meeting specifications by shifting the process mean from 82.5 to 80.

At the same time, the process capability index C_{pk} increases from 0.1984 to

$$\text{Min } \{(85 - 80) / [(3)(4.2)], (80 - 75) / [(3)(4.2)]\}$$
$$= \text{Min } \{0.3968, 0.3968\} = 0.3968$$

which is in fact the C_p.

FIGURE 9.13 Improvement from the Mean Shift

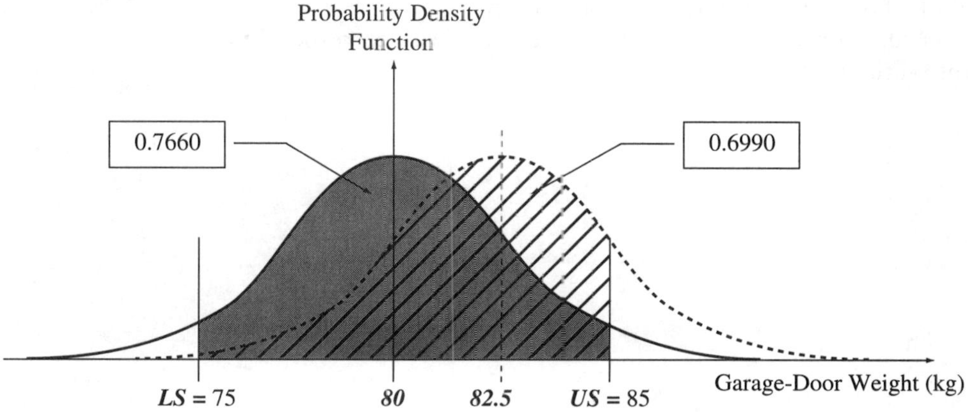

Thus, centering the process appropriately improves its capability. Any further improvement must come from a reduction in variability.

9.6.2   Variance Reduction

Currently, as measured by the standard deviation of 4.2 kg, there is too much variability in weight from one door to the next. This lack of consistency may be due to any number of causes—perhaps the door fabrication equipment is too old, poorly maintained, and imprecise; perhaps the operator has not been trained properly; or perhaps the steel rolls delivered by the supplier are inconsistent from batch to batch due to imprecision in the rolling mill.

If such causes of variability were corrected—through investment in better equipment, training, or supplier selection—the process output would be more consistent. In turn, that consistency would be reflected in a smaller standard deviation and a greater concentration of the frequency distribution around the mean. A greater fraction of output would fall within specifications. In this case, reducing the process average is much easier and can be done quickly by the appropriate worker (or at least the appropriate supervisor). Reducing process variability, however, requires considerable time, effort, and investment and is therefore management's responsibility. Sometimes even reducing process mean may require considerable effort. For example, reducing average unit flow time in manufacturing or waiting time in a service operation usually requires considerable investment and process improvement.

EXAMPLE 9.10

Returning to our door weight problem at MBPF, if we can reduce σ from its current estimate of 4.2 kg to 2.5 kg, the proportion of output meeting specifications will increase to

$$\text{Prob}(75 \leq W \leq 85) = \text{Prob}(-2 \leq Z \leq 2) = 0.9544$$

with corresponding

$$C_p = (85 - 75) / [(6)(2.5)] = 0.67$$

Figure 9.14 shows improvement in proportion meeting specifications that comes from reducing the process variability.

If we need 99% of our output within specifications, how far must we reduce σ? To achieve this level, σ must be such that, the upper and lower specifications must be $z = 2.58$ standard deviations from the mean. In other words, we must have

$$2.58\,\sigma = 5$$

or

$$\sigma = 1.938 \text{ kg}$$

with corresponding

$$C_p = 0.86$$

FIGURE 9.14 Improvement from Variability Reduction

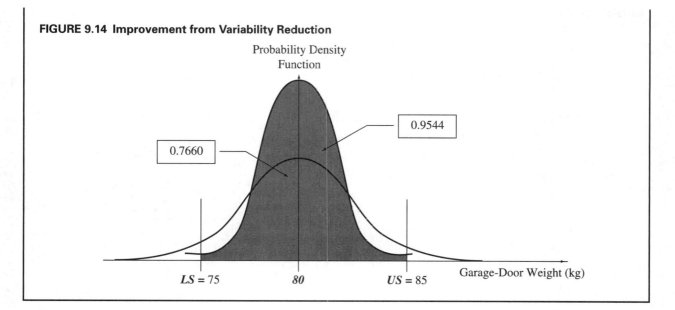

9.6.3   Effect on Process Control

It is important to note that, as the process capability is improved by shifting its mean μ or reducing its variability σ, its control limits must also be adjusted accordingly.

EXAMPLE 9.11

Upon adjusting the process mean from 82.5 kg down to 80 kg, the new control limits on subgroup averages would be

$$80 \pm (3)(1.6) = (75.2, 84.8)$$

From now on, we would compare observed average weights in samples of five doors against these new control limits to identify the presence of an assignable cause.

Similarly, if we reduce the standard deviation from 4.2 kg to 2.5 kg, we need to revise control limits on $\overline{X}$ as well, because as σ changes, so will $\sigma_{\overline{x}}$,

the standard deviation of $\overline{X}$ (recall that the relationship between the two standard deviations is $\sigma_{\overline{x}} = \sigma/\sqrt{n}$, where n is the number of observations in a sample). For example, in the garage door problem, because $n = 5$, reducing σ to 2.5 kg would yield new

$$\sigma_{\overline{x}} = 2.5 / \sqrt{5} = 1.118 \text{ kg}$$

and the new control limits on average weights would be

$$80 \pm (3)(1.118) = (76.646, 83.354)$$

Thus, process control limits should be readjusted each time the process parameters are changed. It is also important to note that process control plots and limits involve *averages and ranges* of observations within subgroups, whereas process capability refers to the ability of the process to meet specifications on *individual* units; the two should not be mixed on the same plots. Figure 9.15 shows the progression in managing process variability from being (a) out of control to (b) in control by eliminating structural and abnormal variability, and then to (c) greater capability through proper centering and lower normal variability.

FIGURE 9.15 From Control to Capability

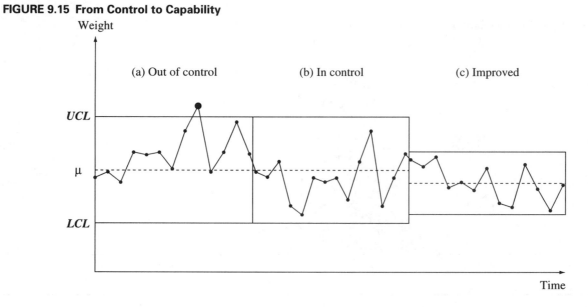

Although progression from (a) to (b) can be achieved in the short run, further improvement from (b) to (c) is a long-term journey. The next section indicates some steps in that direction through improved design of products and processes.

9.7 PRODUCT AND PROCESS DESIGN

Often, sources of performance variability can be traced to the design of the product and process. In this section we indicate two general principles of design for minimizing process variability and its impact on product performance.

9.7.1 Design for Processing

We outline three general principles of designing products and processes that minimize chances of process variability: simplification, standardization, and mistake-proofing.

Simplification   As the term suggests, the objective here is to simplify the product (or process) so that it has fewer parts (or processing stages), which would require fewer suppliers, and reduce chances of confusion and error. Suppose that a product (process) contains n parts (stages) and that each has probability p of working properly. The probability that the entire product (process) will perform satisfactorily—that all n parts (stages) will work—is p^n. This probability decreases geometrically as n increases.

Product simplification without foregoing product variety can be achieved through use of interchangeable parts and modular designs. They not only permit greater variety at the final assembly stage, but also simplify materials handling and inventory control. Recall from chapter 7 the benefits of inventory pooling that results from parts commonality, which reduces the amount of inventory needed. Process simplification by eliminating non-value-adding steps not only reduces processing cost and flow time but also reduces opportunities for making mistakes. In general, "keep it simple, stupid" (KISS) is an important design principle that requires ingenious and innovative ways of identifying opportunities to eliminate unnecessary, non-value-adding parts and processing steps.

Standardization   Although product proliferation provides greater variety to customers, it increases the complexity of processing, which leads to higher cost, longer flow times and lower quality. Using standard, proven parts and procedures removes operator discretion, ambiguity, and opportunities for mistakes. Likewise, standard operating procedures simplify the tasks of recruiting and training and improve employee productivity as well as performance consistency. As discussed in chapter 2, flow shops producing limited variety products in high volumes enjoy low cost, flow time and product consistency advantages. Finally, even in service operations, as we saw in chapter 8, reducing variability in processing times through standardization reduces customer waiting times, which improves their perception of service quality.

Mistake Proofing   By minimizing the chance of human error, foolproofing improves quality, reduces rework, and thus reduces both flow time and processing cost. Product design for ease of assembly is critical in assembly operations, since they account for two-thirds of all manufacturing costs, and are a major source of quality problems. Fasteners, for instance, are widely known as potential problem sources and can be replaced with self-locking mechanisms. In product assembly, parts that have to be fitted together should be designed with either perfect symmetry or obvious asymmetry to prevent the possibility of misorientation. Workers and equipment should always have adequate clearance, unobstructed vision, and easy access to facilitate assembly. Such techniques as alphanumeric coding, color coding, and bar coding of parts help to make processing operations error-resistant. Use of automation generally reduces labor costs, as well as chances of human error, and increases processing speed and consistency.

9.7.2   Robust Design

Until now, we focused on ways to eliminate abnormal variability in the short run and reduce normal variability in the long run. Sometimes, however, variability reduction may not be possible or economical. Another approach to dealing with variability is called robust design. The idea is to design the product in such a way that its actual performance will not suffer despite any variability in the production process or in the customer's operating environment. The goal is to develop a design that is robust in resisting effects of variability.

In general, product performance is determined not only by internal (process-related) and external (environment-related) noise factors, but also by its own design parameters. The designer's goal is to identify a combination of design parameters that will protect product performance from the internal and external noise factors to which it may be subjected. In statistically planned experiments, different combinations of design factors are tested in conjunction with combinations of different levels of noise factors. The challenge is to identify the right combination of design parameters (without trying them all) that works well on average in spite of noise factors. More details may be found in Taguchi and Clausing (1990).

9.8   LEVERS FOR CONTROLLING PROCESS VARIABILITY AND IMPROVING CAPABILITY

In this chapter, we have seen that deviation from desired process performance may be due to normal and abnormal variability. Although process variability will always plague every system, it becomes troublesome when it leads to instability, lower process capability, and excess costs. Managers should be aware of at least three levers for controlling process variability and improving capability:

1. *Feedback control to detect and eliminate abnormal variability:*
   - Set control limits on acceptable variability in key performance measures, and
   - Monitor actual performance and correct any abnormal variability.
2. *Decrease normal process variability*: Design products and processes for ease of processing (simplify, standardize, and mistake-proof).
3. *Immunize product performance to process variability*: Robust design to desensitize performance to sources of variability.

Problem Set

9.1 Costello Labs supplies 500 cc bottles of treated Elixir plasma solution to Mercy Hospital. Several factors are important in assessing plasma quality, such as purity, absence of AIDS or hepatitis virus, and bacterial count. The most important quality characteristic, however, is protein concentration. Protein concentration is measured by a sophisticated electronic process known as electrophoresis. AMA standards specify that a 500 cc plasma bottle should contain between 30 and 35 grams of protein. Both concentrations under and over this range may be hazardous to a patient's health.

Hospital administrators have instructed Costello Labs to reorganize its plasma-production operation and to demonstrate evidence of tighter process controls prior to the renewal of its supply contract. Costello's plasma-production equipment consists of a protein injector and a mixer that together determine protein concentration in each bottle. Process capability depends on the precision of these two pieces of equipment.

a. Suppose that the hospital and the lab have agreed that at least 98% of the plasma bottles supplied by Costello should conform to AMA specifications (the bottles should contain between 30 and 35 grams of protein). Determine the following:
   - The precision of Costello's protein injector, as measured by , and
   - The standard deviation of the amount of protein that it must inject into each bottle to produce 98% of process output within the specifications.

   Also compute corresponding process capability ratio C_p.

b. Costello Labs production manager Phil Abbott wants to establish statistical process control (SPC) charts to monitor the plasma-injection process. Set up these control charts based on average protein readings taken from randomly selected samples of 12 bottles from each batch.

9.2 Natural Foods sells Takeoff, a breakfast cereal, in 1-lb boxes. According to FDA regulations, a 1-lb box must contain at least 15.5 oz cereal. However, Natural Food's box-filling process is not perfect: Its precision, expressed in terms of the standard deviation of the weight of a 1-lb box filled, is 0.5 oz.

a. Where should Natural Foods center its process to ensure that 98% of boxes filled meet FDA requirements? What proportion of boxes would be overfilled beyond 16 oz?

b. While underweight boxes might prompt FDA action, overweight boxes certainly cost Natural Foods in terms of higher materials costs. Therefore, quality control manager Morris Nerdstat wants to monitor the cereal-filling process to ensure that its mean does not deviate from the level established in part (a). He plans to weigh nine randomly selected boxes at regular time intervals and plot the average weight on a chart. At one point, he finds an average weight of 15.9 oz. The company's legal staff is pleased that this performance is better than the FDA requirement of 15.5 oz. What action, if any, should Nerdstat take?

9.3 In measuring and evaluating the quality of banking services, analysts have found that customers regard accuracy, timeliness, and responsiveness as the most important characteristics. Accordingly, First Chicago Bank constantly monitors and charts almost 500 performance measures of these quality characteristics. Accuracy, for example, is measured by the error/reject rate in processing transactions, timeliness by delays in collecting funds, and responsiveness by speed in resolving customer inquiries or complaints. For each measure, First Chicago also sets a level called minimal acceptable performance (MAP), which serves as an early warning signal to management, as a basis for comparison with the banking-industry competition, and as a constantly upgraded goal for ensuring continuous improvement of service quality.

Over a six-month period, First Chicago recorded, on a weekly basis, errors per 1,000 items processed in all types of collection transactions. The resulting 26 numbers were as follows: 0, 2, 0, 17, 2, 4, 0, 2, 1, 0, 0, 5, 6, 5, 15, 5, 10, 5, 2, 2, 0, 2, 0, 0, 0, 1. The Bank Administration Institute (BAI) reports that the average error rate for such transactions is 1.5%.

a. Determine one or the other:
  • The appropriate process control limits on the fraction of transactions in error, or
  • The number of errors per 1,000 transactions.

b. By way of comparison, plot the observations, process average, control limits, and industry standard. Is First Chicago's process in control? How does its performance compare with the industry standard?

References

Deming, W. E. 1986. *Out of the Crisis.* Quality Press, Milwaukee, WI.

Grant, E. L., and R. S. Leavenworth. 1988. *Statistical Quality Control.* 6th ed. McGraw-Hill, New York, NY.

Hauser, J., and D. Clausing. 1988. The house of quality. *Harvard Business Review:* May–June.

Joiner, B., and M. Gaudard. 1990. Variation, management, and W. Edwards Deming. *Quality Progress,* Special Issue on Variation, December.

Juran, J. M., and F. M. Gryna. 1980. *Quality Control Handbook.* 4th ed. McGraw-Hill, New York, NY.

———. 1980. *Quality Planning and Analysis.* 2nd ed. McGraw-Hill, New York, NY.

Ott, E. R., and E.J Schilling. 1990 *Process Quality Control: Troubleshooting and Interpretation of Data.* 2nd ed. McGraw-Hill, New York, NY.

Taguchi, G., and D. Clausing. 1990. Robust quality. *Harvard Business Review:* January–February.

Wadsworth, H. M., K. Stephens, and B. Godfrey. 1986. *Modern Methods for Quality Control and Improvement.* John Wiley and Sons, Inc., New York, NY.

Process Integration

CHAPTER 10

Process Synchronization
and Improvement

CHAPTER

10

Process Synchronization and Improvement

We present an integrated view of an organization and its supply chain as a *processing network,* which has the overall goal of matching its output with customer demand in the most economical way. Ideally, every organization strives to develop, produce, and deliver a wide variety of high-quality products in a short time, at a low cost, as customers demand them. Any deviation from this ideal represents an opportunity to improve the process by eliminating *waste* in the form of defects, delays, and excess costs. In this chapter, we study *lean operations* to improve process performance first at the *plant* level and then extend it to include improvements in the entire *supply chain.* Improvement on either level means increasing process flexibility, reducing variability, and synchronizing different processing stages to ensure an accurate and fast flow of information and materials for continuous processing.

Approaching ideal performance can be accomplished in two ways: continuous improvement and radical reengineering. In either case, process improvement requires making long-term investment in technology, equipment, workers, and suppliers; benchmarking the best business practices; and bringing about and adjusting to the organizational change involved.

10.1 INTRODUCTION

As discussed in chapter 1, any organization can be viewed as a business process that transforms inputs into outputs to satisfy customer needs. Total customer satisfaction with a firm's output requires providing customers what they want, when they want it, where they want it, and at a price they are willing to pay for it. Theoretically, satisfying all of these criteria simultaneously would require developing, producing, and delivering individually customized products of the highest quality, in the shortest time, and at the lowest cost. In reality, of course, given the firm's capabilities and constraints, compromises must be made. In most industries, as discussed in chapter 2, there exists an efficient frontier in the competitive space defined by the four dimensions of product cost, quality, variety, and response time, which reflects the optimal tradeoffs among them given the current state of technology and management practices. Competition forces firms operating below the industry's efficient frontier to improve and move toward the frontier. World-class firms already operating at the frontier can stay ahead of competitors only by improving and pushing the frontier further. Thus, firms at every level have

FIGURE 10.1 Product Flows in a Processing Network

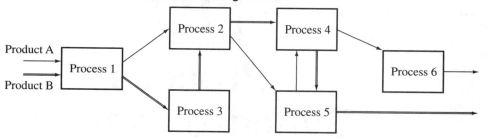

scope and necessity to improve process performance along the four dimensions that customers value.

In parts II and III of this book, we studied specific levers for improving cost, quality, variety, and flow time. In this chapter we acknowledge that customers typically demand satisfaction in all of these areas. Moreover, our focus in earlier chapters was mostly on single processes that supply single products which serve as building blocks in processing networks. In reality, firms typically develop, produce, and deliver varieties of products through networks of processes. When a customer purchases a box of detergent in a supermarket, this event is the last stage in a long sequence of processes that starts with the manufacturer's chemicals supplier and culminates in the checkout-counter operation, and each of these processes may be handling other products as well. To improve ultimate customer satisfaction with product cost, quality, and availability, the firm must therefore improve all of these intermediate processes. Finally, firms with multiple products flowing through them must ensure that the information and material flows among processes are well coordinated, accurate, and fast.

In this chapter, we show how the concepts and principles that we have developed thus far for individual processes can be extended to improve performance of a **processing network** *that consists of information and material flows of multiple products through a sequence of interconnected processes.* Figure 10.1 illustrates two product flows through a typical processing network. The overall goal of this network is to satisfy customer demand in the most economical way by producing and delivering the *right* products in the *right* quantities at the *right* times to the *right* places. It involves efficiently synchronizing flows between processes.

Plants and Supply Chains   Our discussion will focus on performance at two different levels—plant and supply chain—depending on where we draw process boundaries. A **plant** is *any singly owned, independently managed and operated process* such as a manufacturing, service, or storage facility. A **supply chain** refers to *an entire network of interconnected plants of diverse ownership with flows of information and materials between them, with the objective of coordinating production and consumption of goods and services.* For example, the supply chain that makes the detergent available to customers in a supermarket will include chemical plants, warehouses for storing chemicals, factories for producing and packaging detergents, distributors, wholesalers, and finally retailers—all of whom together constitute a connected network of processes.

We may also view each plant in the supply chain as a processing network. Within the detergent maker's factory, the purchasing, production, storage, and shipping departments can all be considered as processes, each handling a variety of detergents and cleaners. In this chapter, we first examine how to manage processing network operations within a single plant and then extend the key principles to coordinate operations of the entire supply chain of interconnected plants. The core ideas that apply to both levels of operation are the same, and draw upon the process improvement levers that we have discussed in earlier chapters. The operational details, however, differ because of differences in scale, scope, geographical dispersion, and incentives of diverse process owners involved.

In section 10.2 we characterize the ideal performance of a processing network in meeting customer requirements in terms of flow synchronization and cost efficiency. In section 10.3 we view any deviation from this ideal as waste and examine its sources and consequences. We define the goal of process improvement as bringing its performance closer to the ideal by identifying and eliminating waste. Section 10.4 studies methods of lean operations designed to improve plant-level performance by increasing flexibility, reducing variability, and improving information and material flows, all at lowest cost. Throughout this section we link the concepts and methods of process improvement to the practical levers described in earlier chapters of the book. In section 10.5 we extend the same ideas to supply-chain management. We also show how poor supply chain design and operation can lead to a significant loss of synchronization and efficiency. Finally, section 10.6 compares two general approaches to attaining ideal performance: continuous improvement and process reengineering. We also indicate the role of benchmarking in setting process improvement goals and the importance of managing the organizational change that always accompanies process improvement.

10.2   THE PROCESS IDEAL: EFFICIENCY AND SYNCHRONIZATION

Ideally, customers would like to have available a wide variety of high-quality products at low prices, as needed in terms of their quantity, time, and location requirements. An ideal process would enable a firm to satisfy all these needs in the most economical way. We may therefore summarize process performance in terms of two closely related operating characteristics:

1. Process **synchronization** refers to *the ability of the process to meet customers' demand in terms of their exact quality, quantity, time, and location requirements.*
2. Process (cost) **efficiency** is measured in terms of *total processing cost, the ideal being to develop, produce, and deliver products at the lowest possible cost.*

The Four "Just Rights" of Synchronization   A well-synchronized detergent supply chain would produce and deliver defect-free boxes in sufficient quantities to widely dispersed supermarkets, so that the detergent is available to satisfy all customer demand without delay. In the case of manufactured goods, this can always be achieved by producing in advance and carrying large inventories of all products, of verified quality, in all locations. This approach, however, may be prohibitively expensive and thus quite cost inefficient. We therefore define a perfectly synchronized process as one that is *lean* in that it develops, produces and delivers only on demand:

- Exactly *what* is needed (not wrong or defective products),
- Exactly *how much* is needed (neither more nor less),
- Exactly *when* it is needed (not before or after), and
- Exactly *where* it is needed (not somewhere else).

In short, a perfectly synchronized process always supplies just the right *quality* product, in just the right *quantity,* at just the right *time,* and in just the right *place*—just as desired by customers. These four "just rights" of synchronization lay at the heart of the *just-in-time (JIT)* paradigm that stresses production of only necessary flow units in necessary quantities at necessary times. Together with cost efficiency, the "just rights" of synchronization define the **process ideal** *in matching supply with demand in the most economical way.* With multiple products, synchronization means supplying different products to different customers to meet respective demands for the right quality, quantity, time, and place. We may imagine such a process as one in which various products appear in necessary quantities at desired locations just as customers wish to purchase them—without any defects, delays, excess inventories, or stockouts.

To achieve such a goal, a process must be able to produce and deliver any product, in any quantity, at any time, in any place, precisely *in synch* with the demand for them— hence the term *synchronization.* These four criteria define the ultimate in process capability, flexibility, and speed. Producing any product without defects requires the process to be extremely versatile and precise. The ability to produce any desired quantity requires flexibility to produce one flow unit at a time. To satisfy demand arising at any time—without entailing inventories—a process must have instant, complete, and accurate information on demand and must be able to react by producing and delivering instantly. An ideal process can satisfy all these requirements and do so at the lowest possible cost. In short, an ideal process is infinitely capable, flexible, fast, and frugal.

Synchronized Networks   This concept of an ideal process extends naturally to a network of processes—once we recognize that in such a network, the outflow of one process (a supplier) is the inflow of another (a customer). Thus, perfect synchronization of an entire network of suppliers and customers means a precise match of the supply and demand of various flow units at each processing stage. It means that each stage must satisfy—precisely—the quality, quantity, time, and place requirements of the next stage.

We can define *synchronization* at the level of an individual process (as a network of activities), a plant (as a network of processes), or a supply chain (as a network of plants). In each case, the goal of ideal performance requires that individual processing stages be capable, flexible, fast, and frugal. Processes must also be tightly linked—informationally as well as physically—so that each stage knows and provides, quickly and accurately, what and how much its successor stage needs, and when and where it needs it. The result is a precisely balanced system of inflows and outflows at all stages through which units flow smoothly and continuously without disruption or accumulation. In particular, the output of the last stage will precisely match (external) end-customer demand. In an ideal network, this synchronization of processing stages is achieved at the lowest possible cost.

Although the ideal may seem unattainable in a practical sense, the long-run goal and challenge of process management should be to approach this ideal by improving products, processes, and practices. In the next section, we examine the causes and consequences of failure to attain the ideal.

10.3   WASTE AND ITS SOURCES

Why is it so important to understand an ideal level of performance that we can, in reality, only approximate? Because anything short of ideal performance represents an opportunity to improve the process—or for the competition to move in. Operationally, low efficiency is reflected in high processing costs. Lack of synchronization manifests in unwanted or defective products, high inventories, long delays, and frequent stockouts.

In processing networks, lack of synchronization means uneven flows between processing stages. As a result, excess inflows cause inventory buildups at some stages, while insufficient inflows of required units starve others.

Sources of Waste   Regarding *any such deviation from the ideal* as **waste,** we may paraphrase the goal of process improvement as *the elimination of all waste.* Thus, waste means producing inefficiently, producing wrong or defective products, producing in quantities too large or too small, delivering products too early or too late—basically, failing to match customer demand most economically. Taiichi Ohno, the main architect of the Toyota Production System (TPS), classified seven types of waste in manufacturing (1988):

- Producing defective products,
- Producing too much product,
- Carrying inventory,
- Waiting due to unbalanced workloads,
- Unnecessary processing,
- Unnecessary worker movement, and
- Transporting materials.

All this waste results in high costs, low quality, and long response times, ultimately leading to customer dissatisfaction and loss of business to the competition. Producing and delivering defective flow units results not only in unhappy customers but also in the additional cost and time required to receive, inspect, test, rework, and return those flow units. Producing too much product or producing it too early builds up excess inventory, which increases not only holding costs (including the costs of capital, storage, and possible obsolescence) but also increases unit flow time. In turn, long flow times mean long delays in responding to changes in customer tastes and in getting new product designs to market. Inventories also occupy valuable floor space and hide defective units, delaying their exposure, detection, and correction of root causes, during which more defective flow units are being produced. In processing networks, inventory buffers between stages increase total flow time, thus delaying feedback on quality problems, obstructing traceability of root causes, and diffusing accountability for errors.

Thus, in addition to financial costs, producing excess inventories means operational inefficiencies due to long flow times. Conversely, producing too little product too late results in stockouts, delays, and increased expediting costs. In processing networks, insufficient inflows idle some stages, resulting in inefficient utilization of resources. Finally, delivering wrong products to wrong places creates excess inventories of wrong products, shortages of right ones, or both. Necessary corrective transfers also result in additional costs and delays.

The sources of all this waste can ultimately be traced to underlying process imperfections, environmental variables, or management practices. As discussed in chapter 4, *non-value-adding activities* such as transportation, movement, inspection, and rework increase theoretical flow time and processing costs. As discussed in chapters 5 and 8, *insufficient capacity* at bottlenecks reduces process throughput and increases waiting time. From chapter 6, *lack of flexibility* to switch between products, measured in terms of fixed setup (or changeover) costs, necessitates processing in batches even though demand is continuous (a mismatch giving rise to cycle inventories). As discussed in chapter 7, *stochastic variability* in supply and demand, together with long and uncertain lead times, requires us to hold safety inventory to protect against stockouts. In processing networks, cycle and safety inventories are inserted to decouple consecutive processing stages so that their operations are relatively independent of one another. Each stage can then operate at its own economical scale regardless of the demand pattern of its subsequent stage. Moreover, each stage is less vulnerable to variability in flow from the preceding stage. If all stages were flexible in processing different products as well as predictable in terms of operating without variability, buffer inventories would be unnecessary and flows would be synchronized. As discussed in chapter 8, it is the *variability* in inflows and processing that causes both waiting and inflow inventory, thereby requiring safety capacity at an added cost. Chapter 9 explained that *insufficient process capability* in terms of high normal variability results in defective units. Abnormal variability in terms of *process instability* over time also necessitates expensive statistical process control. Finally, lack of synchronization from delivering wrong products to wrong locations is often due to inadequate transmission of materials and information through the network.

Waste Elimination   Thus, cycle and safety inventories, safety capacity, safety time, and many non-value-adding activities (including transportation, inspection, rework, and process control) are short-term tactical actions that process managers must take to work with imperfect processes suffering from inflexibility, variability, and inefficient logistics. In the short term, we accept these process limitations as given and try to deal with them by processing flow units in batches, keeping safety inventory (capacity), employing process control, and correcting defects. All of these measures, however, increase total cost, inventory, and flow time, leading to loss of synchronization, and cost efficiency, resulting in less-than-ideal performance, and more waste.

A more fundamental long-term strategy would be to improve the underlying process itself to make it more flexible, predictable, and stable, which would eliminate the need for such temporary measures as batch processing, safety allowances, and process control. For example, recall from chapter 6 that the optimal batch size (hence, the cycle inventory and flow time) are directly related to the (square root of) the setup cost. A long-term solution to reducing cycle inventories, then, is to reduce the setup cost and changeover time itself (improve process flexibility) so that we could process different flow units in small batches economically, which would then automatically reduce cycle inventory and flow time and improve synchronization.

Similarly, recall from chapters 7 and 8 that the amount of safety inventory and safety capacity needed to provide a given level of service depend directly on the degree of variability in the system. Our long-term solution would call for making flows more regular and predictable and reducing variability. This would reduce our safety cushion requirement, thereby reducing cost while improving synchronization.

In chapter 9 we identified two principles governing the relationship between variability and process stability. In the short run:

1. Greater normal variability results in more defective products, and
2. More abnormal variability requires tighter process control to maintain stability.

It follows, then, that increasing process capability and stability (reducing variability) would

1. Decrease the number of defective products, inspection, and rework, and
2. Reduce the need for on-line process control, thereby improving synchronization and reducing overall cost.

The long-term goal of process improvement should therefore be to isolate and eliminate the fundamental *sources* of waste—process imperfections such as rigidity and variability—rather than to compensate for these imperfections with short-term solu-

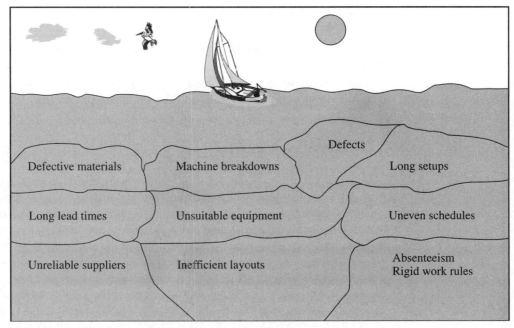

FIGURE 10.2 The River Analogy: Waste and Its Sources

tions. The basic idea is to diagnose and remove the roots of an ailment, seeking a permanent cure rather than superficially treating symptoms with temporary fixes.

The River Analogy   Figure 10.2 illustrates the concept of waste and its sources by using a *river analogy* that has been popularized in the literature on the Toyota Production System. Visualize process imperfections—unreliable suppliers, defective materials, long lead times, long setup times, unreliable equipment, untrained workers, unstable processes, inefficient layouts—as rocks lying on a river bed. The water level in the river represents short-term measures in the form of cycle and safety inventories, safety capacity, safety time, safety quality, inspection, rework, and process control. Such measures permit smooth sailing of day-to-day operations for the process manager despite underlying problems. The correct long-term response should be to expose and pulverize these rocks so that we could sail smoothly even in shallow water (which symbolizes lean operations). Three factors, however, divert us from achieving the long-term solution: (1) water level covers up rocks, reduces *visibility* and thus clouds the root causes on the bottom, (2) smooth sailing dampens our *incentives* to look for the problems, and (3) lack of adequate *problem-solving skills* makes it difficult to eliminate these problems. The challenge of process management is to overcome these three obstructions and bring actual performance closer to the ideal.

In the next two sections, we examine specific methods for improving process synchronization and efficiency, first within a plant and then within an entire supply chain. Although the operational details in the two contexts will be different, the following basic principles are the same:

TO IMPROVE PROCESS SYNCHRONIZATION
- Streamline flows of information and material.
- Increase resource flexibility,
- Reduce process variability.

TO IMPROVE PROCESS EFFICIENCY
- Reduce processing cost and flow time by eliminating non-value adding activities.

These improvements at the plant and the supply chain level require a long-term investment in the process, including equipment, technology, workers, and suppliers. In the concluding section, we then outline two philosophies for implementing such process improvement—one continuous and the other discontinuous.

10.4 IMPROVING FLOWS IN A PLANT

Any plant, whether a manufacturing or a service facility, is a network of processing stages through which materials or customers flow before emerging as finished products or serviced customers. An ideal plant is synchronized and efficient: The outflow of each stage meets—precisely and economically—the inflow requirements of the next, without defects, inventories, delays, or stockouts. Methods for achieving this level of synchronization and efficiency within a plant have been discussed in the operations management literature under such headings as *lean operations, just-in-time (JIT) production, synchronous manufacturing, agile manufacturing,* and the *Toyota Production System (TPS).*

The basic objective of TPS is "to shorten the time it takes to convert customer orders into deliveries" (Ohno, 1988). Although this goal can be achieved by building large finished-product inventories of all models, Toyota aims to achieve it at much lower cost through lean operations by synchronizing production with customer demand. Because there will always be a gap between actual and ideal degrees of synchronization, the process of approaching the ideal is an important aspect of lean operations. TPS strives to make small but constant changes and improvements (called *kaizen*) by continuously identifying and eliminating sources of waste (by gradually lowering the water level in the river analogy to expose the rocks at the bottom). We discuss this philosophy of continuous improvement further in section 10.6. In this section we focus primarily on the concrete methods of lean operations to achieve synchronization and efficiency.

Essentially, the ongoing goal of lean operations involves four points:

1. *To improve process logistics* through efficient plant layout and fast and accurate flow of information and material,
2. *To increase process flexibility* by reducing equipment changeover times and instituting cross-functional training,
3. *To decrease process variability* in flow rates, processing times, and quality, and
4. *To minimize processing cost by eliminating non-value-adding activities* such as transportation, inspection, and rework.

The first three goals aim to improve process synchronization and the fourth relates to cost efficiency. These goals are achieved through the process-improvement levers discussed in parts II and III, and require long-term investments in processes, people, and procedures. Although the methods for achieving them will often be illustrated in the specific context of (automobile) manufacturing, the basic ideas are also applicable in service industries. In fact, they work well in any stable, high-volume, limited-variety, sequential-processing environment.

The classic example of synchronization and efficiency for mass production was Henry Ford's Rouge, Michigan, plant in the 1910s described in chapter 2. The plant was a totally integrated facility (including steel mills and glass factories) with modern machine tools, electrical systems, and an automated assembly line operated by highly paid, well-trained workers. Process efficiency was achieved by applying Frederick W. Taylor's principles of "scientific management," including time-and-motion studies, work rationalization, and best work methods indicated in section 2.7. Streamlined to minimize the total flow time and cost, the moving assembly line was the ultimate in synchronizing production without buffer inventories between workstations. In fact, as indicated in Example 2.4 the roots of TPS can be traced to Ford's system, except for one vital distinction: the ability to handle product *variety*. Whereas the Ford plant produced only Model T (and only in black because that color dries fastest), modern automobile manufacturers must offer a wide variety of models and options, all of which must be of high quality and competitively priced, to satisfy contemporary customers' ever-rising expectations. We explore some of Toyota's tactics for meeting this challenge in the following sections. However, we keep our exposition at a more general level to address how any plant can achieve synchronization and efficiency through lean operations. To start with, the first two sections indicate how to improve process logistics through efficient plant layout and flow control.

10.4.1   Improving Process Organization: Cellular Layout

A plant's *process architecture* (the network of activities and resources, including their layout) has a significant impact on flow of work through the process and hence its ability to synchronize production with demand. As indicated in section 1.4.2, in a conventional **functional layout,** resources (stations) that perform the same function are physically positioned together. Depending on their individual processing requirements, different product types are then routed differently through these resource pools, and each flow unit may be sent to any available station in the pool. A functional layout of the MBPF garage-making factory, for example, would group all roof-making stations in one area, all base-making stations in another, and all final-assembly stations in a third.

A major advantage of the functional layout is that it pools all available capacity for each function, thereby permitting fuller utilization of the whole resource pool in producing a variety of products. It also facilitates worker training and performance measurement in each well-defined function. Most importantly, it benefits from division of labor, specialization, and standardization of work within each function, thereby increasing the efficiency of each function. Finally, as indicated in section 1.4.2, it is ideal for job shops that process wide variety of products in small volumes.

In terms of synchronization, however, the functional layout has several drawbacks. Flow units may have to travel significant distances between various resource pools, so their flow times are longer and it is more impractical to move them in small lots. The result is an intermittent jumbled flow with significant accumulation of inventories between stages. In addition, because each worker tends to be narrowly focused on performing only a part of the total processing task, he or she rarely sees the whole picture, leading to fragmented, unsatisfying jobs. Specialized workers are also less likely to make broad product-focused improvements as they are to make narrow, technology-focused process improvements.

An alternative to the process-based functional layout is the product-based **cellular layout,** in which *all workstations that perform successive operations on a given product (or product family) are grouped to form a "cell."* To facilitate a streamlined, efficient flow of information and materials, stations within the cell are located next to one another and laid out sequentially. As indicated earlier, Henry Ford's assembly line for mass production of Model T is a classic example of such a product layout, which on a smaller scale is referred to as a cell. At MBPF, a cell would consist of one roof station, one base station, and one assembly station, each located next to the others. MBPF might then replicate one or more copies of such a three-station cell (e.g., one for each type of garage). Recall Figure 1.3 which illustrates the distinction between process-based functional layouts and product-based cellular layouts.

The cellular layout facilitates synchronous flow of information and materials between processing stations. Physical proximity of stations within a cell reduces transportation between them, and makes it feasible to move small lots of flow-units (as small as one) quickly. It also facilitates communication among stations and improves synchronization by permitting each station to see and produce parts only if and when the next station needs them. Moreover, because any differences in workloads borne by different stations become immediately apparent, targeted improvements can be made to balance them. Similarly, if a station encounters a defective unit, that information can be reported to the supplier station immediately; because the supplier station has just handled the unit in question, the cause of the defect can be determined more easily. Thus, cellular layout improves defect visibility, traceability, and accountability, which in turn leads to fast detection, analysis, and correction of quality problems.

Close interaction among different functions within a cell also encourages cross-functional skill development and teamwork among workers, which leads to more satisfying jobs. Because the entire team works on the same product, workers can experience a sense of ownership of total product and process. The interchangeability of flexible workers also allows them to cooperate and smooth out any flow imbalances resulting from station variability. Finally, a cross-trained workforce also improves synchronization by making it possible to adjust production volume to conform to changes in demand.

Disadvantages of Cellular Layouts   Because resources are dedicated to specific cells, they cannot be used by other cells. Consequently, we lose the advantage of resource pooling. The required duplication of resources for each product line is justified only if product volume is sufficiently high. In addition, resource pooling in a functional layout better absorbs variability that exists from station to station. For example, if a worker at a specific station calls in sick or if a machine breaks down, other similarly skilled operators and similarly tooled machines can be substituted. In a cellular layout, contending with such disruptions would require not only a flexible, trained workforce but also general-purpose machines, which increase cost and lower efficiency.

The stronger interdependence of cellular stations also means that worker incentives must be based on team—rather than individual—performance. Because individual effort is only indirectly related to the team performance and rewards, workers have less incentive to do their share of work. One solution to this "free-rider problem" relies on peer pressure to control productivity of some team members. Another problem with teams working in cells is that not all workers like to work with others or take on the challenging cross-functional jobs involved. Some people prefer to work individually at well-defined, routine tasks, and forcing them to work closely with others in a cell would be counter-productive.

Thus, there are advantages and disadvantages to both functional and cellular layouts. Ideally, cellular structure is appropriate for products or product families with similar work-flow patterns and sufficiently high volume, as in automobile and electronic-goods manufacturing. It would be inefficient to set up a cell to handle a variety of products that entail different work-flow requirements and high changeover times and costs, as in a job shop. There, the functional layout would be more appropriate. From the viewpoint of synchronization, however, cellular layout facilitates flow of information and materials.

10.4.2   **Improving Information and Material Flow: Demand Pull**

Given a system of interconnected stations in a processing network, managing flows means informing each station about what to produce, when to produce, and how much to produce. There are two approaches to managing flows: push and pull. In the conventional **supply push** approach, *input availability triggers production or work,* the emphasis being on "keeping busy" to maximize resource utilization as long as there is work to be done. For example, in production scheduling with *material requirements planning (MRP),* the end-product demand is forecasted and "exploded" backwards to determine parts requirements at upstream stations, based on the product structure ("bills of materials"), processing lead times, and levels of inventories on hand at those stations. A centralized production plan then tells each station when to produce and how much to produce, so that its output will meet the planned (not the actual) requirements of downstream stations. In implementing the plan, each station processes whatever input quantity is on hand and "pushes" the resulting output on to the next station. This push operation will synchronize supply with demand at each stage, but only under the following conditions:

- *If* all information (about the product recipe, processing lead times, and parts inventories) is accurate,
- *If* forecasts of finished goods are correct, and
- *If* there is no variability in processing.

Failure to meet any one of these conditions at any stage will disturb planned flow and destroy synchronization throughout the process, which will then experience excess inventories and/or shortages at various stages. Because each process bases output not on demand but on input availability, it is not surprising that production often fails to synchronize with demand.

An alternative method for ensuring synchronization is **demand pull** in which *output need triggers production,* so that each station produces only on demand from its customer station. Work at an upstream station is initiated by actual demand downstream. Flow units, therefore, are "pulled" from each process by its customer process as the customer needs them, rather than "pushed" by the supplier process on to customer process as the supplier produces them. With demand pull, the supplier does not plan to produce or deliver anything until the customer really needs it, and thus avoids inventories of unwanted outputs by refraining from processing inputs even if they are available.

Toyota's Taiichi Ohno (1988) characterized the pull system in terms of supermarket operations:

> From the supermarket, we got the idea of viewing the earlier process in a production line as a store. The later process (customer) goes to the earlier process (supermarket) to acquire the required parts (commodities) at the time and in the quantity needed. The earlier process immediately produces the quantity just taken (restocking the shelves).

The distinction between the push and the pull systems of work flow is illustrated in Figure 10.3. Note that material flows in the push system are determined by a central plan based on the end-product demand forecast. Information needed to determine flows in a pull system, on the other hand, is local from the succeeding station only, and flows are controlled in real time in decentralized fashion.

Supply Push: Input availability triggers production

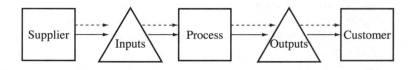

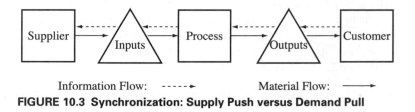

Demand Pull: Output need triggers production

Information Flow: ----►   Material Flow: ——►

FIGURE 10.3 Synchronization: Supply Push versus Demand Pull

The two key requirements to making a pull system work are as follows:

1. Each process must have a well-defined customer, and each customer must have a well-defined supplier process.

2. Each process must produce only in the quantity needed and only when signaled to do so by its customer.

Demand Signaling   In a push system, input availability is sufficient to trigger production. In a pull system, however, the customer needs a *signaling device* with which to inform the supplier of its need.

One example of such a signaling device is the continuous review system of inventory control discussed in chapters 6 and 7. Recall that with this method, the fall of inventory level below a reorder point (ROP) triggers placement of an order of economic order quantity (EOQ). In a perfectly synchronized world, a customer would signal demand as soon as a unit is needed and the supplier would instantly produce it, which translates into setting $ROP = 0$ and $EOQ = 1$. In reality, the supplier needs *replenishment lead time* in which to fill demand, and there may be variability in supply, demand, and lead time. It is therefore a good idea to maintain an inventory buffer between the two stages—hence, the ROP must be greater than zero. Moreover, if changeover costs dictate economies of scale, the supplier's production quantity EOQ may have to be greater than one. The maximum size of the buffer, then, is $ROP + EOQ$. Under a pull system, therefore, a station will not produce if its output buffer is full (signaling lack of demand) even if it has plenty of inputs available. As soon as demand depletes inventory to ROP (signaling lack of supply), the station will produce EOQ units to replenish precisely the amount withdrawn. In turn, producing those EOQ units requires inputs that the supplier station must withdraw from its supplier station, which then signals production upstream, and so on.

The EOQ-ROP system is thus a demand-pull operation that tries to match supply with demand by signaling production at each station in response to actual (rather than anticipated) demand from the following station. The system works, however, only when the supplier has discipline to hold production down to *EOQ* (and nothing more) and to produce only when the inventory buffer is down to *ROP* (and no earlier).

Kanbans   In a cellular layout with workstations located next to each other—each station signals demand by picking up a part from its input buffer. Its supplier station, seeing the transfer, produces a new unit as a replacement in the buffer. Toyota has formalized its information and material pull system with cards called **kanbans.** Kanbans are attached to output flow units in the buffer between customer and supplier processes, and each card lists the following information:

- Customer process,
- Supplier process,
- Parts description, and
- Production quantity.

As the customer withdraws output flow units from the buffer, the attached kanban goes back to the supplier; it signals an authorization for the supplier to produce the listed quantity to be replaced in the buffer. Upon producing the stipulated quantity, the supplier returns the output with an attached kanban to the buffer. (There are actually two types of kanbans—one to authorize withdrawal and one to authorize production. We will, however, skim over the details.) Because each kanban corresponds to a fixed quantity of flow units to be produced and passed on, the number of kanbans in the buffer between the customer and the supplier determines the size of the buffer. A station can produce a prescribed quantity only if it receives a production-authorization kanban. Thus, kanbans control buffer inventory and provide information and discipline to the supplier as to when and how much to produce. The end-customer's demand starts a chain reaction of withdrawals and replenishments of intermediate parts that ripples back through upstream stations.

In the case of a process that handles multiple products, in addition to when and how much to produce, each supplier station must also know *what* to produce next. In an automobile assembly plant, for example, cars of different colors and options have different parts and processing requirements. A station that installs inner trim in 1 of 10 options needs to know which trim to install in the car next in line; likewise, its supplier needs a signal to produce that particular trim. One solution for handling variety is to create separate kanbans for each option—create a system in which 10 different buffers are controlled by 10 different kanbans. As the assembly station installs a particular trim, the released kanban signals its supplier to replenish that unit.

In order for the assembly station to know which trim unit to install on the car at hand, it needs to know the exact production sequence of cars rolling down the line. There is an alternative to maintaining multiple kanbans and complete information at each station if the trim supplier's response time is short enough. Suppose that the supplier can produce the trim and deliver it to the assembly station in the period between the time at which the production sequence is fixed and the time at which the car reaches the assembly station. Then the supplier can deliver different trims in the correct sequence. Knowing that the delivered trim sequence matches the car sequence coming down the line, the assembly station can simply pick up the trim at the head of the buffer and install it into the next car without knowing the entire production sequence. In this case, only the trim supplier needs to know the production sequence to determine what to produce and in what sequence to deliver it. This approach requires a greater capability on the part of the supplier process. At the same time, however, it achieves, with minimal flow of material and information, synchronization within a plant.

10.4.3 Improving Process Flexibility: Batch-Size Reduction

In addition to knowing what and when to produce, each station in a processing network needs to know *how much* to produce—a specification that affects the process output buffer and thus the degree of process synchronization. Consider an automobile assembly line that produces two different models—sedans and station wagons. Suppose that monthly demand for each model is 10,000 units. One way to meet this demand would be to spend the first half month producing 10,000 sedans and the second half producing 10,000 station wagons. Because actual monthly demand is unlikely to follow this pattern, production will not synchronize with demand. This approach will place an uneven workload on the upstream processes (typically, suppliers) that feed parts for the two models—whereas parts suppliers for station wagons will have no orders in the first half of the month, those for sedans will have no orders in the second half of the month.

Level Production   At the other extreme, if we could alternate sedan and station wagon production one at a time, we could achieve perfect synchronization, with stable demand, for both models. This achievement results in *level production,* (*Heijunka* in TPS terminology) which refers to producing small quantities frequently. If monthly demand called for 10,000 sedans and 5,000 station wagons, a level-production would call for producing two sedans followed by one station wagon and then repeating the sequence. If the demand pattern is stable, level production will achieve perfect synchronization, producing flow units exactly on demand and in the quantity demanded. Moreover, level production will place an even workload on the production process itself and on all the supplier processes feeding it.

Changeover Costs and Batch Reduction   Having level production in a multiproduct setting means reducing the batch size of each product produced at one time. As observed in chapter 6, this reduction is economical only if we can reduce the key driver of scale economies—the fixed cost associated with producing each batch. The fixed cost in this case results from the changeover cost and time required to switch production from one model to the other. Thus, a fundamental requirement of level production is reduction of changeover cost. If changeover costs are not reduced before batch sizes are reduced, excessive changeover costs will drive up total production costs, thereby reducing cost efficiency.

This requirement is one of the major aspects of TPS that Toyota impresses on its suppliers when introducing them to lean operations. Changeover costs can be reduced by studying and simplifying the changeover process itself, using special tools to speed it up, customizing machines, and keeping extra machines that are already set up. By focusing on improvements to the changeover process itself, Toyota and other automakers have successfully reduced changeover times and costs by orders of magnitude. The result is an increased flexibility to produce small batches economically while simultaneously maintaining throughput and reducing both flow time and inventory.

The concept of small-batch production within a plant can be extended to small-batch pickups and deliveries made from several suppliers to several plants. One of two procedures is normally used: Either a single truck from one supplier carries deliveries to multiple plants, or a single truck destined for one plant carries small quantities of supplies from multiple suppliers. In either case, it is feasible to ship in smaller batches because the fixed cost of a shipment is spread over several suppliers or several plants.

We should reemphasize, however, that although level production is the goal of synchronization, it can be achieved only through reduction of the fixed setup (changeover) or transportation costs associated with each batch. Recall that reduction in this area was among the key levers explained in chapter 6, and that it may not be optimal for every process to achieve level production with batches of one. In automobile manufacturing, for instance, expensive parts such as seats are produced and delivered in batches of one. Windshield wipers, fasteners, and other low-cost items arrive in larger batches, because it is not economical to reduce batch sizes if the costs of doing so outweigh the benefits of small inventories. Reducing batch sizes is generally beneficial for large, expensive inputs; smaller, less expensive inputs are better handled in larger batches.

10.4.4 Reducing Quality Variability: Defect Prevention and Early Detection

Synchronization means more than supplying correct quantities at correct times as required by customers. It also means meeting their quality requirements. Supplying defective flow units increases average flow time and cost because it necessitates inspection and rework. To avoid starving the customer station, the production process must compensate for defective units by holding extra safety inventory in the buffer. This requirement further increases average flow time and cost; otherwise, defective flow units would choke the system downstream. Thus, a key requirement of lean, synchronous operations is producing and passing only defect-free flow units between workstations. Synchronization requires planning and controlling quality at source rather than after the fact (in the final inspection), and can be accomplished in two ways:

1. By preventing defects from occurring in the first place, and
2. By detecting and correcting them as soon as they appear.

Defect Prevention   As discussed in chapter 9, defect prevention requires careful design of product and process. The goal is to simplify, standardize, and mistake-proof the process to minimize the chance of errors. TPS guards against defects by stressing mistake-proofing (*poka yoke*) and intelligent automation (*jidoka*). Thus, parts are designed to minimize chances of incorrect assembly, and machines are designed to halt automatically when defective units are fed into them. Product and process design for defect prevention requires clearly defining and documenting the processing steps involved, thus removing worker discretion to the extent possible. Integrated design requires joint cooperation and input of all players: customers, designers, engineers, suppliers, and production workers. Each of them may have unique ideas and suggestions for product and process improvement that should be encouraged and rewarded.

Defect Visibility   Even though all defects cannot be prevented, both their early detection and correction are more effective and economical than catching them later during final inspection. Early detection of defects not only improves the chances of tracing them to their sources, but also minimizes waste of economic value that was added during the process until they are caught and discarded as scrap. Early detection contributes to better synchronization and lower costs in the long run by reducing the number of defective flow units introduced into the process stream.

Fast detection and correction of quality problems require constant vigilance and feedback. As discussed in chapter 9, statistical process control can be used to monitor process performance on line, so that any abnormal variation can be detected and eliminated early to maintain process stability, which is a prerequisite for high quality.

In addition, employees must be empowered with both the authority and the means to identify and correct problems at the local level without administrative and bureaucratic delays. The main idea behind making problems visible is to minimize the cost and delays associated with searching for, identifying, and eliminating their sources. In a Toyota plant, for example, workers can stop production by pulling a rope conveniently located next to their stations if they detect anything suspicious. Pulling the rope lights a lamp (called an *andon*) on a signboard that immediately calls the supervisor's attention to the worker's location (like a flight attendant's light in an airplane). The supervisor can then rush to the station to help correct the problem on which everybody's attention is focused. (One should consider the trade-off between the benefits of detecting and fixing problems early and the costs of lost production due to line stoppages.) Compare this practice with that of conventional plants in which resource utilization is given the top priority, work stoppage is permitted only on rare occasions, and only managers are empowered to take action. Often, in a typical conventional plant, line workers do not feel ownership, motivation, or security to point out problems. The typical attitude is "It's not *my* job."

In summary, poor quality hinders flow synchronization and can be avoided by:

1. Preventing defects through better product and process design, and
2. Highlighting problems as soon as they occur.

The goal is to take permanent, corrective action immediately and minimize future recurrences of defects to ensure quality at source.

10.4.5 Reducing Supply Variability: Maintenance and Safety Capacity

Variability in supply often results from equipment malfunction and breakdown. Not surprisingly, operations that maintain no inventories are vulnerable to downstream work stoppages caused by equipment failure. Preventive maintenance, therefore, is an important prerequisite for synchronizing supply and demand. In fact, TPS calls for workers themselves to perform light maintenance of their equipment on an ongoing basis; more complete maintenance is then scheduled off-hours.

It is impossible to eliminate all sources of variability; some are simply beyond any manager's control. For example, labor strikes, foul weather, fires, and other acts of nature can disrupt supply deliveries. As discussed in chapters 7 and 8, there are only two practical means of dealing with variability in supply or demand: carrying safety inventory or maintaining safety capacity. Although generally one should consider trade-off between carrying safety inventory and safety capacity, lean operations tend to avoid carrying safety inventory because it increases flow time, and jeopardizes synchronization. Instead, they maintain some safety capacity as protection against equipment breakdown.

Safety capacity may be in the form of keeping available extra machines, workers, or overtime. Toyota, for example, does not schedule production for all 24 hours in the day. The residual capacity is used as overtime if scheduled production is not completed by the end of the day. Thus, if there is any loss of synchronization in a given hour, overtime capacity is used to restore synchronization by the end of the shift. Developing a flexible workforce through cross-functional training may also be viewed as keeping safety capacity of one kind in another form.

In addition to keeping excess production capacity, the plant may choose to procure its materials externally from multiple suppliers to increase the reliability of their deliveries. In case one supplier fails to deliver the materials, another supplier can be called to deliver them. Thus, multiple sourcing may be viewed as a strategy of maintaining safety capacity as protection against supply variability. The advantages of increased reliability that derive from relationships with many suppliers should be balanced against the disadvantages of such a policy—particularly in terms of diluting the strength of relationships with suppliers. As we shall see, suppliers play an important role in every firm's quest for synchronization.

10.4.6 Managing Human Resources: Employee Involvement

Implementing synchronization of various processes within a plant requires cooperation, contribution, and commitment on the part of all employees. Managing human resources is therefore a critical factor in lean operations.

Mechanistic Approach   A conventional approach to workforce management can be traced to a combination of Frederick W. Taylor's "scientific management" principles and Frank Gilbreth's "best work methods" as applied in the early part of the twentieth century to the model of worker as an "economic man." Both Taylor and Gilbreth sought to break down a job into its constituent activities, develop best work methods for performing them, establish time standards for performing each activity, assign each activity to an individual, and reward individuals according to their performance in relation to these standards.

This approach was based on the premise that workers themselves, having no ability or initiative to plan their own work, must be told exactly what to do and closely monitored to make sure that, motivated by monetary incentives alone, they performed their assigned tasks. Hence the concept of the **plan-do-check-act cycle:** Industrial engineers plan and assign work, workers perform assigned tasks, inspectors check results, and supervisors take corrective or punitive actions. As a result, workers performed repetitive, narrowly defined tasks under close supervision and exercised little control over their work environment.

Given the uneducated workforce of the time—and, more importantly, the emphasis on efficient mass production—such a mechanistic approach to human resources management was more or less natural. The downside, however, was the proliferation of unskilled, fragmented, unsatisfying jobs for workers subject to centralized planning and hierarchial control of work.

Behavioral Approach   Theories variously labeled as *Theory Y, Theory Z,* or *Quality of Work Life* proposed job enlargement and job enrichment as keys to more meaningful, challenging, and satisfying work. Specifically, the behavioral approach argues that combining (rather than dividing) job activities and expanding (rather than specializing) worker responsibilities increase both job satisfaction and the likelihood of positive worker contributions to process improvement. In lean operations, job responsibilities are expanded to include performing light preventive maintenance, equipment setups, quality checks, and material-handling tasks. In a cellular layout, workers are cross-trained to provide the company with flexible workers and to give workers greater variety through job rotation. In other cases, teams of multiskilled workers produce entire products with minimum supervision. In addition to their regular jobs, these autonomous work teams may also be authorized to perform certain managerial duties such as scheduling work and vacations, ordering material, and even the hiring of new workers.

Behavioral studies since Elton Mayo's famous Hawthorne experiments at Western Electric in the 1940s have shown that if workers are involved in the decision-making processes that affect their jobs, they are better motivated to contribute substantially to productivity improvement. The key concept behind these theories of employee involvement is the recognition that workers have talents, education, and experience that can be harnessed to improve the process.

Worker participation in problem solving and process improvement efforts (as in quality circles) is an important component of lean operations. Workers might be able to make suggestions about how to reduce equipment setup times or improve product or process design for easier manufacturing and better quality. Based on the premise that the workers closest to the job have the most expertise to provide suggestions for improvement, the employee-involvement approach tries to involve workers in all four phases of the plan-do-check-act cycle. It also argues that employees possess the most current and accurate information about a given problem. Therefore, providing them the necessary training and tools—and, just as important, empowering them with the authority and responsibility to make job-related decisions—is the fastest method of implementing decentralized control. The authority to pull the rope and stop the line in TPS is an example of such an approach.

Worker participation in such initiatives requires that employees have basic skills and education, a willingness to learn multiple tasks and to work in team environments, and a commitment to the success of the entire process. Lean operations place a great importance on the recruiting and training of workers with these attributes. Given the long-term investment that firms make in their workers—and to make workers feel secure enough to make process-improvement suggestions—some firms now provide employment security.

10.4.7 Supplier Management: Partnerships

Outsourcing materials—*buying* them from someone else's process rather than *making* them—provides a flexible alternative to vertical integration, which would require greater process capability and organizational complexity in plant management. In modern manufacturing, purchased materials not only account for more than one-half of all product costs, but also represent a major source of quality problems. With lean operations, reliable on-time deliveries of defect-free parts assume critical importance. External suppliers constitute an essential resource that, if managed carefully, can contribute significantly to the control of product cost, quality, flow time, and therefore to process synchronization.

A conventional approach to supplier management calls for selecting several suppliers, making them compete against one another on price alone, and then monitoring them closely to ensure that they do not neglect quality and timely delivery. It is an approach that often leads to adversarial, and even hostile, relationships between the supplier and the manufacturer. The modern approach to supplier management calls for choosing only a few capable, reliable suppliers with whom to cultivate cooperative, long-term relationships. The buyer works to make the suppliers an extension of the plant by sharing information, by helping them to improve their own processes through training and technical and economic assistance, and by extending long-term contracts as incentives to induce cooperation in synchronizing flows of inputs with the plant requirements.

In terms of actual deliveries, the conventional approach seeks quantity discounts by purchasing in large volumes, and tries to ensure quality through extensive inspection of incoming material. Lean operations involve processing without inventories or quality inspection. Plant synchronization requires defect-free material that is delivered frequently, in small batches, and directly to the point of usage. In turn, small, frequent, reliable deliveries require supplier proximity and simplified buying and accounts-payable procedures. They also require that the supplier's process be able to produce small quantities on demand—that the supplier's plant be synchronized with the buyer's. Ensuring quality at source (without the non-value-adding activity of inspection) requires supplier capability and commitment to producing quality parts. It also requires open communication between the buyer's plant and the supplier on such matters as product design changes and possible improvements.

Supplier management involves treating suppliers as partners, which is a change from the conventional approach that regarded suppliers as outsiders not to be trusted. Even now, firms often interpret lean operations within a plant to mean requiring suppliers to produce and hold the parts inventory, while delivering just in time to the plant. In essence, it amounts to simply pushing the plant's raw-materials inventory back on to the suppliers. The goal of lean operations should be to integrate and synchronize the entire supply chain that consists of both the supplier's process and the buyer's process. It is thus critical to manage suppliers as a part of one's business, working with them closely to help them improve material quality, delivery, and cost, so that they will be able to meet the plant's input requirements and still remain economically viable.

In summary, lean operations aim to synchronize flows by three closely related means:

1. *Efficient logistics* by means of cellular layouts and demand pull mechanisms to facilitate material and information flows, (sections 10.4.1 and 10.4.2)
2. *Increased flexibility* by means of fast changeovers that permit smaller batches to level production, (section 10.4.3)
3. *Reduced variability* by means of improved supply reliability and quality, coupled with safety capacity, preventive maintenance, and fast feedback and correction. (Sections 10.4.4 and 10.4.5)

These strategies require long-term investment in equipment, workers, and suppliers (sections 10.4.6 and 10.4.7). Any efforts to implement just-in-time operations that ignore these prerequisites are sure to fail, as many companies have realized. If a process has high setup cost and a high degree of variability, it will be uneconomical and inefficient to operate without cycle or safety inventories (for further discussion see Zipkin, 1991). Finally, cost efficiency—the second aspect of ideal performance—is achieved through elimination of non-value-adding activities (chapter 4).

10.5   IMPROVING FLOWS IN A SUPPLY CHAIN

Producing and distributing goods to meet customer demand involves flows through a complex network of processes that include raw-materials suppliers, finished-goods producers, and their wholesalers, distributors, and retailers. This entire value-adding network of plants is called a **supply chain.** Its goal is to synchronize flows throughout the network to meet the end-customer demand most economically. Managing a supply chain involves storing and moving products and information along the entire network to make products available to customers when and where they are desired at the lowest possible cost.

In the previous section we discussed key issues in achieving synchronization and efficiency within a plant, which is just one node in the entire supply chain. As discussed, however, the plant itself can be considered a network of processing stages through which raw materials, components, and subassemblies flow to emerge as finished products. Its structure is thus similar to that of a supply chain, so the concepts that we have studied at the plant level should be equally applicable to synchronizing flows in whole supply chains. There are, however, three special challenges in managing a supply chain:

1. *Scale magnification* implies that issues which arise within a plant (relating to economies of scale, inventory levels, flow times, and so forth) are magnified in a supply chain. For example, flow times between nodes in a supply chain could be orders of magnitude larger than those between processes within a plant. Similarly, economies of scale in transporting goods from one node to another in a supply chain are much larger because of the geographical distances involved.

2. Because different nodes in a supply chain may have separate ownership, each with its own objectives, the supply chain consists of *multiple decision makers*. Aligning incentives among different agents is more difficult, which results in suboptimization of nodes—locally optimal decisions made at one node may not be globally optimal for the entire supply chain.

3. Each (independent) decision maker may possess only *private information* and may lack the global information necessary to synchronize its flows with the rest of the supply chain. Thus, even if a decision maker wishes to act in the best interests of the chain, he or she may not be able to do so.

In this section, we discuss the consequences of unsynchronized flows in a supply chain, identify their root causes, and propose some measures for improving synchronization and efficiency in a supply chain by coordinating various plants involved.

10.5.1 Lack of Synchronization: The Bullwhip Effect

From the flow perspective, supply-chain performance can be studied by analyzing product and information flows. While products flow from suppliers to consumers, information flows generally in both directions. Whereas customer-order information flows from retailers to suppliers, order-status information (regarding availability, lead times, and so forth) flows in the opposite (downstream) direction. Although matching supply and demand involves balancing product flows, it should be clear that information flows also play a crucial role in achieving that balance.

Figure 10.4 shows typical order patterns faced by each node in a supply chain that consists of a manufacturer, a distributor, a wholesaler, and a retailer. The retailer's orders to the wholesaler display greater variability than the end-consumer sales, the wholesaler's orders to its distributor show even more oscillation, and, finally, the distributor's orders to the manufacturer are most volatile. Thus, the pattern of orders received at upstream stages becomes increasingly more variable than consumption patterns at the retail end.

This phenomenon of variability magnification is often referred to as the **bullwhip effect** and indicates lack of synchronization among supply-chain members. Even a slight perturbation in consumer sales ripples backward in the form of magnified oscillations upstream, as a flick of a bullwhip handle would result. In a perfectly synchronized supply chain, the order pattern at each stage would mimic the consumption pattern at the retail end. Because the supply patterns do not match the demand patterns, the resulting lack of synchronization means inventory accumulation at various stages, and shortages and delays at others. Such a bullwhip effect has been observed by firms in numerous industries, including Procter & Gamble in consumer products, Hewlett-Packard in electronics, General Motors in automobiles, and Eli Lily in pharmaceuticals.

10.5.2 Causes of the Bullwhip Effect

Four main causes of the bullwhip effect have been identified by Lee, Padmanabhan, and Whang (1997):

1. Demand signal processing,
2. Batch purchasing,

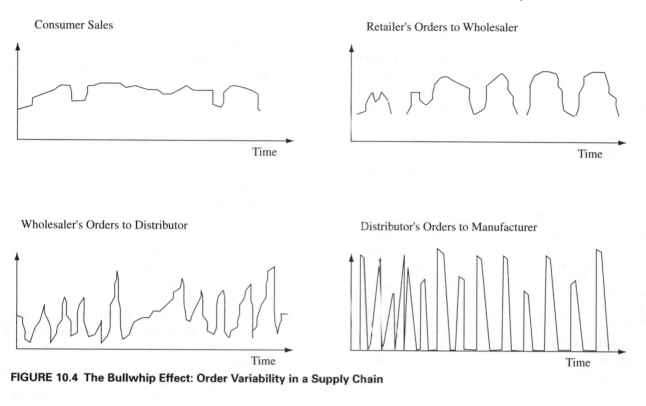

FIGURE 10.4 The Bullwhip Effect: Order Variability in a Supply Chain

3. Price fluctuations, and

4. Rationing or shortage gaming.

In the following subsections, we discuss each cause briefly and show how it leads to an increase in the variability of the order pattern as compared with the demand pattern faced by each node in the supply network. The bullwhip effect is then a result of these four causes, as the variability cascades across the nodes as orders move upstream.

Demand Signal Processing   Most firms rely on some form of demand forecasting to plan procurement, production, and capacity. Usually, short-term forecasting involves extrapolating the history of past sales and demand, with every observation of current demand factored into future demand projections. Consider a retailer who satisfies end-customer demand by ordering from a wholesaler. If demand during the current period is higher than the forecast, our retailer will adjust the forecast of future demand during the supply lead time (including both the mean and the error). Clearly, the new forecast will be adjusted upward. Because current realized demand is significantly different from the previous forecast, the estimate of forecast error will also increase. The retailer's order with the wholesaler should account not only for the higher mean lead-time demand that has been forecast, but also for the larger safety stock that will be needed to compensate for the increased error in the forecast. The retailer's order will be higher than realized demand. This increased variability is exacerbated by the delay in material and information flow between the two stages. The same phenomenon recurs when the wholesaler receives the retailer's order—the wholesaler's order to its supplier is also amplified. Thus, order amplifications cascade upstream in the supply chain.

Conversely, if current demand is lower than the forecast amount, the retailer will adjust downward the forecast of lead-time demand. This adjustment may also lead to a reduction in order, thus creating a distortion in the ordering pattern. Observe that the order amplification is exacerbated by the fact that each stage in the supply chain makes plans according to a different information set—the order stream from the immediate downstream stage—and not according to ultimate customer demand. We therefore see an interplay of the three difficulties discussed in section 10.5—scale magnification, diverse decision makers, and private information.

Batch Purchasing   The practice of batch purchasing occurs when a node in the supply chain places large and infrequent orders. Firms may place orders in some periodic fashion such as on a weekly, biweekly, or monthly basis. This practice usually results from some form of economy of scale in procurement, production, or transportation. In chapter 6 we saw that batch purchasing is also optimal when ordering entails fixed costs. Firms may also place orders in large batches in response to incentives (e.g., quantity discounts) offered by a supplier.

Although batch purchasing may be optimal for the buyer, it creates a distortion in the demand pattern experienced by the supplier. As in chapter 6, when demand rates are known and constant, the buyer may use the economic order quantity (EOQ) model to create order patterns that display large spikes in the supplier's demand pattern. If a supplier expects this pattern of ordering from a buyer (perhaps through information sharing), then he or she can account for the variability, but this is often not the case. The situation is further complicated when multiple buyers ordering from the same supplier may generate drastically different order patterns.

In short, when a process at one stage in the supply chain places orders in batches, the process at the upstream stage does not know if the batching is due to economies of scale or to a genuine increase in demand. If the upstream stage mistakenly assumes the latter, the bullwhip effect results. Moreover, the effect is exaggerated when multiple retailers place large orders simultaneously with the same upstream supplier (numerous retailers, for instance, may place their orders every Monday).

Price Fluctuations   When prices offered by an upstream stage to a downstream stage fluctuate often, the downstream stage may order more than its immediate needs. It will buy when prices are low and postpone purchases when they are high, leading again to the bullwhip effect. In chapter 6 we showed how buyers increase order quantities when suppliers offered short-term price discounts. We saw, too, that even a small price decrease could inspire large increases in order quantities.

Recall from chapter 6 that the practice of placing larger or additional orders to take advantage of low prices is called **forward buying.** Because of the frequency and intensity of manufacturers' promotions, forward buying is quite common in the grocery industry. When retailers "forward buy" to take advantage of price discounts, they also create large inventories in the supply chain and thus increase both product flow time and the costs of doing business. Ironically, this situation occurs even if end-consumer demand is stable, thereby creating a highly variable order pattern upstream.

Rationing and Shortage Gaming   When total orders placed by retailers exceed product availability, manufacturers use some form of rationing to allocate their products to buyers. If retailers know that a product will be in short supply (and thus rationed), they may exaggerate their needs when placing orders. When demand turns out to be lower than that suggested by inflated order quantities, retailers start canceling orders, leaving large levels of inventories with manufacturers. This pattern can set in even if shortages are not real—orders may be amplified at the slightest perception of a shortage by retailers. Because orders do not reflect actual consumer demand, such "gaming" behavior on the part of downstream stages produces the bullwhip effect.

During the 1992 and 1993 Christmas seasons, Motorola struggled to meet demand for its handsets and cellular phones. As a result, many distributors were forced to turn away business. Anticipating future shortages, some distributors drastically over-ordered for the 1994 season. Motorola produced accordingly and reported record last-quarter earnings for 1994. Because actual customer demand in 1994 turned out to be lower than it had been in 1992 and 1993, dealers who had over-ordered were swamped with inventory. Once Wall Street evaluated the situation, Motorola's stock tumbled almost 10%.

10.5.3   Levers to Counteract The Bullwhip Effect

A typical supply chain is characterized by independent players who optimize their own objectives according to limited private information. As we have seen thus far, even when these players behave rationally, information distortion in the supply chain can produce the bullwhip effect. Having understood some of the causes of the bullwhip effect, we can now outline some levers to counteract these causes. We know already that the root causes of the bullwhip effect can be traced to the following factors:

1. Inefficient processes (resulting, for example, in long flow times between stages or in high fixed costs),
2. Inconsistency of available information (due to poor timing and inaccuracy), and
3. Local actions by individual players that are suboptimal for the overall system.

Likewise, we can put the levers for counteracting the bullwhip effect into three categories:

1. Operational effectiveness,
2. Information sharing, and
3. Channel alignment.

Operational Effectiveness   Throughout this book, we have considered operational effectiveness in terms of cost, quality, and response time. Various levers have been suggested in the earlier chapters to achieve effectiveness in these terms. We begin by taking a quick survey of these levers:

- *Reduce (material and information) flow time* As discussed, when the bullwhip effect results from demand signal processing, it is exacerbated when material and/or information flow times between stages are long. Reducing flow times, therefore, will reduce the magnitude of the bullwhip effect. Some technologies are available to facilitate this strategy. Electronic data interchange (EDI) technology permits various stages in the supply chain to transmit information electronically, thereby reducing delays in information flows. Cross-docking, which is widely practiced by Wal-Mart and many other firms (see Example 2.1), calls for moving material directly from receiving to shipping with minimum dwell time in the warehouse—a practice that helps to decrease the transportation flow time and pipeline inventory between suppliers and retailers.

- *Reduce economies of scale* We have also seen how economies of scale contribute to the bullwhip effect by encouraging batch purchasing. The various levers for managing economies of scale that we have already described can also be applied at various levels in the supply chain—for a single product within a firm, across multiple products within a firm, or across multiple firms united in various alliances:

  - *Reduce fixed costs of ordering* Fixed procurement, production, and transportation costs create the bullwhip effect by encouraging large batch-order sizes. By placing orders electronically, encouraging more frequent ordering, and reducing per-order batch size, EDI reduces fixed procurement costs, as may several of the principles that we have attributed to lean operations. For example, the *single minute exchange of die (SMED)* and *flexible manufacturing systems (FMS)* permit level production (*Heijunka*) by reducing the production changeover costs. (Note that full-truckload constraints may still produce transportation economies and large transfer batches.)

- *Give discounts for assortments* Suppliers usually offer quantity discounts when they enjoy economies of scale in production or distribution. They offer such discounts, however, for individual items and in so doing they induce buyers to increase order sizes for those products, and thereby distort ultimate demand information. If suppliers offered discounts on assortments of items, there would be little need to exaggerate orders for individual items. Such a policy would reduce distortion in item-level demand information while still permitting the supplier to exploit economies of scale in transportation. Procter & Gamble, for example, offers discounts to distributors who order assortments of different products.

- *Enter logistical alliances* Another way to exploit transportation economies is to form an alliance with a third-party logistics firm. Such providers achieve economies of scale in transportation by consolidating needs of multiple suppliers and customers. Consolidating shipments lessens the need to increase batch sizes by allowing each supplier and customer to ship or receive less than a full truckload of quantities. Firms should consider other coordination and strategic issues before deciding to outsource the logistics function.

Information Sharing   As discussed, the presence of multiple decision makers working with private information affects the product and information flows in the supply chain. Sharing the following information among supply-chain members can reduce the magnitude of the bullwhip effect:

- *Share consumption information with upstream players* Each stage in the supply chain processes its demand information to construct a forecast for the future (a strategy labeled *demand signal processing*). Because information travels upstream in a sequential fashion, each upstream stage is processing information passed on to it from its immediate downstream stage. At any stage, information is always an outcome of similar processing done by a downstream stage. Only the last stage in the chain is privy to consumption data regarding the end-consumer demand, which is usually collected through *point-of-sale (POS)* technology. Consequently, each stage in the chain is trying to forecast demand based on a different set of data. A first step in information sharing is to make consumption, or POS, data available to all players in the supply chain so that every member's plans are based on the same data set. In fact, several computer companies (including IBM and Hewlett-Packard) require resellers to share POS data.

- *Share availability information with downstream players* Shortage gaming results when retailers do not know the actual availability or capacity of their suppliers. Although sharing capacity and availability information will eliminate mistaken perceptions of shortages, it will also reveal the existence of real shortages. Thus, sharing of availability information may not be a perfect instrument for counteracting the bullwhip effect. When shortages do exist, allocation policies should be modified.

Channel Alignment   Although operational improvements and information sharing may assist independent supply-chain players in making decisions that improve their own performance, these practices alone are usually insufficient to synchronize the entire supply chain. Other explicit coordination and incentive mechanisms are needed to align the priorities of individual members with those of the system:

- *Coordinate replenishment and forecasting decisions* What would happen if the consumption information collected through POS technology were made available to all supply-chain players? Even if every stage in the chain possessed the same data, differences in fore-casting methods and buying practices could still lead to fluctuations in orders. One solution is for an upstream stage to control the replenishment of material to the downstream stage. This tactic works when the upstream stage has access to downstream demand and inventory information, and replenishes its stock accordingly. These practices are now being implemented in the consumer-products industry under such techniques as the *vendor managed inventory (VMI)* and the *continuous replenishment program (CRP)*. Campbell Soup, for example, uses a CRP program with its retailers, and P&G uses a VMI program to supply Wal-Mart with diapers.

Under such programs, however, a downstream stage no longer decides on how much to order and may perceive a loss of control. Another solution is to adopt a consistent fore-casting methodology for every stage in the chain. Collaborative Forecasting and Replenishment (CFAR), developed by the consulting firm of Benchmarking Partners Inc., offers a standardized procedure by which manufacturers and merchants can cooperate to generate forecasts over the Internet.

- *Stabilize prices* We have already observed that short-term price reductions are a major factor in the bullwhip effect. Such reductions provide an incentive to the retailers to forward buy and thereby distort the supplier's demand information. A manufacturer can reduce forward buying by one of the following methods:

  1. Establishing a uniform wholesale-pricing policy,
  2. Limiting the amount that can be purchased under forward buys, or
  3. Crediting retailers for promotional discounts based on customer sales during a given period rather than on orders placed.

  In the grocery industry, for instance, major manufacturers such as P&G and Kraft have adopted everyday low pricing (EDLP) strategies.

- *Change allocation policies* We have already observed that sharing upstream capacity and availability information is not a perfect instrument for reducing the bullwhip effect due to gaming. Allocation mechanisms based on current orders encourage downstream stages to exaggerate their orders. Other allocation mechanisms—such as GM's policy of basing allocations on past sales—may remove incentives to inflate orders.

To summarize, the ability to synchronize flows in a supply chain is affected by such factors as operational efficiency, information availability, and level of coordination. Organizations must understand the root causes of the inefficiencies that result from the bullwhip effect and take measures to remedy them. Implementation of such solutions as those proposed in this chapter is challenging because the process often involves interorganizational issues in coordination, information sharing, and change of incentive structures.

10.6   THE IMPROVEMENT PROCESS

In part I of this book we identified processes as core technologies of all organizations for developing, producing, and delivering goods and services to satisfy customer needs in terms of product cost, quality, variety, and availability when and where desired. In part II we related these product measures to process measures in such operational terms as number of processing cost, defects, inventory, flow time, and flow rate and showed their relationship to financial measures.

In parts II and III we also identified levers for improving these performance measures in a single process. In this chapter thus far we have extended our discussion of levers to cover the management of flows in networks of processes, both within a plant and in a supply chain. We can summarize the ideal of any processing network as perfectly synchronizing supply with demand at the lowest cost by identifying and eliminating waste. Because actual process performance usually falls short of this ideal, we must constantly improve the process to approach the ideal.

Although we have identified throughout the book various levers for process improvement (i.e., *what* to do), we have yet to describe any process or framework for achieving such improvement (i.e., *how* to do it). In this section, then, we conclude by discussing the *process* of process improvement. We describe a process that begins by maintaining process stability in the short run, and then gradually improves the process over time while occasionally revamping it in the long run.

In section 10.6.1 we summarize process stabilization. In sections 10.6.2 and 10.6.3 we define and contrast the concepts of continuous improvement and process reengineering. Finally, in section 10.6.4 we describe the benchmarking technique for setting concrete process improvement goals, and conclude in section 10.6.5 with some comments about managing the change that so often accompanies any process improvement.

10.6.1 Process Stabilization: Democratizing the Plan-Do-Check-Act Cycle

We can improve a process only if it is stable and we have a reliable measurement of its performance in relation to the ideal. Because process performance usually displays variability, reliable measurement requires that the observed performance be *statistically predictable*—that its variation be *normal.* As discussed in chapter 9, statistical process control involves monitoring performance over time and providing fast feedback when variation appears to be *abnormal.* This practice not only helps us keep the process in a stable state by identifying and correcting sources of variation, but also ensures that our estimates of its performance characteristics are reliable.

Also in sections 9.4 and 10.4 we indicated the steps in implementing process control through the plan-do-check-act (PDCA) cycle. In this context, we stress only the importance of delegating all four phases of the PDCA cycle to the person performing the activity. Being closest to the job—and armed with necessary experience and training—workers can observe and act swiftly and accurately to identify and correct any performance abnormality. This decentralization of information and decision-making authority promotes fast feedback and quick corrective action to maintain a process in the stable state that we need before we can consider improving it. Worker involvement in process control, with the empowerment to act without administrative approval, minimizes delays in passing information and making decisions. The supervisor therefore becomes more of a facilitator than a decision maker. Such "democratization of the workplace" not only requires workers with the necessary tools and training, but also gives them the authority and responsibility for managing their own work environment. However, the system works only if it features highly flexible work rules and a trained workforce that is willing and able to take the initiative in process stabilization and improvement.

10.6.2 Continuous Improvement: Management by Sight and Stress

Process stability is a necessary but not sufficient condition for process improvement, which involves closing the gap between actual and ideal performance. This goal may be achieved by constantly making incremental improvements and steadily bringing process performance closer to the ideal. Such **continuous improvement** is an important aspect of lean operations and TPS; it is often referred to as *kaizen,* or "a good change." One functional definition characterizes it as "continuous, incremental improvement in the process by everyone involved" (Imai, 1986).

Management by Sight   The process of continuous improvement is based on the philosophy of making problems and opportunities visible and providing incentives to eliminate the former and take advantage of the latter. Recalling our discussion of the river analogy in section 10.3, a natural short-term tendency in process management is to cover up process imperfections (inflexibility or variability) by building in safety cushions (cycle or safety inventory). Unfortunately, this approach hinders synchronization, obstructs our view of process imperfections and reduces the sense of urgency in removing them. The principle of continuous improvement calls for *removing*—not inserting—inventory to *expose*—rather than protect against—process problems, each of which is treated as an opportunity to improve the process. We can thus refer to the concept of promoting problem visibility as the principle of **management by sight.**

Management by Stress   As the water level is lowered, new problems surface and we are forced to deal with them. As soon as we have solved these newly visible problems, water level is lowered again, exposing yet more rocks to face. Our goal is to refuse to be content with smooth sailing in ample water, and to continue reducing the level, relentlessly exposing more problems and eliminating their root causes. Our philosophy is to keep ourselves under constant pressure to improve the process by gradually removing the security blanket. This philosophy may be called **management by stress.**

The management by stress philosophy teaches us that by keeping the system under constant stress, we force new problems to become visible and so increase our own responsibility for eliminating root causes rather than simply reacting to them as they occur. At Toyota, for example, the rope-pull (*andon*) system is a tool for making problems visible. If a problem repeatedly prompts rope pulls, it is clearly in the supervisor's best interest to get to the root cause of the problem and eliminate it entirely. To ensure sufficient visibility, Toyota tracks the number of rope pulls per shift. Similarly, the process is kept under constant stress by removing kanbans (and hence the inventory buffer) between stages, so that stages or nodes are forced to work with increasingly less inventory.

Recall, however, that the success of continuous improvement requires a *gradual* lowering of the water level; otherwise the boat will suddenly hit a rock and sink. In fact, the failure to appreciate this fact is one reason why lean operations sometimes fail in practice: Firms set arbitrarily high targets for inventory reduction without correspondingly improving the process. Ultimately, it is process improvement—not merely inventory reduction in itself—that is the goal of such principles as just-in-time operations. Inventory reduction is merely a means for exposing problems. Meanwhile, continual reduction of inventories by constantly exposing problems, keeps the process under constant pressure to resolve them.

Recall, too, that the workers closest to the job are in the best position to identify opportunities for process improvement, so they should be encouraged—even prodded—to make suggestions for process improvement. Including workers in the continuous-improvement strategy means making them feel not only comfortable and secure in exposing and facing up to new problems, but also trained, disciplined and ambitious enough to overcome any complacency in approaching the ideal.

Management By Objective   Another approach to regular continuous improvement (every quarter or every year) is to set *targets* for critical performance measures. These targets should reflect both the demands of the marketplace and the performance of competitors. The purpose of such targets is to guide the firm in its efforts to do better than competitors with the same level of resources or to do as well with fewer resources. In either case, targets, once achieved, are then revised, and the process (and the pressure) continues. This approach to continuous improvement is sometimes called **management by objective.** The major difference between this approach and that of management by sight and stress is a matter of focus. In managing by sight and stress, we focus on making problems visible and then treat them as drivers for change. In management by objective, we focus on achieving an objective—a set of targets—more than on solving problems; the desire to hit targets is the change driver. In either case, the basic tool kit for process improvement contains the same levers that we have been describing throughout this book.

10.6.3   Business Process Reengineering: Process Innovation

Sometimes gradual improvement toward the ideal process may not be enough—a significant jump in process performance may be necessary to catch or overtake the competition. In that case, the solution might be **reengineering,** which Hammer and Champy (1993), who popularized the term in the early 1990s, define as "fundamental rethinking and radical redesign of business processes in order to achieve dramatic improvements in critical contemporary measures of performance such as cost, quality, service and speed."

Consider some of the key terms of this definition:

- *Fundamental* rethinking means reexamining and questioning traditional practices and assumptions, which may have become obsolete, erroneous, or inappropriate over time. At each stage of a business process, one asks why it is done and how it can be done differently or, better yet, eliminated completely.

- *Radical* redesign means reinventing a process from scratch, not just tweaking the existing one. It means channeling a new river without rocks rather than trying to uncover and crush the rocks in the current river. Radical redesign thus requires starting with a clean slate and asking what an ideal process would look like.

- *Dramatic* improvements mean quantum—not incremental—jumps aimed at 10-fold—not 10%—improvements in performance measures. For example, the goal of a typical reengineering project would be to design, produce, and deliver a product with half as many defects in half as much time, at half as much cost as the one we now market. The six-sigma philosophy discussed in chapter 9 is an example of setting such stretch goals. Improvements of such magnitude require "out-of-the-box," innovative thinking.

- *Critical* measures of performance that are important to the customer—cost, quality, and response time, should be the focus of process improvement. It is a waste of energy to make improvements that the customer does not see or value.

Reengineering versus Continuous Improvement   As a framework for process improvement, reengineering differs from continuous improvement in three elements: magnitude and time frame of desired improvement and change drivers. In continuous improvement, the change drivers (visibility or targets) are internal components of the existing process. In process reengineering, a complete rethinking of the process itself is forced by something external—either a dramatic change in customer needs or a change in technology. We strive not merely to make the existing process better but, potentially, to invent a new process that will do the job significantly better than the current process.

Hammer and Champy (1993) cite the accounts-payable process at Ford Motor Company as a classic example of successful reengineering, as described in chapter 4. By eliminating invoices and basing payments on receipts of shipments, Ford could radically alter the entire procurement process, with a 75% reduction in the personnel. Although the popular press tended to equate "reengineering" with "downsizing" in the early 1990s, reducing head count and cost are not the only projects in which reengineering may be useful. Reengineering may also make dramatic improvements in terms of time, quality, and flexibility. Hammer and Champy (1993) discuss several illuminating examples.

Conversely, reengineering and continuous improvement are not necessarily antithetical approaches. Both may be valuable components of the same long-term process improvement program. Among the results of a reengineering effort should be a design for a new process and a program for continuous improvement. Whereas continuous improvement takes a process toward ideal performance in regular, incremental steps, reengineering is needed occasionally to make a radical change—especially when changes in the external environment appear to prompt industrywide changes. Thus, the rationale for reengineering: The driver for radical change is generally external (not part of the process) and is due to either a dramatic change in customer expectations or a change in technology that makes possible a completely different process design.

10.6.4   Benchmarking: Learning from the Voices of the Best

Process improvement requires setting and approaching specific goals—a project that can be aided greatly by studying others' processes and emulating their best practices—it is not always necessary to reinvent the wheel. Robert Camp (1995) defines **benchmarking** as "the process of continually searching for the best methods, practices, and processes, and adopting or adapting the good features to become 'the best of the best.' " We may benchmark someone else's products (in terms of price, quality, response time), key processes (in terms of cost, flow time, inventory turns), or support processes (such as warehousing, billing, or shipping).

In search of best practices, we may look either within our own organization or to outside competitors. We may even turn to noncompetitors in other industries. We have already seen, for instance, how Japanese manufacturers devised the pull system of material flow based on observations of U.S. supermarket operations. Xerox Corporation benchmarked mail-order retailer L. L. Bean for its efficient logistics and distribution system. In an effort to expedite airport turnaround times, Southwest Airlines studied NASCAR pit stops in auto racing. The use of bar coding, so prevalent at supermarket checkout counters, is now widely used by manufacturers to manage parts inventories and flows.

The key to successful benchmarking is not merely duplicating the activities of others: Benchmarking means understanding the basic concepts underlying what world-class companies do, understanding the essence of how they do it, and adapting what we have learned to our own situation. It requires external orientation, open-mindedness, and the ability to perceive underlying similarities in apparently dissimilar situations.

10.6.5   Managing Change

Above all, process improvement means changing our way of doing business. It therefore entails uncertainty despite the fact that we are naturally inclined to like and keep things as they are. In managing change, then, the challenge is to encourage people to accept change and to motivate them to take the kinds of risks that bring about change for the better.

Ironically, it is easier to motivate people to change when "times are bad"; change is then perceived more as a survival imperative rather than an option. By that time, however, it may be too late to improve the firm's competitive position merely by making marginal improvements to the existing process; it may be necessary to reengineer the whole process. It is also unfortunate that when "times are good," the natural tendency is to be complacent and probably oblivious to potential environmental changes and competitive threats looming on the horizon. The challenge then is to make people feel dissatisfied with the status quo and yet secure enough to suggest a change. As we saw in our discussion of continuous improvement, this motivational balance can be spurred by gradually reducing available resources (management by stress) or gradually raising goals—demanding the same level of performance with fewer resources or a higher level of performance with the same resources (management by objective). Finally, any organizational change is easier to bring about if everyone affected by it is involved in a participatory spirit, in a nonthreatening environment, with open lines of communication.

References

Camp, R. 1995. *Business Process Benchmarking.* ASQ Quality Press, Milwaukee, WI.

Hammer, M., and J. Champy. 1993. *Reengineering the Corporation: A Manifesto for Business Revolution.* Harper Press, New York, NY.

Imai, M. 1986. *Kaizen: The Key to Japan's Competitive Success.* Random House, New York, NY.

Lee, H. L., V. Padmanabhan, and S. Whang. 1997. Information distortion in a supply chain: The bullwhip effect. *Management Science* 43: 546–558.

Ohno, T. 1988. *Toyota Production System: Beyond Large-Scale Production.* Productivity Press, Cambridge, MA.

Schoenberger, R. 1982. *Japanese Manufacturing Techniques: Nine Hidden Lessons in Simplicity.* The Free Press, New York, NY.

Spear, S. 1998. "A Field-based Study of Toyota Production System: An Organizationally Modular Architecture Fostered by Problem Solving Based Learning Leading to Superior Performance." Seminar presented at Northwestern University, Evanston, IL.

Zipkin, P. 1991. Does manufacturing need a JIT revolution? *Harvard Business Review,* January–February.

MBPF Checklist

Here we provide a summary of key points from the book. This appendix is meant to serve as a checklist for managing business process flows.

A1.1 PROCESS-FLOW MEASURES

- *Key concepts* Flow time (T), inventory (I), throughput (R), process cost (c)
- *Key relation* Inventory = Throughput × Flow time: $I = R \times T$
- *Key management activity* Select process-flow measures to manage for improvement
- *Key metric* Net present value, return on total assets

Because the three operational measures (flow time, inventory, throughput) are interrelated, defining targets on any two of them defines a target for the third. The basic managerial levers for process improvement are:

1. Increase in throughput (decrease in flow time),
2. Decrease in inventory (decrease in flow time), and
3. Decrease in process cost.

A1.2 LEVERS FOR MANAGING THEORETICAL FLOW TIME

- *Key concepts* Critical path, critical activity, theoretical flow time
- *Key management activity* Identify and manage activities on all critical paths
- *Key metric* Length of critical paths

Because the theoretical flow time of a process is determined by the total work content of its critical path(s), the only way to decrease it is by shortening the length of *every* critical path. The basic approaches to decreasing the work content of a critical path are:

1. Reduce the work content of an activity on the critical path.
   - Eliminate non-value-adding aspects of the activity ("work smarter"),
   - Increase the speed at which the activity is done ("work faster"),
     - Acquire faster equipment.
     - Increase incentives to work faster.
   - Reduce the number of repeat activities ("do it right the first time"), and
   - Change the product mix to produce products with smaller work content with respect to the specified activity.
2. Move some of the work content off the critical path.
   - Move work from a critical path to a noncritical path, and
   - Move work from a critical path to the outer loop (pre- or postprocessing).

A1.3 LEVERS FOR MANAGING THEORETICAL CAPACITY

- *Key concepts* Throughput, capacity (theoretical and effective), bottleneck resource
- *Key management activity* Identify and manage bottleneck resource(s)
- *Key metric* Contribution margin per unit time on bottleneck(s)

To increase the *effective* capacity of a process

- Decreasing the availability loss ("eliminate availability waste")

To increase the *theoretical* capacity of a process we must increase the theoretical capacity of *every* bottleneck resource pool. The three basic approaches to increasing the theoretical capacity of a resource pool can be summarized as:

1. Decrease the unit load on the bottleneck resource:
   - Decrease the work content of an activity performed by a bottleneck resource by working smarter, working faster, doing it right the first time, or changing the product mix,
   - Move some of the work content to a nonbottleneck resource, and
   - Invest in flexible resources.
2. Increase the size of load batches at a bottleneck resource ("increase scale of resource"),
3. Increase the scheduled availability of a bottleneck resource ("work longer"), and
4. Increase the number of bottleneck resource units ("increase scale of process").

A1.4 LEVERS FOR REDUCING WAITING TIME

- *Key concepts* Waiting time, buffer, variability, flow-time efficiency, cycle inventory, safety inventory, safety capacity.
- *Key management activity* Manage buffers to reduce waiting time
- *Key metric* Waiting time in buffers

Buffers build up primarily because of batching or variability. The basic approaches to reducing waiting time can be summarized as:

1. Reduce cycle inventory (reduce batch size):
   - Reduce setup or order cost per batch, and
   - Reduce forward buying.
2. Reduce safety inventory:
   - Reduce demand variability through improved forecasting,
   - Reduce the replenishment lead time,
   - Reduce the variability in replenishment lead time,
   - Pool safety inventory for multiple locations or products through either physical/virtual centralization or specialization or some combination thereof,
   - Exploit product substitution,
   - Use common components, and
   - Postpone the product differentiation closer to the point of demand.
3. Manage safety capacity:
   - Increase safety capacity,
   - Decrease variability in arrivals and service, and
   - Pool available safety capacity.
4. Synchronize flows:
   - Manage capacity to synchronize with demand,
   - Manage demand to synchronize with available capacity, and
   - Synchronize flows within the process.
5. Manage the psychological perceptions of the customers to *reduce the cost of waiting*.

A1.5 LEVERS FOR CONTROLLING PROCESS VARIABILITY

- *Key concepts* Normal and abnormal variability, process capability, robust design
- *Key management activity* Monitor and adjust process performance dynamically over time. Reduce variability and its effects.
- *Key metrics* Quality, cost, time, inventory

1. Measure, prioritize, and analyze variability in key performance measures over time,
2. Feedback control to limit abnormal variability:
   - Set control limits of acceptable variability in key performance measures, and
   - Monitor actual performance and correct any abnormal variability.
3. Decrease normal process variability:
   - Design for processing (simplify, standardize, and mistake-proof).
4. Immunize product performance to process variability through robust design.

A1.6 LEVERS FOR MANAGING FLOWS IN PROCESSING NETWORKS

- *Key concepts* Waste, non-value-adding activities, product (cellular) layout, demand pull, quality at source, employee involvement, supplier partnership, bullwhip effect, information flows, incentives, level production, river analogy, continuous improvement, reengineering.
- *Key management activity* Synchronize process flows while maintaining efficiency. Set up a framework for process improvement.
- *Key metrics* Cost, quality, time, flexibility

1. Managing flows in a plant:
   - Process structure: Cellular layout,
   - Information and material flow: Demand pull system,
   - Level production: Batch size reduction,
   - Quality at source: Defect prevention, visibility, and decentralized control,
   - Supplier management: Partnership with information sharing and aligned incentives,
   - Supply consistency: Maintenance of safety capacity, and
   - Human resource management: Employee involvement.
2. Managing flows in a supply chain:
   - Reduce information and material flow times through technology and efficient logistics,
   - Reduce fixed costs of ordering and quantity discounts,
   - Share information on customer demand and product availability,
   - Coordinate forecasts between various parties, and
   - Stabilize prices.
3. Improve processes:
   - Frameworks: Continuous improvement and reengineering, and
   - Tools: Increased visibility, incentives, improvement engine (PDCA cycle), benchmarking.

APPENDIX 2

Background Material in Probability and Statistics

This appendix summarizes some basic material in probability and statistics that is used in the text.

A2.1 RANDOM VARIABLES, MEAN, VARIANCE, AND COVARIANCE

Random Variable   A random variable (r.v.) is a numerical outcome whose value depends on chance. We will denote random variables by script capital letters X, Y, Z and lowercase letters for their values.

Density and Distribution Functions of a Random Variable   The expression $\{X \leq x\}$ is the event that the r.v. X assumes a value that is less than or equal to the real number x. This event may or may not occur, depending on the outcome of the experiment or phenomenon that determines the value for the r.v. X. The probability that the event occurs is written $\text{Prob}\{X \leq x\}$. Allowing x to vary, this probability defines a function

$$F(x) = \text{Prob}\{X \leq x\}, \qquad -\infty < x < +\infty$$

called the **distribution function** of the r.v. X. (We may write $F_X(\cdot)$ to denote the correspondence between the r.v. and its distribution function.) The distribution function contains all the information available about a r.v. before its value is determined by experiment. A r.v. X is called **discrete** if there is a finite or denumerable set of distinct values $x_1, x_2, \ldots$ such that $p_i = \text{Prob}\{X = x_i\}$ for $i = 1, 2, \cdots$ and $\Sigma_i p_i = 1$. The function

$$f(x_i) = p_i \qquad \text{for } i = 1, 2, \cdots$$

is called the **probability mass function** of the r.v. X and is related to the distribution function via

$$F(x) = \sum_{x_i \leq x} f(x_i)$$

A r.v. X is called **continuous** if $\text{Prob}\{X = x\} = 0$ for every value of x. Then its distribution function $F(x)$ is a continuous function of x. Often there exists a **probability density function** $f(x)$ such that

$$F(x) = \int_{u=-\infty}^{u=x} f(u)\,du$$

Mean   The mean or "expected value" of a r.v. X is

$$E(X) = \begin{cases} \Sigma_i x_i f(x_i) & \text{if } X \text{ is discrete r.v.} \\ \int_{u=-\infty}^{u=x} u f(u) du & \text{if } X \text{ is continuous r.v.} \end{cases}$$

Often the mean of a r.v. X is also denoted as μ_X.

Variance   The variance, $V(X)$, of a r.v. X measures the average squared deviation of X from its mean, μ_X. Thus:

$$V(X) = E\left[(X - \mu_X)^2\right]$$

Standard Deviation   The standard deviation of a r.v. X, σ_X, is the positive root of its variance, $V(X)$. That is,

$$\sigma_X = \sqrt{V(X)}.$$

Coefficient of Variation   The coefficient of variation of a r.v. X, denoted by C_X, is the ratio of its standard deviation to its mean.

$$C_X = \frac{\sigma_X}{\mu_X}$$

The variance, standard deviation, and the coefficient of variation are all measures of the amount of uncertainty or variability in X.

With these basic definitions we can now consider some concepts and results that involve multiple random variables.

A2.1.1 Independence of Random Variables

Two random variables X_1 and X_2 are said to be independent if and only if knowledge about the value of X_1 does not change the probability of any event involving X_2. Formally, *two random variables X_1 and X_2 are* **independent** *if and only if for any two events A and B,*

$$\text{Prob}\{X_1 \in A \text{ and } X_2 \in B\} = \text{Prob}\{X_1 \in A\}\text{Prob}\{X_2 \in B\}$$

If the above relationship is not satisfied, then X_1 and X_2 are said to be dependent. It follows that if X_1 and X_2 are independent, then

$$E(X_1 X_2) = E(X_1)E(X_2).$$

A2.1.2 Covariance and Coefficient of Correlation

Let X_1 and X_2 be two random variables with means of μ_1 and μ_2 and standard deviations σ_1 and σ_2 respectively. The *covariance* of X_1 and X_2 is defined to be the expected value of $(X_1 - \mu_1)(X_2 - \mu_2)$. Thus:

$$Cov(X_1, X_2) = E[(X_1 - \mu_1)(X_2 - \mu_2)].$$

The *coefficient of correlation*, ρ, is defined as

$$\rho = \frac{Cov(X_1, X_2)}{\sigma_1 \sigma_2}.$$

The value of the correlation coefficient always lies between -1 and $+1$. A positive covariance or correlation coefficient between X_1 and X_2 implies if X_1 increases, then, on average, so does X_2. Alternately, a negative covariance or correlation coefficient implies that if X_1 increases then X_2 decreases, on average. If X_1 and X_2 are independent then $Cov(X_1, X_2) = 0$.

2.1.3 Sums of Random Variables

Consider two random variables, X_1 and X_2. Then,

$$E(X_1 + X_2) = E(X_1) + E(X_2)$$
$$V(X_1 + X_2) = V(X_1) + V(X_2) + 2Cov(X_1, X_2)$$

Recall that if X_1 and X_2 are independent, then $Cov(X_1, X_2) = 0$. It then follows that *the expected value and variance of sums of independent random variables is equal to the sum of their expectations and variances, respectively.*

Also, if X_1 and X_2 have identical distributions (and thus identical means and standard deviations) but are correlated with a correlation coefficient ρ, then the standard deviation of the sum $X_1 + X_2$ is

$$\sigma_{X_1 + X_2} = \sqrt{2(1 + \rho)}\sigma$$

where σ is the standard deviation of X_1 and X_2.

A2.2 SOME PROBABILITY DISTRIBUTIONS

2.2.1 The Poisson Probability Distribution

Consider a sequence of random events occurring in time. Suppose that these events occur at an average rate of R events per unit time. Let $N(t)$ be the r.v. representing the number of events that occur in a time interval of duration t. We say that $N(t)$ follows a *Poisson distribution* if

$$\text{Prob}\{N(t) = n\} = e^{-Rt}\frac{(Rt)^n}{n!}$$

The mean number of events in time period t is given by $E[N(t)] = Rt$ and the standard deviation of the number events in time period t is also given by Rt. Thus, the coefficient of variation of a Poisson r.v. is equal to 1.

2.2.2 The Exponential Probability Distribution

Consider a sequence of random events occurring in time. Let T be a r.v. representing the time elapsed between two consecutive events. If the mean elapsed time between two consecutive events is given by m, then the probability density function of T, $f(t)$, is said to be exponentially distributed if

$$f(t) = \frac{1}{m}e^{-t/m}$$

The standard deviation of the elapsed time between consecutive events is also m. Therefore, the coefficient of variation of an exponential r.v. is equal to 1.

From the previous definitions, one may guess that there should be a relationship between the Poisson and the exponential distributions. In fact, if the distribution of the number of events in a time interval is Poisson, then the times are independent and exponentially distributed.

2.2.3   The Normal Probability Distribution

A continuous r.v. X has a normal distribution if for some μ and $\sigma > 0$, the probability distribution function $f(x)$ of the r.v. X is given by:

$$f(x) = \frac{1}{\sigma\sqrt{2\pi}} \exp\left[-\frac{(x-\mu)^2}{2\sigma^2}\right]$$

The mean of a normally distributed r.v. X is μ and its variance is σ^2. It is often denoted as $N(\mu, \sigma^2)$. The normal r.v. $N(0, 1)$ is called the standard normal random variable. Two important properties of the normal distribution are that

- It is symmetric around its mean, and
- A sum of a fixed number of normally distributed random variables is also normally distributed.

We now discuss methods to compute the probability, say q, that a r.v. X is smaller than a given quantity x, using a technique called **standardization.** A modification of this technique also helps us to find the quantity x given a specific probability q.

To find a probability q given a quantity x   Let X be normally distributed with mean μ and standard deviation σ, denoted as $X \sim N(\mu, \sigma)$. To find the cumulative probability $q = \text{Prob}\{X \leq x\}$ given a quantity x, transform X and x into

$$Z = \frac{X-\mu}{\sigma} \quad \text{and} \quad z = \frac{x-\mu}{\sigma}$$

Then Z is a standard normal random variable ($Z \sim N(0, 1)$) and

$$q = \text{Prob}\{X \leq x\} = \text{Prob}\{Z \leq z\}$$

For any given z, the value of q can be read from Table A2.1. Note that $\text{Prob}\{Z \leq -z\} = 1 - \text{Prob}\{Z \leq z\}$.

To find a quantity x given a probability q   Given a probability q, to find the quantity x such that $\text{Prob}\{X \leq x\} = q$, first read z from Table A2.1 such that $\text{Prob}\{Z \leq z\} = q$. Then compute the quantity x as:

$$x = \mu + z\sigma$$

TABLE A2.1 The Cumulative Standard Normal Distribution

z	0.00	0.01	0.02	0.03	0.04	0.05	0.06	0.07	0.08	0.09
0.0	0.5000	0.5040	0.5080	0.5120	0.5160	0.5199	0.5239	0.5279	0.5319	0.5359
0.1	0.5398	0.5438	0.5478	0.5517	0.5557	0.5596	0.5636	0.5675	0.5714	0.5753
0.2	0.5793	0.5832	0.5871	0.5910	0.5948	0.5987	0.6026	0.6064	0.6103	0.6141
0.3	0.6179	0.6217	0.6255	0.6293	0.6331	0.6368	0.6406	0.6443	0.6480	0.6517
0.4	0.6554	0.6591	0.6628	0.6664	0.6700	0.6736	0.6772	0.6808	0.6844	0.6879
0.5	0.6915	0.6950	0.6985	0.7019	0.7054	0.7088	0.7123	0.7157	0.7190	0.7224
0.6	0.7257	0.7291	0.7324	0.7357	0.7389	0.7422	0.7454	0.7486	0.7517	0.7549
0.7	0.7580	0.7611	0.7642	0.7673	0.7704	0.7734	0.7764	0.7794	0.7823	0.7852
0.8	0.7881	0.7910	0.7939	0.7967	0.7995	0.8023	0.8051	0.8078	0.8106	0.8133
0.9	0.8159	0.8186	0.8212	0.8238	0.8264	0.8289	0.8315	0.8340	0.8365	0.8389
1.0	0.8413	0.8438	0.8461	0.8485	0.8508	0.8531	0.8554	0.8577	0.8599	0.8621
1.1	0.8643	0.8665	0.8686	0.8708	0.8729	0.8749	0.8770	0.8790	0.8810	0.8830
1.2	0.8849	0.8869	0.8888	0.8907	0.8925	0.8944	0.8962	0.8980	0.8997	0.9015
1.3	0.9032	0.9049	0.9066	0.9082	0.9099	0.9115	0.9131	0.9147	0.9162	0.9177
1.4	0.9192	0.9207	0.9222	0.9236	0.9251	0.9265	0.9279	0.9292	0.9306	0.9319
1.5	0.9332	0.9345	0.9357	0.9370	0.9382	0.9394	0.9406	0.9418	0.9429	0.9441
1.6	0.9452	0.9463	0.9474	0.9484	0.9495	0.9505	0.9515	0.9525	0.9535	0.9545
1.7	0.9554	0.9564	0.9573	0.9582	0.9591	0.9599	0.9608	0.9616	0.9625	0.9633
1.8	0.9641	0.9649	0.9656	0.9664	0.9671	0.9678	0.9686	0.9693	0.9699	0.9706
1.9	0.9713	0.9719	0.9726	0.9732	0.9738	0.9744	0.9750	0.9756	0.9761	0.9767
2.0	0.9772	0.9778	0.9783	0.9788	0.9793	0.9798	0.9803	0.9808	0.9812	0.9817
2.1	0.9821	0.9826	0.9830	0.9834	0.9838	0.9842	0.9846	0.9850	0.9854	0.9857
2.2	0.9861	0.9864	0.8968	0.9871	0.9875	0.9878	0.9881	0.9884	0.9887	0.9890
2.3	0.9893	0.9896	0.9898	0.9901	0.9904	0.9906	0.9909	0.9911	0.9913	0.9916
2.4	0.9918	0.9920	0.9922	0.9925	0.9927	0.9929	0.9931	0.9932	0.9934	0.9936
2.5	0.9938	0.9940	0.9941	0.9943	0.9945	0.9946	0.9948	0.9949	0.9951	0.9952
2.6	0.9953	0.9955	0.9956	0.9957	0.9958	0.9960	0.9961	0.9962	0.9963	0.9964
2.7	0.9965	0.9966	0.9967	0.9968	0.9969	0.9970	0.9971	0.9972	0.9973	0.9974
2.8	0.9974	0.9975	0.9976	0.9977	0.9977	0.9978	0.9979	0.9979	0.9980	0.9981
2.9	0.9981	0.9982	0.9982	0.9983	0.9984	0.9984	0.9985	0.9985	0.9986	0.9986
3.0	0.9987	0.9987	0.9987	0.9988	0.9988	0.9989	0.9989	0.9989	0.9990	0.9990
3.1	0.9990	0.9991	0.9991	0.9991	0.9992	0.9992	0.9992	0.9992	0.9993	0.9993
3.2	0.9993	0.9993	0.9994	0.9994	0.9994	0.9994	0.9994	0.9995	0.9995	0.9995
3.3	0.9995	0.9995	0.9995	0.9996	0.9996	0.9996	0.9996	0.9996	0.9996	0.9997

- If $X \sim N(\mu, \sigma)$, to find $P(X \leq x)$, transform X into $Z = (X - \mu)/\sigma$.

  Then $Z \sim N(0,1)$ and

  $P(X \leq x) = P(Z \leq z) = (x - \mu)/\sigma)$,

  which can be read from the table.

  Note: $P(Z \leq -z) = 1 - P(Z \leq z)$

- Conversely, given probability p, to find x such that $P(Z \leq z) = p$, read z from the table such that $P(Z \leq z) = p$. Then $z = (x - \mu)/\sigma$, so compute $x = \mu + z \sigma$.

Index

"As Is" License Agreement and Limited Warranty

READ THIS LICENSE CAREFULLY BEFORE OPENING THIS PACKAGE. BY OPENING THIS PACKAGE, YOU ARE AGREEING TO THE TERMS AND CONDITIONS OF THIS LICENSE. IF YOU DO NOT AGREE, DO NOT OPEN THE PACKAGE. PROMPTLY RETURN THE UNOPENED PACKAGE AND ALL ACCOMPANYING ITEMS TO THE PLACE YOU OBTAINED THEM. *THESE TERMS APPLY TO ALL LICENSED SOFTWARE ON THE DISK EXCEPT THAT THE TERMS FOR USE OF ANY SHAREWARE OR FREEWARE ON THE DISKETTES ARE AS SET FORTH IN THE ELECTRONIC LICENSE LOCATED ON THE DISK:*

1. GRANT OF LICENSE and OWNERSHIP: The enclosed computer programs «and any data» ("Software") are licensed, not sold, to you by Prentice-Hall, Inc. ("We" or the "Company") in consideration of your adoption of the accompanying Company textbooks and/or other materials, and your agreement to these terms. You own only the disk(s) but we and/or our licensors own the Software itself. This license allows instructors and students enrolled in the course using the Company textbook that accompanies this Software (the "Course") to use and display the enclosed copy of the Software on an unlimited number of computers at a single campus or branch or geographic location of an educational institution, for academic use only, so long as you comply with the terms of this Agreement. You may make one copy for back up only. We reserve any rights not granted to you. This version of ProcessModel is not a LAN version, so it is not recommended that you install it on your network.

2. USE RESTRICTIONS: You may <u>not</u> sell or license copies of the Software or the Documentation to others. You may <u>not</u> transfer, distribute or make available the Software or the Documentation, except to instructors and students in your school who are users of the adopted Company textbook that accompanies this Software in connection with the course for which the textbook was adopted. You may <u>not</u> reverse engineer, disassemble, decompile, modify, adapt, translate or create derivative works based on the Software or the Documentation. You may be held legally responsible for any copying or copyright infringement which is caused by your failure to abide by the terms of these restrictions.

3. TERMINATION: This license is effective until terminated. This license will terminate automatically without notice from the Company if you fail to comply with any provisions or limitations of this license. Upon termination, you shall destroy the Documentation and all copies of the Software. All provisions of this Agreement as to limitation and disclaimer of warranties, limitation of liability, remedies or damages, and our ownership rights shall survive termination.

4. DISCLAIMER OF WARRANTY: THE COMPANY AND ITS LICENSORS MAKE <u>NO</u> WARRANTIES ABOUT THE SOFTWARE, WHICH IS PROVIDED "<u>AS-IS</u>." IF THE DISK IS DEFECTIVE IN MATERIALS OR WORKMANSHIP, YOUR ONLY REMEDY IS TO RETURN IT TO THE COMPANY WITHIN 30 DAYS FOR REPLACEMENT UNLESS THE COMPANY DETERMINES IN GOOD FAITH THAT THE DISK HAS BEEN MISUSED OR IMPROPERLY INSTALLED, REPAIRED, ALTERED OR DAMAGED. THE COMPANY DISCLAIMS ALL WARRANTIES, EXPRESS OR IMPLIED, INCLUDING WITHOUT LIMITATION, THE IMPLIED WARRANTIES OF MERCHANTABILITY AND FITNESS FOR A PARTICULAR PURPOSE. THE COMPANY DOES NOT WARRANT, GUARANTEE OR MAKE ANY REPRESENTATION REGARDING THE ACCURACY, RELIABILITY, CURRENTNESS, USE, OR RESULTS OF USE, OF THE SOFTWARE.

5. LIMITATION OF REMEDIES AND DAMAGES: IN NO EVENT, SHALL THE COMPANY OR ITS EMPLOYEES, AGENTS, LICENSORS OR CONTRACTORS BE LIABLE FOR ANY INCIDENTAL, INDIRECT, SPECIAL OR CONSEQUENTIAL DAMAGES ARISING OUT OF OR IN CONNECTION WITH THIS LICENSE OR THE SOFTWARE, INCLUDING, WITHOUT LIMITATION, LOSS OF USE, LOSS OF DATA, LOSS OF INCOME OR PROFIT, OR OTHER LOSSES SUSTAINED AS A RESULT OF INJURY TO ANY PERSON, OR LOSS OF OR DAMAGE TO PROPERTY, OR CLAIMS OF THIRD PARTIES, EVEN IF THE COMPANY OR AN AUTHORIZED REPRESENTATIVE OF THE COMPANY HAS BEEN ADVISED OF THE POSSIBILITY OF SUCH DAMAGES. SOME JURISDICTIONS DO NOT ALLOW THE LIMITATION OF DAMAGES IN CERTAIN CIRCUMSTANCES, SO THE ABOVE LIMITATIONS MAY NOT ALWAYS APPLY.

6. GENERAL: THIS AGREEMENT SHALL BE CONSTRUED IN ACCORDANCE WITH THE LAWS OF THE UNITED STATES OF AMERICA AND THE STATE OF NEW YORK, APPLICABLE TO CONTRACTS MADE IN NEW YORK, AND SHALL BENEFIT THE COMPANY, ITS AFFILIATES AND ASSIGNEES. This Agreement is the complete and exclusive statement of the agreement between you and the Company and supersedes all proposals, prior agreements, oral or written, and any other communications between you and the company or any of its representatives relating to the subject matter. If you are a U.S. Government user, this Software is licensed with "restricted rights" as set forth in subparagraphs (a)-(d) of the Commercial Computer-Restricted Rights clause at FAR 52.227-19 or in subparagraphs (c)(1)(ii) of the Rights in Technical Data and Computer Software clause at DFARS 252.227-7013, and similar clauses, as applicable.